LISZT, CAROLYNE, AND THE VATICAN

AMERICAN LISZT SOCIETY STUDIES SERIES No. 1

Frontispiece: Liszt in Munich, a photograph by Franz Hanfstaengl (1858).

LISZT, CAROLYNE, AND THE VATICAN

The story of a thwarted marriage

by

ALAN WALKER

as it emerges from the original Church documents

edited and translated by

GABRIELE ERASMI

with additional commentaries by Alan Walker

AMERICAN LISZT SOCIETY STUDIES SERIES No. 1

General Editor: Michael Saffle

PENDRAGON PRESS
STUYVESANT, NY

Other Titles in the American Liszt Society Series

No. 2   Michael Saffle, *Liszt in Germany, 1840-1845.*

No. 3   Keith T. Johns, *The Symphonic Poems of Franz Liszt.*

No. 4   Ronald E. Booth, Jr., *Gieseking.*

—

Library of Congress Cataloging-in-Publication Data

Walker, Alan, 1930-
    Liszt, Carolyne, and the Vatican: the story of a thwarted marriage as it
emerges from the original Church documents edited and translated by Gabriele
Erasmi / by Alan Walker: with additional commentaries by Alan Walker.
        p. cm. -- (American Liszt Society studies series; no. 1) Includes
    documents translated from French, Russian, and German. Includes
    bibliographical references and indexes.
    ISBN 0-945193-09-2
        1. Liszt, Franz, 1811–1886. 2. Sayn-Wittgenstein, Carolyne de, 1819–1887.
    3. Composers--Biography. 4. Marriage--Dispensations--History--19th century.
    5. Catholic Church--Doctrines--History--19th-century. I. Erasmi, Gabriele.
    II. Title. III. Series.
        ML410.L7W293 1991
        780′ .92--dc2067
        [B]   91-24067
                                                                 CIP
                                                                 MN

CONTENTS

ILLUSTRATIONS

ACKNOWLEDGEMENTS

Thanks are due to Cardinal Ugo Poletti of St. John Lateran, and Monsignor Charles Burns, Head of the Archivio Segreto Vaticano, for so kindly giving us permission to publish the files in their care; to Monsignor John Hanly, former Head of the Irish Seminary in Rome; to Father John Hayes, parish priest of San Carlo al Corso; to Professor Germano Gualdo, archivist in the Vatican Archives; to Monsignor Agostino Lauro of the Congregation for the Clergy; to Monsignor Joseph Metzler, Prefect of the Archivio Segreto Vaticano; and to Monsignor Gabriele Crognale, archivist at the Archivio Storico del Vicariato di Roma, in St. John Lateran. We would also like to thank Pauline Pocknell and Professors Nina Kolesnikoff and Gerry Chapple of McMaster University for their help on textual and translation problems relating to the French, Russian, and German documents.

A.W., G.E.

Plate 1. Princess Carolyne with her daughter Princess Marie. A lithograph by Carl Fischer (1844).

PREFACE

For more than one hundred and twenty-five years the whereabouts of the Vatican's files on the thwarted marriage of Liszt and Princess Carolyne von Sayn-Wittgenstein remained shrouded in mystery. Although a Holy Congregation of Cardinals was convened by Pope Pius IX on two separate occasions in order to review the case for an annulment of her marriage to Prince Nicholas,[1] no record of those convocations appeared to have been kept, and no document containing their judgement appeared to have been issued. That always aroused interest among Liszt scholars; after all, the question of Liszt's marriage to Carolyne was one of the central issues of his life, and the presence of documents in Rome would be of fundamental interest to his biographers. All inquiries made through the labyrinthine organization of the Vatican Archives, however, invariably encountered a negative response. The suspicion soon arose in Lisztian circles that the Vatican was part of a conspiracy to suppress information. In which case, what were its motives?

In the summer of 1985 I located two of the "missing files" in two quite separate archives. The story of how that came about is not without interest, for it is symptomatic of the complex position in which Liszt scholarship finds itself today. A year earlier, while attempting to track down the birth certificate of Daniel Liszt in Weimar, I had come across a rare copy of his obituary notice written by Princess Carolyne von Sayn-Wittgenstein and printed by her in a limited edition for private circulation among Liszt's friends in Germany. In it she happened to mention the name of the church in Rome in which Daniel was baptised—San Luigi de' Francesi—a vital piece of information that she could only have received from Liszt himself, and without which all previous attempts to track down Daniel's birth certificate had foundered. Weimar and Rome are neighboring cities in the field of Liszt research, although in reality they are separated by a thousand miles. Eventually I arrived in the Eternal City and the church of San Luigi de' Francesi, only to learn from the clerics there that the church records had long since been removed to the Vicariato di Roma, in San Giovanni in Laterano. And it was at the Vicariato that I received an unexpected "bonus" for my efforts. For not only did the archive contain Daniel's baptismal records, but also the vastly more important cache of long-lost documents surrounding the nuptials of Liszt and Princess Carolyne.[2] But where were the annulment documents? This question led me to make further inquiries at the Vatican library itself, where about forty additional documents relating to Carolyne's annulment came to light among the papers of Cardinal Antonino De Luca, in the Archive of the Nunciature of Vienna, for the years 1860–61. The file bears the description "Special Annex: The Matrimonial Case of Wittgenstein versus Iwanowska," and it relates mainly to the long struggle leading up to the annulment of Carolyne's marriage and to the issuing of the decree itself.[3] When conflated, the documents from both archives allow us to review the tortured history of the case with some precision, and they prove three things:

(a) it was Liszt's firm resolve to marry Carolyne;

(b) he did not abandon her at the altar;

(c) it was not the fault of the Catholic Church that the marriage did not take place; in fact, the Church issued a decree of annulment to Carolyne which was upheld by Pius IX.

Any one of these conclusions would give Liszt's biographers pause for thought. Taken together, they call for nothing less than a major rewriting of the story of Liszt's life, or at any rate that part of it which unfolded during the years 1848–61. All this by way of illustrating that the modern Liszt scholar must deserve his luck.

---

[1] On September 22 and December 22, 1860, respectively.

[2] AVR.

[3] ASV, NV.

Nor did the trail of discovery end there. It soon became evident that it would be necessary to call in an expert to transcribe and translate these church documents (couched as some of them are in the arcane language of canon law), and present them in a form that made them accessible to the English reader. I invited Professor Gabriele Erasmi to undertake this task, and he readily agreed. During much of the period 1989–90 he and I discussed every aspect of Carolyne's case—its tortured chronology, its legal foundations, and its unsatisfactory outcome. From the chain of evidence at our disposal we concluded that there must be still more documents lurking in the Vatican Archives and that there was a good chance they might be found in the files of the Congregation of the Council, where the issue had been twice debated in 1860. Armed with this knowledge Professor Erasmi returned to the Vatican Archives and, thanks to the generous collaboration of the Prefect and the Archivist, succeeded after several frustrating attempts in locating the still uncatalogued file of the Congregation of the Council.[4] These three files—from the archives of the Vicariato di Roma, the Nunciature of Vienna, and the Congregation of the Council—contain more than a hundred documents in all, and they permit the re-construction of the complicated legal story of Carolyne's marriage annulment in greater detail than has hitherto been possible.

The entire case turned on the question of perjury. Anyone who was knowingly about to bear false witness on a matter so grave as a second Catholic marriage-service had to be made aware of the legal and ethical consequences of such testimony. And where the annulment of a previous marriage was an issue, as it was in this case, false evidence could lead to charges of bigamy. Now bigamy, in the Rome of Pius IX, was not only a mortal sin but a crime as well, and it was usually punished both by excommunication and a long term of imprisonment. Before Liszt and Carolyne could marry, therefore, they would both have been subjected to questioning by clerics charged with such tasks. And the documents prove that such questioning did indeed take place. Their case was both complex and notorious; whatever the outcome, the Catholic Church itself was also on trial.

It is clear from a perusal of the Vatican files that yet more documents may one day come to light. After all, several high-ranking clerics were involved in the case—Archbishop Wenceslas Żyliński, (Metropolitan of St. Petersburg), Bishop Christophe Kött (Bishop of Fulda), and Monsignor (later Cardinal) Gustav Hohenlohe—and they are directly represented in the dossier. But while a search of their individual archives might add more detail to the case, the main outlines of that case are now in place. The position of the Catholic church is clearly stated; so, too, is the position of the Wittgenstein and Hohenlohe families, who were opposed to it. As for Liszt and Carolyne, their views will emerge from the pages which follow.

ALAN WALKER
Spring 1990

---

[4]ASV, CC.

CHRONOLOGY

Liszt, Carolyne, and the Vatican
between the years 1847 and 1887

1847

February 14: Liszt gives a recital in the Great Hall of Kiev University, and Carolyne hears him for the first time. She invites him to her château at Woronince in order to join in the tenth birthday celebrations of her daughter Princess Marie, on February 18.

July: Liszt meets Carolyne again in Odessa and spends several weeks there with her while giving the final concerts of his *Glanzzeit*. In Odessa he meets Carolyne's estranged husband Prince Nicholas von Sayn-Wittgenstein, who is attending the Russian army manoeuvres in his capacity as aide-de-camp to Tsar Nicholas I, and also her mother Pauline Iwanowska.

September: Liszt announces his retirement from the concert platform and gives his last recital for money in Elisabetgrad. Carolyne returns to Woronince, where Liszt has promised to join her for an extended holiday.

October: Liszt arrives at Woronince and stays as a guest of Carolyne for three months. Prince Nicholas spends the winter in Berlin. Carolyne and Liszt exchange vows of love and plan their future together.

1848

January: Liszt sets out for Weimar in order to take up his fulltime duties as Court Kapellmeister. Carolyne travels to Kiev and arranges the sale of some of her properties in Ukraine.

April: Princess Carolyne returns to Kiev and gives notice that she wishes to commence proceedings for the annulment of her marriage. She then closes down her property at Woronince and flees with her daughter and several million roubles across the Russian border into Austria. Liszt meets her at Kryzanowicz, the mountain-castle of his friend Prince Felix Lichnowsky.

July: After a nostalgic trip to Vienna, Eisenstadt, and Raiding (Liszt's birthplace), where Liszt shows Carolyne the places associated with his childhood and youth, the pair take up residence in Weimar. In order to keep up appearances, Carolyne and her daughter move into the Altenburg while Liszt stays in the Erbprinz Hotel.

May 12: Carolyne's petition for an annulment is heard by the Consistory of Mohilow which, after taking evidence from a number of witnesses, concludes that the Princess has a *prima facie* case which should be brought to trial.

1849

January: Since Carolyne's annulment appears to be imminent, Liszt moves into the Altenburg with her and they live together as man and wife.

September: Carolyne falls ill with a form of blood-poisoning, and Liszt takes her to Bad Eilsen for a water-cure.

October: Princess Marie falls ill with typhus.

1850

October: Carolyne again falls ill and stays at Bad Eilsen for the next nine months, while Liszt commutes back and forth from there to Weimar.

November: Carolyne's mother, Pauline Iwanowska, dies.

1851

November 6: The issue of Carolyne's annulment comes before the Consistory of Luck-Zhitomir, Carolyne's own diocese, which declares the marriage valid. *This is the judgement in the first instance.* It automatically goes to appeal.

1852

September: Anticipating that the annulment will shortly be decreed, Prince Nicholas visits Carolyne in Weimar in order to work out a property settlement. Princess Marie is made a ward of the Weimar court as part of the agreement.

November 13: The Consistory of Mohilow hears the appeal and reverses the judgement of Luck-Zhitomir: the marriage is null and void. *This is the judgement in the second instance.* However, this declaration is not sanctioned by the Metropolitan Archbishop of St. Petersburg, Ignaz Holowinski, who insists that the judgement of Luck-Zhitomir, issued on November 6, 1851, be upheld. The question whether Archbishop Holowinski has the legal authority to withhold his sanction becomes a bone of contention in the years ahead.

1853

January: The Tsar's emissary (Prince Peter von Oldenburg) arrives in Weimar with orders to arrest Carolyne for non-compliance with the property settlement (1852) and to return her and Princess Marie to Russia. Carolyne catches the overnight train to Paris and begs Napoleon III to offer her and her daughter his protection. (There is talk of a possible betrothal between Marie and Count Talleyrand, French ambassador to Weimar, in which case Marie would have received diplomatic immunity.)

1854

Tsar Nicholas I once more orders Carolyne to return to Russia in order to handle her affairs in person. Fearing for her personal liberty she refuses, and the Tsar sequesters all her lands and estates.

1855

March: Tsar Nicholas I dies and is succeeded by Alexander II, who strips Carolyne of her citizenship and condemns her to exile. Her estates are put into trust for Princess Marie.

Prince Nicholas, tired of waiting for a Catholic annulment, commences proceedings for a Protestant divorce.

September: The Metropolitan of St. Petersburg, Archbishop Holowinski, dies.

1856

January: Prince Nicholas re-marries within the Protestant church. Archbishop Holowinski is succeeded as Metropolitan of St. Petersburg by Archbishop Wencelas Żyliński.

1857

In light of Holowinsky's death the Princess is persuaded to take up her case once more, and it is brought before the Consistory of Mohilow. The court upholds Holowinsky's earlier decree, however.

June 23: Liszt is admitted to the Order of St. Francis as a "Confrater" by the Hungarian Franciscans.

1858

December: Liszt resigns from his position as Kapellmeister to the Weimar court.

1859

February: Liszt sends Pius IX a specially bound copy of his "Gran" Mass, and receives a flattering reply from the Pontiff.

June: Carolyne receives a visit from Wladislaw Okraszewski, one of her landed tenants in Ukraine, who informs her of a way out of her legal impasse and takes charge of her case. The costs, he warns her, could amount to 70,000 silver roubles.

August 8: Acting on a formal command of Pope Pius IX, Archbishop Żyliński re-opens the case. He himself heads the Consistory of Mohilow which is charged with the task of reviewing all the evidence and submitting a definitive sentence to the pope.

In this same month Pius IX elevates Liszt to the rank of Commander of the Order of St. Gregory the Great.

October 15: Princess Marie von Sayn-Wittgenstein marries Prince Konstantin von Hohenlohe in the Catholic Church in Weimar. The marriage, reluctantly approved by Carolyne, appears to be part of a complex agreement between the Wittgenstein and Hohenlohe families to retain control of Marie's fortune in exchange for their complicity in securing Carolyne's annulment.

1860

February 24 (O.S.): Archbishop Żyliński issues the final decree of annulment, which sends shock waves throughout the hierarchy of the Catholic church. The decree is immediately suspended by the Bishop of Fulda (in whose diocese Weimar falls) on the authority of the Papal Nuncio to Vienna, Monsignor De Luca.

May 17: Carolyne sets out for Rome in order to plead with the Vatican to have Fulda's suspension lifted. She arrives in the Eternal City on May 24, 1860, and takes rooms in the Piazza di Spagna. It is rumored that she bribed the judges of the Mohilow consistory to secure her annulment, which she and Archbishop Żyliński deny.

September 9: Carolyne is granted an audience by Pius IX, who agrees to look into her case. Monsignor Gustav Hohenlohe (the brother of Konstantin, her son-in-law) acts behind the scenes to jeopardize Carolyne's actions.

September 22: The Holy Congregation of Cardinals is convened, and it upholds Żyliński's annulment and rules in Carolyne's favor. Owing to the joint machinations of Monsignor De Luca, Monsignor Hohenlohe, and the Bishop of Fulda, this ruling is challenged.

December 22: The Holy Congregation of Cardinals is convened for a second time. Once more it rules in Carolyne's favor.

1861

January 7: Pius IX ratifies the judgement of the Cardinals, and it is released the following day. Liszt and Carolyne are now legally free to marry within the Catholic church.

October 20: Liszt arrives in Rome, in readiness for his marriage to Carolyne which is planned to take place in the church of San Carlo al Corso two days later, his fiftieth birthday. The pair go to the Vatican in order to swear out statements and to have the reading of the banns waived. Monsignor Hohenlohe has meanwhile procured witnesses from Ukraine to testify that the annulment was obtained through perjured evidence.

October 21: Carolyne receives a message from San Carlo church that the wedding must be postponed. Shortly afterwards she moves into apartments on the Via Babuino. Liszt takes up separate quarters at 113 Via Felice.

1862

Liszt decides to stay in Rome and enters into the city's musical life. He becomes a familiar figure in the homes of the upper clergy, including Monsignor Francesco Nardi. He is also introduced to the powerful Caetani family.

August 10: Liszt completes his oratorio *St. Elisabeth.*

September 11: His daughter Blandine dies.

1863

June: Liszt moves into the Madonna del Rosario, on the Monte Mario, just outside Rome. In this isolated retreat he finishes a number of his compositions, including the oratorio *Christus.* He is visited by Pius IX to whom he plays one of his newly composed "Franciscan Legends."

From this time Liszt becomes better acquainted with Pope Pius IX. He plays before the music-loving pontiff a number of times at the latter's special request, both in the Vatican and at the Pope's summer residence in Castel Gandolfo. Pius clearly enjoys these encounters and takes to calling Liszt "my dear Palestrina." It is often rumored that Liszt is to become director of music at St. Peter's in Rome, but Liszt himself expresses no interest in the idea.

1864

March: Prince Nicholas von Sayn-Wittgenstein dies. However, there is no further talk of a marriage between Liszt and Carolyne.

June: Liszt agrees to a request from Pius IX to take part in a great charity concert for Peter's Pence at the camp of the Pretorian Guard.

July: He accepts an invitation to visit the Pope at his summer retreat in Castel Gandolfo, and he plays for the Pontiff and his entourage. He also travels to the old town of Albano, whose Canon he later becomes.

1865

April 25: Liszt receives the tonsure from Monsignor Hohenlohe and moves into the latter's apartments in the Vatican.

June 21: Liszt plays in the festival hall of the Vatican Library before Pius IX and his court, in honor of the 19th anniversary of the pontiff's coronation.

July 30: He is admitted to the minor orders of the priesthood—Doorkeeper, Lector, Exorcist, and

Acolyte. Again it is Gustav Hohenlohe who officiates at the ceremony, this time in his private chapel at Tivoli. Henceforth, Liszt is known by the title of "Abbé."

1866

February 6: Liszt's mother dies in Paris.

March 4–May 22: Liszt visits Paris for a performance of his "Gran" Mass in the church of Saint Eustache (March 15).

June 22: Gustav von Hohenlohe is made a cardinal and quits his apartments in the Vatican. Monsignor de Mérode takes over his position as Grand Almoner to Pius IX. Liszt returns for a few months to his old quarters at the Madonna del Rosario. As the years roll by, the friendship between Hohenlohe and Liszt becomes closer. His adversarial role in Liszt's marriage plans to Carolyne seems to be forgotten.

November 22: Liszt moves to new apartments in the Santa Francesca Romana, overlooking the Forum.

1867

The Compromise between Austria and Hungary is achieved. Liszt composes his "Hungarian Coronation Mass," which is performed on June 8 for the coronation of the Emperor Franz Josef as King of Hungary, in the Matthias Church, Budapest.

August 28: Liszt conducts his oratorio *St. Elisabeth* in the Wartburg, to celebrate the 800th anniversary of the castle.

1868

June 21: Liszt plays to Pius IX for the 22nd anniversary of the latter's coronation.

July–August: Liszt travels to Grottamare with Don Antonio Solfanelli, who gives him serious religious instruction.

November: Cosima deserts Hans von Bülow, after years of unhappiness, and elopes to Switzerland with Richard Wagner. Liszt breaks off relations with his daughter and Wagner, his former friend.

1869

Liszt accepts an invitation from the Grand Duke Carl Alexander to return to Weimar for three months of each year in order to conduct advanced masterclasses in piano playing. He lives in the Hofgärtnerei.

October: Hohenlohe sets aside a suite of rooms for Liszt in the Villa d'Este (Hohenlohe's home in Tivoli, near Rome), where the composer henceforth prefers to stay whenever he is in Italy.

December 8: Pius IX opens the First Vatican Council, and the doctrine of papal infallibility is proclaimed the following year.

1870

Italian troops enter Rome and the city becomes the capital of a united Italy. Until his death, eight years later, Pius IX remains a prisoner within the Vatican.

May 29: Liszt attends the Allgemeiner Deutscher Musikverein in Weimar, and conducts a performance of Beethoven's "Choral" symphony.

August 25: Cosima marries Richard Wagner in a Protestant ceremony in Lucerne, after being divorced from Hans von Bülow and renouncing her Catholic faith. Liszt, who had no dealings with his daughter for more than a year, learns of this development from the newspapers.

December 16: To mark the one hundredth anniversary of the birth of Beethoven, Liszt conducts the "Choral" symphony and the Violin Concerto, with Reményi as soloist.

1871

Gustav von Hohenlohe falls out of favor with Pius IX for expressing liberal views on the way the Church should conduct its affairs. For the next few years he hardly sets foot in Rome.

June 13: Liszt is appointed a Royal Hungarian Counsellor. He receives a pension of 4000 forints for life.

September 3–7: Liszt attends the annual general meeting of the Cäcilienverein in Eichstätt. He becomes friendly with its founder, Franz Witt.

1872

Liszt patches up his long-standing quarrel with Wagner. Wagner and Cosima visit him in Weimar (September). The following month Liszt reciprocates by visiting them in Bayreuth, where they now live.

1873

May 29: Liszt conducts the first complete performance of *Christus* at Weimar. Wagner and Cosima are in attendance.

November 8–11: A national celebration is mounted in Budapest to mark the fiftieth anniversary of Liszt's artistic career.

1874

March 25: Liszt conducts his Coronation Mass in the Budapest parish church.

May: Visits Hans von Bülow in Florence.

1875

March 10: Liszt and Wagner appear at a concert in Budapest in aid of the Bayreuth Festival Fund. Liszt plays Beethoven's "Emperor" Concerto, conducted by Hans Richter.

March 30: Liszt is appointed first President of the Royal Academy of Music, Budapest (official opening November 14). Apart from his administrative duties, he also directs some piano master classes.

1876

March 5: The death of Countess Marie d'Agoult, in Paris.

March 26: Liszt's pupils give their first concert in the Academy building (4, Hal tér).

1877

March 16: Liszt participates in a concert in aid of a monument for Beethoven in Vienna. He performs Beethoven's "Emperor" Concerto. The eleven-year-old Busoni is present in the audience.

March 24–April 3: Liszt visits Wagner in Bayreuth and stays with him and Cosima at Wahnfried; Liszt performs his Sonata in B minor (April 2). Wagner returns the compliment by giving Liszt a signed copy of his autobiography.

July 12: Volume nine of Carolyne's *Causes intérieures* is placed on the Index by a decree of Pius IX.

1878

Death of Pius IX, who is succeeded to the papacy by Leo XIII. Gustav von Hohenlohe now returns to Rome and is appointed Archbishop of Santa Maria Maggiore.

1879

February 3: Volume three of Carolyne's *Causes intérieures* is placed on the Index by a decree of Leo XIII.

August: Gustav Hohenlohe is inducted as Bishop of Albano. Shortly afterward (October 12) he makes Liszt an honorary Canon of Albano.

1880

March 14: Liszt's Hungarian pupils give their first concert in the new Academy building in Budapest (67, Sugár utca).

September 16–25: Liszt visits Cosima and Richard Wagner in Siena.

1881

May 1: Liszt's oratorio *Christus* is performed at the music festival in Freiburg.

July 2: Liszt falls down the stairs of the Hofgärtnerei. His general health, until now good, starts to decline.

1882

November 19–January 13 (1883): Liszt stays with Cosima and Wagner in Venice.

1883

February 13: The death of Richard Wagner, in Venice.

May 22: Liszt helps to mount a memorial concert for Wagner on the latter's birthday, in Weimar. He conducts the Prelude and the "Good Friday Music" from *Parsifal.*

November 24: Cardinal Hohenlohe visits Liszt in Weimar.

1884

February 25: Liszt conducts a performance of his Hungarian Coronation Mass in Pressburg cathedral.

May 18: Liszt hears his oratorio *Christus* conducted by Carl Riedel in Leipzig.

May 25: Liszt conducts for the last time, in Weimar, at the congress of the Allgemeiner Deutscher Musikverein (Bülow's *Nirvana*).

1885

May 27–June 1: Liszt attends the Tonkünstlerversammlung at Karlsruhe and hears a performance of his *Dante* Symphony conducted by Felix Mottl.

1886

March: Liszt visits Paris.

April: Liszt visits London for the first time since 1841. He is received with acclaim and plays the piano for Queen Victoria at Windsor castle. His oratorio *St. Elisabeth* is performed at St. James's Hall (April 6) and again at Crystal Palace (April 17).

July 31: Liszt dies in Bayreuth while lending support to the Wagner Festival there. He is buried in that city against the wishes of many of his friends and supporters.

1887

March 9: Death of Princess Carolyne in Rome. Cardinal Hohenlohe officiates at her funeral service in the church of Santa Maria del Popolo. She is buried in the German Cemetery in the Vatican.

SYMBOLS AND ABBREVIATIONS USED IN THE DOCUMENTS.

[ ]	Words abbreviated in the original.
< >	Editorial corrections and insertions.
{ }	Phrases and words erased in the original.
( )	When containing one or two letters, they enclose a misspelling in the original.

ASV, NV	File from the Nunciature in Vienna.
ASV, CC	File from the Holy Congregation of the Tridentine Council.
AVR	File from the Vicariate of Rome.
ASV, SS	Documents in the Archives of the Vatican Secretary of State.

LISZT, CAROLYNE, AND THE VATICAN

The story of a thwarted marriage

by ALAN WALKER

I

Carolyne Iwanowska was born on February 8, 1819 (New Style),[1] at Monasterzyska, a remote village in Ukraine, in the house of her maternal grandfather. She was the only child of an immensely rich Polish landowner, Peter Iwanowsky, and his wife Pauline Podowska. The Iwanowskys were Roman Catholics and their estates, which were of unimaginable vastness, lay mainly in the province of Podolia, in Polish Ukraine; it took several days to traverse their borders on horseback. Brought up in isolation, on the fringe of the civilized world, Carolyne was allowed to roam free by her doting father. La Mara would later describe her as "a child of the steppes."[2]

The Iwanowsky domains encompassed such communities as Staniscince, Bielaski, Buchny, Iwanki, Woronince, Tencki, and Polok. Thirty thousand serfs were required to work these far-flung territories, and over this desperate sea of humanity the Iwanowskys exercised total control. The climate was extreme. In summer there was tropical heat; in winter cold so intense that the inhabitants had to wear masks with holes for their eyes. It was not uncommon to send a servant for purchases in the next village, only to discover him the following morning frozen to death in the back of his cart. These serfs knew no other way of life. After the Polish insurrection of 1830 their lot became particularly harsh. All travel to nearby provinces was curtailed, and many families were separated. Simply to visit one's kith and kin without travel documents was to risk a Russian bullet through the head.

When Carolyne was eleven years old her parents separated. By nature Peter Iwanowsky was a recluse, and his wife Pauline had soon discovered

that life in a remote Ukrainian village with a man who preferred to be alone left much to be desired. She spent years of her married life pining for the social whirl of the large cities she had known as a girl. Pauline and her daughter now traveled to Central Europe, where they turned up in the brilliant salons of Berlin and Vienna and at a number of fashionable watering spas. Pauline Podowska, in fact, was renowned for her beauty and for her musical talent. She was a welcome guest in Metternich's salon, where she charmed the cream of Viennese society; both Spontini and Meyerbeer complimented her on the purity of her singing voice, and Schelling praised her in his poetry. By contrast, Carolyne herself was exceedingly plain, and this cast a shadow across her childhood from which she never escaped. Indeed, the difference between mother and daughter was so disconcerting that it frequently drew comment. So upset was Pauline at the trick that nature had played on her that her sensitive daughter, painfully aware that she was the cause, attempted to console her by urging her to wait until the Resurrection, after which Carolyne would be transformed into a great beauty.

On her return to Ukraine, Carolyne divided her time between her father and her mother. Her education was supervised by her father, who hired a French governess, Madame Patersi de Fossombroni—who would later educate Franz Liszt's daughters. Peter Iwanowsky was a book-worm by nature, and he attempted to forget his matrimonial troubles by sitting up half the night browsing in his library, smoking large cigars. His daughter would often join him there, and they would read his learned tomes together, the father thinking nothing of offering a cigar to his young charge. As she grew older, her favorite pas-

---

[1]Until she left Ukraine, Carolyne invariably celebrated her birthdays on January 27 (Old Style). See her unpublished letter to Liszt dated January 27, 1848, in which she tells him that today is her twenty-ninth birthday. WA, Kasten 33.

[2]LSJ, p. 10.

time was to debate with her father, and they would argue the night away in his smoke-filled library. Carolyne's later reputation as a blue-stocking, her love of disputation, and her addiction to tobacco can all be traced back to this early environment. It is typical of her industrious nature that when she was only nine years old, she had already drawn up for herself a table of laws that rewarded the crime of idleness with capital punishment.

II

Concerned for the welfare of his daughter, who would one day inherit his fortune, Iwan-owsky trained her in the daily affairs of his business. Caro-lyne became a skilled horsewoman, and under her father's tutelage she assumed greater responsibility for the grain transactions on which the family's wealth ultimately rested. But Iwanowsky was also anxious to secure a marriage for her; if the family fortune were to be protected, she must produce an heir. She was only seventeen years old when she received an offer of matrimony from the 24-year-old Prince Nicholas, the youngest son of Field Marshal Ludwig Adolf Peter von Sayn-Wittgenstein.[3] The Wittgensteins were Protestants, and they owned a few small properties which bordered on the Iwanowsky domains. Iwanowsky knew full well that the Wittgensteins wanted to marry money, but he also recognized that his strait-laced daughter would never be wooed by a more eligible suitor. Three times Nicholas proposed and three times Carolyne rejected him. Frustrated and angry, Nicholas pro-tested to the father. According to the Vatican docu-ments, Iwanowsky put an end to further speculation by making an outright promise of his daughter's hand in marriage to Prince Nicholas, and he then summoned the recalcitrant Carolyne to his home in Starostince. There he subjected the unfortunate girl to intense verbal pressure and, when that failed, he threatened to disinherit her.[4] Witnesses later came forward to testify to the fact that Iwanowsky used fustigation against his daughter in his efforts to break her will. Despite her tears and entreaties not to marry Nicholas Wittgenstein, the marriage plans went forward, and the ceremony itself took place in Starostince on April 26, 1836 (Old Style). Many years later, Carolyne told Liszt that before the wed-ding she had "wept for a whole night" in her father's room, "and a few steps further on I gave up my happiness—hardly conscious of what I was doing and what I was accomplishing. What an initia-tion into the science of life!"[5] During the ceremony Iwanowsky never left his daughter's side lest she leave the church. These were the circumstances that would later form the basis of Carolyne's case for an annulment of her marriage, her petition al-leging *vis et metus*—force and intimidation. Moreover, there were other irregularities. It later transpired that the marriage service was conducted outside Carolyne's own parish, by a cleric she did not know, and without the prior consent of her own parish priest. These grave improprieties Carolyne later used to bolster her case. And what of Caro-lyne's mother during this traumatic time? She in-terceded in her daughter's behalf, but to no avail. Reluctantly she set out to attend the service but fell ill en route and was observed to remark: "I really do not have the courage to attend my daughter's wed-ding, for I know that she will be as unhappy as I am."[6]

Immediately after the wedding, Prince Ni-cholas took his child-bride to Kiev, where he held a position as captain in the Russian cavalry and aide-de-camp to the governor of that city. Carolyne found life there so unsettling that after only a few

---

[3]The field-marshal (1769-1843) had defended St. Petersburg against Napoleon in 1812. In 1834 he and all his descendants had been made princes of Prussia by King Friedrich Wilhelm III, despite the fact that they were Russian subjects. It is worth noting that neither Nicholas nor Carolyne was born into the upper aristocracy. She acquired the title of Princess almost by accident, as it were, because of marriage to a man who had only acquired it himself when he was twenty-two years old.

[4]ASV, NV Doc. No. 36.

[5]WA, Kasten 33, unpublished letter dated February 13, 1848. Before we cast Peter Iwanowsky in the role of villain, deter-mined at all costs to sacrifice his daughter on the altar of his own ambition, we should remember that "arranged" marriages of this sort were a commonplace in the nineteenth century. Indeed, it was perfectly normal among the upper classes to con-sider matrimony as an extension of business. The Wittgenstein-Iwanowska marriage seemed like a perfect bargain for both parties: Carolyne became a Princess, while Nicholas acquired property and a great deal of money. The fact that they made one another unhappy was irrelevant. Life offered a plentiful supply of diversions to those couples who were willing to make the necessary accommodations and compromises—especially if (as here) money was no impediment.

[6] ASV, CC Doc. No. 8.

months she returned to Woronince, the country estate that her father had given her as part of her wedding dowry. It was at Woronince that she gave birth to her only daughter, Princess Marie, on February 18, 1837 (New Style), a mere nine months after the wedding. To please his young wife, Nicholas relinquished his cavalry commission and joined her there.[7] The marriage soon failed, however, owing to their incompatible natures, and within four years they had agreed upon a permanent separation.

On October 4, 1844, Peter Iwanowsky suffered an apoplectic stroke while attending mass and died on the floor of the church because, claimed his daughter, he knew himself to be responsible for her misfortune.[8] Distraught with grief, Carolyne sealed his house in Starostince and entombed within it every book, picture and piece of furniture exactly as he had left them. More than three years were to elapse before she mustered the courage to unlock its doors again.[9] At the moment of Iwanowsky's death Carolyne inherited fourteen estates and became one of the wealthiest women in Ukraine.

III

After the death of her father, which had followed so hard on the failure of her marriage, Carolyne learned the full meaning of adversity. Scarcely had the body of Peter Iwanowsky been lowered into the grave than her three cousins (the daughters of Iwanowsky's brother, Dyonis) confronted her with a false will purporting to name them as beneficiaries. They knew that Iwanowsky had threatened to disinherit his daughter, and now that he was dead they were determined to do their best to make that threat become a reality. Because the document bore a watermark postdating his death, however, she was able to expose them.[10] The Wittgensteins were equally hostile. Fearing to lose all control over her fortune, they kept a careful watch on her affairs from their home just beyond her borders. These family squabbles turned Carolyne into a recluse. She escaped into her library, like her father before her, seeking consolation from the philosophers. There she read Kant, Fichte, and Goethe, writing a long commentary on *Faust*. A light always burned at her window as she read or scribbled the night away. And all the while she yearned secretly for her liberator.

Woronince is all but impossible to find on modern maps. It lies 49°40′ north and 20°10′ east. That places it, roughly speaking, about one hundred and fifty miles south-west of Kiev. Carolyne's château was situated in a park with a wide avenue of trees and a lake. The house was plainly furnished and devoid of taste. According to Princess Marie, who lived there until she was eleven years old, the walls of the dining-room were painted with parrots.[11] The ground floor was oblong, containing a library, a music-room, and a billiards room. Several busts of philosophers and poets stood like sentinels at the doorways and along the corridors. Carolyne's bedroom, on the first floor, was dominated by a large wooden crucifix hanging on the wall before a prayer stool. One or two flame-colored sofas stood out garishly against the dull grey wallpaper. Surrounding the house were the miserable huts in which the serfs led an animal-like existence. Clumps of bushes hid these wretched hovels from the eyes of visitors, as if to deny their very existence. The château itself was overrun with domestic servants who would unroll their mattresses at dusk and lie down in the dark corridors, or spend the night propped against the walls. Just outside the château Carolyne had built a "house chapel" for her family, her servants, and passing wayfarers. In the absence of the itinerant priest, she and her daughter frequently read the text of the mass, in Latin, to the motley congregation. Liszt himself delivered one such reading while he was a guest at Woronince.

---

[7]LSJ, p. 12.

[8]MAL, pp. 162 and LAG, p. 29. The Vatican documents support Carolyne's statement. When the case came to trial, Peter Iwanowsky himself was reported to have said before witnesses who had known him well that he bitterly regretted the unhappiness that he had introduced into his daughter's life. "Her father, seeing that his daughter's revulsion for her husband had not diminished with the passing of time, would often say to those who were close to him that he regretted having forced his daughter into a marriage against her will." See ASV, CC Doc. No. 7.

[9]WA, Kasten 33, February 13, 1848 (Old Style).

[10]LSJ, pp. 15-16. This information was given to La Mara by Princess Marie, Carolyne's daughter.

[11]LSJ, p. 13.

IV

In the winter of 1847 the Princess undertook her annual journey to Kiev in order to negotiate the prices on her forthcoming grain harvest. She herself has left a vivid account of this difficult 150-mile journey, which was made in a horse-drawn sled through snow-covered terrain, across frozen lakes, and with the constant howling of wolves in the background. These trips were not without physical danger, in fact, and they could sometimes take a week or more, especially if the traveler had the misfortune to be trapped in a blizzard.[12] Hundreds of Ukrainian farmers used to converge on Kiev's Corn Exchange, or "Contract Hall" as it was sometimes called, in which bargains were struck and loans were raised against next year's crops. What made Carolyne different was that she was a woman functioning in a man's world. Peter Iwanowsky had trained his daughter well, however, and she often aroused the admiration of her male competitors in the grain business. "Madame," remarked one of them, "you work more laboriously than any of us. I wish my son were man enough to undertake such a journey in this season."[13]

One day, when she was leaving Contract Hall, Carolyne happened to overhear her colleagues talking about a piano recital that had been given in the building a few days previously by Franz Liszt. The famous pianist was just then in the middle of a concert tour which had brought him from Western Europe, through the Danube Principalities, and into Ukraine. Her curiosity aroused, she attended his next recital at Kiev University.[14] A few days later she heard his *Pater noster* sung in the cathedral, and was so moved by it that she sent him an anonymous donation of 100 roubles for his charity subscription. Liszt insisted on knowing the identity of his anonymous benefactress so that he could thank her in person, and that is how they came to be introduced.

V

When Liszt first met Carolyne he was thirty-five years old, and he had been on the road more or less continuously since 1839. He was now regarded as the world's greatest pianist and the whole of Europe lay at his feet. The story of Liszt's life has been told so often that it is unnecessary to repeat it here. It is sufficient only to recall that scholars still refer to that brief eight-year period from 1839 to 1847 as the "years of transcendental execution," when Liszt unfolded a virtuoso career unmatched in musical history. That is a large claim, but it can be sustained. And had he died in 1847, the year in which he and Carolyne first met, the title of "the first modern pianist" could not have been withheld from him. His stage-presence was already the stuff of legends. Audiences were enslaved by him and there were times when they seemed to succumb to mass hysteria. Liszt's emotionally charged concerts were not unlike seances which strove for contact with the metaphysical. Hans Christian Andersen was present at one of his Hamburg recitals, in 1842, and described it this way:

> As Liszt sat before the piano, the first impression of his personality was derived from the appearance of strong passions in his wan face, so that he seemed to me a demon nailed fast to the instrument whence the tones streamed forth—they came from his blood, from his thoughts; he was a demon who would liberate his soul from thraldom; he was on the rack, his blood flowed and his nerves trembled; but as he continued to play, so the demon vanished. I saw that pale face assume a nobler and brighter expression: the divine soul shone from his eyes, from his every feature; he became as beauteous as only spirit and enthusiasm can make their worshipers.[15]

With his mesmeric personality, good looks, and Byronic manner, Liszt swept all before him. Swooning female "fans" attempted to take cuttings

---

[12]During one such journey, undertaken in March 1847, the Princess and her maidservant were trapped in their coach while a blizzard raged around them. "Have you ever seen a blizzard?" she asked Liszt. "It is a fine moment of nature's folly. The sun sometimes appears in it like a flash of intelligence promptly blotted out. Then everything is white and dark, yet simple and pure and wild." (WA, Kasten 33, unpublished letter dated March 21, 1847, Old Style).

[13]Ibid.

[14]The concert took place on February 2, 1847 (Old Style). Carolyne preserved the program and after her death it was donated to the Weimar Liszt Museum by her daughter, Princess Marie (LSJ, p. 21).

[15]*A Poet's Bazaar*, Vol. 1, pp. 50-51.

of his hair. Others carried glass phials into which they poured his coffee dregs. Some even collected his cigar butts, which they hid in their cleavages. Heine labeled the phenomenon "Lisztomania," and the term has stuck. Few of his encounters with the opposite sex were anything more than passing affairs, but by the time he met Princess Carolyne they had colored his reputation. One or two had created a scandal, particularly the Lola Montez episode, which he never really succeeded in living down. It was gossip about Lola Montez that had finally put an end to his long-standing liaison with Countess Marie d'Agoult, in 1844, by whom he had three children. As Marie put it, she did not mind being his mistress, but she objected to being one of his mistresses. In 1846 Marie avenged herself by publishing her autobiographical novel *Nélida*, in which Liszt is depicted as an artistically impotent painter named Guermann Regnier. Liszt always refused to recognize himself in *Nélida*. He called the character of Guermann "a stupid invention." That he was hurt by the book, however, cannot be denied.

It is difficult to imagine the impact that such a magical personality as Liszt must have had on Princess Carolyne. For years she had lived as a recluse at Woronince. The only members of the opposite sex she now met were the dull "gentleman farmers" of Ukraine, her business colleagues. Liszt was the dazzling antithesis of everything that they stood for, a sophisticated man of the world who swept everyone before him. And there was something else, too. The Princess was one of those women who are destined to love but once. Such females seem fated to go through life locked in limbo, their emotional life a frozen wasteland. But should they meet the man who sets both heart and body aflame, they are his for eternity. And Liszt had one other advantage for Carolyne. He was not only a man with whom she could go through life, but he was also a musical genius of the front rank. Henceforth, she now had a mission: to make life softer for him, to sacrifice herself on the altar of his artistic ambitions.

VI

After their first meeting Carolyne invited him to visit her at Woronince in a few days' time. The ostensible reason for this invitation was the tenth birthday celebration of Princess Marie, which was held on February 18. We say "ostensible," because there is evidence that from the moment Carolyne set eyes on Liszt she was in love with him. Years later she revealed to him the cause of that fatal attraction: she saw in him the spirit of her dead father. "It was as clear as daylight, in my mind's eye, that the Lord was sending you to take the place my father had left vacant."[16] Liszt stayed at Woronince as Carolyne's guest for a mere ten days. We shall probably never know for certain what happened during this brief eternity, but the force of their encounter was strong enough to produce a lasting consequence. When the time came for Liszt to resume his concert tour of Ukraine, it was already understood that he and Carolyne would rendezvous later in the year in Odessa. Meanwhile, his travels were to take him through Lemberg, Czernovsty, Jassy, and Galatz, culminating in a month-long visit to Constantinople, in June 1847, where he played in

the Tchiraghan Palace before the Turkish Sultan, Abdul-Medjid Khan. He then sailed from Constantinople across the Black Sea aboard the cruiser *Peter the Great*, which docked in Odessa in mid-July. There he and Carolyne were reunited.

Accompanying Carolyne was her husband, Prince Nicholas, who had come to Odessa to observe the Russian army maneuvers. There is no suggestion that Nicholas played the role of an outraged husband at this time. Quite the contrary. The trio were often seen together in Odessa's fashionable society. Did Nicholas know that his wife was enamored of Liszt? If so, his "civilized" behavior can only be explained by the fact that he saw in the great pianist the solution to his life's problem. This is borne out by the fact that when Carolyne invited Liszt to spend three months with her at her château in Woronince, Nicholas not only did not stand in her way but tacitly encouraged the arrangement by going off to Berlin in pursuit of his own pleasures. Nicholas's aggression towards both Liszt and Carolyne came later, when her case for an annulment became mired in

---

[16]WA, Kasten 34, from a letter dated July 13, 1853. The entire text of this letter has meanwhile been published in *Silences: Liszt* (Paris 1986), pp. 23-25.

legal difficulties and it began to look as if he might lose control over her fortune.

In September 1847 Liszt made a momentous decision. He resolved to give up his life as a wandering minstrel and turn his back on the concert platform for good. The idea had long been germinating in his mind for he wanted leisure to compose. He was undoubtedly supported in this resolve by Princess Carolyne who saw in him a great artist whose irregular lifestyle was harming his work. As early as 1842 he had been given the position of Kapellmeister at the court of Weimar. The thought of taking up residence there held many attractions for him. Weimar was one of the most cultured cities in Germany. It throve under the benign patronage of the Grand Duchess Maria Pawlowna, the sister of Tsar Nicholas I of Russia. Already it could boast of more than a century's unbroken association with the arts. Bach had lived and worked there; so too had Goethe and Schiller. Moreover, Weimar possessed an orchestra and an opera house. It was an attractive offer, and Liszt now decided to take it up. The last concert that he ever gave for money took place in the Ukrainian city of Elisabetgrad, in September 1847. He was still only thirty-five years old.

VII

In the meantime, the Princess had traveled back to Woronince in order to prepare her "little cottage," as she put it, for Liszt's arrival. She reached Woronince on September 11 (Old Style),[17] and Liszt himself got there a week later. Liszt spent his thirty-sixth birthday at Woronince. On October 22 Carolyne gave a large birthday party for him to which she invited hundreds of her peasant workers from the surrounding areas. As a special surprise she also invited a local gypsy band to play for him. Liszt was always susceptible to gypsy music, and he later wrote about this particular occasion in his book *The Gypsies and their Music in Hungary*.[18] This visit to Woronince was not harmful to his work. Carolyne had installed a piano in his room until his own arrived from Odessa. Among the works he brought to completion were his *Glanes de Woronince*, which he dedicated to Princess Marie, and much of his great cycle *Harmonies poétiques et religieuses*, which he dedicated to Princess Carolyne.

The three months that Liszt and Carolyne spent at Woronince—a honeymoon by any other name—changed the course of his life. It was there that Carolyne resolved to throw in her lot with his and follow him to Weimar. Liszt made only one stipulation: that before leaving Ukraine she should make over to her daughter one half of her fortune so that the child's inheritance be secured.[19] Both Liszt and Carolyne were confident that her marriage could be annulled and that they would soon be free to marry. They knew that their chief obstacle was Tsar Nicholas I, who, as the titular head of the Russian Orthodox Church, exercised absolute authority over the dissolution of marriages.[20] But was not Liszt's most powerful ally in Weimar Maria Pawlowna, the tsar's sister? And would not she intercede in behalf of her genius Kapellmeister?

The first winter snows now started to fall, and Liszt and Carolyne were marooned from the outside world. Vows of eternal love were ex-

---

17WA, Kasten 33, u. 1.

18RGS, Vol. 6, pp. 157-59.

19LSJ, p. 23.

20There was no love lost between Tsar Nicholas and Liszt. Once, when the great pianist was giving a recital in St. Petersburg, the monarch arrived late and started talking to one of his aides. Liszt stopped playing and sat at the keyboard with bowed head. When Nicholas inquired the cause of the silence, Liszt replied: "Music herself should be silent when Nicholas speaks." It was a chilling rebuke which set the whole of St. Petersburg talking. Not long afterwards, Nicholas asked Liszt to give a concert for the survivors of the Battle of Borodino. It was a tactless idea and Liszt felt obliged to refuse. "I owe my education and my celebrity to France," he said. "It is impossible for me to make common cause with her adversaries." This reply angered the Tsar, who made it known that "the [long] hair and the political opinions of this man displease me." Liszt retorted: "I let my hair grow in Paris and shall cut it only in Paris. As for my political views, I have none and will have none until the day the tsar deigns to put at my disposal three hundred thousand bayonets." (RLKM, Vol. 2, p. 186.) We cannot properly appreciate the impact of Liszt's retort until we put it into some sort of historical perspective. This encounter with Tsar Nicholas took place in 1841, less than thirty years after his elder brother, Tsar Alexander I,. had defeated Napoleon in Russia and had pursued the remnants of the French army all the way back to Paris. Liszt's remark was tantamount to saying that the only reason people listened to Nicholas's views was because he had inherited an army. He could hardly have guessed that the fates would one day entrust his personal happiness to this despot.

changed, and the Princess gave Liszt a Gordian knot of pure gold, which symbolized a union that could not be broken.[21] The time had now come to lift the veil of silence that Liszt had drawn around his relationship with Carolyne. The European newspapers had picked up rumors of a forthcoming betrothal; the story was premature and it embarrassed him.[22] On December 22 he broke the news of his new relationship to Marie d'Agoult. Ever since their rupture, three years earlier, they had maintained a sporadic correspondence, if only because the fate of their three children still bound them together. He told her that he had met "a great character united with a great spirit...Attribute the change in my location to a very real change in my life..."[23] "Nélida's" reply was scathing. "So, a new apparition has seized your imagination and your heart? So much the better. This woman of great character (so you say) will not consent to share your life." And with a bitter reference to her earlier *cri de coeur*, she went on: "She will not want to be *one of your mistresses*."[24] Liszt showed the letter to Carolyne, whose forthright rejoinder deserves to be better known: "On the contrary, I would be happy for her to know that one really wants to be *one of the mistresses*, for there are devotions without limits."[25]

Early in January 1848 the lovers of Woronince took their leave of one another. Liszt journeyed to Weimar in order to begin his fulltime duties there, while Carolyne herself set out on one of those nightmare journeys to Kiev. Her primary purposes were to sell off some of her estates and commence legal proceedings for an annulment of her marriage. That this action weighed heavily on her mind cannot be doubted. She wrote: "The bells of Kiev have often formed a solemn midnight accompaniment to the muffled sobbing of my heart."[26] One of the most painful aspects of this journey was to return to the old property of her father at Starostince. When she broke the seals on the door, placed there three years earlier, she entered his study and found everything as it had been on the day of Peter Iwanowsky's death, as if frozen in time—the table covered with his papers, the half-turned chair, the antique desk that he had inherited from his own father, and the blond curl he had cut from Carolyne's infant head twenty-five years earlier still hanging from the crucifix on the wall, which bore the inscription: "I am the Way."[27] It distressed her to part with her lands, for to her it was like breaking faith with her ancestors. "Today I have just sold one of my lands, one of the first that my grandfather bought, one of the cornerstones of that fortune amassed so laboriously and honestly by the hard work and sincere efforts of two generations of men...I burst into tears when it passed into other hands."[28] One of her last acts was to deposit with the clerical authorities in Kiev a petition for the annulment of her marriage; this petition was at once forwarded to Archbishop Ignaz Holowinski, the Metropolitan of St. Petersburg, whose response we shall come to shortly. Then, the main purpose of her journey accomplished, she returned to Woronince, closed up the house, and fled with her daughter across the Russian border into Austria.[29]

Her journey must have been filled with high adventure. Europe was in a state of revolutionary upheaval and Russia was about to close its borders. The tsar's troops were everywhere. Liszt himself had a hand in the design of Carolyne's getaway coach,[30] which was stuffed with precious stones and the money she had raised on the sale of her properties; this would form the basis of her personal wealth in the years to come.

[21]It is reproduced in Robert Bory's *La vie de Franz Liszt par l'image* (Geneva 1936), p. 130.

[22]He wrote to Baron von Gutmansthal: "As for the *Journal de Francfort*, it announces the marriage of a famous pianist with a Russian Princess, but it is only a rumour that I am not at all in a position to confirm to you" (GSL, p. 30).

[23]ACLA, Vol. 2, p. 390.

[24]ACLA, Vol. 2, p. 417.

[25]Unpublished letter dated January 27, 1848 (Old Style), WA, Kasten 33. Carolyne had already read Marie d'Agoult's novel *Nélida* the previous spring, not long after she had first met Liszt, as is proved by the derogatory remarks she had made about the book to her friend Marie Potocka. "It takes courage to expose oneself in something less than a shirt," she observed sarcastically (LAG, p. 34).

[26]Unpublished letter dated January 20, 1848 (Old Style).WA, Kasten 33.

[27]Unpublished letter, dated February 13, 1848 (Old Style). WA, Kasten 33.

[28]Unpublished letter dated January 25, 1848 (Old Style). WA, Kasten 33.

[29]During Carolyne's long absence in Kiev, the eleven-year-old Princess Marie had stayed with her grandmother, old Frau Wittgenstein. When she went to collect her daughter, Carolyne made no mention of her imminent departure for Germany. By this single act Carolyne made lifelong enemies of the Wittgenstein family, and of Nicholas in particular, who later not only accused his wife of kidnapping their daughter but attempted to reciprocate the act (see p. 10).

[30]HLSW, p. 23.

VIII

When Liszt got to Weimar, towards the end of January 1848, he moved into the Erbprinz Hotel in the Marktplatz, not far from the Court Theatre. This was to be his official address throughout his thirteen-year stay in Weimar. Even after he had moved into the Altenburg with Carolyne, his mail was always forwarded to the Erbprinz, and messages from the Court were delivered there as a matter of course. This arrangement was meant to save the Court from embarrassment: the problem of Liszt's *ménage à deux* was solved by the simple expedient of not recognizing it.

Almost from the moment that Liszt had arrived in Weimar, he was plunged into a busy round of rehearsals and concerts. On February 16 he conducted a performance of Flotow's *Martha* at the Court Theatre in honor of Maria Pawlowna's birthday. A few days later he appeared as soloist in a Henselt piano concerto, and between times he had to give four or five singing lessons a week to Duchess Sophie (the wife of Carl Alexander, the future grand duke). He also had a number of private audiences with Maria Pawlowna, at which he brought her up to date about Carolyne and asked her to intercede with Tsar Nicholas in their behalf.

Meanwhile, Carolyne was en route from Russia. As she crossed the frontiers of Podolia for the last time, on April 2, she felt no remorse. "I am about to leave the country which has held me in its shrewish bosom for fifteen years, and whose milk has turned to vinegar and bile."[31] She wrote to Liszt every day and kept changing the place of their rendezvous, perhaps to confuse the censors. Liszt finally traveled to the Austro-Russian border and they were re-united at Kryzanowicz, the mountain castle of his friend Prince Felix Lichnowsky, about the middle of April. After a brief trip to Vienna, Eisenstadt, and Raiding (where Liszt showed Carolyne the humble cottage in which he had been born), the couple got back to Weimar in July 1848. Liszt returned to his bachelor quarters in the Erbprinz Hotel, while the Princess rented the Altenburg, a large house on the outskirts of the city. A year later, when their wedding looked as far distant as ever, Liszt moved in with her, and they lived in the Altenburg as man and wife for the next twelve years.

IX

Carolyne's original plea for an annulment was brought before the consistory of Mohilow, in the vicinity of St. Petersburg, on May 4, 1848, one month after she had fled Russia. The basis of her case was that she had been forced into marriage by her father, and her petition alleged *vis et metus*—that is, "violence and fear." This ecclesiastical court of three judges had appointed one Deacon Mierzwinski to be the Defender of the Marriage Bond, and the case was tried on May 12 (Old Style). Drama and confrontation must have characterized the occasion: ten family witnesses were called for Prince Nicholas and five for Princess Carolyne, including her mother.[32] The case for the Princess was flimsy, Mierzwinski argued. She had been married for twelve years before filing her petition. Why had she not begun these proceedings at once? Moreover, there was a child of the union, which further strengthened the matrimonial bond. Carolyne, for her part, made it clear through written documentation that she was only seventeen at the time of her marriage, that it was her father (not Prince Nicholas) who had coerced her; and there were witnesses within the family circle to testify to that fact. One of them, a servant named Julianna Stolarczuk, claimed that fustigation had been used against Carolyne; another, named Peter Slobodiany, confirmed this and asserted that he had listened to it through the door. Carolyne further argued that the wedding had taken place at Starostince, where she was not a parishioner; consequently, the marriage service had not been blessed by her own parish priest, who had been told nothing about it (a highly irregular practice in the Catholic church). Moreover, it was claimed that Carolyne had continued to live with Prince Nicholas for no other reason than that of not displeasing her father.

Deacon Mierzwinski responded by pointing out that the word of servants could hardly be

---

[31]Unpublished letter dated April 3 (Old Style). WA, Kasten 33.

[32]ASV, NV Doc. No. 36.

trusted, since they all knew that their very livelihood depended on their testimony. For all his eloquence, however, he failed to convince the court; Carolyne's case was upheld, and it was then referred to her own diocese of Luck-Zhitomir, in Ukraine, where the evidence (which included a written protest from Mierzwinski)[33] was re-examined. More than three years elapsed before the Luck-Zhitomir court brought forth its decision: "that the matrimonial bond between Prince Wittgenstein and Carolyne Iwanowska be declared valid." Carolyne now had two court decisions, one in her favor and one against. A year later her case was referred once more to the consistory of Mohilow, which, after reviewing the case, upturned the earlier decision and ruled again in Carolyne's favor. The judges actually issued a decree of annulment on November 13, 1852. It was at this point that the Metropolitan Archbishop Ignaz Holowinski refused to give his sanction and halted Carolyne's motion in its tracks.[34] This was devastating news for the Princess. The case had been heard in Mohilow (1848), struck down in Luck-Zhitomir (1851), restored in Mohilow (1852), and finally ruled against by the Metropolitan of St. Petersburg (1852). After four years of emotional turmoil, she had nothing whatever to show for her efforts.

The situation was just as bleak for Prince Nicholas. There is ample evidence to suggest that by now he was at one with Carolyne in his desire for an annulment. The only point of dissension between the pair was the sort of property settlement he would receive from the Iwanowsky fortune. In the summer of 1852, at the very moment when the case looked as if it was at last taking a favorable turn, Nicholas decided to enter into direct negotiations with his wife. The go-between was the Russian ambassador to Weimar, Baron von Maltitz, from whom we gain some unusual insights into the matter. Caro-

lyne had turned her annulment into a crusade, and Maltitz (who by virtue of his official position was her nearest target) had been deluged with letters, briefs, and memoranda, all of which were designed to bring him to a fuller understanding of her plight. She had even offered him money in an attempt to speed the process along, a ploy he found objectionable.[35] Through the offices of the governor-general of Kiev it was finally arranged that Nicholas would journey to Weimar in person and bring with him a proposal for a financial settlement. Nicholas arrived in Weimar on September 12, 1852, and made his way to the Altenburg the following day. The document was drafted in the presence of the court marshal, Baron von Vitzthum, and it was witnessed by Nicholas, Carolyne, Princess Marie, and Liszt. It was the first time that Nicholas and Carolyne had seen one another since she had fled Russia, and the meeting must have been a painful one. Liszt, we know, had resisted this visit in a vain attempt to spare Carolyne's feelings, and he even threatened to use force to keep Nicholas away from the Altenburg.[36] He felt that Carolyne was being used, and later events were to bear him out.

The essential points embodied in the agreement were these:

1. In the event that Carolyne re-married,

    a. one-seventh of her fortune would pass to Nicholas;

    b. six-sevenths would pass to Princess Marie;

    c. Carolyne would receive 200,000 roubles in cash.[37]

2. The Grand Duchess Maria Pawlowna would meanwhile take over the guardianship of Princess Marie and ensure that the morals of the young girl were protected.

This last proposal was a sensitive one, and it was meant to humiliate. Nicholas was determined to reg-

---

[33]It was Mierzwinski's duty, as Defender of the Marriage Bond, to appeal all decisions affecting the bond to a higher court. The role of *Defensor Vincali Matrimoni* was more than a hundred years old at this time, having been introduced by Benedict XIV in his papal bull *Dei miseratione* of 1741. There was no more powerful symbol of the profound importance attached to the annulment proceedings than the presence in court of "God's advocate," whose holy task it was to defend the sanctity of the marriage bond by all legal means.

[34]This was not only irregular, it was possibly illegal too. There was nothing in canon law to validate such an arbitrary action. The judges who made up a consistory had an equal vote, and

majority decisions prevailed. Holowinski's veto was to become a bone of contention in the years ahead, and it was eventually upturned.

[35]BLTB, Vol. 2, p. 138.

[36]BLTB, Vol. 3, pp. 139-40.

[37]The properties that Carolyne was expected to yield included Starostince, Bielaski, Buchny, Iwanki (in the environs of Kiev), Woronince, Tencki, Cetwukowce (in the district of Litin), Wonlowce, Wolfwodowska, Polok (in the district of Berislawl), and Bielany, Szendrowska, Kislicku, and Lozowa (in the districts of Mohilow and Jampol.)

ister his objection to the fact that his adolescent daughter was growing up under the roof of his wife's paramour. He described the Altenburg, and the atmosphere of sycophantism that surrounded Liszt there, as "a drug." That Carolyne signed the document at all must be regarded as a measure of her desperation to sever the chains that still bound her to the Wittgensteins. Accordingly, the fourteen-year-old Princess Marie, together with her governess "Scotchy" Anderson, was removed from the Altenburg and given a room in the royal castle. Liszt joked with Marie about her misfortune in an attempt to revive her flagging spirits, and he nicknamed her spartan quarters "the Bastille." This unhappy arrangement lasted for two years, when it was brought to a sudden and dramatic end. In the summer of 1854 Weimar experienced a series of exceptionally heavy thunderstorms. The castle tower was struck by lightning in the middle of the night, and Princess Marie was discovered senseless on the floor of her room. She suffered intensely from this traumatic event and was brought back to the Altenburg to recover; she never returned to "the Bastille."

Scarcely any of the documents relating to Prince Nicholas's visit to Weimar during the late summer of 1852 have survived. Control over Carolyne's fortune was still the Wittgensteins' primary aim, of course; but Nicholas, if not his family, wanted a swift and amicable end to the impasse. We know that as early as 1852 he wanted to re-marry and no longer wished Carolyne "to go on bearing my name."[38] Despite the paucity of original sources, however, there are some scattered pieces of information which, when drawn together, help us to reveal the background of tension and mistrust which prevailed at the Altenburg when Nicholas crossed the threshold on September 13. One such source is the diary of Theodor von Bernhardi, politician and military historian, who was in Weimar for much of 1851 and 1852 and was an eye-witness to these extraordinary comings and goings. There was a confrontation between Liszt and Prince Nicholas which nearly ended in blows. Nicholas later expressed the desire not to meet Liszt again "in order to avoid an

encounter that might be unfortunate for him rather than for me."[39] Were Liszt and Carolyne under threat of physical force during these years? It seems so, to judge from a letter that Carolyne wrote some time later to Baron von Maltitz. In it she complains that not only was she menaced by police at her husband's behest, but that these same police, "furnished with imperial orders," attempted a brutal kidnapping of Princess Marie.[40] The Tsar eventually sent his plenipotentiary Prince Peter von Oldenburg to Weimar in the early part of 1853 in order to enforce his will. At the heart of the matter lay the fact that the property settlement between Carolyne and Nicholas carried the authority of the tsar; the issue of an arrest warrant was the Russian autocrat's clumsy way of ensuring that the terms of the agreement were enforced. Carolyne panicked at the thought that she and her daughter might well be arrested and returned to Russia forcibly. (Since she knew that her husband had always maintained that she had "kidnapped" their daughter from Ukraine and had taken her without his consent to Weimar, the fear that her in-laws might reciprocate was a real one.) She caught the overnight train to Paris in order to seek the protection of Napoleon III.[41] We shall probably never know the full extent of this human tragedy, but it is clear from these occasional clues that there must have been some appalling scenes at the Altenburg in which Liszt was inextricably involved.

In 1854 the Princess was summoned back to Russia in order to explain her non-compliance with the terms of the property settlement. She refused to obey this directive (after all, her marriage to Nicholas had still not been annulled), whereupon the Russian minister of justice recommended that the full rigor of the law be applied against her, and Tsar Nicholas I sequestered all her lands and estates. The following year, 1855, his successor, Tsar Alexander II, stripped her of her citizenship and condemned her to exile. The Iwanowsky estates were eventually put into trust for Princess Marie until she reached her majority; meanwhile, the girl received 75,000 roubles a year from the profits. Carolyne's means were now drasti-

[38]BLTB, Vol. 2, p. 142. The current object of Nicholas's attentions was a widow from Berlin, Frau Kosens. He appears to have tired of her, as of his other amours.

[39]BLTB, Vol. 3, pp. 139-40.

[40]HFL, p. 180.

[41]RL, p. 94. One of Princess Marie's suitors at this time was Baron Charles-Angélique Talleyrand, the French ambassador to

Weimar. Had the pair become betrothed, the diplomatic protection enjoyed by Talleyrand could have been extended to Marie as well, and the Wittgensteins would not have wanted to risk creating a diplomatic incident. In the event, Carolyne's attempt to gain an audience with Napoleon III came to nothing. See TOS-W, pp. 218-19.

cally diminished, and she frequently had to turn to her daughter to settle her debts. Her exile was particularly hard for her to bear. This mark of imperial disfavor was transmitted to the court at Weimar, with which Carolyne was already persona non grata, and she became a pariah, untouchable by anyone with court connections. What this meant in such a small town as Weimar can hardly be imagined. One story may stand for all the others. On September 4, 1859, Carolyne was invited to observe the unveiling of the Goethe-Schiller monument from the home of her friend Henriette von Schorn, whose windows offered a grandstand view of the ceremonials. The whole of Weimar's establishment was gathered in the central square outside, and the grand duke and duchess themselves were in attendance. The moment that Carolyne entered the room, all the ladies of the court got up and left. This painful snub was immediately seen by Liszt, who advanced towards Henriette, kissed her hand in grateful acknowledgement of her support, and then led Carolyne to the square outside where they took their seats in full glare of the court officials gathered there.[42] During the Weimar years,

Liszt and Carolyne often had to brazen it out on formal occasions.

And there the matter might have rested, an uneasy stalemate among the principal contenders—the Russian court on the one hand, the Weimar court on the other, and Carolyne and Liszt in the middle.

But in 1855 two very important developments occurred. Holowinski died and was succeed by Archbishop Wenceslas Zyliński, who knew the details of this case very well. That same year, too, Prince Nicholas secured a Protestant divorce, and in 1856 he re-married.[43] Carolyne's legal advisers informed her that the complexion of her case now looked somewhat different. Hitherto she had been fighting two adversaries, the Wittgensteins and the Church. Now she would only have to fight one, since Nicholas had dropped his defense the moment he re-married and had no further interest in the outcome. In 1857 they brought it once more before the lower consistory of Luck-Zhitomir, the court that had originally denied her petition. That court, however, upheld its earlier decision and, by implication, Holowinsky's veto.

X

This was the dismal history of the legal wrangle when the case took a dramatic turn. In the spring of 1859 Carolyne received a visit from one of her tenant-farmers in Ukraine, a lawyer named Władislaw Okraszewski, who persuaded Carolyne to appeal directly to the new archbishop, Zyliński. For this plan to be effective, Okraszewski told her, it would require the payment of 70,000 silver roubles in fees and disbursements.[44] This was an enormous sum of money which the Princess was obliged to borrow from her daughter, who now controlled her former

fortune. Furthermore, Zyliński would have to seek a special dispensation from Pius IX to re-open the case. This he did, and Pius issued that document through the Holy Congregation of the Council on August 8, 1859.[45] The Mohilow court was duly reconvened towards the end of the year and, after a thorough review of all the original documents, Archbishop Zyliński issued a decree of annulment on February 24, 1860 (Old Style).[46] On the basis of this document alone, Carolyne and Liszt were free to marry. Unfortunately, the annulment was at once

---

[42]SZM, pp. 92-93.

[43]Nicholas's second marriage took place in January 1856; his new wife was Marie Michaïloff, a twenty-six-year-old nurse to the children of Prince Souvaroff, governor of Riga.

[44]Okraszewski appears to have lost no time in taking up Carolyne's case with Zyliński. The Vatican files contain a letter from Zyliński to Okraszewski, dated June 13, 1859, which indicates that the latter had already launched the first of a series of detailed attacks on the way in which that case had been handled in the past [ASV, CC Doc. no. 5].

[45]The three-month delay was caused by the fact that Zyliński was obliged to direct his request through the Imperial cabinet in St. Petersburg. Russian prelates were not permitted to communicate directly with the Holy See.

[46]ASV, NV Doc. No. 6. Zyliński selected three high-ranking clerics to serve on his consistory: Maximilian Staniewski, Bishop of Platen; Andreas Dobszewicz, Provost of Szydlow; and Monsignor Moszezynski, Prelate Deacon of Minsk. After reviewing the case in great detail, Zyliński and his colleagues made two pronouncements which are worth recording here.

(a) "On the basis of these findings, [we] unanimously decreed the marriage of Carolyne Iwanowska to be null and void.

(b) "Accordingly, through the present letters, in the absence of any other impediment which His Holiness thought might be an obstacle, we state, pronounce, declare, and moroever issue, a definitive sentence attributing to the aforesaid Carolyne full faculty to contract a new marriage freely and legitimately."

suspended by the Bishop of Fulda (in whose diocese both Carolyne and Liszt were living) on the authority of the Papal Nuncio to Vienna, Monsignor Antonino De Luca.[47] Lurking in the background was the powerful figure of Monsignor (later Cardinal) Gustav von Hohenlohe, who lived in the Vatican, and whose family was determined at all costs to prevent a marriage between Liszt and Carolyne from taking place.

What was the basis of Gustav's hostility? A few months earlier, Carolyne's 24-year-old daughter Princess Marie had married Gustav's younger brother, Prince Konstantin Hohenlohe. The marriage had taken place in Weimar after a courtship of only a few weeks.[48] From the moment that Marie had become his bride, Konstantin exercised complete control over the fortune that had passed to her through her mother as her wedding dowry. The first thing he did was to renege on the debt of 70,000 silver roubles. This caused Carolyne many problems, and in the end she was obliged to send Liszt to Vienna to withdraw some of the money from capital she had invested years earlier with Liszt's lawyer-cousin Eduard, in Vienna. But why should Konstantin refuse to allow his young wife to discharge a debt-of-honor to her own mother? He feared that if Carolyne succeeded in gaining an annulment, Marie could be declared illegitimate, and the marriage contract so laboriously drawn up between Carolyne and the Hohenlohes might come to be regarded as null and void.[49] More serious still were the possible consequences of a marriage between Liszt and Carolyne. In 1860 Carolyne was still only forty-two years old and was theoretically capable of bearing Liszt a child. This offspring would certainly be regarded by the church as legitimate and would therefore be a strong claimant to Carolyne's fortune, the possession of which the newly-illegitimate Marie might be forced to relinquish. Such were the dark thoughts that turned Konstantin into Carolyne's adversary within weeks of becoming her son-in-law. It was not merely that he did not want her to marry Liszt; he did not want her to marry *anyone*. Carolyne knew that she would now have to look to Rome, and Pius IX, to have Fulda's suspension lifted.

XI

On May 17, 1860, Carolyne set out from Weimar in the company of Okraszewski and her maid Augusta. The trio made their way down to Marseilles and boarded ship for Italy. (The name of the vessel was *The Quirinal* which Carolyne took to be a happy omen, since it was the name of one of the summer residences of the popes.) The crossing was rough, the Princess tells us, and the passengers "were pitched about like parcels."[50]

It was not until Carolyne arrived in the Eternal City, on May 24, 1860, that she learned the full extent of her plight. Gustav Hohenlohe had developed a twin strategy against her. First he had raised doubts in De Luca's mind about Okraszewski's "fee" of 70,000 silver roubles and suggested that it must have

[47]ASV, NV Doc. No. 12. From the time of the Reformation, Fulda had been the centre of Roman Catholic administration in Thuringia. Since Carolyne and Liszt were domiciled in Weimar, they were part of the diocese of Fulda and were bound by the bishop's suspension.

[48]The ceremony was held in the small Catholic church in Weimar, on October 15, 1859.

[49]The fear that Marie could be declared illegitimate on the dissolution of her mother's marriage was a real one. We are dealing here with the concept of annulment, not divorce. Divorce acknowledges that a marriage once existed but is now ended. Annulment is a retrospective admission that the marriage had never existed in the first place, since the ceremony itself was based on some grave impropriety, offensive both to God and to the church. The offspring of such unions often had to protect their inheritance rights by means of legally binding contracts drawn up at the time of dissolution. Carolyne, Konstantin, and Marie herself had all foreseen such difficulties, of course. One month before she married, Marie had petitioned Pope Pius IX to declare her the legitimate off-spring of a legitimate marriage. While the petition for Marie's legitimacy is in the Vatican file [ASV, CC Doc. 11] the response is not. Moreover, Żyliński did not address the matter in his decree of annulment, dated February 24, 1860. Given Princess Marie's powerful connections within the Hohenlohe family, however, there is no reason to suppose that her petition for legitimacy was not granted. But if it was, the information appears to have been withheld from Carolyne who, for a time, became frantic about the matter. The first inkling that Carolyne had that her daughter could be stigmatized as a bastard, and that she herself could be branded as a bigamist, comes in one of her unpublished letters to Liszt, dated August 30, 1860 (WA, Kasten 36). There is no doubt that she was reflecting some views fed to her by high-ranking clerics. In the Vatican files there is a memorandum to Pope Pius IX which states that "By contracting [a second marriage] she would make herself a concubine" (ASV, CC Doc. No. 33). The position of the Catholic Church is very well expressed in ASV, CC Doc. 7.

[50]The details of the Princess's journey are preserved in an unpublished letter to Liszt dated May 24, 1860 (WA, Kasten 37).

been used for the purpose of bribing the judges who sat on the St. Petersburg consistory.[51] (It is clear from the documents that Hohenlohe regarded Okraszewski as nothing but "a meddler," and he came to regard him as "quite a scoundrel.")[52] The charge of bribery was one of the most serious that could be leveled against a consistory and it was strenuously denied by Archbishop Żyliński, whose forthright response deserves to be quoted: "It causes me the greatest pain that I and the judges of this Diocese could have been suspected of bad faith...I pray and wish that Your Most Reverend Excellency be completely persuaded that the petitioner's solicitor did not give out a farthing...to corrupt the judges and dishonestly obtain a favorable outcome of the case."[53] Secondly, Hohenlohe had found a witness who was present at Carolyne's wedding, a cousin named Denise Poniatowska, who denied that coercion had been used. If the testimony of this witness were accepted, Carolyne knew that she herself would be found guilty of perjury, with all the aforementioned penalties.

At first Hohenlohe had worked behind the scenes. He was politeness itself to Carolyne's face. Indeed, not long after she arrived in Rome, he received her as an honored guest at his quarters in the Vatican, where she was won over by his charm. During a long conversation with him about the legal complexities of her case, she noticed that his mitre, while studded with precious stones, was lacking in emeralds, so she later presented him with two such jewels from her own collection.[54] For a time the pair met almost daily, and Gustav took her on various sight-seeing expeditions and generally played the part of host. Occasionally, they even traveled outside Rome and went to visit Hadrian's Villa and the Villa d'Este. Although Carolyne did not at first know it, practically every conversation that she had with Hohenlohe was reported back to Konstantin in Vienna. Gustav proved himself to be a master of duplicity who, in the matter of the Iwanowsky fortune, was determined to place the interests of his brother first. By August 1860, however, the Princess knew that the source of most of her difficulties in Rome was Hohenlohe himself. In an unpublished letter to Liszt she speaks of Gustav's "unbelievable treason" and goes on to accuse him of having broken her confidences and of having "exercised an influence on the pope that was disastrous for me."[55] It was at this juncture that Carolyne appealed directly to Pius IX, and the pontiff granted her an audience on September 9. She begged the Holy Father for his blessing, told him that her marriage was indeed the result of parental constraint, and pleaded with him for his intervention. "Mia cara figlia, non ti di-

---

[51]Letter of De Luca to Żyliński, dated April 24, 1860 [ASV, NV Doc. No. 15]. The allegations of bribery first began to surface just over a month after the judgement of February 24, 1860 had been issued. It appears that the Bishop of Fulda had been sent a damaging letter by a Domenican monk, a certain Father Filippo Guidi, who was a professor of Dogmatic Theology in the University of Vienna. This worthy claimed that while on a recent visit to Rome he had been approached by some "high-ranking clerics" who wished to remain anonymous and who told him that Carolyne's annulment was obtained through bribery [ASV, NV Doc. No. 7]. Guidi was enjoined by them to return at once to Vienna and report the matter to the papal nuncio, which he did, requesting that his identity be protected through anonymity. This was the cloak-and-dagger atmosphere against which Carolyne's case henceforth unfolded. Who were the high-ranking clerics? We cannot be sure. But Gustav Hohenlohe had been in touch about this case with Father Guidi, a fact that is proved by the former's letter to De Luca, dated "The Vatican, April 19, 1860." [ASV, NV Doc. No. 14]. Hohenlohe would certainly have benefitted from the mantle of anonymity, since he could hardly afford to be seen publicly meddling in a matter that concerned a member of his own family.

[52]Letters from Hohenlohe to De Luca, dated April 19 and October 11, 1860 [ASV, NV Docs. No. 14 and 27]. Hohenlohe appears to have been offended not only by Okraszewski's fiscal cunning, but also by his personal idiosyncrasies. Not

long after their arrival in Rome, the Princess sent Okraszewski to Hohenlohe's apartments in the Vatican with a message. Hohenlohe was not at home, so Okraszewski scribbled it on the wall by the door to let his distinguished friend know that he had been there. A man with the courage to leave graffiti in the corridors of the Vatican was not to be trifled with. (Unpublished letter from Carolyne to Liszt, dated May 24, 1860, WA, Kasten 36).

[53]ASV, NV Doc. No. 21. A question-mark still hovers over the matter of the 70,000 silver roubles, however. For what possible purpose did Okraszewski demand such a large sum of money? And why was the Princess so ready to hand it over without question? We know of two other occasions on which the Princess tried to reward people connected with her case. The first concerned her offer of money to Baron von Maltitz, during the Weimar years, already mentioned above. The other was the strange business of the papal title that Carolyne tried to secure for Anton Hohmann, the parish priest in Weimar, in recognition of his help in securing her annulment [ASV, NV Doc. No. 28]. The Bishop of Fulda, to whom Carolyne directed this latter request, refused point blank to have anything to do with it.

[54]WA, Kasten 37. Unpublished letter to Liszt dated June 1, 1860.

[55]WA, Kasten 37. Unpublished letter to Liszt dated August 30, 1860.

mentichero!" he reassured her,[56] and undertook to convene a Holy Congregation of the Council to examine the question. This audience with Pius IX was an important turning-point in the disposition of Carolyne's case.

Would Gustav Hohenlohe have behaved differently if his brother had not become obsessed with keeping the Iwanowsky fortune? The documents suggest that he might have done. He had first met Okraszewski in July 1859, a year earlier, well before his brother's marriage to Marie Witt-genstein, and he appears to have gone out of his way to be helpful. It was Hohenlohe who asked Monsignor Quaglia, the Secretary of the Holy Congregation, to provide a full report of Okra-szewski's case to the Pope "in order that the question be solved as quickly as possible," and the context makes it clear that he thought it should be solved in the Princess's favor.[57] It was only after the marriage of his brother to Marie Wittgenstein that his attitude changed. The old saying "money talks" was never truer than here.

XII

While Carolyne was in Rome, exerting all the influence that she could muster to have the Bishop of Fulda's suspension lifted, Liszt himself was fighting an important rearguard action in Weimar itself. He persuaded Carl Alexander to intervene directly in the case, a move that caused Carolyne's enemies some troubled moments. What influence, it might be asked, could a Protestant monarch have over a Roman Catholic bishop? Under normal circumstances, very little. But since Fulda lay in the domains of the grand dukes of Weimar, Carl Alexander's authority was very powerful, and Bishop Kött could hardly ignore it. Indeed, he must have reeled with dismay when he received a communication from Weimar's Minister of State, Dr. Gottfried Stichling, inviting him to perform the marriage service in Fulda itself. ("...the Princess and Dr. Liszt have turned to His Royal Highness, the Grand Duke, requesting that their wish be brought to your attention.")[58] This letter was immediately forwarded to Monsignor De Luca in Vienna with a request for advice. Later, when Carolyne's adversaries in the Vatican looked as if they were gaining the upper hand, Liszt wrote a heartfelt letter to Carl Alexander which leaves no doubt as to the important part the monarch played in this matter:

Weimar, August 19, 1860

Save me, sire—you can do it! Wherever the obstacle might be, you are in a position to remove it. My gratitude is of such little use that I forbear to mention it at this moment. But the feeling of having done a good and noble thing will bear a reward worthy of you, and God who rules our conscience will bless you.

Do not abandon me, then. You know that in this union with the Princess lies all the honor and all the happiness to which [I] aspire and hope in this world.

Your very respectfully devoted and grateful servant,

F. Liszt.[59]

In October 1860, Liszt even traveled down to Vienna in order to meet Gustav Hohenlohe and discuss the ramifications of Carolyne's case. The interview was strained, and Liszt was left in no doubt that Hohenlohe was acting for the Wittgenstein family; in fact he told Carolyne that the Wittgensteins had given Hohenlohe their "power of attorney" in the case. While he was in Vienna he petitioned Monsignor De Luca for an audience, and was received on or about October 16.[60] According to Liszt, De Luca "rode on his high horse" and claimed that the decision from Rome contradicted certain articles in the Concordat of Vienna—the point being that Liszt was an Austro-Hungarian citizen, and these articles governed his case. Liszt listened patiently to the lecture, and assumed the mock conviction necessary "when one knows in advance that white must be black, and that the moon is indisputably made of green cheese."[61]

[56]"My dear daughter, I shall not forget you!" (LAG, p. 425).

[57]ASV, CC Doc. No. 1. Letter dated August 2, 1859.

[58]ASV, NV Doc. No. 17. Letter dated August 2, 1859.

[59]LBLCA, p. 95.

[60]ASV, NV Doc. No. 29.

[61]ASV, DA unpublished fragment of a letter written to Agnes Street-Klindworth, dated November 8, 1860.

XIII

When the Holy Congregation met on September 22, 1860, it had before it the Decree of Nullity issued by Archbishop Żyliński on February 24, 1860. After due deliberation the Cardinals voted overwhelmingly in favor of the Princess (with the exception of Cardinal Teodulfo Mertel, who abstained): the Russian annulment would be upheld. Two days later Pius IX gave his formal assent.[62] To this decision De Luca, Fulda, and Hohenlohe objected in the strongest terms, and their joint voices were powerful enough to persuade Pius to re-convene the Holy Congregation of the Council. On December 22, 1860, they reassembled in order to consider the appeal, and they confirmed their earlier decision.[63] The annulment first granted in Mohilow in 1852, and upheld in St. Petersburg in 1860, would stand. Pius IX ratified this decision on January 7, 1861, and the Cardinals issued the decree of annulment the following day. A thirteen-year-old struggle was at an end.

Carolyne could not contain her jubilation, and wrote to Liszt on January 11: "A triumph, a complete triumph...Through his resistance Monsignor De Luca has only earned himself a letter, infinitely more peremptory than the first, which enjoins him to obey [the Holy Congregation] and does so in such a way that he is left with no possibility of a refusal."[64] There was now no legal impediment whatsoever standing in the way of a marriage between Carolyne and Liszt. The only matter to be decided was where to hold the ceremony itself. If at that moment the couple had decided to be married by a local priest in some small town or village, well away from Rome, the débâcle which occurred at the church of San Carlo al Corso on October 21, the eve of their wedding, might have been avoided. But they vacillated, and with the passing of time they were delivered once more into the hands of their enemies.

XIV

And what of that débâcle? Liszt arrived in Rome on Sunday, October 20, 1861.[65] Although the wedding was due to take place on October 22, his fiftieth birthday, the Princess had not yet arranged to have the banns read.[66] This was an extraordinary decision that can only be explained by Carolyne's constant fear of last-minute intervention by the Hohenlohes who, as we have seen, stood to lose millions of roubles if the ceremony went ahead. In her near-paranoia Carolyne reasoned that a series of public announcements could only invite disaster. But without a waiver of the banns no marriage ceremony could proceed. Together, Liszt and Carolyne went from her apartment on the Piazza di Spagna to the Vatican, where they sought a special dispensation from Monsignor Bernardino Maggi, who was ob-

viously expecting them. What took place in those chambers deserves to be stated with force. With the Holy Gospels in his hand, Liszt swore (a) that he was single, (b) that he had not taken vows to become a priest, (c) that he was not promised in marriage to another, and (d) that he had come to Rome for the specific purpose of contracting matrimony. He then affixed his signature to the document; and after similar oaths had been sworn by Carolyne, she affixed hers.[67] A separate document was drawn up requesting the waiving of the banns. The grounds were ominous: the couple wished "to join in holy matrimony in haste and secrecy on account of just and legitimate reasons presented verbally..."[68] This waiver must have been communicated to the pastor of San Carlo church, Father Francesco Morelli, for he received the

---

[62]ASV, CC Doc. 42.

[63]Nine cardinals took part in these deliberations, and the vote was far from unanimous. Cardinals Cagiano, D'Andrea, Milesi, Marini, Silvestri, and Bofondi voted in favor, although the record showed that the last-named expressed reservations; Cardinals Santucci and Mertel abstained. The President of the Congregation, Cardinal Caterini, voted against the resolution. [ASV, CC Doc. No. 59]

[64]Unpublished letter dated January 11, 1861. WA, Kasten 37. Something of the embarrassing dilemma in which Monsignor De Luca now found himself is indicated in the letter he wrote to the Bishop of Fulda on February 6, 1861 [ASV, NV Doc. No. 40].

[65]We know this for certain from his "Memento-Journalier" (VLKN, p. 86).

[66]AVR Doc. No. 6.

[67]AVR Doc. No. 8. The facsimile of this document is reproduced in Volume Two of my ongoing Liszt biography (*The Weimar Years, 1848-1861*, Appendix II, doc. [f].). It happens to be the only legal testimony we have in which Liszt himself declares before witnesses his intention to marry Carolyne.

[68]AVR Doc. No. 6. We know that this undated request to waive the banns for a ceremony that was supposed to take place only two days later could not have been made before October 20, because it mentions the fact that Liszt was already in the city, and his "Memento-journalier" confirms that this was the day of his arrival.

couple on the early evening of October 21 in order to celebrate a pre-nuptial communion. What happened next has become a part of the Liszt mythology. Late that night Morelli received a communication from the Vatican that the marriage ceremony planned for the following morning must be postponed, and he in turn dispatched a messenger to the Piazza di Spagna to inform the Princess. New objections had been raised which would have to be examined. What were they? Unknown to Carolyne, at the very moment that she and Liszt were swearing out their statements before Monsignor Bernardino Maggi, one of her Russian cousins was seeking an urgent audience with Cardinal Prospero Caterini, the prefect of the Holy Congregation of the Council, which had reviewed Carolyne's case on December 22, and who had himself voted against it. The cousin's name was Kalm-Podowska, and he was accompanied by two of Carolyne's female relatives.[69] This powerful deputation carried with it a message which confirmed the one brought by Denise Poniatowska, the cousin who had unsuccessfully conspired against Carolyne in the summer of 1860. The Wittgenstein-Iwanowska marriage was not forced, as Carolyne insisted that it was, but was entered into freely. Kalm-Podowska had actually been present at the first introductions between Carolyne and Nicholas in 1836, so he claimed, and he had observed their courtship and nuptials unfold without constraint.[70] The annulment granted for

vis et metus should therefore be quashed since it rested on perjured evidence. It remains only to observe that the testimony of such witnesses could never have reached the ears of Cardinal Caterini at this late stage without the backing of a powerful cleric. The finger of guilt points directly towards Gustav Hohenlohe.[71] In the archives of the proceedings of the Holy Congregation there is a letter that proves Hohenlohe's complicity beyond doubt. It is addressed to Cardinal Caterini and is dated Friday, October 18, 1860—that is, two days before Liszt's arrival in Rome. In it, he introduces the Polish bearers of the letter, Father Semenenko of San Claudio de' Polacchi, in Rome, and Count Potoczki [sic] who, he tells Caterini, will present new evidence against the annulment and thus "forestall a great scandal".[72] Father Semenenko was a Polish priest who for some years had been attached to an order of Polish seminarians at the church of San Claudio, and he appears to have been present in order to confirm the identity of Carolyne's relatives. Why, it may be asked, were these worthies so eager to testify against her? They had never forgiven her for exposing their fraudulent claims against her father's estate.[73] That painful episode had created a permanent divide between the two halves of the family. Gustav Hohenlohe had no difficulty at all in recruiting Carolyne's relatives to his cause.[74]

[69]RLKM, Vol. 3, pp. 10 and 434. The two female relatives are identified only as "Princess O" and "Countess B." We surmise that the former must have been Princess Orloffsky, the married name of the second of Dyonis Iwanowsky's daughters.

[70]RLKM, Vol. 3, pp. 10-11; LSJ, p. 42. This information derives ultimately from Carolyne herself. Years later Carolyne told Lina Ramann that the pope's last-minute intervention was the result of "scheming Russian intrigues" (RL, p. 89). This conversation took place in Rome, in June 1876, not long after Lina Ramann had begun work on her Liszt biography.

[71]If the Vatican documents do nothing else, they show conclusively that Gustav Hohenlohe was not the innocent bystander depicted by certain biographers of Liszt. We now know of four previous occasions when Hohenlohe actively meddled in the case. He was involved in procuring the testimony of Father Filippo Guidi which charged the Russian consistory with corruption [ASV, NV Docs. No. 7 and 14]; he wrote directly to Pius IX and charged the Russian consistory with receiving bribes [ASV, CC Doc. No. 16, dated "March 26,

1860]; he questioned the motives and smeared the reputation of Carolyne's factotum Władislaw Okrasewski [ASV, NV Doc. No. 27]; and he tried to persuade De Luca not to send the annulment file to Carolyne's strongest ally Cardinal Antonelli, "for I have some reason to think that [he] does not have very clear ideas about this business" [ASV, NV Doc. No. 38].

[72]ASV, CC Doc. No. 72.

[73]See p. 3.

[74]Cardinal Caterini would have received the evidence of Father Semenenko, Kalm-Podoska and the others verbally. Since there are no further depositions on file in the archives of the Holy Congregation, there is no sworn written testimony of what Semenenko actually said. Caterini was evidently waiting for Carolyne to appeal against the ban on the marriage, at which point he would have convened the Holy Congregation to examine these fresh charges and there would be a record of the proceedings. But Carolyne did not appeal. Hohenlohe's letter is the very last document to be deposited in the file, on November 12, 1861. From the standpoint of the church, the case was now closed.

XV

The crisis of October 21 appears to have had a devastating effect on the Princess. After thirteen years of litigation her nerves were shattered; for the first time her will failed.

The intervention of Kalm-Podowska and his entourage could not have been strong enough to do more than postpone the marriage by a week or two (the problem of perjury had already been examined by the Cardinals), and there is no evidence in the Vatican file to suggest that the document of annulment was ever upturned. Carolyne was free to rebut these latest charges, like all the others she had rebutted in the past, but she did not bother to do so. The marriage between Liszt and Carolyne did not take place because Carolyne herself lost heart. The Iwanowskys were against her, the Wittgensteins were against her, the Hohenlohes were against her. And now even her daughter was against her, a particularly hard blow for her to bear. Marie had recently given birth to her first child, Franz Josef, and Carolyne had been neither allowed to see her grandchild nor been invited to the baptism.[75] The nightmare scenario in which Carolyne's grandchildren might be deprived of their legacy (as the "illegitimate" half of her family line) loomed large with everyone. Would Carolyne's remarriage expose them to endless litigation in the years ahead? Even though Carolyne protested that it would not, she could not be sure. Nobody could. Time changes many things.[76]

But Carolyne also faced a more immediate difficulty. She and her legal advisers knew full well that once an annulment had been granted, and a remarriage had taken place, the case could be reopened by anyone, at any time, providing the evidence warranted it. Canon law, as expressed in the Papal Bull *Dei miseratione*, makes that point perfectly clear: because marriage is a sacrament, annulment cases are never closed. Given the hostility of her immediate family, Carolyne doubtless feared being hounded into perpetuity.

The burden simply became too much for the Princess to bear. Thereafter she had many opportunities to marry Liszt, but after October 21 the matter was allowed to subside. The essential correctness of this view is borne out by the fact that when Prince Nicholas died, in March 1864, the last remaining obstacle to Carolyne's union with Liszt was removed, and yet their marriage plans were never revived. Carolyne herself has told us that she refused to marry Liszt "as soon as that refusal became possible for me."[77] Liszt himself corroborates the idea that it was a mutual decision. In 1864 he made his first return to Weimar since exchanging the city for Rome, and while he was there he was re-united with Carl Alexander, the grand duke of Weimar. During the course of their conversation, the grand duke inquired about Carolyne and the prospects of their much-postponed marriage. Liszt's little-known response is worth quoting: "[The grand duke] was unable to imagine that one might have pursued a goal for fifteen years only to withdraw from it at the moment when nothing more opposed its realization."[78]

"...only to withdraw from it." The decision not to proceed with the wedding, Liszt seems to be saying, was his and Carolyne's alone. A few months later there was a postscript to Liszt's interesting conversation with the grand duke. Carl Alexander told him that now Prince Nicholas was dead, there was "no longer any human reason, nor earthly power which could oppose your union. If it is not accomplished, the reason lies in you, or in her."[79] To which Liszt responded with Pascal's famous

---

[75]Franz Josef had been born in July 1861. Carolyne left him a small bequest in her will, drawn up in October that same year (WFL, Vol. 2, p. 565). Altogether there would be five grandchildren: Franz Josef (1861), Dorothea (1862), Konrad (1863), Philipp (1864), and Gottfried (1867).

[76]One of the most difficult situations that Carolyne was called upon to face while obtaining her annulment was the deteriorating relationship with her daughter. After Marie's wedding, in October 1859, there was an ever-widening rift betweeen the pair. Carolyne blamed Konstantin for poisoning the atmosphere by making an issue of the 70,000 silver roubles, and she convinced herself that he was intercepting her mail to her daughter. It never seems to have occurred to her that Marie had much to lose in the fanatical battle that was being waged with the church. In desperation Marie had turned to Liszt, and in the summer of 1860 had written to her "dear, great, and impartial judge" for help. Carolyne, she told Liszt, expected her daughter to obey her without hesitation even "if she ordered me to throw my fortune into the Danube...I suffer cruelly, for the rapid torrent of circumstances makes me more and more incapable of being good for anything. It is as much as I can do to maintain my peace of mind, confidence, and serenity....Burn this letter, dear Great One, and do not reply to it. The negotiations are secret." (WA, Unpublished letter of July 16, 1860.)

[77]EKFL, p. 68.

[78]LLB, Vol. 6, p. 55.

[79]LLCA, p. 127.

aphorism: "The heart has its reasons of which reason knows nothing."[80]

With this simple phrase Liszt absolves the Wittgensteins, the Hohenlohes, and above all the Roman Catholic Church. It is an unexpected coda to our strange and complex tale, but it comes to us from Liszt and Carolyne themselves. We must surely leave the last word with them.

XVI

What became of Liszt and Carolyne in their later years? Carolyne remained at the Piazza di Spagna for a few months, and then moved into apartments at 89, Via del Babuino (in the parish of Santa Maria del Popolo),[81] where she remained until her death more than twenty-five years later. Here she became a recluse and allowed her many eccentricities full play. Thick velvet curtains were perpetually drawn against the daylight, and the gloomy interior was lit by flickering candles. No fresh air was allowed to penetrate the apartment for fear she might catch a chill, and the atmosphere soon became choking on account of the cigars she perpetually smoked. During the day she often stayed in bed; during the night she scribbled away at her writing-desk. Pictures and busts of Liszt adorned every room, icons to the memory of their lost life together, which evidently assuaged some of the pain. From this heart of darkness there emerged the first faint glimmer of her psychological salvation. Carolyne became obsessed with Canon Law, and she began to fill her rooms with theological tomes over which she pored incessantly. She was preparing herself for the task of writing her magnum opus *Interior Causes of the External Weakness of the Church in 1870*—a monumental project which eventually ran to twenty-four volumes and took twenty years to write. Parts of it were so controversial that two of the volumes were placed on the Index,[82] and she made enemies among the higher clergy—not a new situation for her. We shall only come to understand this strange book if we regard it as a therapy, so to speak, a gigantic rationalization of her differences with the theologians.

There was no question of Carolyne resuming her former *ménage à deux* with Liszt, and a moment's reflection will tell us why. That kind of life had been difficult enough in Weimar; in Rome it would have been impossible. She now lived under the very nose of the Vatican, she was known to the church's leading clerics, and during her long battle to secure her annulment she had rested her case on the sanctity of the marriage bond. Under such circumstances, to resume her old liaison with Liszt would have been to flaunt defiance, not in the face of the world (which she had never minded) but in the face of the church itself, and that she could never have brought herself to do.

XVII

As for Liszt, he appears to have taken the wedding fiasco calmly. We say appears because there is not a single letter, document, or diary-entry that would allow us to divine his true feelings.[83] Perhaps Liszt thought that he and Carolyne merely faced a temporary setback, indistinguishable from dozens of others they had experienced across the years. But with the passing weeks, and with Carolyne's fundamental change of heart, it must have quickly dawned on Liszt that this particular setback would be permanent. At first he took apartments at 113, Via Felice, which is today's Via Sistina, leading to the Piazza di Spagna, so that he could see Carolyne daily and offer her some consolation in this period of crisis. But his own life was soon to reach an important turning-point. In September 1862 his eldest daughter Blandine died, aged 26, and her death was a devastating blow, coming as it did so soon

---

[80]LLCA, p. 128.

[81]Second floor. Later on she moved to the third floor, which had more spacious accomodation.

[82]On July 12, 1877, volume nine was placed on the Index by decree of Pius IX. Two years later, on February 3, 1879, the same fate was meted out to volume three by decree of Leo XIII. The *Causes intérieures* have appeared in all subsequent editions of the Index, the last one being in 1961.

[83]His "Memento-Journalier" entry for October 22 (VLKN, No. 2, p. 86) consists mainly of a series of aphorisms of the kind that he had always liked to collect in order to mull them over at leisure:

"I am a Roman citizen!"

"All misfortune is conquered through suffering."

"Unless an order comes expressly from the Pope, I plan to go on doing what I am doing" (Montalembert).

There is not the slightest hint in all this of a spiritual crisis.

after that of his 20-year-old son Daniel.[84] By the beginning of 1863 Liszt had entered a deep depression. His sense of boundless optimism temporarily deserted him, and he became introspective. In order to bring some repose into his troubled life he appealed to an old acquaintance, Father Agostino Theiner, to help him find somewhere else to live, away from the hustle and bustle of Rome.[85] Theiner suggested that they should journey up the slopes of the Monte Mario, beyond the city limits, and visit the Madonna del Rosario, not far from where he himself lived. From the moment that Liszt caught sight of the old monastery he knew that he had found the perfect retreat. He took up residence there on June 20, 1863, and remained there until 1868.[86] The Madonna del Rosario was run by Domenican monks, and it was quite cut off from the world. Liszt was given a small cell at the front of the monastery, with whitewashed walls, whose floor space was a mere fifteen feet by twelve feet. His only furniture was a wooden bed, a work-table, a bookcase, and a small piano. His windows commanded some panoramic views of Rome, however; from one side he could see the dome of St. Peter's shining in the distance, from the other the Albano Hills stretching along the horizon. In these inspirational surroundings Liszt spent much time in meditation. He even joined the monks in their ministrations, and during mass he sometimes played the harmonium. Nor was the Madonna del Rosario harmful to his work. It was there that he brought to completion his great oratorio *Christus*, his two Franciscan Legends for piano, and his keyboard transcription of Beethoven's Ninth Symphony.

Three weeks after Liszt had moved into the Madonna del Rosario, there occurred an event that put the isolated monastary on the map and set the whole of Rome talking. On July 11, 1863, Liszt was visited in his cell by Pope Pius IX, in the company of Monsignors Hohenlohe and de Mérode. Liszt himself left a description of the occasion.[87] After chatting for a brief period to his dear Palestrina, as he called Liszt, the music-loving Pontiff asked the great pianist to play something for him. Liszt sat down at his piano and delivered the first of his newly-composed Fran-

ciscan Legends—"St. Francis preaching to the birds." Then followed a performance of the aria "Casta Diva," from Bellini's *Norma*. The pope was so moved by this melody that he sprang to his feet, went to the keyboard, and in his fine baritone voice sang the aria from memory, with Liszt accompanying. Afterwards he admonished Liszt in the most gracious manner possible to strive after heavenly things in earthly ones, and to use his temporal harmonies as a means of preparing himself for the timeless ones.[88] A few days later, Liszt was received in audience at the Vatican, and the pope gave him a beautiful cameo depicting the Madonna.

It was in the peaceful surroundings of the Madonna del Rosario that Liszt prepared himself for one of the gravest decisions of his life, that of entering the lower orders of the priesthood. To the outside world this decision has always represented a paradox. Here was a supreme man of the world who had rubbed shoulders with kings and princes; most of his life he had commanded luxury and power; he had only to open a piano and audiences swooned; he had enjoyed the favors of beautiful women, and his illicit union with Marie d'Agoult had produced three children. How could such a man become a cleric? Predictably, Liszt was accused of a lack of sincerity. His detractors, doubtless recalling his clanking medals and the Lola Montez episode, took it to be a superb coup de théâtre by a master showman. The charge will hardly withstand scrutiny, however. Liszt had pondered his decision for a long time. As he himself put it, it harmonized with all the antecedents of his youth. Indeed, in his Will (1860) he had confessed that he had always felt the Church to be his true vocation "from the age of seventeen when, with tears and supplications I begged to be permitted to enter the seminary in Paris, and I hoped that it would be given to me to live the life of the saints and perhaps die the death of the martyrs."[89] To reverse the previous question: How could such a man not become a cleric?

Liszt entered the ecclesiastical state on April 25, 1865, when he received the tonsure in the private chapel of Monsignor Gustav Hohenlohe at the Vatican.[90] Shortly afterwards he wrote:

[84]The harrowing details of Daniel's death are given in Volume Two of my life of Liszt, WFL, pp. 474-79.

[85]Father Theiner was the Prefect of the Secret Archive of the Vatican Library.

[86]With one exception: from April 1865 until June 1866 he occupied quarters in the Vatican.

[87]LLB, Vol. 2, p. 46.

[88]*Loc. cit.*

[89]LLB, Vol. 5, p. 52.

[90]Only three people knew in advance about his decision. Gustav Hohenlohe, Pope Pius IX, and Princess Carolyne had been informed as early as April 2 (LBLB, p. 328).

Convinced as I was that this act would strengthen me in the right road, I accomplished it without effort, in all simplicity and uprightness of intention...To speak familiarly, if the cloak does not make the monk, it also does not prevent him from becoming one; and, in certain cases, when the monk is already formed within, why not appropriate the outer garments of one?

But I am forgetting that I do not in the least intend to become a monk, in the severe sense of the word. For this I have no vocation.[91]

The tonsure placed Liszt under no obligations to proceed any further in his spiritual Odyssey. Nonetheless, on July 30 he entered the four minor orders of the priesthood—Doorkeeper, Lector, Exorcist, and Acolyte. Once again, Gustav Hohenlohe officiated at the ceremony—this time, in his private chapel at Tivoli. The limited extent to which Liszt had committed himself to the church should be clearly understood. Although he was now called an "Abbé," he could not celebrate Mass nor could he hear confession. He undertook no vows of celibacy, and at any time he was free to retract. Always he made it clear that he had no desire to become a monk "in the severe sense of the word." Nevertheless, there is evidence that Liszt was interested in pursuing the Sub-Deaconship—the next order in the sequence of steps towards the priesthood—and for a few months he entered a fairly intensive study of theology towards that end, under a private tutor especially assigned to him for that purpose, Father Antonio Solfanelli.[92] He eventually abandoned the idea, for it would have imposed obligations on him

that he was not prepared to fulfil and, as he himself pointed out, it would have robbed him of leisure for composition, which daily became more precious to him.

The fact that it was Gustav Hohenlohe who performed the ceremony has given rise to a "conspiracy theory" in the Liszt literature.[93] What better way to keep Liszt and Carolyne apart than to have Liszt enter the priesthood? And who better to seduce Liszt into the arms of the church than Gustav Hohenlohe, who by now had got to know the musician very well? In light of Hohenlohe's past behavior, and the way in which he had meddled in Carolyne's affairs, he certainly had a vested interest in the outcome. Yet in this instance, Hohenlohe appears to carry no blame. It was Liszt himself who desired to don the cassock (as a knowledge of his life proves, especially the early part of it), and he was under no outside pressure from anyone to do so.[94] The conspiracy theory is further weakened when we consider the warm friendship that now began to develop between Liszt and Hohenlohe, which was based on mutual respect and admiration. Just before Liszt received the tonsure, Hohenlohe had offered Liszt accomodation in his comfortable quarters in the Vatican itself, and it was in these privileged surroundings that Liszt entered the ecclesiastical state. From 1869 Hohenlohe also gave Liszt the use of rooms at the Villa d'Este in Tivoli, and the composer generally preferred to stay there whenever he was in Italy, away from the hustle and bustle of Rome. Its gardens were world-famous. Here, amidst the towering cypress trees and hundreds of gushing fountains, Liszt

---

[91]LLB, Vol. 2, p. 81.

[92]After the four minor orders, come the three major ones: Sub-Deacon, the Diaconate, and the Priesthood. Incidentally, the major orders, unlike the minor ones, are regarded as part of the sacrament, and they involve vows of celibacy. Seminarians entering the last two orders must be ordained by a bishop.

[93]According to this theory, the Hohenlohes conspired to prevent Liszt's marriage to Carolyne by playing on his vanity. They knew of his lifelong ambition to reform church music, and they held out before him the prospect of one day taking over the direction of music at St. Peter's itself—the most prestigious musical position in the Roman Catholic Church. In order to do this, however, Liszt would have had to remain single and he would have had to take holy orders. Carolyne, in short, was to be sacrificed on the altar of Liszt's ambition. The only thing wrong with this theory is that it required the participation of Liszt himself, and there is no evidence that it was forthcoming. The present director of music at St. Peter's was Salvatore Meluzzi, and it would not have been possible to dismiss him without cause. Nor is there any evidence that Liszt

coveted such a position. He once wrote that he "neither expected nor wished for an appointment or title of any kind at Rome." And he added that he was "under no illusions as to the difficulty and vexations of such a task." LLB, Vol. 7, p. 73.

[94]For authentic information on Liszt's lifelong connection with the Franciscans, see the writings of Father Všesvlad Gajdoš, and in particular his *František Liszt a františkani* [Franz Liszt and the Franciscans], Bratislava 1936, and his "War Franz Liszt Franziskaner?" *Studia Musicologica* 6 (1964), pp. 299-310.

That Liszt was anxious to explain the limited nature of his commitment to the church is shown by his letters to his friends, of which the following extract, to Agnes Street-Klindworth, is typical.

"I think that I need hardly tell you that I have not changed to any extent, still less have I forgotten anything. It is only that my life is ordered more simply—and that the Catholic devotion of my childhood has become a regular and guiding sentiment" (LLB, Vol. 3, p. 161).

composed some of the best keyboard music of his old age.[95] Then, in 1879, not long after Hohenlohe had been made Bishop of Albano, he elevated Liszt to the rank of honorary Canon of Albano. These were generous favors which caused comment. To the charge that Liszt had been bought, there is only one reply: he gave nothing in return except his friendship. Least of all did he give Hohenlohe any undertakings as to how he would henceforth conduct his private life. It was Carolyne who regarded Hohenlohe as the enemy, and it was she, not Liszt, who gave Hohenlohe what he wanted when she decided not to re-open her case after the débâcle of October 1861.

From 1869 until his death seventeen years later, Liszt lived "a threefold life," as he put it, dividing his time more or less equally between Weimar, Budapest, and Rome in an endless circle. In Weimar he started his world-famous masterclasses to which students flocked from the four quarters. He taught some of the best talents of the second half of the nineteenth century—including Friedheim, Rosenthal, Sauer, and Lamond—and he never charged a penny for his services. In Budapest he became the first Director of the newly-formed Royal Academy of Music, which today bears his name, and again he gave his services freely to that institution. And everywhere he wore his Abbé's soutane. He became a familiar figure in Rome, walking through the cobbled streets of the old city, with his long gray hair streaming in the wind and his Abbé's soutane fluttering behind him. Gregorovius, the Roman historian, once observed him getting out of a hackney carriage, and described him unforgettably as "Mephistopheles disguised as an Abbé. Such is the end of Lovelace!"[96]

His generosity to others, particularly to young and struggling musicians, became the stuff of legend. He gave freely and fully to a variety of musical causes, even if they did not always coincide with his own interests. He also did much good by stealth. His Hungarian pupil Janka Wohl once observed him putting banknotes into a pile of envelopes, for distribution among needy colleagues.[97] He called it "playing Providence." The rest of the world might call it folly; the poor, after all, are always with us. In both word and deed, however, Liszt was a true Franciscan, and he had come to understand the real meaning of the life of St. Francis: that poverty is the gateway to riches. Whenever he was in Rome he never failed to visit Carolyne, although he looked forward less and less to entering her stuffy apartments. All her visitors (including Liszt himself) had to wait in the ante-room until the cold air they brought with them had warmed up to the temperature of her chambers. For most of the rest of the year Liszt was in Budapest or Weimar, and he remained the most faithful of correspondents, sometimes despatching long letters to her at the rate of two or three a week. These letters number nearly thirteen hundred and occupy four volumes of his collected correspondence. As for Carolyne's replies, more than two thousand of them are preserved in the Weimar archive, but they remain unpublished except for a few scattered fragments. When this vast correspondence is read side by side it presents an indispensable chronicle of their life together. To the end of his days, Liszt continued to disclose to Carolyne more about himself and his work-in-progress than to any other single individual—a clear enough indication of how important she continued to be to him.

XVIII

As Carolyne entered her old age she became ever more reclusive. Her daughter tells us that she hardly ever ventured out of doors because she entertained irrational fears of catching malaria. She was in any case convinced that she suffered from a permanent condition that she described as "fever of the blood," and avoided physical activity. Those who knew her felt that it was her unhealthy regimen that determined many of her ailments, and not the ail-

ments that determined her regimen, as she herself insisted. Adelheid von Schorn has told us that Carolyne did not believe any doctor who found her pulse regular, and if the thermometer had existed at that time she would not have believed it either.[98] In the early days of her stay in Rome she had at least visited friends, or had found her way to the many monuments or picture galleries in which she was interested. But with the passing years these outings were

---

[95]Including "Les jeux d'eaux à la Villa d'Este," and the two pieces entitled "Aux cyprès de la Villa d'Este," threnodies I and II.

[96]GRT, p. 300.
[97]WFLR, p. 219.
[98]SZM, p. 274.

reduced to short walks along the neighboring streets, and in time even they ceased. She spent a great deal of time in bed, from where she wrote much of her considerable literary output.[99] Since she insisted on working in a darkened room by candlelight, often at night, her eyesight grew progressively worse, and she had to employ one of her footmen to read to her. In desparation she sought a private audience of Pius IX and asked him for his blessing on her weak eyes. She impulsively seized the pontiff's hands and placed them on her eyelids. That evening, after she had returned to the Via Babuino, she was able to read without difficulty. Carolyne always referred to the event as a miracle.[100] Her apartments were filled with books on every conceivable topic, and the occasional visitor took away the memory of walls and corridors lined with volumes like a library; there were even piles of books in the corridor and stacked around the bed. Her eccentricity made her vulnerable, and in December 1868 thieves broke into her apartment and robbed her of some jewellry. They also took away some of Liszt's orders and decorations which he had left with her for safe-keeping.[101] On the death of Pius IX she went into mourning, and for the duration of the conclave she wore over her bonnet a black crêpe veil which went right down to her feet. She was oblivious to the ridicule to which this exposed her, for she herself thought that such behavior was perfectly natural. Towards the end of her life she developed some very peculiar ideas and claimed that her living room was inhabited with benevolent spirits that kept her from becoming lonely. Once, when she attended mass at Sant'Andrea della Fratte, she saw clouds of angels hovering around her.[102] It is not a very flattering image, and it is hardly surprising that it has colored so many biographies of Liszt. Princess Carolyne in old age always made "good copy." To Ernest Newman, one of Liszt's English biographers, she was "a half-cracked blue-stocking," and that description still haunts the literature today.

On two occasions only were relations between Liszt and Carolyne strained to breaking point. The first had to do with Cosima, Liszt's second daughter, who was unhappily married to Hans von Bülow. In 1868, after a notorious affair that had gone on for at least five years, Cosima eloped with Richard Wagner, and in 1870 she married him in a Protestant ceremony after securing a Protestant divorce. Carolyne was so incensed at what she considered to be a devious and expedient way of solving one's matrimonial problems, that she tried to force Liszt to break off all connections with his daughter. This he refused to do, although he had much sympathy for Carolyne's point of view. For what Cosima had done (namely, renounce her Catholic faith) was something that Carolyne and Liszt had often been urged to do, but had always steadfastly refused to contemplate. The other matter had to do with his two books, on Chopin and on Gypsy music respectively, which had first been published in the 1850s. We know that Carolyne collaborated with Liszt on the writing of part of the texts, and when the question of new editions arose in the late 1870s, Liszt entrusted them to her. Without his knowledge and consent, she lengthened both books, and in the case of the Gypsy book she added some inflammatory material about the Jews. This caused Liszt many problems, and there was an outcry in the European press.[103] Liszt bore the brunt of the criticism in silence and never once indicated that the Princess was to blame. We shall never know for sure what passed between the couple on either of these issues, but the correpondence suggests that a serious rift developed which was bridged with difficulty. Adelheid von Schorn once visited Rome and witnessed a violent quarrel between the pair which ended in tears and pleas for forgiveness on both sides. It was doubtless one of many such episodes.

XIX

The circumstantial account of Liszt's death, given in the diary of his pupil Lina Schmalhausen, makes unhappy reading, and it is a standing indictment against those who were in a position to ease his last moments.[104] He had gone to Bayreuth in July 1886, in order to attend the Wagner festival in fulfilment of a promise made earlier in the year to his daughter Cosima (who, since Wagner's own death in 1883, was now in charge of the Wagner festival). The overnight train journey upset him, and when he ar-

---

[99]At least 44 volumes flowed form her pen.

[100]MAL, p. 185.

[101]HLC, pp. 262-63 and note.

[102]MAL, pp. 191-92.

[103]For a fuller account of this difficult episode see WFL, Vol. 2, pp. 379-90.

[104]WA, Ramann's Liszt-Bibliothek No. 330. A curtailed version of this 84-page diary was published in RL, pp. 370-78.

rived in Bayreuth he had to take to his bed with a high fever and a racking cough. For the first day or two hardly anybody knew that he had arrived. On July 23 he made a valiant effort to get up, and he attended the first of the *Parsifal* performances. Two days later there was a performance of *Tristan* (the first time that this opera had ever been mounted at Bayreuth). Liszt sat at the back of the Wagner family box, slumped in the shadows, with a handkerchief clasped to his mouth. Somebody spotted him when the lights went up during an interval, and he came forward to receive an ovation. It was the last time that he was seen in public. He passed away during the night of July 31, 1886, after a violent death-struggle. The funeral took place on August 3. Liszt's wishes, contained in his Will (1860), were not carried out. He was not given extreme unction, he did not receive a requiem mass, and he was not buried in the habit of the Order of St. Francis. There was a final irony when a minister of the Protestant faith offered prayers over the coffin. Most of the "mourners" who lined the route to the cemetary were in fact visitors to the Wagner festival who had come to the funeral merely out of curiosity. So all Bayreuth celebrated Wagner while Liszt was lowered into the ground. There was something peculiarly Franciscan about it all. The self-effacement that Liszt had so assiduously

cultivated for the last twenty years of his life seemed to achieve its highest expression at his funeral.

Immediately after the burial a monumental quarrel broke out about his last resting-place. Everyone knew that Bayreuth was the worst place in the world for Liszt to be buried, because the city was inseparably bound up with Wagner and his music. The Franciscans of Budapest claimed the body; so too did the Grand Duke of Weimar. There was even a debate in the Hungarian legislature (on February 26, 1887) on the question of when, and if, Liszt should be brought home to Hungary. Princess Carolyne, who had always disapproved of Liszt's Wagner connections, was especially incensed that Liszt's body might have to rest in "Pagan Bayreuth," as she put it, and consulted lawyers in Vienna. But it all came to nought because Cosima refused to allow her father's body to leave Bayreuth. What no one knew at that time (and what Carolyne herself had forgotten) was that Liszt had once written a letter in which his own view is stated with force: "Let my body be buried, not within a church, but in some cemetary, and let it not be removed from that grave to any other. I will have no other place for my body than the cemetary in use in the place where I die."[105] Liszt in short, wanted to be buried where he fell.

XX

When news of Liszt's death was brought to Princess Carolyne, she took to her bed and never left it. She appears to have suffered a seizure which partially immobilized her. Her mental energies also began to decline, and she was visited by dropsy and intermittent fevers. However, her will to work was as strong as ever, and she continued to write a mass of correspondence on such matters as Liszt's last resting-place and the disposition of his will. This cost her a great deal of physical pain, for she had difficulty in holding the pen in her swollen hand which

was ravaged by rheumatism, her old enemy. She managed to complete work on her magnum opus, however: the twenty-fourth and final volume of her *Causes intérieures* was finished just two weeks before her death. It concludes with the date February 23, 'Ash Wednesday,' Rome, 1887.

Carolyne drew her last breath on the evening of March 9, 1887, only a few months after Liszt himself had expired. Princess Marie described her last days on earth.[106] At the beginning of March, Marie had come down from Vienna in response to

---

[105]LLB, Vol. 6, pp. 228-29. The letter is dated "Rome, November 27, 1869."

[106]In a letter to Emma Herwegh, Princess Marie revealed some of the details surrounding her mother's last months. Marie mourned the fact that with the death of her mother all the "heroes" of the Altenburg years were gone, and that she herself felt like a hyphen between a vanished past and future which was yet to take shape. "After Liszt's death," she wrote, "my mother asked to remain alone. She was afraid that my visits would upset her too much. From then on, she only wanted to be isolated in her sorrow and silence. She hardly saw anyone all winter, complained a great deal about little

things; but we were used to that. It was only in February that her complaints became more sorrowful, and some friends in Rome wrote to me that they were fearful about her condition.

"I rushed to Rome and was frightened to find her suffering from dropsy, when nothing had prepared me for that. The enormous affection that she had formerly felt for me, revived then; she greeted me, radiant with joy. The doctor predicted a long illness, but God was merciful to her. A high fever broke out and managed to burn up her feeble resistance in a few days. She was not aware of death's approach and fell gently asleep, without suffering during the night of March 9.

"Vienna, Easter Saturday, 1887" (HSD, p. 125).

an urgent summons from friends to look after her mother at Via Babuino. She was shocked when she entered the stifling sick-room and saw that Carolyne's body was bloated by dropsy. A doctor was summoned, but he could do little except to ease her last moments. On March 9, Cardinal Hohenlohe called on his sister-in-law, and they began to discuss the possibility of sending for Carolyne's confessor. As they were chatting, the chamber-maid entered and said: "There is a deathly silence in the bedroom."[107] When they opened the door they saw her head slightly inclined, an expression of great calm on her face. She had slipped into the arms of death without a sound. Because certain parts of the *Causes intérieures* had been placed on the Index, there were difficulties about her receiving the last rites. The funeral services for such people were traditionally held at the church of Santa Maria del Popolo, which took a lenient view of the "black aristocrats" of Catholicism, and which also happened to be Carolyne's parish church. Cardinal Ho-

henlohe officiated at the requiem mass, and during the service Liszt's Requiem Mass for Male Voices was performed. (By a supreme irony, Carolyne was blessed in death by the very priest who had blighted her in life.) Carolyne was buried in the German cemetary inside the Vatican, behind St. Peter's Basilica. On her tombstone we read the following inscription:

> Here rests in Peace
> Carolyne
> Princess von Sayn-Wittgenstein
> of the Iwanowska line
> born February 8, 1819
> died March 9, 1887
> Per Angusta-ad-Augusta[108]

Beneath this inscription lies a simple marble slab, bearing the epitaph "Jenseits ist meine Hoffnung"—"Eternity is my hope."

---

[107]SZM, p. 469.

[108]"Through suffering to greatness."

THE VATICAN ARCHIVES

Plate 2. The Altenburg, a watercolor by Carl Hoffmann, December, 1859.

THE VATICAN ARCHIVES

The Vatican documents that are assembled here, most of them for the first time, come from two different archives: the Archivio Storico del Vicariato di Roma (AVR) and the Archivio Segreto Vaticano (ASV).

The first archive belongs to the Vicar General of Rome, who performs some of the Pope's functions as the Bishop of Rome. The Vicariato di Roma is therefore the place where the marriage records for the diocese of Rome are to be found. As Liszt and Carolyne were to be married there in 1861, away from their respective parishes, they had to present documents testifying to their single status, their baptism, and their confirmation. Moreover, they had to obtain some special dispensations. Bearing the shelf mark 4477, the Vicariato di Roma holds a file that contains nine documents pertaining to Liszt and Carolyne, the most important of which is a copy of the decree dated January 8, 1861, issued, with Papal approval, by the Holy Congregation of the Council. This decree upholds the annulment of Carolyne's previous marriage, which was issued by the Archbishop of Mohilow on February 24, 1861. On the basis of the documents presented here and the dispensations that were granted, this file is the equivalent of a licence to marry, although the marriage never took place.

The Archivio Segreto Vaticano, on the other hand, is the general historical archive of the Roman Catholic Church in Rome. It is composed of a daunting number of separate archives pertaining to the different branches of the complex governmental structure of the Roman Catholic Church and State. One of these archives, organised by year and location, contains the papers of the different Apostolic Nunciatures (or embassies of the Vatican State) around the world. The nuncio (or papal ambassador) is entrusted with the relations between the Apostolic See and the civil goverment of the state to which he is attached. He also acts as an intermediary between the local churches and the Holy See. When Carolyne, then residing in Weimar, started proceedings to reopen her annulment case, she found herself under the jurisdiction of the Diocese of Fulda (the centre of Catholic ad-

ministration in Germany), even though her case was to be reviewed in the Diocese of Mohilow, the seat of the Archbishop Metropolitan of Russia. The Diocese of Fulda in turn was controlled by the papal nuncio to Vienna, Monsignor Antonino De Luca. That is why, during the years 1860–61, De Luca became embroiled in Carolyne's case, which involved Rome, St. Petersburg, Fulda, and the Ukrainian diocese of Luck-Zhitomir, where Carolyne's first marriage had been performed. The resulting correspondence is preserved in a file for the Diocese of Fulda, and it bears the shelf mark No. 427. With the exception of three documents, the entire file is dedicated to Carolyne's efforts to obtain an annulment. De Luca played an adversarial role in the case, and his letters had a very important impact on the final outcome. The file contains 44 documents, and they allow us to follow the case as it unfolded after Carolyne had obtained a sentence of annulment from the Metropolitan of Mohilow, in February 1860. The most important documents are a copy of the Mohilow sentence that was sent to De Luca by the Bishop of Fulda (Doc. 6), the defense of that sentence provided by the Archbishop of Mohilow (Doc. 21), and a long description of the 1851 proceedings of the case as it was debated in the first instance in the Diocese of Luck-Zhitomir (Doc. 36). The latter is the only account of that trial to come down to us.

De Luca's correspondence with Rome was mainly with the Secretary of the Holy Congregation of the Tridentine Council. In 1859 this Congregation had issued the Papal rescript which authorised the Archbishop of Mohilow to reopen the case, and it was this same Congregation that, in 1860, was entrusted by Pope Pius IX with the task of pronouncing on the validity of that sentence.

The Congregation of the Council was one of the 11 permanent departments constituting the Vatican Curia. It had been created in 1564 by Pius IV for the purpose of supervising the reforms instituted by the Council of Trent. Its original executive function was soon expanded, and the Congregation assumed the role of in-

terpreter of the decisions of the Council and arbiter in controversial questions related to those decisions. The Congregation thus dealt with the rights and duties of bishops, cathedral chapters, parishes, confraternities, religious vows, and also impediments and irregularities in marriage cases. Besides its ordinary powers, the Congregation often obtained extraordinary powers and continued over the centuries to deal with marriage cases. This prerogative was even expanded by Benedict XIV, who made the Congregation the last court of appeal in marriage cases, although, as an alternative, one could appeal to the Sacra Rota. The Congregation of the Council was directed by a prefect, acting as chairman, and its business was normally conducted by the Secretary. All its deliberations were submitted to the Pope for his approval.

As one can imagine, given the very large scope of the activities of this Congregation, its archives are divided into numerous sections, each constituting a separate archive. Moreover, such archives have become part of the Vatican Archives only in recent times and, as it happens, not all its catalogues are kept there; some are to be consulted in the Library of the Congregation for the Clergy. The records of Carolyne's case, given its delicacy, were kept as part of the Secret Archive of the Congregation, and the latter is neither properly organised nor catalogued. In fact, the file, which had probably never been opened since 1861, was not found there. Though it should have been contained in a volume marked with the letter "Z" (for the Diocese of Zhitomir, where the case was originally debated), there was no such volume, and the file was eventually found on a shelf containing uncatalogued material emanating from the Congregation and originally kept at the Torre Borgia. It was for this reason that the file had never been discovered, let alone perused and given a proper archive location. These materials have now been deciphered, organised and cross-referenced in the pages that follow.

De Luca, as a Nuncio, was bound to report to the Secretary of State, Cardinal Antonelli; moreover, Liszt and Carolyne had been known to have a friendly rapport with this cleric. The huge archives pertaining to the Secretary of State do indeed hold several documents concerning Liszt and Carolyne, even though Antonelli was not directly involved in their case. These were, for the most part, gathered by László Eősze in his *119 római Liszt dokumentum* (Budapest: Zeneműkiadó, 1980), so we have included here only those few documents directly related to the events taking place between 1859 and 1861, together with references to documents catalogued but not yet found.

One of the major problems encountered in the process of editing and translating these documents is that of a consistent transcription of Slavic personal and place names. Many such names exist in alternative forms—Polish, Russian, and Ukrainian. Thus Mohilow, the spelling used most consistently in the documents, is the Ukrainian form, whereas the Russian one to be found in most atlases is Mogilev. Luck, the normal form in Ukrainian, often appears in the literature written as Luk, whereas the atlas provides the spelling pronunciation Lutsk. As for Zhitomir, which is the Russian form in an atlas, it can appear as Zytomir, Zitomir, Zytomierz, Zytomirien, Zitomerien, etc. To compound the problem, there are errors which have been placed there by scribes in the course of adapting such names to Latin, the language of a large number of the documents. The situation is worse for place names of small towns, usually appearing in the documents in a Latin participial form. Is Carolyne's native village Starosteine, as it is sometime named in the literature, or is it Starostince (one of the many variant spellings in the documents), or is it perhaps Starostenetse, as it is called in a Russian document? There is no permanent solution to such problems. They reflect ethnic usage which goes back, in some cases, for centuries.

G.E.

ARCHIVIO SEGRETO VATICANO

Archivio della Nunziatura di Vienna: File No. 427

From the Secret Vatican Archives, Nunciature of Vienna, 1860–61, Vol. 427. The file of Monsignor Antonino De Luca (papal nuncio to Vienna) for the diocese of Fulda, containing a special annex: The Matrimonial Case of Wittgenstein versus Iwanowska

Plate 3. Princess Carolyne in Rome, in the clothes she wore at her audience with Pope
Pius IX on September 9, 1860

**Document No. 1: Inscription on the spine of the volume containing De Luca's
file from Vienna.**

CARDINAL A. DE LUCA
VOLUME 55
427
VARIOUS DIOCESES
OF PRUSSIA AND GERMANY
ARCHIVE OF THE NUNCIO'S SEE
IN VIENNA
427

CARD[INAL] A. DE LUCA
VOL LV.
427
VARIE DIOCESI
DELLA PRUSSIA E DELLA GERMANIA
ARCHIVIO DELLA NUNZIATURA DI
VIENNA
427

Document No. 2: File Title. Italian. Leaf No. 76.[1]

No. 2. DIOCESE OF FULDA

Which includes special documentation pertaining
to:

The Wittgenstein-Iwanowska marriage case.

2. DIOCESI DI FULDA

con annessa posizione speciale:

Causa matrimoniale Wittgenstein-Iwanowska.

Document No. 3: De Luca to Kött, April 11, 1860. Latin. Leaf No. 77.

To: The Most Illustrious and Reverend
Monsignor Christophe Florenz Kött,
Bishop of Fulda
Fulda

No. 1458/1
Vienna, April 11, 1860
Most Illustrious and Reverend Monsignor:

The newspapers are talking a lot but provide hardly any good news about the present
spiritual needs of the Catholic community in
Bockenheim near Frankfurt and, knowing well
Your Most Illustrious and Reverend Excellency's
graciousness, I earnestly request that you brief
me in general about the state of Catholicism in
the Elector's Principality of Hesse and in particular in the above mentioned community.

I have heard nothing more about that most
valuable idea of erecting a Seminary in Fulda,
near the tomb of the German Apostle,[2] where
younger or recently ordained priests could be

Ill[ustrissi]mo et R[everendissi]mo D[omi]no
D[omi]no Christoforo Florenti(n)o Koett
Episcopo Fuldensi
Fuldam
Fulda
N. 1458/1
Viennae die XI Aprilis 1860
Ill[ustrissi]me et R[everendissi]me D[omi]ne.

Cum publicae Ephemerides multa et quidem
haud sane laeta nuntient de spirituali penuria in
qua nunc versatur Parochia catholica in pago
Bockenheim prope Francofortum, rogo ex-
ploratam Dominationis vestrae Ill[ustrissi]mae et
R[everendissi]mae benignitatem ut mihi, comunicare velit quomodo res catholica in toto electorali
Hassiano Principatu generatim et speciatim vero
in praedicto Pago sese habeat.

Nil ultra rescivi de perutili consilio Fuldae
ad sepulcrum Germanorum Apostoli Seminari-
um erigendi in quo juniores sacerdotes, vel
saltem sacris ordinibus initiati, tirocinium

---

[1]Volume 55 contains other files. File No. 427, pertaining to
the Diocese of Fulda, is reproduced here in full. Leaves in
this particular file are numbered from 76 to 159. Leaf num-
bers omitted in the following pages refer to blank sheets.

[2]The apostle of Germany was Saint Boniface (680-754), born
with the name of Wynfrith in Devonshire. In 719 he set out
as a missionary to the Germans, where he was very success-

ful. He was made bishop in 722; following even greater
success he was made archbishop in 732. He reformed the
Frankish Church and in 742 presided over the first German
Council. On June 5, 754 he was assassinated with his com-
panions near Dockum. His remains were later buried in
Fulda.

trained before being sent to minister to Catholic Parishes in the Northern regions of Germany and the United States. Such a desirable institute, built on the model of the celebrated ones existing already in Paris, in Ireland, and also in Italy in Milan, would train strong, proven missionaries, accustomed to the laws of discipline

I beg, therefore, your Excellency to let me know whether there are any bright hopes that this project may come to light. The Catholic religion in Germany and people everywhere would derive the greatest advantage from such an initiative.

With the expression of my deepest respect, I remain

....

<Antonino De Luca,
Archbishop of Tarsus,
Apostolic Nuncio in Vienna>

deponerent antequam ad regendas Parochias catholicas in Nordicis Germaniae et in Americae Foederatis Regionibus discederent. Huiusmodi salutare Institutum, ad instar celeberrimi Parisiis jamdudum extantis, tum in Hibernia, tum etiam Mediolani in Italia fundatum, strenuos et probatos Missionarios accomodatis disciplinae legibus instruit.

Precor igitur ut Dominatio Vestra me certiorem facere velit an spes effulgent fore ut hujusmodi consilium ad effectum deduci possit. Ita maximum Religionis catholicae emolumentum in Germania et ubivis gentium hujusmodi incoeptum vergeret.

Cum peculiaris observantiae cultu permaneo....

<Antoninus De Luca,
Archiepiscopus Tarsensis,
Nuntius Apostolicus Viennae>

Document No. 4: Kött to De Luca, October 31, 1860 (Answer to Document No. 3, with note on the verso penned by De Luca). Latin. Leaves No. 78–79.[3]

<To: Monsignor Antonino De Luca,
Archbishop of Tarsus,
Apostolic Nuncio in Vienna>
Fulda, October 31, 1860.
Most Excellent and Reverend Monsignor!

The people overseeing the pious Societies in this Diocese of ours have entrusted into my hands, on behalf of the members of these same pious Societies, the enclosed letters to the Most Holy Father in order that I may pass them on to Your Excellency. They add their most humble prayers that you deign yourself to present them at the holy feet of the Most Holy Father.

As I comply most happily with this request, I avail myself of this occasion to profess my personal feelings of good will and veneration toward Your Most Illustrious and Reverend Excellency and with these sentiments I remain
Your Excellency's
most humble and devoted
x Christophe Florenz Kött,
Bishop of Fulda

<Antonino De Luca
Archiepiscopo Tarsensi
Nuntio Apostolico, Viennam>

Excellentissime ac Reverendissime Domine, Domine!

Qui praesunt Societatibus piis, quae in hac nostra Diocesi vigent, nomine Sociorum Piarum Societatum literas adjacentes ad Sanctissimum Patrem manibus meis tradiderunt, ut eas Excellentiae Vestrae transmittam, precibus humillimis adjectis, ut Ipsa dignetur, ad pedes sacratos Sanctissimi Patris eas deponere.

Hisce precibus lubentissime obsecundans, et hac occasione utor, ut intimos meae voluntatis et venerationis erga Excellentiam Vestram Reverendissimam et Illustrissimam sensus declarem, quibus persisto Excellentiae Vestrae humillimus et addictissimus

x Christophorus Florentius <Koett>,
Episcopus Fuldensis

[3]These first two documents represent the first contacts between Kött and De Luca. The issues involved here will be forgotten as the rest of the file is devoted entirely to the

question of Princess Carolyne's marriage annulment. There is one brief mention of these matters in Doc. No. 16.

Monsignor the Bishop of Fulda. October 31, 1860
He sends a letter for the Holy Father on behalf of the Pious Societies of his Diocese.

Fuldae, 31 Oct[o]br[i]s 1860

M[onsi]g[no]r Vescovo di Fulda, li 31 Ottobre 1860
Invia un indirizzo pel S[anto] Padre a nome delle Pie Società della sua Diocesi.

Document No. 5: File Title. Leaf No. 81.

Special Annex:
The case for annulment of the Wittgenstein-Iwanowska marriage.
DIOCESE OF FULDA.

Posizione Speciale:
Causa matrimoniale Wittgenstein-Iwanowska

DIOCESI DI FULDA.

Document No. 6: Copy of Żyliński's annulment decree, February 24 (O.S.) =March 7, 1860 (Enclosed by Kött with Document No. 11, Kött to De Luca, April 10, 1860). Latin. Leaves No. 82–83–84. For the text see ASV, CC file, Doc. No. 28.

Document No. 7: Copy of Father Guidi's letter to Kött, March 29, 1860 (Enclosed with Document No. 8: Kött to De Luca, April 3, 1860). Latin. Leaf No. 86. For the question of bribery, see ASV, CC Docs. No. 16 and 17.

Copy of the letter from the Reverend Father Filippo Guidi of the Order of Preachers, Professor of Dogmatics in Vienna.

Exemplar literarum R[everendi] P[atris] Phil[ippi] Guidi O[rdinis] Pr[aedicatorum] Professoris dogm[aticae]. Vienn[ae].

Vienna, from the Dominican Monastery, on the 29th of March, 1860.

Illustrissimo et Reverendissimo Christophoro Florentio Koett Episcopo Fuldensi, Fuldam

When, on the occasion of the holidays at the end of the first academic semester, I went to Rome to take care of some personal matters, I was approached there by some highly-placed prelates[4] and asked to return to Vienna in order to attend quickly to those things that would put a stop to the decision reached in *the second trial for the validity or invalidity* of the marriage of the Illustrious Princess Carolyne Wittgenstein, born Iwanowska. Indeed, unquestionable evidence did reach Rome to the effect that some individual from Poland, a Monsieur Władislaw Okraszewski, had promised, in so far as a second trial could be held in the same Curia, that he would easily corrupt the judges by means of a

Quum occasione feriarum post Primum Scholasticum Semestre occurrentium ad quaedam negotia peragenda Romam me contulerim, ibi a quibusdam gravissimis Ecclesiaticis viris mandatum accepi, ut Vindobonam reversus ea expedite curarem, quae decisionem *alterius processus de valitudine aut nullitate* matrimonii Ill[ustrissi]mae Principis[sae] Karolinae Wittgenstein natae Iwanowska impedirent. Etenim Romam indubia argumenta pervenerant quemdam Polonum D[ominum] Ladislaum Okrazowski mediante Summa 70 millium Rublorum promisisse se facile, dummodo alius processus ab eadem curia institui posset, iudices esse corrupturum, ut invalidum praecedens matrimonium praefatae Dominae

---

[4]It can be easily surmised from the unfolding documentation that the "highly-placed" prelates included Gustav von Hohenlohe. See Doc. No. 14.

sum of 70,000 roubles and would have them rule for the invalidity of the aforesaid Lady Carolyne's previous marriage, during which a daughter had been born to her. Secondly, once she obtained the annulment, the aforementioned Carolyne would proceed to marry a Monsieur Franz Liszt, with whom she has already been living scandalously for ten years as an adulteress. Things being so, those highly-placed prelates thought that, at the end of the trial, the Episcopal Curia should issue no decree, but would take steps in order that the pope be able to reserve the final decision for himself, which doubtless would be the case.

As soon as I reached Vienna, I diligently inquired into these matters, and it was reported to me that the Curia had already issued the *decree* and it had been sent to Your Most Illustrious and Reverend Excellency, without a doubt in order that, there being a decree for the annulment of the previous marriage, the aforesaid Carolyne might be able to marry Monsieur Franz Liszt who lives in Weimar, a part of the Diocese of Fulda. Monsieur Okraszewski has already requested the first installment of the promised sum and, if I am not mistaken, he is also at present in Weimar.

But given that the previous marriage, as it was recognised at the first trial and has now been absolutely ascertained in Rome, is *valid* without any possible doubt and, moreover, the most recent decree for the annulment of the previous marriage is the result of corruption, while I am appraising those eminent Roman prelates of these facts, I inform also your Most Illustrious and Reverend Excellency so that, if, in the Lord's name, it will seem proper to you, you may suspend everything until either instructions will come to your Most Illustrious and Reverend Excellency or I get an answer from Rome. The matter is of such gravity that I am sure that Your Excellency will prudently choose to delay the whole thing.

Should there be such a delay, I request that the true cause be kept secret and that, in any event, my name be meanwhile withheld. On both accounts silence is necessary.

Humbly leaning to kiss your holy hands, with the greatest veneration I am
Friar Filippo Maria Guidi

Karolinae, quae ex illo Filiam genuerat, decernerent, qua nullitate decreta, praedicta Karolina nuptura erat cuidam D[omino] Francisco Liszt, cum quo iam per decennium adultere ac scandalose vivit. Quibus stantibus eorum gravissimorum Ecclesiasticorum mens erat, ut peracto processu Curia Ep[iscopa]lis nullum decretum ferret, sed curasset ut Summus Pontifex sibi illud reservaret, quod certo evenisset.

Vix Vindobonam perveni, de re diligenter inquisivi atque mihi renunciatum est iam *decretum* ab ea curia fuisse latum, atque ad Ill[ustrissi]mam ac R[everendissi]mam Dominationam Vestram transmissum; procul dubio ut, stante Decreto illo de nullitate praecedentis matrimonii, praedicta Karolina nubere possit cum D[omino] Francisco Liszt, eo quod iste Weimarii degat, quae urbs ad Dioecesim Fuldensem spectat. Iam D[ominus] Okrazowski primam ratam promissae pecuniae expostulavit, atque nisi fallor, ipse quoque in praesentiarum Weimarii moratur.

Quum vero matrimonium praecedens, prout ex primo processu constiterat et, ut Romae nunc absolute constat, absque ullo prorsus dubio *validum* sit ac nuperrimum decretum pro nullitate praecedentis matrimonii ex venalitate processerit, dum illos gravissimos Romanos viros moneo, etiam Ill[ustrissiman] ac Rev[erendissi]mam Dominationem Vestram de eadem re certiorem facio, ut, si sibi in Domino videbitur, omnia suspendat, quoadusque Roma vel ad Ill[ustrissi]mam ac R[everendissi]mam Dominationem Vestram instructio vel ad me responsum venerit. Res adeo gravis est ut pro certo habeam praelaudatam Dominationem V[estram] prudenter omnia fore dilaturam.

Quae dilatio si fiat, oro ut de vera causa huiusce dilationis secretum servetur, atque saltem pro interim *meum nomen* reticeatur. De utroque silentium necessarium est.

Humillime s[anctas] manus osculans maxima cum veneratione sum
Fr[ater] Philippus M[ari]a Guidi

Vindobonae, ex Conventu Dominic[anorum],
die 29 Martii 1860.

For the authenticity of the copy:
x Christophe Florenz Kött
Bishop of Fulda.

Pro copia
x Christophorus Florentius <Koett>.

**Document No. 8: Kött to De Luca, April 3, 1860, with note on the verso penned
by De Luca. Doc. No. 7 is enclosed. Latin. Leaves No. 87–88.**

<To: Monsignor Antonino De Luca,
Archbishop of Tarsus and
Apostolic Nuncio in Vienna.>
Fulda, April 3, 1860.
Most Excellent and Reverend Monsignor!

I received not long ago from the Dominican
Monastery in Vienna a letter which I have tran-
scribed and enclosed with this one; it was written
on March 29 by the Reverend Father Friar Filippo Maria Guidi of the Order of Preachers, Professor of Dogmatic Theology at the University. It
says more or less that the case of the validity or
invalidity of the marriage of the Illustrious
Princess Carolyne Wittgenstein, born
Iwanowska, has been reopened, and that the
judges have been corrupted to the tune of 70,000
roubles by a Władislaw Okraszewski from Poland
in order that they vote for invalidity, while the
validity of the marriage has become truly apparent in Rome. The decree, moreover, has already been issued and sent to me. He asks,
therefore, that I take steps to suspend the sentence; he has been requested to do these things
by highly placed prelates in Rome, whose names
he does not wish to mention. I have no doubt at
all that the letter written by the aforementioned
Professor is genuine and truthful, since there is
not one argument that appears to deny its
authenticity and veracity. But I have not yet ex-
plored the *impossibility* of a fraud; nor have I
thus far received that decree for the annulment
of the marriage, which is mentioned in this letter.

Things being so, I turn to Your Excellency
and ask you in all humility either, in your prudence, to refute the things reported in this letter
or to confirm them with your authority and,
should you have some insight about this case,
please let me know as soon as possible.

<Antonino De Luca
Archiepiscopo Tarsensi
Nuntio Apostolico Viennam>

Excellentissime ac Reverendissime Domine!

Pervenere nuper ad me ex Conventu
Dominicanorum Viennensi literae, quas de-
scriptas huic epistolae addidi, datae a R[eve-
rendo] P[atre] Fr[atre] Philippo M[aria] Guidi
Ordinis Praedicatorum in Universitate
Theol[ogiae] Dogmat[icae] Professore de die
29 Martii, quae haec fere habent: processum de
valore aut nullitate matrimonii Ill[ustrissi]mae
Principis[sae] Karolinae Wittgenstein natae
Iwanowska iterum institutum, auctore
D[omino] Ladislao Okrazowski Polono 70 milli-
bus Rublorum corruptionem iudicum factam ut
nullitas decerneretur, dum valor nunc certo
constaret Romae; hoc decretum vere iam factum et ad me transmissum; unde rogare sese ut
executionem curarem suspendendam; haec
denique omnia ut ageret, mandatum ipsi esse a
viris quibusdam gravissimis ecclesiasticis Ro-
manis, quorum tamen nomina silentio premit.
Haud dubito quin literae a praefato P[atre]
Professore datae genuinae sint et veraces;
siquidem non unum tantum argumentum et
genuinitatem et veracitatem suadere videtur.
Sed *impossibilitas* fraudis nondum explorata
mihi est; neque hucusque decretum illud nullitatis matrimonii, quod commemoratum inveni-
tur in literis istis, ad me pervenit.

Quod quum ita sit, ad officium Excellentiae Vestrae recurro et humiliter rogo ut, quae
relata istis literis sunt, ea discutere pro Sua
prudentia, et auctoritate confirmare et si quae
forte hac de causa Ipsa sentiat, quam fieri potest
citissime mecum velit communicare.

Furthermore, just as I must keep silent about the person involved in this matter, so, I entreat you, may it please your Excellency to keep the secret.

I am very happy to use this occasion to declare my personal feelings of good will and respect toward Your Most Illustrious and Reverend Excellency, and in this spirit I remain Your Excellency's
most humble and devoted,
x Christophe Florenz Kött
Bishop of Fulda

Monsignor the Bishop of Fulda. April 3, 1860.
On the Wittgenstein-Iwanowska marriage case.

Ceterum sicut ego rem et auctorem sileo, ita, quaeso, etiam Excellentiae Vestrae secretum placeat servare.

Libentissime hac occasione utor, ut intimos voluntatis atque venerationis meae erga Excellentiam Vestram Illustrissimam et Reverendissimam sensus declarem, quibus persisto Excellentiae Vestrae
Humillimus et addictissimus
x Christophorus Florentius <Koett>
Episcopus Fuldensis
Fuldae, die Aprilis III. 1860.

M[onsi]g[no]r Vescovo di Fulda, 3 aprile 1860.
Su la causa matrimoniale della Principessa Carolina Wittgenstein.

Document No. 9: Quaglia to De Luca, April 4, 1860 (with note on the verso penned by De Luca). Enclosed with Doc. No. 10. Italian. Leaves No. 90–91. The draft of this document is in ASV, CC Doc. No. 18. For the context, see ASV, CC Docs. No. 16, a petition by Monsignor Hohenlohe, and 17, a memorandum to the Pope on the question of bribery. De Luca's answer, not preserved in this file, is in ASV, CC Doc. No. 21.

To: Monsignor Antonino De Luca
Archbishop of Tarsus,
Apostolic Nuncio, Vienna
Rome, April 4, 1860
Most Illustrious and Reverend Excellency:

During the month of August of last year, Princess Carolyne Iwanowska, Catholic, from the Diocese of Luck-Zhitomir in Russia, presented a petition to the Holy Father through the offices of this Holy Congregation of the Council stating that she had already requested, a few years ago, from her own Ordinary Office a judgement declaring her marriage to Prince Nicholas Wittgenstein, non Catholic, null and void on account of its being contracted in a situation of violence and intimidation provoked by her father, and that a sentence proclaiming its validity was issued by that Curia in 1851.

She added also that she appealed against that sentence to the so-called Consistory of the Metropolitan Curia of Mohilow, from which she said she obtained an opinion in favor of the annulment; the latter was not, however, adopted by the Vicar General of the then Metropolitan. The case being suspended, because in the meantime

Monsign[or] Antoni[n]o De Luca,
Arciv[escov]o di Tarso
Nunzio Apostolico
Vienna
Ill[ustrissi]mo e Rev[erendissi]mo Signore.

La Principessa Carolina Iwanowska Cattolica della Diocesi di Luk-Zitomir in Russia rappresentava nell'Agosto del decorso anno per organo di questa Sacra Congregazione del Concilio al S[anto] Padre di avere già da alcuni anni promosso innanzi al proprio Ordinariato giudizio di nullità di matrimonio, comeché per violenza e timore incussole dal suo genitore, da lei contratto col Principe Nicola Wittgenstein eterodosso, ed essersene emanata in quella curia nel 1851 sentenza per la validità.

Aggiungeva pure di avere appellato innanzi al così detto Concistoro della Curia Metropolitana di Mohilow, dal quale riferiva avere ottenuto un opinamento per la nullità, che però non venne adottato dal vicario generale del Metropolitano di quel tempo; onde la stessa esponente (essendo rimasta

the aforesaid Metropolitan had died and, Prince Nicholas having entered a new marriage in the Lutheran sect, the appellant turned to the present Archbishop for a definitive sentence. He told her that he could not deal with the case without a specific authorization from the Holy See, probably because that Consistory had already issued an opinion. So the Princess requested that the said Archbishop be authorized to deal again with the case for annulment and provide a definitive sentence.

These facts, corroborated by a declaration of the Metropolitan himself, were presented by me to His Holiness for his decision at an audience given on August 8, 1859.[5] I was authorized by His Holiness himself to issue a rescript of the following tenor:

"The Holy Father kindly condescends to empower the present Metropolitan of Mohilow, whereas there be nothing to the contrary, to take up again the aforesaid case of marriage annulment, review it, and issue a definitive sentence according to the level of appeal, observing otherwise what is to be observed according to the Law and especially the Bull *Dei miseratione* issued by the late Benedict XIV."

This rescript was forwarded to the Archbishop; and the interested party, through an agent of hers who was sent to Rome, obtained an authenticated copy of the same.

It has now been intimated to the Holy Father by some respectable individuals that Princess Carolyne Iwanowska, in endeavoring to obtain the annulment of her marriage, may have induced her daughter Marie to yield to her eighty thousand roubles from her dowry before she married Prince Konstantin von Hohenlohe; of this amount, fifty thousand would be used for the abominable purpose of bribing and corrupting those judges. It has also been pointed out that the very individual chosen to represent her in Rome, a Monsieur Okraszewski, is now active

sospesa la causa, avvenuta nel frattempo la morte dell'anzidetto Metropolitano, e passato il Principe Nicola ad altre nozze nella setta Luterana) si rivolse all'odierno Arcivescovo per ottenere una sentenza definitiva. Ma avendole questi significato di non potersi ingerire in tal causa senza una particolare autorizzazione della S[anta] Sede, forse perché quel Concistoro aveva in antecedenza emesso un opinamento, quindi la medesima Principessa supplicava affinché fosse abilitato quell'Arcivescovo a trattare nuovamente detta causa di nullità fino alla definitiva sentenza.

Questi fatti corroborati da una esposizione dello stesso Metropolitano vennero da me rappresentati a Sua Santità nell' udienza degli 8 Agosto 1859 per le opportune provvidenze e fui dalla Stessa Santità Sua autorizzato ad emettere il rescritto del tenore che siegue:

"P[ater] S[anctissi]mus benigne annuit, ut, contrariis quibuscumque non obstantibus, modernus Metropolitanus Mohilowiensis enunciatam causam super nullitate matrimonii, reassumere, cognoscere, ac per sententiam definitivam dijudicare valeat in gradu appellationis, servatis ceteroquin de jure servandis, ac praesertim Constitutione Sa[nctae] Me[moriae] Benedicti XIV *Dei Miseratione*."

Questo rescritto venne notificato all'Arcivescovo; e la parte interessata per mezzo di un suo Agente spedito in Roma ottenne copia autentica del medesimo.

Ora per parte di ragguardevoli personaggi si è rappresentato al S[anto] Padre che la Principessa Carolina Iwanowska nell'intendimento di ottenere l'annullamento del suo matrimonio inducesse la sua figlia Maria prima di sposarsi al Principe Costantino D'Hohenlohe a cederle ottantamila scudi della sua dote, dei quali cinquantamila verrebbero impiegati al riprovevole scopo di comprare e corrompere quei giudici, facendosi anche rimarcare che lo stesso Procuratore, tal Okraszewski, che venne inviato a Roma, ora trovasi ad agire presso quel Concis-

---

[5]For Carolyne's appeal see ASV, CC Docs. No. 2-10, the last of which contains the papal rescript. The Bull *Dei miseratione* can be found in *Bullarium Benedicti XIV*, tome I, pp. 69-74.

It sets the basic procedures in annulment cases, the levels of jurisdiction, and the notion that at least two sentences in favor of annulment are necessary to dissolve a marriage.

around that Consistory. On the basis of this, it has been requested that the trial be moved away from that Curia and the case be dealt with by the Holy See.

The Holy Father could not accede to such a request, both because it would not be proper to do so given the above mentioned rescript and, though it may have been possible that the Princess had the intention of bribing those judges, it did not follow that their accepting a bribe could be taken as a fact; moreover, there was no evidence whatsoever to give credit to such a suspicion.

The Holy Father, however, in his desire to show some concern for these fears, ordered me to inform Your Most Illustrious and Reverend Excellency for the sole purpose that you may write a letter to that Monsignor Archbishop of Mohilow and make him aware of what I have told you with respect to the alleged machinations whose aim is to corrupt those judges and, with that prudence that distinguishes you, you might alert him about them and then ask him for a categorical answer which you should in turn be so kind as to convey at the appropriate time to this Holy Congregation.

Having discharged my duties with respect to the Pontifical command, all that remains for me to do is to express to You my feelings of the most singular and respectful esteem and declare myself
Your Most Illustrious and Reverend Excellency's
Most Devoted and Obliging Servant,
Angelo Quaglia,
Secretary to the Holy Congregation
of the Council

Monsignor Secretary of the Council,
April 4, 1860.
On the marriage case of Princess Carolyne Wittgenstein discussed in the Metropolitan Curia of Mohilow.
Answered on April 14 enclosing a copy of the Mohilow Sentence.

toro, e su questa base si è domandato che venisse richiamato il processo da quella Curia per essere giudicata la causa dalla S[anta] Sede.

Il S[anto] Padre non poteva accogliere tale dimanda sia perché non trattavasi di cosa integra stante il rescritto sopra ricordato, sia perché, quantunque fosse possibile nella Principessa Iwanowska l'intendimento di subornare quei giudici, non ne seguiva però che potesse ritenersi come un fatto la loro prevaricazione, e d'altronde, nemmeno il sospetto veniva convalidato da un qualche documento.

Tuttavia il S[anto] Padre, volendo pure avere un qualche riguardo a siffatte apprensioni, mi ha ordinato far conoscere tutte queste cose a V[ostra] S[ignoria] Ill[ustrissi]ma e Rev[erendissi]ma al solo effetto, che Ella con una lettera porti a notizia di Monsig[nor] Arcivescovo di Mohilow quel tanto che io Le ho qui esposto in ordine alle asserte machinazioni tendenti a corrompere quei giudici e, con quella prudenza che L'è propria, lo ponga in guardia sulle medesime, e provochi una di Lui categorica risposta, che poi Ella dovrebbe avere la bontà di rimettere a suo tempo a questa S[anta] Congr[egazion]e.

Adempiuto così al Pontificio comando non mi rimane che porgerle i sensi di mia distinta ed ossequiosa stima e rassegnarmi

Di V[ostra] S[ignoria] Ill[ustrissi]ma e
    Rev[erendissi]ma
Dev[otissi]mo Ob[bligatiss]imo Servo
Angelo Quaglia, Seg[reta]rio della
S[anta] C[ongregazione] del Concilio.
Roma, li 4 Aprile 1860.

M[onsi]g[no]r Seg[reta]rio del Concilio,
4 Aprile 1860.
Su la causa matrimoniale della P[rincipe]ssa Carolina Wittgenstein presso la Curia Metropolitana di Mohilow.
Risp[osto] li 14 Aprile soccartandogli la copia della Sentenza di Mohilow.

Document No. 10: Hohenlohe to De Luca, April 6, 1860, with note on the verso penned by De Luca. Enclosing Doc. No. 9. Italian. Leaves No. 92–93.

To: Monsignor <Antonino> De Luca,
Apostolic Nuncio in Vienna.
Vatican, April 6, 1860
Most Venerable Monsignor:

Monsignor Secretary of the Holy Congregation of the Council has asked me to forward, with today's courier, the enclosed letter to Your Most Reverend Excellency. I do so with great pleasure for it gives me a welcome chance to wish you a most happy Easter and, as I respectfully bend to kiss your holy ring, I confirm myself
Your Most Reverend Excellency's

most devoted and obliging servant
Gustav von Hohenlohe,
Archbishop of Edessa

P.S.: I beg Your Most Reverend Excellency to tell Canon Sapri that I wish to know whether he has sent to Canon Prisac in Aachen that letter that I sent to him in Vienna a few weeks ago.

Monsignor Hohenlohe, April 6, 1860
He sends a letter from the Secretary of the Holy
    Congregation of the Council

Mo[nsi]gnor <Antonino De Luca>
Nunzio Ap[osto]lico di Vienna.

Monsignore Veneratissimo.

Mo[nsi]gnor Segretario della S[anta] Congregazione del Concilio mi prega di spedire col corriere d'oggi l'acclusa lettera a V[ostra] E[ccellenza] R[everendissima]. Io lo faccio con vero piacere mentre mi dà la felice occasione di augurarLe la Pasqua felicissima e con alta considerazione baciandoLe il S[acro] anello mi confermo di V[ostra] E[ccellenza] R[everendissima]
D[evotissi]mo obl[igatissi]mo servo
G[ustavo] d'Hohenlohe,
Arciv[escov]o d'Edessa
Vaticano, 6 Aprile 1860

P.S. Prego V[ostra] E[ccellenza] R[everendissima] di dire al Sig[no]r Canonico Sapri che desidero sapere se ha mandato quella lettera al Canonico Prisac in Aquisgrana, ch'io gli spedii a Vienna settimane fa.

M[onsi]g[n]or Hohenlohe, 6 Aprile 1860
Spedisce una lettera del Segr[eta]rio del
    Concilio.

Document No. 11: Kött to De Luca, April 10, 1860 (Enclosing a copy of Document No. 6, a copy of Żyliński's decree. See Doc. No. 6 and ASV, CC Doc. No. 22. The text of the decree is in ASV, CC Doc. No. 28). Latin. Leaf No. 94.

<To: Monsignor Antonino De Luca,
Archbishop of Tarsus and
Apostolic Nuncio in Vienna>
Fulda, April 10, 1860
Most Excellent and Reverend Monsignor:

I hope you have received the letter I wrote you on April 3 in which I had asked Your Most Illustrious and Reverend Excellency to confirm whether or not the letter sent to me by a Dominican father, professor at the great University of Vienna, is to be believed and, assuming the truthfulness of the things reported therein, to instruct me as to what should be done.

Today the man from Poland, one Monsieur Władislaw Okraszewski mentioned in that letter,

<Domino Antonino De Luca
Archiepiscopo Tarsensi
Nuntio Apostolico
Viennam>
Excellentissime ac Reverendissime Domine!

Datis de die tertio Aprilis literis et, ut spero, acceptis Excellentiam Vestram Illustrissimam et Reverendissimam rogaveram, ut Patris cuiusdam Dominicani, Professoris in alma universitate Viennensi, Philippi Guidi epistolae mihi missae fidem faceret certam, et supposita veritate eorum quae eadem epistola relata erant, quid consilii capiendum esset, innueret.

Hodie qui in dicta epistola commemoratus erat D[ominus] Ladislaus Okraszewski Polonus

actually came to see me and, on presenting to me a decree issued by his most illustrious and reverend Excellency the Archbishop of Mohilow, Wenceslas Żyliński, which annuls the marriage between Carolyne Iwanowska and Prince Wittgenstein (Your Excellency will find a copy of this decree enclosed with this letter of mine), he requested on behalf of this same Carolyne that I myself consent to bless, as soon as possible, her new forthcoming marriage with Liszt.

Promising that I would respond in writing, I put off a definite answer until eight days from now.

For this reason, I am most concerned that I should know whether Your Excellency is aware of any decision of the Holy Apostolic See so that, with that information, I can either forbid the celebration of this marriage or, in the meantime, I can further postpone it.

Given the gravity of the matter, I earnestly request Your Most Illustrious and Reverend Excellency to deign to answer me immediately upon receiving this letter if it is at all possible.

My inclination and veneration toward Your Excellency are and will be the same as they have been in the past.
Your Excellency's
most humble and devoted
x Christophe Florenz <Koett>,
Bishop of Fulda.

revera me adiit, et decreto R[everen]d[issi]mi et Excell[entissi]mi D[omi]ni Archiepiscopi Mohiloviensis Venceslas Żyliński de nullitate matrimonii Karolinae Iwanowska cum Principe Wittgenstein, cuius decreti exemplar his literis meis adnexum invenit Excellentia Vestra, prolato, nomine istius Karolinae petiit, ut novis nuptiis cum isto Lisztio celebrandis benedicere quam citissime ego ipse vellem.

Distuli equidem certum responsum, octavo, ab hodierno si computamus, die me rescripturum esse promittens.

Quamobrem magis mihi cordi est audire, si quid sententiae Apostolicae Sedis Excellentiae Vestrae innotuerit, quo communicato habeam, unde nuptias celebrandas vel negem[6] vel longius interim differam.

Pro rei gravitate Excellentiam Vestram Illustrissimam ac Reverendissimam oro rogoque, ut, si fieri potest, statim post acceptas has literas mihi respondere dignetur, qui eadem qua fui erga Excellentiam Vestram voluntate et veneratione, etiamnunc sum et semper ero

Excellentiae Vestrae
Humillimus et addictissimus
x Christophorus Florentius <Koett>,
Episcopus Fuldensis.
Fuldae, die Aprilis X ann[i] 1860

Document No. 12: De Luca to Kött, April 11, 1860 (Answer to Document No. 8: Kött to De Luca, April 3, 1860). Latin. Leaf No. 96.

To: The Most Illustrious and Reverend
<Monsignor Christophe Florenz Kött,>
Bishop of Fulda, etc.
Vienna, April 11, 1860
Most Illustrious and Reverend Excellency:

After rather much consideration I set out to answer, in my own hand, the most humane letter written by Your Most Illustrious and Reverend Excellency on the 3rd day of this present April.

Ill[ustrissi]mo et R[everendissi]mo
<Domino Christoforo Florentio Koett>
Episcopo Fuldensi, etc.
Viennae, die XI Aprilis 1860
Ill[ustrissi]me et R[everendissi]me Domine.

Consultius duco autographum responsum dare humanissimis literis a D[ominatio]ne V[estr]a Ill[ustrissi]ma et R[everendissi]ma die 3 labensis mensis mihi inscriptis.

---

[6]Kött lightly corrected *haberem* and *negarem*, originally written, into *habeam* and *negem*.

written by Your Most Illustrious and Reverend Excellency on the 3rd day of this present April.

The letter sent to Your Excellency on the 29th of last February by the well known professor is genuine and truthful.

The matter under discussion had already come to my knowledge, and I took extensive counsel on it, though this action on my part had neither legal nor official sanction but was private.

I definitely think that under no circumstances can the decree for the marriage annulment, should it be presented to Your Most Reverend Excellency, be carried out. Therefore I ask that you communicate to me in the most confidential way anything that may eventually transpire on this subject. Nothing should be done without it being confirmed or ordered on the authority of the Holy Roman See, properly and through legitimate channels.

....

<Antonino De Luca,
Archbishop of Tarsus and
Apostolic Nuncio in Vienna>

Epistola D[ominatio]ni Vestrae die 29 praeterlapsi mensis a noto Professore data genuina et verax est.

Mihi negotium de quo est sermo, jamdudum innotuerat et penitiorem rei habui consilium non juridico seu officiali, verum privato modo.

Equidem reor decretum de invaliditate matrimonii si forte D[ominatio]ni V[estr]ae R[everendissim]ae exhibitum fuerit executioni mandari nullomodo posse. Ideoque secretissime rogo ut mecum comunicare velit quidquid hac super re eventurum sit. Nil perficiatur quin auctoritate S[anctae] Romanae Sedis et *legitima* via rite firmetur aut decernatur.

....

<Antoninus De Luca
Archiepiscopus Tarsensis
Nuntius Apostolicus
Viennae>

Document No. 13: De Luca to Kött, April 14, 1860 (Answer to Document No. 11: Kött to De Luca, April 10, 1860). Latin. Leaf No. 97.

To: His Most Illustrious and Reverend Excellency,
Monsignor Christophe Florenz Kött,
Bishop of Fulda
Fulda
No.: 1463/1
Vienna, April 14, 1860
Most Illustrious and Reverend Excellency:

Without any delay, I set out to answer the second letter written to me on the 10th of the present month by Your Most Illustrious and Reverend Excellency. I received it today.

The present Archbishop of Mohilow, through an official rescript issued on August 9 of last year[7] by the Reverend Father Secretary of the Holy Congregation of the Council, has received the mandate and the appropriate faculties in order that, "whereas there be nothing to the

<Ill[ustrissi]mo et R[everentissi]mo

D[omi]no Christophoro Florenti(n)o Koett
Episcopo Fuldensi
Fuldam>
N. 1463/1
Viennae, die XIV Aprilis, 1860
Ill[ustrissi]me et R[everendissi]me Domine.

Nulla interposita mora, meum duco responsum dare alterae epistolae D[ominatio]nis V[estr]ae Ill[ustrissi]mae et R[everendissi]mae die X labentis mensis mihi inscriptae, et hodie a me receptae.

Modernus Archiepiscopus Mohilowiensis per Rescriptum a R[everendo] P[atre] S[anctae] C[ongregationis] Concilii Segretario Romae die 9 Augusti anni praeterlapsi dato mandatum et facultates opportunas recepit ut "contrariis quibuscumque non obstantibus enunciatam causam super nullitatem matrimonii (inter principem Nic[olaum] Wittgenstein et

[7]Actually August 8. See ASV, CC Doc. No. 10.

genstein and Princess Carolyne Iwanowska, and after studying it, be empowered to issue a definitive sentence, according to the level of appeal, observing otherwise what needs be observed, especially with reference to the Bull *Dei miseratione* issued by the late Benedict XIV, etc."

But since in the aforementioned Bull, as your Excellency well knows, it was clearly and deliberately stated that there should be an appeal against a second sentence of annulment if it be such that an individual, in his conscience, may not deem it possible to acquiesce in it and since, according to the above mentioned Pontiff, marriage cases are never adjudicated once and for all,[8] it is quite clear that the decree of annulment newly issued by the Archbishop of Mohilow cannot be carried out and that Princess Carolyne cannot be permitted to marry again.

Indeed, serious rumors about the corruption of judges through bribes have continued to spread. In the course of their marriage, the two parties managed to live peacefully for many years and produced a daughter. The arguments in favor of the annulment are subjective rather than objective in nature, namely *violence and intimidation*, and the truth of such things is very difficult to prove, especially after so many years have passed since the inception of the marriage.

Therefore, Your Most Illustrious and Reverend Excellency will see that, before we go much further into this matter, it is only right that a report be sent to the Reverend Father Secretary of the Holy Congregation of the Roman Council, together with a copy of the aforesaid sentence issued by the Metropolitan of Mohilow. Instructions should also be requested from the Most Holy Father as to the manner of proceeding in this very difficult matter.

....
<Antonino De Luca,
Archbishop of Tarsus and
Apostolic Nuncio in Vienna>

Principissam Carolinam Iwanowska) reassumere, cognoscere ac per sententiam definitivam dijudicare valeat in gradu appellationis, servatis ceteroquin de jure servandis, ac praesertim Constitutione Sa[nctae] Me[moriae] Benedicti XIV *Dei miseratione* etc."

Cum vero in praedicta Constitutione, prout Dominatio Vestra recte novit, dilucide et expressis verbis praescribatur a secunda sententia super nullitate appellandum esse, si huiusmodi sit, ut ei salva conscientia acquiescendum non putetur et, cum juxta praelaudatum Pontificem causae matrimoniales nunquam transeant in rem judicatam, liquide constat decretum de nullitate ab Archiepiscopo Mohilowiensi noviter prolatum executioni mandari non posse neque potestatem Principissae Karolinae faciendam esse ad alias nuptias convolandi.

Non vani etenim percrebuerunt rumores de corruptione judicum per pecuniae oblationem. In Matrimonio per plurimos annos pacifice perdurarunt partes et filiam progenuerunt. Argumenta pro nullitate non objectivae naturae sed mere subjectivae sunt, nempe *vis et metus*, quorum veritas difficillime potest probari, praesertim cum multi ab inito matrimonio anni praeterlapsi.

Recte igitur Dominatio Vestra Ill[ustrissi]ma et R[everendissi]ma perspiciet, antequam ulterius in hac re progrediatur, relationem trasmittendam esse R[everendo] P[atri] Secretario S[anctae] C[ongregationis] Concilii Romani una cum exemplo commemoratae sententiae a Metropolitano Mohilowiensi prolatae et mandatum a Sanctissimo Patre exquirendum de ratione procedendi in huiusmodi arduo negotio.

....
<Antoninus De Luca
Archiepiscopus Tarsensis,
Nuntius Apostolicus,
Viennae>

---

[8]This is a key phrase for an understanding of the legal problems encountered by Carolyne. Benedict XIV states in *Dei miseratione* (paragraph 11, p. 72) that, while after two analogous sentences in favor of annulment, the parties in the annulled marriage are allowed to remarry, it is a firmly established principle that marriage cases are never adjudi-

cated once and for all (*numquam transeant in rem judicatam*) no matter how much time has elapsed since the judgement for, if some new element that had not been considered or was not known is brought to light, the case may be reopened.

Document No. 14: Hohenlohe to De Luca, April 19, 1860, with note on the verso penned by De Luca. Italian. Leaves No. 98–99. De Luca's answer is not in the files.

To: Monsignor Antonino De Luca,
Apostolic Nuncio in Vienna etc. etc. etc.
Vatican, April 19, 1860
Most Venerable Monsignor:

Your Most Reverend Excellency must have received the letter from Monsignor Secretary of the Holy Congregation of the Council in which, with respect to the very serious case pertaining to the marriage of Princess Carolyne von Sayn-Wittgenstein, formerly Iwanowska, you were to receive the proper instructions for Monsignor Archbishop of Mohilow, who had received very *extensive* powers in dealing with that case.

Following the telegraphic dispatch I sent him before yesterday, the Reverend Father Guidi from the Preachers' Order must have informed Your Most Reverend Excellency of the orders His Holiness gave me in a most holy audience on April 17 for Your Most Reverend Excellency, which it is my duty to reproduce here in writing, namely that you should write to Monsignor the Bishop of Fulda in order that he inform the aforementioned Princess Carolyne that it is the Holy Father's will that, for the time being, she does not proceed to contract a new marriage; this in order to prevent a great scandal, since the first marriage of the above mentioned Princess Carolyne with Prince Nicholas von Sayn-Wittgenstein (still alive) is, according to the best information we now have, valid, and the declaration of annulment lately issued by the Archiepiscopal Curia of Mohilow can be deemed, in all probability, false and procured through the services of some meddler.

You know better than I that these are not the kind of dispensations that the Holy See can give, and that it is rather a question of declaring the marriage between the aforesaid Princess Carolyne and the above named Prince Nicholas null and void. But this is a marriage contracted many years ago, characterized by cohabitation, consummated many years ago, and with *issue*; but now we are supposed to believe there was lack of consent on the part of the woman!

Mons[ignor] <Antonino> De Luca
Nunzio Apostolico a Vienna
etc., etc., etc.
Monsignore Veneratissimo.

Vostra Eccellenza R[e]v[erendissi]ma avrà ricevuto la lettera di M[on]s[i]g[no]re Segretario della S[anta] Congreg[azion]e del Concilio nella quale, in riguardo alla gravissima causa matrimoniale della Principessa Carolina di Sayn-Wittgenstein nata Iwanowska, Ella riceve le opportune istruzioni per M[on]-s[i]g[no]re Arcivescovo di Mohilow il quale per quella causa aveva ricevuto delle facoltà assai *estese*.

In seguito del mio dispaccio telegrafico dell'altro ieri il R[everendo] Padre Guidi de' Predicatori avrà informato V[ostra] E[ccellenza] R[everendissima] dell'ordine di Sua Santità datomi nell' udienza santissima del 17 Aprile per V[ostra] E[ccellenza] R[everendissima] che qui mi faccio un dovere di ripeterLe in iscritto, cioè ch'Ella scrivesse a M[on]-s[i]g[no]re Vescovo di Fulda onde questo significhi alla sudd[ett]a Principessa Carolina, che è volontà del Santo Padre che per ora *non procedat ad alias nuptias*; e ciò per impedire uno scandalo inaudito perché il primo matrimonio della sudd[ett]a Principessa Carolina col Principe Nicolao di Sayn-Wittgenstein (tuttora vivente) è, secondo tutte le notizie che ora abbiamo, valido, e la dichiarazione di nullità emanata ultimamente dalla Curia Arcivescovile di Mohilow con tutta probabilità può riputarsi come falsa e procurata da qualche intrigante.

Ella meglio di me conosce che non si tratta di dispense che possa dare la Santa Sede, ma più tosto di dichiarare nullo il matrimonio della suddetta Principessa Carolina col sopranominato Principe Nicolao,—matrimonio contratto da molti anni, con coabitazione, consumato da molti anni e con *prole*,—ed ora si vorrebbe supporre la mancanza del consenso per parte della donna!

Because of all this, it is the express will of His Holiness that, notwithstanding the powers given to the Archbishop of Mohilow, the case be brought to the Holy See for review and for a definitive sentence. For this purpose, you will be able to take the best measures.

Your Most Reverend Excellency can see that this is a very serious case; it is even more serious because it was partially dealt with in Russia, where this matter is well known and where those schismatics will not miss a chance to denigrate the Catholic Church.

I trust that Your Most Reverend Excellency will wish to honor myself and Monsignor the Secretary of the Holy Congregation of the Council with a prompt answer and, as I lay a respectful kiss upon your hands, I declare myself, with high consideration and esteem,
Your Most Reverend Excellency's
most humble and devoted servant
as well as most affectionate friend,
Gustav von Hohenlohe,
Archbishop of Edessa

Monsignor Hohenlohe, April 19, 1860

He asks that the Bishop of Fulda be notified of the suspension of the annulment sentence in the Wittgenstein-Iwanowska case.
Answered on April 28 stating that the Bishop of Fulda had received the order not to proceed.

Per il che è volontà espressa di Sua Santità che, malgrado le facoltà concesse all'Arciv[escov]o di Mohilow, venga la causa riportata in via di revisione e per una definitiva sentenza alla Santa Sede, onde Ella potrà prendere le opportune misure.

Vede bene Vostra Eccellenza R[e]v[erendissi]ma trattarsi d'una causa assai grave in sè, e gravissima ancora perché trattata in parte e conosciuta in Russia dove non si tralascia nissuna occasione per parte di scismatici onde denigrare la Chiesa cattolica.

Mi lusingo che V[ostra] E[ccellenza] R[everendissima] voglia onorare me e Mons[ignor] Segretario della S[anta] Congreg[azione] del Concilio d'una sollecita risposta e, baciandoLe rispettosamente le mani, passo a dichiararmi con alta considerazione e stima di Vostra Eccellenza Reverendissima
umilissimo devotissimo servo ed amico
aff[ezionatissi]mo
G[ustavo] d'Hohenlohe,
Arciv[escov]o d'Edessa
Vaticano, 19 Aprile 1860

M[onsi]g[no]r Hohenlohe, 19 Aprile, 1860
Chiede che si notifichi al V[escov]o di Fulda la sospensione della sentenza di nullità del matrimonio Wittgenstein-Iwanowska.
Risp[osto] il 28 Aprile con dirgli che il Vescovo di Fulda aveva ricevuto l'inibizione.

Document No. 15: De Luca to Żyliński, April 29, 1860.[9] Latin. Leaf No. 101.

To: The Most Excellent and Reverend Monsignor
Wenceslas Żyliński
Archbishop of Mohilow, etc. etc. etc.
St. Petersburg
Prot. No. 1477/I[wanowska]
Vienna, April 29, 1860
Most Excellent and Reverend Monsignor:

I have recently received a copy of a decree issued by Your Most Reverend Excellency in St. Petersburg on the 24th of February of this year, whereby the marriage between Princess Carolyne Iwanowska

Exc[ellentissi]mo et R[everendissi]mo Domino

D[omi]no Venceslao Żyliński
Archiepiscopo Mohiloviensi ,etc. etc. etc.
Petropolim/St. Petersburg
N.1477/I[wanowska]
Viennae, die XXIX Aprilis 1860
Ex[cellentissi]me et R[everendissi]me Domine.

Nuper ad manus meas pervenit exemplar Decreti Petropoli die 24 Februarii labentis anni ab Excellentia Vestra R[everendissi]ma prolatum quo matrimonium a Domina Karolina Iwanowska cum

---

[9]The draft of De Luca's letter is dated April 29th, 1860; but Żyliński's answer (see Doc. No. 21) implies that the actual letter bore the date of May 2, 1860.

and Prince Nicholas Wittgenstein long since consummated is declared null and void, and the above mentioned lady is granted permission to marry again.

Allow me, please, to present freely to Your Most Reverend Excellency some considerations on this issue of really very grave importance.

The Bull of the late Benedict XIV that begins *Dei miseratione* prescribes most clearly that a second sentence of annulment must always be appealed if it is such that one cannot think of acquiescing in it to the satisfaction of his conscience. Your Excellency is well aware that, according to the teachings of the aforementioned Pontiff, marriage cases are never adjudicated once and for all, and that they can be reopened if new arguments emerge that cast doubt on the validity of the sentence issued in favor of annulment.

In order that I may better come to the point, I feel it is my duty to inform Your Most Reverend Excellency about rumors which are really not to be dismissed and are actually supported by sufficiently valid suppositions. According to them, a Polish layman who is managing the case demanded from the aforesaid Lady Iwanowska a large sum to corrupt the judges and obtain the desired outcome by lawful and unlawful means. For my part, I have no doubt that the judges of that same Metropolitan Diocese of Mohilow, in their deliberations upon this marriage case, brought forth a judgement in accordance with the bidding of their conscience. Nevertheless, it would be an occasion for great scandal among the faithful if, adding to these things and after such rumors, Princess Carolyne were to be granted right there and then permission to marry her lover, with whom she has openly lived for many years as an adulteress.

Add to this the fact that this same couple, Wittgenstein and Iwanowska, led for a long time a quiet life together and even produced a daughter. Therefore, assuming there was a lack of consent at the beginning, after such a long habit of life, it must be deemed that it was sufficiently renewed over and over again.

Principe Nicolao Wittgenstein jamdudum initum tamquam nullum et irritum declaratur et praelaudatae matronae facultas ad alias nuptias transeundi conceditur.

Mihi fas sit super huiusmodi gravissimi sane momenti negotio quasdam animadversiones ingenue Excellentiae Vestrae R[everendissi]mae communicare.

In Constitutione San[ctae] Mem[oriae] Benedicti XIV cuius initium *Dei miseratione*, clarissimis et expressis verbis praescribitur a secunda sententia super nullitate matrimonii semper appellandum esse si huiusmodi sit, ut ei salva conscientia acquiescendum non putetur. Minime Excell[enti]am V[estr]am latet juxta placita superius laudati Pontificis causas matrimoniales numquam transire in rem judicatam et novo subjici posse examini si nova suboriantur argumenta dubitandi de prolata sententia circa nullitatem.

Ut vero ad rem nostram proprius accedam, officio mihi duco Excellentiam V[estr]am R[everendissi]mam certiorem facere de rumoribus non sane futilibus sed e contra satis validis conjecturis suffultis, qui ferunt procuratorem totius negotii Polonum quemdam laicum ingentem pecuniae summam a praedicta matrona Iwanowska exegisse ad corrumpendos judices et ad totam rem ad exoptatum exitum per fas or nefas deducendam. Ego vero mea ex parte nullus dubito quin Judices ipsius metropolitanae Curiae Mohiloviensis in dijudicanda praedicta causa matrimoniali juxta conscientiae propriae dictamen sententiam protulerint. Nihilominus gravissimo scandalo inter fideles daretur occasio, si in hisce rerum adjunctis et posthabitis huiusmodi rumoribus illico et confestim daretur facultas Principissae Karolinae Wittgenstein nubendi amasio, quo cum per plures annos in adulterio publice convixit.

Addatur insuper quod in matrimonio coniuges ipsos Wittgenstein et Iwanowska anteactis temporibus pacificam egisse vitam et filiam procreasse. Ideoque si quis in consensu defectus ab initio extitisset per tam diuturnam vitae consuetudinem satis superque renovatus censendus erit.

By the same token, the arguments brought forth in favor of annulment are not of an objective nature, but merely *subjective* and, therefore, extremely difficult to prove.

From what has been said so far, Your Most Reverend Excellency will easily see that the sentence of annulment that has been issued can be carried out neither in that Metropolitan Diocese nor in the Diocese of Fulda, which Princess Wittgenstein has chosen as her residence, before a report on this whole affair together with a copy of the above mentioned decree is sent by Your Most Reverend Excellency to Rome for the attention of the Most Reverend Father Secretary of the Holy Congregation of the Council and an answer is received from him on the manner to proceed. It was on behalf and on the authority of the aforementioned Holy Congregation of the Council that your Excellency was given the authority and the faculty to deal with this case.

It was my express duty to relate these things to Your Most Reverend Excellency, and I hope that you will be so kind as to send me, as soon as possible, a letter such that it will assuage my preoccupations and anxiety and will restore my peace of mind.

I am very happy for this occasion to acknowledge openly my continued reverence and respect for Your Most Reverend Excellency.

....

<Antonino De Luca,
Archbishop of Tarsus and
Apostolic Nuncio in Vienna>

Argumenta itidem pro nullitate matrimonii allata non objectivae naturae, sed mere *subjectivae* ideoque quam maxime probatu difficilia sunt.

Ex hactenus dictis Excellentia V[estr]a R[everendissi]ma facili negotio perspiciet prolatam de nullitate sententiam executioni mandari non posse neque in ista Metropolitana Archidiocesi neque in Diocesi Fuldensi in qua Domina Principissa Wittgenstein domicilium suum constituit antequam ab Excellentia Vestra R[everendissi]ma relatio de toto hoc negotio una cum exemplari predicti Decreti Romam Rev[erendissi]mo P[atri] Secretario S[anctae] C[ongregationis] Concilii mittatur, et ab eodem responsum recipiatur de ratione ulterius procedendi. Nomine et auctoritate etenim praedictae S[anctae] Congregationis Excellentiae Vestrae officium fuit demandatum et potestas tradita huismodi causam pertractandi.

Haec nuntiare Exc[ellentiae] V[estr]ae R[everendissi]mae officium meum postulabat; et spem foveo fore ut Epistolam, quam citius fieri poterit, mihi humanissime dare velit, quae anxiam animi mei sollicitudinem levare et reficere valeat.

Hac occasione libentissime utor ut observantiae meae cultum Ex[cellenti]ae V[estr]ae R[everendissi]mae profitear usque persistens

....

<Antoninus De Luca,
Archiepiscopus Tarsensis
Nuntius Apostolicus Viennae>

Document No. 16: Kött to De Luca, April 25, 1860 (Answer to Documents No. 12 and 13: De Luca to Kött, April 11 and 14, 1860). Document No. 17, a copy of Stichling's letter to Kött, April 23, 1860, is enclosed. Latin. Leaf No. 102.

To: The Most Excellent and Reverend Monsignor Antonino De Luca
Archbishop of Tarsus, Apostolic Nuncio Vienna.
Fulda, April 25, 1860
Most Excellent and Reverend Monsignor:

I have received your communication dated April 11 of this year, which was written in the hand of your Most Illustrious and Reverend Excellency quite at the right time, since the gentle-

Excellentissimo et Reverendissimo D[omi]no D[omi]no Archiepiscopo Tarsensi
Antoni<n>o De Luca
Nuncio Apostolico
Viennam.
Excellentissime ac Reverendissime Domine!

Literis de die XI Aprilis h[uius] a[anni] ab Excellentiae Vestrae Illustrissimae et Reverendissimae gratia propria manu scriptis opportune acceptis, Okrazowski Polono heic loci

man from Poland, Monsieur Okraszewski, is here awaiting an answer; so I told him that the decree issued by the Archbishop of Mohilow could not be implemented unless it could be shown that it was sanctioned by Our Most Holy Father, and I returned into his hands the decree document.

Since, in your letter of the 14th, Your Excellency wrote toward the end that "before one goes further in this matter, a report must be sent to Rome to the Reverend Father Secretary of the Holy Congregation of the Council, together with a copy of the aforementioned sentence issued by the Metropolitan of Mohilow, and instructions must be obtained from the Holy Father as to the manner of proceeding in this difficult business," I took it to mean that Your Excellency would take care of it. Hence, since it was not said at all that I should do it, I did not wish to bother Your Excellency; but from then on there were no other rumors about the corruption of the judges through offerings of money beside the evidence which was known to me, so I could not place the question on a solid foundation.

But, since Your Excellency wished to be informed of anything new about this matter that might happen, I enclose a copy of a letter whereby the Grand Duke of Weimar seems to wish to interpose his own authority in order that the case be happily resolved according to the desires of Princess Carolyne; therefore this business which is already quite difficult on its own, as Your Excellency rightly put it, becomes even more complicated.

As I am counting on the well known graciousness of your Most Illustrious and Reverend Excellency, I am herewith soliciting you to endeavor as much as possible to speed up the response from Rome and ensure that it be sent to me.

As for a general report on ecclesiastical matters pertaining to this diocese and a specific report about Bockenheim and its seminary, I am going to send you a rather lengthy one in a little while; for the present, if I will not say much

responsum exspectanti, exsecutioni mandari haud posse Archiepiscopi Mohilowiensis decretum, quin agnitum ostendatur a Sanctissimo Dom[i]no Nostro, declaravi eiusque manibus decreti formulam reddidi.

Quod vero literis de die XIV datis sub finem Excellentia Vestra scripsit, "antequam ulterius in hac re progredatur, relationem transmittendam esse R[everendo] P[atri] Secretario S[anctae] C[ongregationis] Concilii Romam, una cum exemplo commemoratae sententiae a Metropolitano Mohilowiensi prolatae, et mandatum a Sanctissimo Patre exquirendum de ratione procedendi in huiusmodi arduo negotio," hoc ita intellexi ut putarem fore ut istud ab Ipsa Vestra Excellentia Illustrissima ac Reverendissima fieret. Hinc enim eo ipso, quod a me illud fieri debere dictum omnino non sit, Excellentiam Vestram ego praeoccupare nolui; inde vero alii rumores de iudicibus pecunia oblata corruptis praeter notum illud indicium mihi quidem minime percrebuerunt, ita ut solido fundamento quaestionem superstruere non possem.

Verum quoniam si quid novi hac in re acciderit, id communicatum Secum Excellentia Vestra voluit, exemplar adiungo literarum, quibus literis Supremus Princeps, Archidux Vimariensis, suam auctoritatem interponere velle videtur ut causa felicem ex voto Principissae Carolinae eventum sortietur; unde negotium, ut vere dixit Excellentia Vestra, in se iam arduum, etiam magis evadit intricatum.

Rogo ergo Excellentiae Vestrae Ilustrissimae ac Reverendissimae celebrem benignitatem ut responsum Romanum acceleret quantum fieri potest, mihique mittendum curet.

De rebus ecclesiasticis diocesanis generatim et de Bockenheimianis atque de Seminario speciatim parva mora interposita fusius relaturus, in praesens etsi aliud non feribam, at insignem qua erga Excellentiam Vestram feror,

more, I will insist in expressing again and again the high esteem which draws me close to Your Excellency.

Your Most Illustrious and Reverend Excellency's very humble and devoted,

x Christophe Florenz Kött,
Bishop of Fulda.

existimationem iterum atque iterum exprimens persistam.

Excellentiae Vestrae Ill[ustrissi]mae ac Rev[er-endissi]mae
Humillimus et addictissimus
x Christophorus Florentius <Koett>,
Episcopus Fuldensis.
Fuldae, die XXV Aprilis 1860

Document No. 17: Copy of Stichling's letter to Kött, April 23, 1860 (Enclosed with Document No. 16: Kött to De Luca, April 25, 1860). German. Leaf No. 103.

Exact copy
<To: His Grace,
Monsignor Christophe Florenz Kött,
Bishop of Fulda>
Weimar, April 23, 1860
Most Honored and Reverend Excellency:

I deeply fear that you may no longer have any recollection of me, for many a year has passed since I had the good fortune of becoming known to you through a business matter of which I may be justified in my hope that it was settled to the satisfaction of both parties. All the greater is my pleasure that, because of a new task—a briefer and simpler one, to be sure—given me by my most gracious Prince, I can seize the present opportunity to recall myself to Your kind memory.

As Your Grace is doubtless aware, the most diverse efforts have been made for years now to facilitate the marriage between Her Serene Highness the Princess Wittgenstein, a divorcee residing here, and the illustrious musician Dr. Franz Liszt, by obtaining the requisite dispensation from Rome. This has finally met with success: the dispensation has been granted, and it is hoped that this long-sought bond of marriage might be consecrated forthwith. It would, however, be of special value to both parties if Your Grace were inclined to perform the consecration Yourself, and this in Fulda. To this end, the Princess and Dr. Liszt have turned to His Royal Highness the Grand Duke, requesting that their wish be brought to Your attention, and His Royal Highness, unhesitatingly and most graciously, commissioned me to convey this wish to

Exemplar descriptum

Hochwürdigester Bischof,

Hochverehrter Herr!

Wohl muß ich fürchten, in dem Gedächtnisse Eu[er] Bischöfl[ichen] Gnaden nicht mehr zu leben, denn manches Jahr ist nunmehr verflossen, seit ich das Glück hatte, Hochderenselben durch einem Geschäftsauftrag bekannt zu werden, von dem ich hoffen zu duerfen glaube, daß er zur Zufriedenheit beider Theile ausgeführt worden. Um so erfreulicher ist es mir, daß ich gegenwärtig durch einen—freilich weit kürzeren und leichteren—neuen Auftrag meines gnädigsten Fürsten und Herrn Gelegenheit erhalte, mich in Hochdero freundliches Andenken zurückzurufen.

Wie Eu[er] Bischöfl[ichen] Gnaden ohne Zweifel bekannt ist, wurden schon seit Jahren die verschiedensten Anstrengungen gemacht, um zur Vermählung Ihrer Durchlaucht, der geschiedenen Fürstin Wittgenstein hier mit dem berühmten Musiker Dr. Franz Liszt den erforderlichen Dispens in Rom zu erlangen. Endlich ist dies nun gelungen, der Dispens ist ertheilt und eine baldige Einsegnung des schon so lange erstrebten Ehebundes wird beabsichtigt. Von besonderem Werthe aber würde es beiden Theilen sein, wenn Eu[er] Bischöfl[ichen] Gnaden geneigt sein wollten, diese Einsegnung Selbst, und zwar in Fulda, zu bewirken. Zu diesem Zwecke haben sich die Fürstin und Dr. Liszt an Seine Königl[iche] Hoheit den Großherzog mit der Bitte gewendet, diesen ihren Wunsch zu Hochdero Kennt-

Your Grace in His name and with His best wishes.

Insofar as I herewith carry out this royal order and request a favorable report of the decision taken, and perhaps as well of the day chosen for the consecration, it is with sincere pleasure that I avail myself of this occasion to reassure you of the most sincere respect with which I shall always remain

Your Grace's
most devoted servant,
D. G. J. Stichling,
Councillor of State
For the authenticity of the copy.
x Christophe Florenz Kött

niß bringen zu wollen, und Seine König[iche] Hoheit haben keinen Anstand genommen, mich gnädigest zu beauftragen, denselben in Höchstseinem Namen mit den besten Grüßen an Eu[er] Bischöfl[ichen] Gnaden weiter zu befördern.

Indem ich andurch dieses höchsten Befehls mich entledige, und eine hochgeneigte Mittheilung der gefaßten Entschließung sowie eventuell des zu wählenden Tags der Einsegnung erbitte, benutze ich mit wahrer Freude diesen Anlaß zur erneuerten Versicherung derjenigen aufrichtigesten Verehrung, mit welcher ich stets verbleiben werde
Eu[er] Bischöfl[ichen] Gnaden
ganz ergebenster
D. G. J. Stichling, Staatsrath.
Weimar, den 23 April 1860
Pro Copia.
x Christophorus Florentius Kött

Document No. 18: Quaglia to De Luca, May 3, 1860. The original draft is in CC Doc. No. 26, which contains an additional paragraph that was not included in this document. For the context see also ASV, CC Doc. Nos. 23, 24, 25. Enclosed with Doc. No. 19. Italian. Leaf No. 107.

To: Monsignor Antonino De Luca
Archbishop of Tarsus,
Apostolic Nuncio in Vienna
Rome, May 3, 1860
Most Illustrious and Reverend Excellency:

As soon as I received with great appreciation the letter of Your Most Illustrious and Reverend Excellency, dated the 14th of last April,[10] regarding the marriage case Wittgenstein-Iwanowska, I hastened to inform the Holy Father and begged him to provide further instructions pertaining to this case.

His Holiness approves your warning Monsignor the Bishop of Fulda that he should not proceed with the implementation of the sentence on this marriage case, and deems it necessary that you yourself forward without delay to the aforementioned Bishop a formal prohibition to this effect until he receives further instructions from the Holy See. At the same time, you are to instruct the Archbishop of Mohilow to suggest to

Monsig[nor] Antonino De Luca
Arcives[cov]o di Tarso
Nunzio Ap[osto]lico in Vienna

Ill[ustrissi]mo e R[everendissi]mo Signore.

Appena ricevuto il pregiato foglio di V[ost]ra Sig[no]ria Ill[ustrissi]ma e R[everendissi]ma dei 14 perduto aprile risguardante la causa matrimoniale Wittgenstein-Iwanowska mi sono recato a premura farne relazione al Santo Padre implorando le ulteriori provvidenze analoghe al caso.

Sua Santità, dopo aver trovato opportuna l'avvertenza da Lei fatta a Monsignor Vescovo di Fulda di non procedere alla esecuzione della sentenza matrimoniale, stima necessario che Ella stessa a nome della Santa Sede trasmetta senza ritardo al prelodato Vescovo formale inibizione all'effetto indicato fino a che non riceverà dalla stessa Santa Sede ulteriori istruzioni. Con la stessa sollecitudine poi dovrà

---

[10]De Luca's draft of this letter is not in this file; for the text see ASV, CC Doc. No. 21.

the Defender of the Marriage Bonds in the Curia that he should present to the Holy See an appeal against that last sentence and accordingly forward the records of the proceedings.

This much it was my duty to communicate to your Most Illustrious and Reverend Excellency by order of His Holiness but, in so doing, I renew my expressions of singular esteem for you and confirm myself
Your Most Illustrious and Reverend
    Excellency's most devoted and obliging
    servant,
Angelo Quaglia,
Secretary of the Holy Congregation
of the Council.

dare istruzioni a Monsignor Arcivescovo di Molikovo (sic), perché insinui al Difensore del Vincolo matrimoniale presso quella Curia d'interporre ricorso innanzi alla Santa Sede contro l'ultima sentenza, e quindi trasmetta gli atti processuali.

Tanto doveva io significare per ordine di Sua Santità a V[ost]ra Sig[no]ria Ill[ustrissi]ma e R[everendissi]ma nell'atto che Le rinnovo i sensi della mia distinta stima, e mi raffermo

Di V[ost]ra Sig[no]ria Ill[ustrissi]ma e
    R[everendissi]ma
Dev[otissi]mo Ob[ligatissi]mo Servo
Angelo Quaglia, Segr[eta]rio della
S[anta] C[ongregazione] del Concilio
Roma, 3 maggio 1860.

Document No. 19: Hohenlohe to De Luca, May 10, 1860, with note on the verso penned by De Luca. Leaves No. 108–109. De Luca's answer is not in the files.

To: Monsignor A. De Luca,
Archbishop of Tarsus,
etc. etc. etc.
Vatican, <May 10>, 1860, the day of St.
    Antoninus
Most Venerated Monsignor:

Your name day gives me the welcome chance to express to your Most Reverend Excellency my most sincere and cordial wishes for your much cherished person, your health, your peace and tranquillity, and your quick elevation to the holy purple, and I beg you to receive these feelings of mine with that graciousness and kindness that are typically yours.

From the bottom of my heart I thank you for your letter and the documents that it was your pleasure to send me, together with the letter for Monsignor the Secretary of the Council. I enclose herewith that Monsignor's answer together with some other letters that I am asking you to forward to their destination. I am sorry to inconvenience you so often, but what can one do in these times so unsafe for gentlemen and their letters?!

M[on]s[i]g[no]r A[ntonino] de Luca
Arciv[escov]o di Tarso
etc., etc., etc.

Monsignore Veneratissimo.

Il giorno della Sua festa mi dà la felice occasione di esprimere a Vostra Eccellenza R[everendissi]ma gli auguri più sinceri e cordiali per la Sua carissima persona, per la Sua salute, per la Sua pace e tranquillità, per una sollecita esaltazione alla S[acra] Porpora, onde La prego di gradire questi miei sentimenti con quella bontà e gentilezza tutta Sua propria.

Ringrazio poi di cuore per la Sua lettera e per i documenti che si è compiaciuto inviarmi unitamente alla lettera per Mo[nsi]g[no]r Segret[ari]o del Concilio. Le mando qui la risposta di esso Monsignore, ed alcune lettere che La prego di fare pervenire al loro destino. Mi dispiace d'incomodarLa così spesso, ma come si fa in questi tempi così poco sicuri per li galantuomini e per le di loro lettere?!

Your Most Reverend Excellency must have been pleased to hear that Princess Carolyne von Sayn-Wittgenstein, formerly Iwanowska, has left for Rome and is expected here any day now; I hope that, in this way, everything will be soon made clear after Your Most Reverend Excellency has brought some order and regularity to this business.

Accept, please, once more my best wishes for your Name day and, while with great respect, I kiss your holy hand, I have the honor of declaring myself
Your Most Reverend Excellency's
most humble and devoted servant and friend,
Gustav von Hohenlohe,
Archbishop of Edessa

Monsignor Hohenlohe. May 10 1860
Answered on the 20th.

Avrà sentito con piacere V[ostra] E[ccellenza] R[everendissima] che la Principessa Carolina di Sayn-Wittgenstein nata Iwanowska è partita per Roma e che si aspetta ogni giorno qui; spero che così tutto potrà mettersi in chiaro ben presto, dopo che V[ostra] E[ccellenza] R[everendissima] ha messo un poco d'ordine e di regolarità in quest' affare.

Gradisca, La prego, di nuovo i miei voti per la Sua festa mentre con alto rispetto baciando la S[anta] mano ho l'onore di sottoscrivermi di
Vostra Eccellenza Rev[erendissi]ma
um[ilissi]mo Obl[igatissi]mo servo ed amico
G[ustavo] d'Hohenlohe
Arciv[escov]o d'Edessa
Vaticano, in die Sancti Antonini 1860.

M[onsi]g[no]r Hohenlohe, 10 maggio 1860
Risp[osto] li 20 d[ello] <stesso mese>.

Document No. 20: De Luca to Kött, May 21, 1860. Latin. Leaf No. 110.

To: The Most Illustrious and Reverend
Monsignor Christophe Florenz Kött,
Bishop of Fulda
Fulda

No. 1530/1
Vienna, May 21, 1860
Most Illustrious and Reverend Monsignor:

With regard to the special and express mandate from our Most Holy Father that was communicated to me in a letter of the Most Reverend Secretary of the Holy Congregation of the Council, the Most Illustrious Princess Wittgenstein, born Iwanowska, is positively to be denied permission to remarry. His Holiness, moreover, deigned himself to refer the whole case to the Supreme Roman Court. For this reason nothing more can be done until this matter is settled by a new sentence on the validity or the invalidity of the marriage of the aforementioned couple.

Ill[ustrissi]mo et R[everendissi]mo D[omi]no
D[omi]no Christophoro Florentio Koett
Ep[isco]po Fuldensi
Fuldam
Fulda
N.1530/1
Viennae, die XXI Maji, 1860
Ill[ustrissi]me et R[everendissi]me D[omi]ne.

De speciali et expresso mandato S[anctissi]mi D[omi]ni Nostri mihi per litteras a R[everendissi]mo Secretario S[anctae] C[ongregationis] Concilii comunicato, facultas transeundi ad alias nuptias erit absolute deneganda Illustrissimae Principissae Wittgenstein natae Iwanowska. Praelaudata Sanctitas Sua insuper ad supremum Tribunal Romanum totam rem et causam avocare dignata est. Quamobrem nil ulterius peragi potest antequam per novam sententiam de validitate aut nullitate matrimonii inter commemoratos coniuges constet.

Excellentissime ac Reverendissime Domine.

Multum venerandas literas Excellentiae Vestrae Reverendissimae, Viennae die 2 Maji currentis anni datas, in duplicato modo, non autem authenticas recepi, et ad communicatas animadversiones, super sententia mea 24 februarii ejusdem anni prolata, qua matrimonium D. Carolinae Iwanowska, cum Principe Nicolao Wittgenstein, nullum irritumque declaravi et dictae Matronae facultas, ad alias nuptias transeundi concessi, praeter quae in decreto diserte jam expressi et narravi, sequentia exponenda duxi.

Quum D. Carolina Iwanowska anno praeterito 10.? hujus nempe, supplicem mihi libellum obtulit, quatenus causam de nullitate matrimonii sui in prima et secunda instantia jam agitatam, denuo pertractandam assumerem, inhaerens stricte praescripto specialis conventionis S. Apostolicam Sedem inter et Augustissimum Imperatorem Russorum, Concordato 1847 anni adjectae et in corpus legum Imperii illatae, Oratricem ad dictam S. Sedem remisi. S. D. N. feliciter modernus Pontifex, precibus ejus benigne annuens, per Secretarium S. Congregationis Concilii mihi causam istam reassumere, cognoscere, ac per definitivam sententiam in appellationis gradu, servatis servandis ac praesertim Constitutione s. m. Benedicti XIV. Dei miseratione dijudicare mandavit. Confecto ad tramitem juris processu, qui diserte verbis expositis

in meo decreto, judices a me delegati DD. Maximilianus Staniewski, Episcopus Plotcensis, Suffraganeus Mohyloviensis; Andreas Dobszewicz, Infulatus Praepositus Sydlo-
viensis et Dominicus Moszczynski, Praelatus Decanus Minscensis, viri probatissimae virtutis, ac nullis nominibus
commendabiles, procul dubio nullis muneribus praeventi
aut corrupti, auditis voce Defensoris matrimonii hujus
D. Basilii Zotek, Professoris R.C. Academiae Ecclesiasticae,
justis allata et sufficienter probata et secundum leges
citatas de nullitate matrimonii, dictae Karolinae, libera ac spontanea suffragia sua protulerunt. Postremum
ego ipse eandem causam, simili ratione, resumpsi, diligentissime totum processum perscrutavi; cognovi; omniaque in eo exposita vera esse ac veritate folii regesti,
suffragia praedictorum judicum, consentanea legibus inveni et approbavi, ac <u>definitivam</u>, prout Sua Sanctitas
jusserat, <u>sententiam</u>, justa dictamen conscientiae meae,
promuntiavi.

Quum autem praelaudatus defensor matrimonii, hujusmodi sententiae acquiescendum putaverit, neque appellandum esse crediderit, aliunde vero notum fuerit,
Principem Nicolaum Wittgenstein, jam dudum ad alias
nuptias, in calviniana secta convolasse, quumque Rescripto S. Congregationis Concilii non imponeretur officium
porrigendae sententiae meae alicui ad approbandum
et ratificandum; quin imo, causa per <u>definitivam sen-
tentiam</u> dijudicanda committeretur, inniens igitur verbis supradictae constitutionis s. m. Benedicti XIV. §. 11:
"Instructo in hunc modum judicio, si secunda sententia, alteri conformis fuerit, hoc est: si in secunda aeque ac in prima, nullum ac irritum matrimonium ju-

dicatum

...dicatum fuerit et ab ea pars vel defensor, pro sua conscientia, non crediderit appellandum... in potestate et arbitrio
conjugum sit, novas nuptias contrahere" haud immerito,
arbitratus eum, in mea potestate fuisse, parti petenti copiam decreti *definitive* *prolati*, legali forma conditam, extradere.

Maximo mihi est dolori, me, judicesque curiae metropolitanae, apud Excellentiam Vestram Reverendissimam venire
in suspicionem de mala fide polonica, quum animadverti-
rim, Excellentiam Vestram Reverendissimam, rumoribus omnino prorsusque futilibus, in praejudicium nostrum temere
divulgatis, aurem praebere non abnuisse, eosque sat validis
conjecturis suffultos agnovisse. Persuasam certo Excellentiam
Vestram Reverendissimam esse volo ac rogo, quod procurator Oratricis, ad corrumpendos judices, remque per nefas,
in curia metropolitana, ad exitum deducendam, ne obolum
truncumve quidem erogaverit.

Dictam mulierem cum amasio, per plures annos, in adulterio, quamvis publice, ast in extima ac remota regione, vixisse,
constare mihi haud potuit, priusquam vice ex litteris Excellentiae Vestrae Reverendissimae rescivi. Caeterum, vita et mores
illius, ut mihi videtur, etsi dissolutissimi essent, ad rem, de
qua hic agitur, minime pertinent; mea enim ac judicum
curae credebatur, cognoscere validum, nec ne, fuerit contractus matrimonium ejus, cum Principe Wittgenstein? Si illa
nunc intendat amasio suo nubere, scandalis, ne eveniant,
obviare, obstacula matrimonium istud impedientia investigare ad Sui Ordinariatum, domicilii eorum, spectabit.

Mihi profecto non latet, causas matrimoniales nunquam
transire in rem judicatam; sed post prolatum decretum,
cui litigantes sese non opponant partes, et defensor acquiescendum

cendum putavit, delicto vitae inhonestae cujus alterius ve partis, rumores tenuere, de corruptione judicum divulgati; non con-
stiterint, ut arbitror, illam rem novam, quae justa placita a m.
Benedicti XIV. necessaria exigerent, ut causa resumeretur, vel causa in judicialem controversiam revocaretur.

Ingenue fateor, me non observare, cujusnam naturae, objectivae an subjectivae, fuerint allata, pro nullitate matrimonii, in
dicta causa argumenta; ego diligenter consideravi et attente per-
pendi et ea firma, fide digna, gravia et sufficientia, in processu rite ac recte confecto, prolata reperii.

Expletis adamussim iis, quae S.D.N. Papa in praelaudato Rescripto S. Congregationis circa negotium istud laudare dignatus
est, relationem una cum exemplari prolatae sententiae Suae
Sanctitati porrigendum et Romam per Ministerium Negotiorum internorum, prout leges Imperii jubent, transmittendam
curavi.

Ne autem officio mihi ab Excellentia Vestra Reverendissima
per epistolam humanissimam injuncto deessem, de hisce omnibus Excellentiam Vestram Reverendissimam certiorem facio,
atque enixe humiliterque rogo ac flagito, ut Excellentia Vestra Reverendissima patrocinio suo validissimo tueri ac fovere me dignetur.

       Excellentiae Vestrae Reverendissimae.

       Obsequentissimus Servulus

       + Sigismundus Felinski

       Archiep. Mohil: Metrop.

1860. Anni Maji 24 d. v.s.

  Petropoli:

Excell.mo ac Reverend.mo Dño

De Luca Arch.Epo Tarsensi

Nuntio Apostolico penes Aulam

Imperatoriam Austriae

It was a duty imposed by my office that I should inform Your Most Illustrious and Reverend Excellency of all these things. I hold the greatest hope that due obedience will be shown in the Diocese of Fulda to the orders from the Most Holy Father.

With the expression of the most singular respect, etc.

<Antonino De Luca,
Archbishop of Tarsus and
Apostolic Nuncio in Vienna>

Haec omnia D[ominatio]ni V[estr]ae Ill[ustrissi]mae et R[everendissi]mae nuntiare officii mei ratio postulabat et spem firmissimam foveo fore ut in Diocesi Fuldensi debita exhibeatur obedientia mandato S[anctissi]mi Patris.

Cum peculiaris etc.

<Antoninus De Luca
Archiepiscopus Tarsensis
Nuntius Apostolicus Viennae>

Document No. 21: Żyliński to De Luca, May 24 (O.S.) =June 5, 1860 (Answer to Doc. No. 15: De Luca to Żyliński, April 24, 1860). Enclosed with Doc. No. 23: Balabine to De Luca, June 24 (O.S.) =July 6, 1860. Latin. Leaves No. 111–112.

To: The Most Excellent and Reverend Monsignor
Antonino De Luca,
Archbishop of Tarsus and
Apostolic Nuncio at the Imperial Court of Austria.
St. Petersburg, May 24, 1860 (O.S.)

Most Excellent and Reverend Monsignor:

I received a non-authenticated copy of your Most Reverend Excellency's venerable letter from Vienna, dated May 2 of this year and, in response to the thoughts you expressed about the sentence I issued on February 24 of this same year, to the effect that the marriage of Madame Carolyne Iwanowska and Prince Nicholas Wittgenstein is declared null and void and the aforementioned lady is given faculty to contract another marriage, I have chosen to leave out what I have already described and explained at length in my decree and deal with the following.

When last year, namely on the 10th of June, Madame Carolyne Iwanowska brought me a petition to review again her case for the annulment of her marriage which had already been dealt with in the first and second instance, I, strictly adhering to the prescription of the special agreement between the Holy Apostolic See and the Most August Emperor of the Russians, which was added to the Concordate of 1847 and included in the Code of Laws of the Empire, referred the petitioner to the Holy See. The Pope presently reigning for our happiness, in kindly assenting to her request, ordered through the

Excel[entissim]o ac Reverend[issim]o D[omi]no
Antonino De Luca
Arch[i]ep[isco]po Tarsensi
Nuntio Apostolico penes Aulam Imperatoriam Austriae.
1860 anni Maji 24 d[ie] v[etere] st[ilo] Petropoli.
Excellentissime ac Reverendissime Domine.

Multum venerandas literas Excellentiae Vestrae Reverendissimae, Viennae die 2 Maji currentis anni datas, in duplicatu modo, non autem authenticas recepi, et ad communicatas animadversiones, super sententia mea 24 Februarii ejusdem anni prolata, qua matrimonium D[ominae] Karolinae Iwanowska cum Principe Nicolao Wittgenstein nullum irritumque declaratur et dictae Matronae facultas ad alias nuptias transeundi conceditur, praeter quae in decreto diserte jam expressi et narravi, sequentia exponenda duxi.

Quum D[omina] Karolina Iwanowska anno praeterito 10 d[ie] Junii nempe supplicem mihi libellum obtulerit, quatenus causam de nullitate matrimonii sui in prima et secunda instantia jam agitatam, denuo pertractandam assumerem, inhaerens stricte praescripto specialis conventionis S[anctam] Apostolicam sedem inter et Augustissimum Imperatorem Russorum Concordato 1847 anni adjectae et in Corpus legum Imperii illatae, oratricem ad dictam S[anctam] Sedem remisi. S[anctus] D[ominus] N[oster] feliciter modernus Pontifex, precibus ejus benigne annuens, per Secretarium

Secretary of the Holy Congregation of the Council that I should take up again this case, review it, and decide on it by issuing a *Definitive Sentence* in the level of appeal, after observing what need be observed and especially the Bull *Dei miseratione* issued by the late Benedict XIV. The trial having been conducted according to the proper legal procedures which I described at length in my decree, the judges whom I selected, namely the worthy fathers Maximilian Staniewski, Bishop of Platen and my assistant in Mohilow, Andreas Dobszewicz, Provost of Szydlow; and Monsignor Moszezynski, Prelate Deacon of Minsk, all men of proven integrity and otherwise commendable and, without a doubt, not bought or corrupted by any gifts, having heard the arguments of the Defender of the Marriage Bond in this case, Father Basil Zottek, Professor at the Roman Catholic Ecclesiastical Academy, cast their votes freely and according to their own judgement in favor of the annulment of the marriage of the aforementioned Carolyne after considering the facts presented and deeming them sufficiently proved and in accordance with the laws relevant to the present case. Afterwards, in a similar way, I reviewed the whole case myself, studied very carefully all the proceedings, and gained a thorough knowledge of it. I found everything that had been brought forth in its favor to be true or consonant with the truth. I found the votes of the judges in agreement with the laws and ratified them and, in accordance with his Holiness's command and the dictates of my conscience, I issued the *Definitive Sentence.*

Since the aforesaid Defender of Marriage Bonds deemed the sentence acceptable and did not think it should be appealed and, on the other hand, it was known that Prince Nicholas Wittgenstein had already for some time contracted a new marriage within the Sect of Calvin and, since, according to the Rescript of the Holy Congregation of the Council, no obligation was imposed that my sentence should be submitted to anyone for approval and ratification, and it was mandated that *the case be decided by a Definitive Sentence*, basing myself, therefore, on the statement of the already mentioned Bull of the late Benedict XIV, article 11:

"Having set up the trial in this fashion, if the second sentence will be in conformity with the first, that is if, in the second as well as in the

S[anctae] Congregationis Concilii mihi causam istam reassumere, cognoscere, ac per *definitivam sententiam* in appellationis gradu, servatis servandis ac praesertim Constitutione s[anctae] m[emoriae] Benedicti XIV *Dei miseratione, dijudicare* mandavit. Confecto ad tramites juris processu, qui disertis verbis exponitur in meo decreto, judices a me delegati, D[omini] Maximilianus Staniewski, Episcopus Plateensis, Suffraganeus Mokyloviensis, Andreas Dobszewicz, Infulatus Praepositus Szydloviensis, et Dominus Moszecsynski, Praelatus Decanus Minscensis, viri probatissimae virtutis, ac multis nominibus commendabiles, procul dubio nullis muneribus praeventi aut corrupti, audita voce Defensoris matrimonii huius D[omini] Basilii Zottek, Professoris R[omanae] C[atholicae] Academiae Ecclesiasticae, juxta allata et sufficienter probata et secundum leges citatas, de nullitate matrimonii dictae Karolinae libera ac spontanea suffragia sua protulerunt. Postmodum ego ipse eamdem causam, simili ratione, rea<s>umpsi, diligentissime totum processum perscrutavi, cognovi, omniaque in eo exposita vera esse ac veritate fulciri reperii, suffragia praedictorum judicum consentanea legibus inveni et approbavi, ac *definitivam*, prout Sua Sanctitas jusserat, *sententiam*, iuxta dictamen conscientiae meae, pronuntiavi.

Quum autem praelaudatus defensor matrimonii hujusmodi sententiae acquiescendum putaverit, neque appellandum esse crediderit, aliunde verum notum fuerit Principem Nicolaum Wittgenstein jam dudum ad alias nuptias in Calviniana secta convolasse, quumque Rescripto S[anctae] Congregationis Concilii non imponeretur officium porrigendae sententiae meae alicui ad approbandum et ratificandum; quin imo, causa per *definitivam sententiam dijudicanda* committeretur, innixus igitur verbis supradictae Constitutionis s[anctae] m[emoriae] Benedicti XIV articuli 11:

"Instructo in hunc modum judicio, si secunda sententia alteri conformis fuerit, hoc est, si in secunda, aeque ac in prima, nullum ac

first instance, a marriage will be judged to be null and void and if neither one of the parties nor the defender, according to his conscience, will think that it should be appealed... the spouses will have the faculty and the freedom to contract a new marriage,"

I concluded it was plainly my prerogative to release to the petitioner a legal copy of the *Final Decree*.

It causes me the greatest pain that I and the judges of this Metropolitan Diocese could have been suspected by Your Most Reverend Excellency of bad faith, as I realise that Your Most Reverend Excellency did not refrain from paying attention to completely and utterly unfounded rumors, rashly spread to our detriment, and took them to be supported by sufficiently valid conjectures. I pray and hope that Your Most Reverend Excellency be completely persuaded that the petitioner's solicitor did not pay out a farthing in this Metropolitan Diocese in order to corrupt the judges and dishonestly obtain a favorable outcome of the case.

I could not have known that the lady in question had lived for several years with a lover in a state of adultery for, though this was public knowledge, it happened in a foreign and distant country, and I became aware of it for the first time from Your Most Reverend Excellency's letter. Moreover, her manner of life, it seems to me, even if were absolutely immoral, is completely irrelevant to the issue under discussion. Was it not the judges' assumption and mine as well that we were entrusted with finding out whether or not her marriage to Prince Wittgenstein had been valid? If she now intends to marry her lover, it will be up to the local Ecclesiastical authorities, where their place of residence is, to investigate eventual impediments to this marriage in order to prevent the possibility of any scandals.

I am well aware of the fact that marriage cases are never adjudicated once and for all; but, after a decree has been issued without it being appealed either by the parties involved or by the Defender of the Marriage Bond, neither the discovery of immoral habits of life on the part of one or the other of the parties involved, nor the spreading of unwarranted rumors about the cor-

irritum matrimonium judicatum fuerit et ab ea pars, vel defensor, pro sua conscientia non crediderit appellandum...in potestate et arbitrio conjugum sit novas nuptias contrahere,"

haud immerito, arbitratus sum, in mea potestate fuisse parti petenti copiam decreti *definitive prolati*, legali forma conditam, extradere.

Maximo mihi est dolori me judicesque Curiae Metropolitanae apud Excellentiam Vestram Reverendissimam venire in suspicionem de mala fide potuisse, quum animadverterim Excellentiam Vestram Reverendissimam, rumoribus omnino prorsusque futilibus, in praejudicium nostrum temere divulgatis, aurem praebere non abnuisse, eosque sat validis conjecturis suffultos agnovisse. Persuasam certo Excellentiam Vestram Reverendissimam esse volo ac rogo, quod procurator oratricis, ad corrumpendos judices, remque per nefas, in Curia Metropolitana, ad exitum deducendum, ne obulum terumciumve quidem erogaverit.

Dictam mulierem cum amasio, per plures annos, in adulterio, quamvis publice, ast in extera ac remota regione, vixisse, constare mihi haud potuit, primaque vice ex literis Excellentiae Vestrae Reverendissimae rescivi. Caeterum, vita et mores illius, ut mihi videtur, etsi dissolutissimi essent, ad rem de qua hic agitur, minime pertinent; meae enim ac judicum curae credebatur cognoscere validum, nec ne, fuerit contractum matrimonium ejus cum Principe Wittgenstein? Si illa nunc intendat amasio suo nubere, scandalis, ne eveniant, obviare, obstacula matrimonium istud impedientia investigare ad Loci Ordinariatum, domicilii eorum, spectabit.

Mihi profecto non latet causas matrimoniales numquam transire in rem judicatam; sed post prolatum decretum, cui litigantes sese non opponant partes, et defensor acquiescendum putaverit, detecta vita inhonesta unius alteriusve partis, rumores temere de corruptione judicum divulgati non constituunt, ut arbitror, illam *rem novam*, quae iuxta placita s[anctae]

ruption of judges constitute, in my view, such a *new element* as to make it necessary, according to the Bull of the late Benedict XIV, to reopen the case and deliberate on its merits again.

I frankly confess I did not inquire whether the arguments brought forth in this case for the invalidity of the marriage were of an objective or a subjective nature, but I considered them carefully and examined them with great attention and found them to be well grounded, believable, serious,and sufficiently proved in the course of properly conducted proceedings.

Having scrupulously fulfilled the mandate which our Most Holy Father condescended to give me, as it was indicated in the aforementioned rescript of the Holy Congregation, I made it my duty to write a report for the Holy Father and, availing myself of the offices of the Minister for Internal Affairs, to send it to Rome together with a copy of the sentence issued.

Lest, moreover, I should fail to comply with the requests made by Your Most Reverend Excellency in your very kind letter, I am informing Your Most Reverend Excellency of all these things and I earnestly and humbly pray, nay beg that Your Most Reverend Excellency condescend to hold and keep me under your most worthy patronage.
Your Most Reverend Excellency's
very obsequious servant,
x Wenceslas Żyliński
Metropolitan Archbishop of Mohilow.

m[emoriae] Benedicti XIV necessario exigerent, ut causa resumeretur, vel rursus in Judicialem controversiam revoceretur (sic).

Ingenue fateor me non observasse cujusnam naturae, objectivae an subjectivae, fuerint allata, pro nullitate matrimonii, in dicta causa argumenta; ego diligenter consideravi et attente perpendidi et ea firma, fide digna, gravia et sufficienter, in processu rite ac recte confecto, probata reperii.

Expletis adamussim iis, quae S[anctissimus] D[ominus] N[oster] Papa in praelaudato Rescripto S[anctae] Congregationis circa negotium istud demandare dignatus est, relationem una cum exemplari prolatae sententiae Suae Sanctitati porrigendam et Romam per Ministerium Negotiorum Internorum, prout Leges Imperii jubent, transmittendam curavi.

Ne autem officio mihi ab Excellentia Vestra Reverendissima per epistolam humanissimam injuncto deessem, de hisce omnibus Excellentiam Vestram Reverendissimam certiorem facio, atque enixe humiliterque rogo ac flagito, ut Excellentia Vestra Reverendissima patrocinio suo validissimo tuere ac fovere me dignetur.
Excellentiae Vestrae Reverendissimae
Obsequentissimus famulus
x Venceslaus Żyliński
Archiep[iscopus] Mohil[oviensis] Metrop[olitanus]

Document No. 22: Kozlowska to De Luca, November 23, 1860, with a note on the verso penned by De Luca. German. Leaves No. 113–114.

To <Monsignor Antonino De Luca,>
Most Reverend Nuncio of the Apostolic See in Vienna.

Kolomyya, November 23, <1860>
Most Reverend Nuncio!

Six years ago I brought my husband, Bartholomeus Sanoyiv, before the Royal and Imperial Court in Stanislaus in order to obtain an annulment of our marriage, proceedings for which were initiated but then broken off, on the basis of the High Imperial Patent of December 8,

An die Hochwürdigste Nunciatur des Hohen apostolischen Stuhles in Wien!

Hochwürdigste Nunciatur!

Bereits vor 6 Jahren habe ich beim bestandenen Stanislaus Landrezette wider meinem Ehegatten Bartholomaeus Sanoyiv die Klage wegen Ungiltigkeits-Erklärung der zwischen uns geschlossene Ehe ausgetragen, worüber auch die Verhandlung eingeleitet dann aber im

1856, and transferred to the Diocesan High Court for Marriage in Bamberg.

Since that time, several years have gone by without my either enjoying any success regarding my repeated requests for expediting this matter or indeed receiving any answer at all.

I turned to You, Most Reverend Nuncio, regarding this matter a year ago, however, also with no success—in my sorry state I nevertheless make so bold as to entreat You, Most Reverend Nuncio, on bended knees to deign most graciously to arrange that this matter be given prompt attention.

x Akafia Sanoyiv, née Kozlowska

per me Stefan Kozlowski

Ahafia Sanoyiv, née Kozlowska, resident of Kolomyya in Galicia requests prompt attention in the matter of the annulment of marriage to her husband Bartholomeus Sanoyiv.

Anna Kozlowska
November 23, 1860
She requests a definitive settlement of her
 marriage case.

Grunde h. kaiserl[ichen] Patentes v[om] 8ten October 1856 abgebrochen und an das h. Bischöfliche Ehegericht in Bamberg abgetretten(sic) wurde.

Seit der Zeit sind bereits einige Jahre verfloßen ohne daß ich über meine wegen Beschleunigung dieser Angelegenheit widerholt gestellten Bitten irgend eines Erfolges und überhaupt einer Antwort mich erfreuen könnte.

Vor einem Jahre habe ich mich diesfalls an Euer Hochwürdigste Nunciatur bittlich jedoch ebenfalls erfolglos gewendet—ich wage es dennoch in meiner traurigen Lage fußfälligst zu bitten Euer Hochwürdigste Nunciatur geruhe die Beschleunigung dieser Angelegenheit gnädigst zu veranlassen.
Kolomia den 23t. Nov[ember 1860]
x Ahafia Kozlowska verehlichte Sanoyiv
per me .....
Stefan Kozlowski

Ahafia Kozlowska verehlichte Sanoyiv zu Kolomia in Galizien wohnhaft bittet um Beschleunigung der Angelegenheit wegen Ungiltigkeits-Erklärung der mit ihrem Ehegatten Bartholomaeus Sanoyiv geschlossenen Ehe.

Anna Kozlowska
23 Novembre 1860
Chiede il regolamento definitivo nella sua
 causa matrimoniale.

Document No. 23: Balabine to De Luca, June 24 (O.S.) = July 6, 1860, with a note on the verso penned by De Luca. (Document No. 21, Żyliński's to De Luca, May 24 (O.S.) = June 5, 1860, is enclosed). French. Leaves No. 117–118.

To His Excellency,
Monsignor De Luca,
Archbishop of Tarsus and
Apostolic Nuncio etc. etc.
No. 860
Vienna, June 24/July 6, 1860

By order of the Imperial Minister for Foreign Affairs, the undersigned, Special Envoy of His Majesty the Emperor of all Russia, has the honor of forwarding herewith to His Excellency Monsignor De Luca, Archbishop of Tarsus and Apostolic Nuncio, the letter addressed to him by

à Son Excellence Monseigneur
<Antonino> de Luca, Archevêque de Tarse,

Nonce Apostolique etc., etc.
No. 860

D'ordre du Ministère Impérial des affaires étrangères le Soussigné, Envoyé en Mission spéciale de Sa Majesté l'Empereur de toutes les Russies, a l'honneur de transmettre ci-près à Son Excellence Monsigneur de Luca, Archevêque de Tarse et Nonce Apostolique, la

Monsignor Wenceslas Żyliński, Metropolitan of the Roman Catholic Church in Russia.

I avail myself of this occasion to offer to His Excellency, the Apostolic Nuncio, my renewed assurance of my high consideration.

F. Balabine

The Russian Envoy to the Royal and Imperial Court. July 6, 1860.
He forwards the answer of Monsignor the Archbishop of Mohilow.

lettre que Lui adresse Monseigneur Wenzeslas Żyliński, Métropolitain de l'Eglise Catholique-Romaine en Russie.

Il saisit cette occasion pour offrir à Son Excellence Monseigneur le Nonce Apostolique l'assurance renouvelée de sa haute considération.
F. Balabine
Vienne, le 24 juin–6 juillet 1860

Il M[inis]tro di Russia presso l'I[mperiale] e R[egia] Corte, 6 luglio 1860.
Trasmette una risposta di M[onsi]g[no]r Arciv[escov]o di Mohilow.

Document No. 24: De Luca to Cardinal Antonelli, July 14, 1860, in response to Document No. 18: Quaglia to De Luca, May 3, 1860, and with reference to Document No. 23: Balabine to De Luca, June 24 (O.S) =July 5, 1860. (A copy of Doc. No. 21 is enclosed. See ASV, CC Doc. No. 27, and also No. 26, whereby Antonelli sends it to Quaglia). Italian. Leaf No. 119.

To: The Most Eminent Secretary of State,
<Cardinal Giacomo Antonelli>
Re: The Wittgenstein-Iwanowska marriage case.
Prot. Number: 1057
Vienna, July 14, 1860
Most Reverend Eminence:

In conformity with the request that was made by Monsignor the Secretary of the Holy Congregation of the Council in his letter of May 3, I have sent without delay, on behalf of the Holy See, to Monsignor the Bishop of Fulda and to Monsignor the Archbishop of Mohilow in St. Petersburg, a formal injunction not to carry out the sentence issued by this latter prelate in virtue of a special Pontifical concession according to which the marriage between Prince Nicholas Wittgenstein (Calvinist) and his putative wife, Princess Iwanowska (Catholic), was declared null and void. I have, moreover, instructed the aforementioned bishop to insinuate to the Defender of Marriage Bonds in that Diocese that he should present an appeal to the Holy See against the latest sentence and accordingly forward the records of the proceedings.

All'Em[inentissi]mo Seg[reta]rio di Stato,
<Card. Giacomo Antonelli>
Causa Matrimoniale Wittgenstein-Iwanowska
N. 1057.
Vienna, 14 luglio 1860
Em[inen]za R[everendissi]ma,

Conformandomi all'invito fattomi da M[onsi]g[no]r Segretario della S[anta] C[ongregazione] del Concilio con sua lettera de' 3 maggio p[rossim]o p[assat]o trasmisi senza indugio a M[onsi]g[no]r Vescovo di Fulda e a M[onsi]g[no]r Arcivescovo di Mohilow in Pietroburgo a nome della S[anta] Sede formale inibizione di procedere all'esecuzione della sentenza, pronunciata da quest'ultimo prelato in virtù di speciale delegazione pontificia, che dichiarava nullo il matrimonio tra il Principe Nicola Wittgenstein (Calvinista) e la sua putativa consorte Principessa Iwanowska (Cattolica). Diedi inoltre al summenzionato Arcivescovo istruzioni perché insinuasse al Difensore del vincolo matrimoniale presso quella Curia d'interporre ricorso innanzi alla S[anta] Sede contro l'ultima sentenza e quindi trasmettesse gli atti processuali.

Monsignor the Bishop of Fulda conformed to the injunction in every way; he even informed me of the voyage to Rome undertaken by Princess Iwanowska.

As for Monsignor the Archbishop of Mohilow, I have received from the Russian legation an official note, dated the 6th of the present month, together with which his answer was forwarded to me. I have the honor of enclosing this latter document with the present letter in order that your Excellency may ascertain its contents and be fully and specifically informed about a matter in which the Imperial Cabinet in St. Petersburg felt it had a duty to intrude, in order to uphold the notion that Bishops and other Catholics in that vast Empire are not allowed to correspond directly with the Holy See.

....

<Antonino De Luca,
Archbishop of Tarsus and
Apostolic Nuncio in Vienna>

M[onsi]g[no]r Vescovo di Fulda si conformò esattamente alla inibizione, anzi mi fece consapevole del viaggio intrapreso alla volta di Roma dalla Principessa Iwanowska.

Quanto poi a M[onsi]g[no]r Arciv[escov]o di Mohilow, ho ricevuto da quella Legazione Russa una Nota officiale de' 6 del corrente colla quale mi si rimetteva la risposta di quel Prelato. Ho l'onore di compiegare, in seno al presente, la copia di quest'ultimo documento acciocché l'Em[inen]za V[ost]ra R[everendissi]ma, prima di comunicarla a M[onsi]g[no]r Seg[reta]rio della S[anta] C[ongregazione] del Concilio, possa conoscerne il contenuto ed avere specificata e piena notizia di un affare nel quale il Gabinetto Imperiale di Pietroburgo ha creduto doversi ingerire per mantenere illesa la massima di non esser lecito a' Vescovi e a' fedeli di quel vasto impero il corrispondere direttamente colla S[anta] Sede.

....

<Antonino De Luca,
Arcivescovo di Tarso,
Nunzio Apostolico in Vienna>

**Document No. 25: Quaglia to De Luca, September 25, 1860. See ASV, CC
Doc. No. 43. For the context, see also ASV, CC Docs. No. 41 and 42.
Italian. Leaf No. 120.**

To: Monsignor Antonino De Luca,
Archbishop of Tarsus and
Apostolic Nuncio in Vienna
Rome, September 25, 1860
Most Illustrious and Reverend Excellency:

After a careful examination of the difficulties that seemed to pose an obstacle to the implementation of the sentence issued by the Archbishop of Mohilow for the annulment of the marriage of Princess Carolyne Iwanowska Wittgenstein, the Holy Father, in the audience of the 24th day of this month, deigned himself to state that, as far as the Holy See is concerned, there is nothing to prevent that judgement from being fully carried out. He then ordered that I should inform Your Most Illustrious and Reverend Excellency about this, which I am doing herewith, so that you may be so kind as to report to Monsignor the Bishop of Fulda, on behalf of His Holiness himself, that he may freely proceed to carry out the aforesaid sentence and grant the

Monsig[nor] <Antonino> De Luca
Arcivescovo di Tarso
Nunzio Apostolico in Vienna

Ill[ustrissi]mo e Rev[erendissi]mo Signore.

Dopo essersi prese in maturo esame le difficoltà che sembravano opporsi alla esecuzione della sentenza emanata dall'Arcivescovo di Mohilow per la nullità del matrimonio della Contessa Carolina Iwanowska Wittgenstein, il S[anto] Padre nella Udienza del 24 corrente si è degnato di dichiarare che per parte della stessa S[anta] Sede nulla osta perché quel giudicato abbia il suo pieno effetto. Mi ha ordinato quindi darne partecipazione a V[ostra] S[ignoria] Ill[ustrissi]ma e Rev[erendissi]ma (al che adempio colla presente) perché abbia la compiacenza di significare, a nome della stessa Santità Sua, a Monsig[no]r Vescovo di Fulda, poter egli liberamente procedere alla esecuzione della menzionata sentenza, permettendo che la lo-

above mentioned Countess (*sic*) permission to marry again, if she so desires.

I take advantage of this circumstance to declare myself once more, with the feelings of the most singular and respectful consideration, Your Most Illustrious and Reverend Excellency's

most devoted, obliging and true servant, Angelo Quaglia, Secretary of the Holy Congregation of the Council

data Contessa passi, ove lo voglia, ad altre nozze. Sarà poi opportuno che di tale risultato renda pur consapevole Monsig[nor] Arcivescovo di Mohilow.

Profitto di quest'incontro per riprotestarmi con sensi della più distinta ossequiosa stima
Di V[ostra] S[ignoria] Ill[ustrissi]ma e Rev[erendissi]ma
Dev[otissi]mo Obb[ligatissi]mo Serv[itor]e vero
Il Segretario della S[anta] Congregazione del Concilio
Angelo Quaglia
Roma, 25 Settembre 1860

Document No. 26: De Luca to Kött, October 10, 1860. Latin. Leaf No. 121.

To His Most Illustrious and Reverend Excellency Monsignor Christophe Florenz Kött
Bishop of Fulda
Fulda
No. 1809/1
Vienna, October 10, 1860
Most Illustrious and Reverend Excellency:

This far too widely known business of the marriage of Princess Carolyne von Sayn-Wittgenstein is causing me and Your Most Illustrious and Reverend Excellency a great deal of trouble. She is even going to Rome herself, and I hear that she will bring back, upon her return, I don't know what kind of Letter which would give Your Most Illustrious and Reverend Excellency the authority to let her enter a new legitimate and approved marriage contract with her lover.

Since we are dealing with a matter that would cause great shock in Germany and in Russia, I earnestly request, should indeed the aforementioned Lady come forth with a Letter or some other Document of whatever kind written, as it is reported, in the name and with the authority of the Holy Congregation of the Council, that Your Most Illustrious and Reverend Excellency, given your well known graciousness, send me immediately a copy of it and await my

Ill[ustrissi]mo et R[everendissi]mo Domino
Domino Christophoro Florentio Koett
Episcopo Fuldensi
Fuldam
N. 1809/1
Viennae, die 10 Octobris 1860
Ill[ustrissi]me et R[everendissi]me Domine

Notissimum negotium de matrimonio Dominae Principissae Carolinae Sayn-Wittgenstein natae Iwanowska haud parvam molestiam et mihi et Dominationi Vestrae Ill[ustrissi]mae et R[everendissi]mae adfert. Romam ipsa se contulit et in notitiam mihi pervenit nescio qualem Epistolam secum in reditu allaturam esse vi cujus Dominationi Vestrae Ill[ustrissi]mae et R[everendissi]mae potestas fieret ejusdem novas nuptias ineundas cum suo amasio tamquam licitas et ratas habendi.

Cum de re agatur quae per Germaniam et Russiam magnam admirationem excitaret, rogo enixe expertam benignitatem Dominationis Vestrae Ill[ustrissi]mae et R[everendissi]mae ut, si reapse superius memorata Matrona Epistolam sive aliud cujusve generis documentum nomine et auctoritate, uti fertur, S[anctae] C[ongregationis] Concilii exaratum exhibuerit, statim illius exemplum ad me transmittere velit et responsum meum expectet, antequam novas

response before a permission to contract a new marriage is granted by your Diocese.

I take advantage of this occasion to express ... etc.

<Antonino De Luca,
Archbishop of Tarsus and
Apostolic Nuncio in Vienna>

nuptias contrahendi facultas ab ista Episcopali Curia tradatur.

Hac occasione etc.

<Antoninus De Luca,
Archiepiscopus Tarsensis
Nuntius Apostolicus Viennae>

Document No. 27: Hohenlohe to De Luca, October 11, 1860. Italian. Leaves No. 125–126. De Luca's answer, not included in this file, is in ASV, CC Doc. No. 41.

To: His Most Reverend Excellency
Monsignor Antonino De Luca,
Archbishop of Tarsus and
Apostolic Nuncio in Vienna
Vienna, October 11, 1860
Most Venerable Monsignor:

Princess Wittgenstein's agent has come to Vienna from Rome and will seek an audience with Your Excellency in order to present to you those papers I mentioned the other day. It will be perhaps advantageous for your Most Reverend Excellency to hold on to those papers in order that you may have a chance to consider beforehand the protests that in a short while may come from some Polish bishops against that *unfortunate* business.

Enough! I know you'll do what, in your wisdom, you will deem best. In the meantime, I wish to express to you my feelings of the greatest and most respectful esteem and I have the honor of professing myself
Your Most Reverend Excellency's
most devoted, obliging and affectionate servant,
Gustav von Hohenlohe,
Archbishop of Edessa

P.S.: The aforesaid agent's name is Okraszewski; he is, as the people from Trastevere would say, "quite a scoundrel."

S[on] E[xcellence] R[e]v[erendissi]me
Monseigneur <Antonino> De Luca
Archevêveque de Tarse
Nonce Apostolique à Vienne

Monsignore Veneratissimo.

E' giunto in Vienna l'agente della P[rinci]p[e]ssa Wittgenstein Iwanowska da Roma e si presenterà da V[ostra] E[ccellenza] R[everendissima] con quelle carte che io Le dissi l'altro giorno. Sarà forse opportuno che V[ostra] E[ccellenza] R[everendissima] tenga a sé queste carte per qualche tempo onde esaminare prima i reclami che da qualche Vescovo della Polonia tra poco potranno venire contro quel *disgraziato* affare.

Basta, farà quel che nella sua saviezza meglio crederà. Ed intanto coi sentimenti della più alta e rispettosa stima e considerazione ho l'onore di ripetermi di V[ostra] E[ccellenza] R[everendissima]

d[evotissimo] obl[igatissi]mo aff[ezionatissi]mo
    servo
G[ustavo d'Hohenlohe] Arciv[escov]o d'Edessa
Vienna 11 Ott[obre] 1860

P.S. Il suddetto agente si chiama Okraszewski ed è, come direbbero i Trasteverini, un "birbacc[ione]..."

Document No. 28: Kött to De Luca, October 15, 1860
(Answer to Document No. 26, De Luca to Kött, October 10, 1860). Latin.
Leaves No. 127–128. A copy of this letter will be sent by De Luca to Quaglia.
See in this file Doc. No. 34, and ASV, CC Docs. No. 46 and 47.

<To: Monsignor Antonino De Luca,
Archbishop of Tarsus and
Apostolic Nuncio in Vienna>
Fulda, October 15, 1860
Most Excellent and Reverend Monsignor:

Having read Your Most Reverend Excellency's letter of October 10, I am completely persuaded that we are going to be enmeshed in a strange and, at any rate, difficult business. The message informing Your Excellency about a decree, according to which the marriage previously contracted by Princess Wittgenstein is indeed going to be declared null and void in Rome as well, is not exactly without some foundation; this is evident also from this telegram that I received very early on the morning of the 14th of this month:

TELEGRAM
Sent from Leghorn on October 11, 1860, at 8:00 a.m.
Received in Frankfurt-on-the-Main on October 12, 1860, at 4:18 a.m.
To: Monsignor the Bishop of Fulda by way of Frankfurt-on-the-Main.

Princess Wittgenstein, about to leave Rome, having achieved the fulfillment of her wishes, entreats the Most Reverend Bishop to be so gracious as to commend to the Roman Pontiff, by means of letters or a telegram to be sent by way of France, the priest of the city of Weimar as one worthy of receiving the title of Papal Camerlengo, an honor which will be bestowed as promised as soon as Your Reverence's commendation and testimony, which the Princess anxiously expects in Rome as quickly as possible, will be received.

Bastogi, on behalf of Torlonia
Piazza di Spagna, 93
Rome

The telegram, if it is genuine and trustworthy, even describes the Princess as "having achieved the fulfillment of her wish."

<Domino Antonino De Luca,
Archiepiscopo Tarsensi,
Nuncio Apostolico
Viennam>
Excellentissime ac Reverendissime Domine!

Excellentiae Vestrae Reverendissimae literis de die Octobris X perspectis, fore ut novis nos negotiis utique salebrosis intricemur, persuasum omnino habeo. Etenim quo nuncio Excellentia Vestra certior facta est de decreto, iuxta quod matrimonium a Principissa Wittgenstein antea contractum nullum etiam Romae declaratum dicatur, eum haud esse penitus ina-nem, hoc quoque telegramma testetur, quod die huius mensis XIV multo mane accepi:

TELEGRAMM[A]
Aufgegeben in Livorno, den 11ten Oct. 1860 - 8 Uhr 0 Min. v[or] Mitt[ag].
Angekommen in Frankfurt a/M den 12ten Oct. 1860–4Uhr 18 Min. v[or] Mitt[ag].
Monseigneur l'Evêque Fulda par Francfort sur Mein.

Principissa Wittgenstein quam primum ab urbe discessura voti compos effecta rogat R[everendissi[mum] Episcopum, ut gratiose commendet literis per Galliam vel telegraphice Pontifici Romano parochum civitatis Weimar tanquam dignum, qui decoretur honore cubicularii pontificii, quod signum honoris iuxta promissa concedetur, accepto vix R[everendissi]mi testimonio et commendatione, quam Principissa vehementer expectat citissime Romae.

Bastogi per incarico Torlonia di Roma
Piazza di Spagna 93.

Quo telegrammate pariter—si genuinum est ac fide dignum—Principissa ista perhibetur voti compos effecta.

I cannot quite really believe that, in Rome, men endowed with so much prudence and integrity could approve something which is not quite consistent with the law and is such that, at this unfortunate time, may just provide the occasion, as far as our enemies and the heretics are concerned, to question somehow the firm determination to uphold the indissolubility of the marriage sacrament that the Holy Apostolic See exhibited for so many centuries. The gravity of the case requires, therefore, that everything be reviewed accurately, and I will be quite happy to take advantage of Your Excellency's humaneness and send to Vienna that letter as soon as I receive it, in order that your Excellency may duly verify the authenticity and truth of that document and most graciously communicate to me what you think should be done.

As for the commendation requested of me in the telegram I reproduced above, its aim is to confer on the priest from Weimar the honor of some Roman title. I will not provide any such thing, and I will not even bother to provide an answer for, not to mention other things, I fear that a dignity obtained by a woman on such an occasion might become a source of embarrassment for the Holy Roman Church and also the Most Holy Father whom I love with all my heart.

For the rest, I hope your Most Reverend Excellency will wish to recognise the sincere feelings I always hold toward you, and I sign myself as

Your Most Reverend Excellency's
most humble and devoted
x Christophe Florenz Kött,
Bishop of Fulda.

Vix vel ne vix quidem credere possum, Romae a viris tanta prudentia et integritate praeditis quidquam fieri, quod cum iure non bene cohaereat quoque specie tenus hominibus inimicis aut hereticis occasio forte praebeatur notissimae illi per saecula Sanctae Sedis Apostolicae in tuenda Sacramenti indissolubilitate firmitati hoc funestissimo tempore vel aliquid detrahendi. Unde causae gravitas postulat, ut omnia accurate discutiantur, lubentissimeque Excellentiae Vestrae humanitate usurus, literas, ubi primum accepero, Viennam transmittam, ut Excellentia Vestra instrumenti genuinitatem et veritatem pro munere Suo recognoscat, et quid censeat agendum, gratiosissime mecum communicet.

Quae vero eo quod commemoraveram telegrammate a me exposcitur commendatio, ut parochus Vimariensis dignitate aliqua Romana decoretur; eam equidem non mittam nihil omnino responsurus, quippe quia, ut alia sileam, timeo, ne dignitas tali occasione per feminam obtenta Sanctae Romanae Ecclesiae Sanctissimoque Dom[i]no Nostro cui toto cordis affectu adhaereo, crimini fortasse vertatur.

Ceterum Excellentia Vestra Reverendissima sinceros animi mei sensus velit agnoscere, quibus semper in eandem feror et huic epistolae subscribo
Excellentiae Vestrae R[everendissi]mae
Humillimus et addictissimus
x Christophorus Florentius Koett,
Episcopus Fuldensis.
Fuldae, die Oct[o]bris XV, 1860.

Document No. 29: Hohenlohe to De Luca, October 16, 1860
(Anticipates Liszt's request in Document 30, Liszt to De Luca, October 16, 1860).
Italian. Leaves No. 129–130.

<To: Monsignor Antonino De Luca,
Archbishop of Tarsus and
Apostolic Nuncio in Vienna>
Vienna, October 16, 1860.
Most Venerable Monsignor:

Monsieur Liszt, known to Your Most Reverend Excellency as an interested party in the

<Monsignor Antonino De Luca,
Arcivescovo di Tarso,
Nunzio apostolico in Vienna>

Monsignore Veneratissimo.

E' giunto in Vienna il Signor Liszt noto a V[ostra] E[ccellenza] R[everendissima] come

case of Princess Wittgenstein Iwanowska, has come to Vienna.

He would like to be received by Your Most Reverend Excellency in order to seek your advice.

I pointed out to him that since marriage cases are never adjudicated once and for all, there is more than just a chance that he and the Princess will meet with great disappointments and anxieties.

He seemed to me somewhat disposed to give up on the idea of this marriage, and since he is not lacking in a certain generous disposition of spirit, he could be swayed this way and, through him, the Princess could be persuaded as well. He is probably going to seek an audience with you tomorrow morning, and so you may condescend to receive him.

As for my trip to Warsaw, I begin to meet with some difficulties. I hope they can be surmounted.

Accept, please, the expression of the great respect I have toward you and, in declaring it, I remain
Your Most Reverend Excellency's
most devoted and obliging servant,
Gustav <von Hohenlohe>,
Archbishop of Edessa

parte interessata nella causa della P[rinci]p[e]ssa Wittgenstein Iwanowska.

Egli vor<r>ebbe presentarsi a V[ostra] E[ccellenza] R[everendissima], per sentire un consiglio.

Io gli ho fatto osservare che le cause matrimoniali non passando giammai *in rem judicatam*, vi è pericolo per esso e la P[rinci]p[e]ssa d'incontrare ancora de' grandi dispiaceri ed angustie di coscienza.

Mi ha (sic) sembrato questo Signore essere disposto di rinunziare a questo matrimonio, e siccome non manca di una certa generosità di carattere, forse vi si potrebbe indurre, e per esso anche la P[rinci]p[e]ssa. Egli viene a presentarsi da V[ostra] E[ccellenza] R[everendissima] probabilmente domani mattina, ed allora Si degnerà forse di riceverlo.

In quanto al mio viaggio a Vars[avia] comincio ad incontrare molte difficoltà. Speriamo che si possano sormontare.

Gradisca i sentimenti di alto rispetto coi quali mi dico di V[ostra] E[ccellenza] R[everensissima]
d[evotissi]mo obb[ligatissi]mo servo

Gustavo <d'Hohenlohe>,
Arciv[escov]o d'Edessa

Document No. 30: Liszt to De Luca, October 16, 1860, with note on the verso penned by De Luca. French. Leaves No. 131–132.

[To: Monsignor Antonino De Luca,
Archbishop of Tarsus and
Apostolic Nuncio in Vienna]
Vienna, October 16, 1860
Monsignor,

I beg Your Excellency to accord me the honor of an audience in order that I may respectfully submit to your attention a question of great importance. My present voyage to Vienna having no other purpose than the solution of this problem, I take the liberty to express my desire that Your Excellency will receive me without too much delay and will let me know when I should present myself.

<à Monseigneur Antonino De Luca,
Archevêque de Tarse,
Nonce Apostolique à Vienne>
Vienne, 16 Ottobre 1860
Monseigneur,

Je viens prier Votre Excellence de m'accorder l'honneur d'une audience à l'effet de lui soumettre respectueusement une affaire à laquelle s'attache une importance majeure. Mon présent voyage à Vienne n'ayant d'autre but que le règlement de cette affaire, j'oserais désirer que Votre Excellence veuille bien me recevoir sans trop de délai et me faire connaître quand je devrai me présenter.

It is, Monsignor, with feelings of deep respect that I have the honor of signing myself
Your Excellency's
most humble and obedient servant,
F. Liszt,

Hotel Kaiserin Elisabeth,
Weihburg Gasse.

Professor Liszt, October 16, 1860.

He requests an audience about the question pertaining to Princess Iwanowska-Wittgenstein (Written in his own hand).

C'est avec les sentimens d'un profond respect que j'ai l'honneur d'être, Monsignor,
De Votre Excellence,
le très humble et obéissant serviteur
F. Liszt
Vienne 16 Octobre 1860
Hôtel Kaiserin Elisabeth
Weihburg Gasse.

Il Prof[essor] Liszt, 16 ottobre 1860.

Chiede un'udienza per l'affare della Principessa Iwanowska Wittgenstein (Autografa).

Document No. 31: De Luca to Quaglia, October 18, 1860
(Answer to Document No. 25, Quaglia to De Luca, September 25, 1860).
See ASV, CC Doc. No. 45. Italian. Leaf No. 133.

To: The Most Illustrious and Reverend
Monsignor Angelo Quaglia
Secretary of the Holy Congregation of the Council,
etc. etc. etc.
Rome
No. 1879/1
Vienna, October 18, 1860
Most Illustrious and Reverend Monsignor:

I was duly shown Your Most Reverend and Illustrious Excellency's precious letter dated the 25th of last month. I beg your pardon if the gravity of the matter compels me to share some reflections with you.

I am not aware of the details of the important trial whose outcome was the declaration that the marriage of Prince Wittgenstein and Princess Iwanowska was null and void. I and quite a few others only know that the sentence issued in the first instance by the Diocese of Zhitomir had been in favor of the validity of this marriage.

At a first glance, therefore, it would seem that the rule prescribed in the Bull *Dei miseratione*, which requires that there be at least two sentences of the same kind in order to proceed to the dissolution of the marriage bond, has not been observed.

All'Ill[ustrissimo e R[everendissi]mo Signore
Monsig[nor] Angelo Quaglia
Seg[reta]rio della S[anta] C[ongregazione] del Concilio
ecc. ecc. ecc.
Roma
N. 1879/1
Vienna, 18 ottobre 1860
Ill[ustrissi]mo e R[everendissi]mo Signore.

Mi fu esibita regolarmente la preziosa lettera di V[ostra] S[ignoria] Ill[ustrissi]ma e R[everendissi]ma del 25 del passato mese. Chiedo pertanto scusa se la gravità dell'affare in parola mi obbliga a comunicarLe alcune riflessioni.

A me sono ignote le particolarità dell'importante processo, il cui risultato si fu la dichiarazione di nullità del matrimonio tra il Principe Wittgenstein e la Principessa Iwanowska. Soltanto si conosce da me e da moltissimi altri che la sentenza nella prima istanza presso la Curia Vescovile di Zytomir era stata favorevole alla validità del medesimo matrimonio.

A prima vista dunque sembrerebbe che in questo affare non si fosse direttamente osservata la regola prescritta nella Bolla *Dei miseratione*, la quale esige almeno due sentenze conformi per lo scioglimento del vincolo matrimoniale.

Let us add, moreover, the notion that the Princess would make use of the permission to remarry that she has been granted and wed Monsieur Liszt, a Hungarian quite well known in his country. Now it was precisely in Hungary that there were, and there are perhaps even now, scandalous instances of sentences of annulment granted quite easily by those Dioceses on account of the chapter on *vis et metus*.

I believe that the Holy Congregation of the Inquisition felt compelled at the time to send to those bishops special instructions from Rome on how to proceed in problematic cases of this kind.

One can well imagine the unfavorable impression these bishops will receive from the permission that has been granted to Princess Carolyne Iwanowska to marry again.

For the above-mentioned reasons, I earnestly beg Your Most Illustrious and Reverend Excellency humbly to present to His Holiness these simple observations and to request from him that pertinent instructions be sent directly to Monsignor the Bishop of Fulda. I will be ready and available to forward them to him.

May it please your Most Illustrious and Reverend Excellency to accept again the protestations of my high and devoted esteem while I remain
Your Most Illustrious and Reverend Excellency's <servant>,
<Antonino De Luca,
Archbishop of Tarsus and
Apostolic Nuncio in Vienna>

Si aggiunga l'avvertenza che la Sig[no]ra Principessa farebbe uso della concessa facoltà di passare a seconde nozze collo sposare il Sig[nor] Liszt ungherese notissimo nella sua patria. Ora per l'appunto nell'Ungheria accadevano e forse non sono ancora cessati gli scandali di sentenze pronunziate dalle Curie Vescovili che scioglievano con grande facilità il vincolo matrimoniale *ex capite vis et metus*.

Penso che la S[anta] C[ongregazione] dell'Inquisizione da Roma ha dovuto inviare a que' vesco<vi> una speciale istruzione sul modo di procedere in somiglianti difficilissime cause.

Si può ben immaginare l'impressione che i predetti vescovi risentiranno dalla licenza accordata alla Principessa Carolina Iwanowska di passare a seconde nozze.

Per le anzidette cose prego caldamente V[ostra] S[ignoria] Ill[ustrissi]ma e R[everendissi]ma di umiliare alla Santità di N[ostro] S[ignore] le precedenti umili osservazioni e d'impetrare la grazia che le analoghe istruzioni sieno inviate direttamente a Mons[i]g[nor] Vescovo di Fulda. Io sarò pronto a farne la trasmissione.

Gradisca da ultimo V[ostra] S[ignoria] Ill[ustrissi]ma e R[everendissi]ma le riproteste della mia distinta e ossequiosa stima, con che mi pregio di confermarmi
Di V[ostra] S[ignoria] Ill[ustrissi]ma e R[everendissi]ma ....
<Antonino De Luca,
Arcivescovo di Tarso,
Nunzio Apostolico a Vienna>

Document No. 32: De Luca to Borowski, October 19, 1860. Latin. Leaf No. 134.

To: His Most Illustrious and Reverend
   Excellency,
Monsignor Caspar Borowski,
Bishop of Luck and Zhitomir etc., etc., etc.
Zhitomir
No. 1820/1
Vienna, October 19, 1860
Most Illustrious and Reverend Monsignor:

Since it is of some importance for me to be able to ascertain with certainty the way in which the canonic trial on the validity or invalidity of

Ill[ustrissi]mo et R[everendissi]mo
   Domino
Domino G[asparo] Borowski Episcopo
Luceoviensi et Zytomeriensi etc.etc.etc.
Zytomirium
N°1820/1
Vindobonae, die 19 Octobris 1860
Ill[ustrissi]me et R[everendissi]me Domine.

Cum mea intersit certo rescire quanam ratione processus canonicus de validitate aut invalid<it>ate matrimonii inter principem

the marriage contracted by Prince Nicholas Wittgenstein and Princess Carolyne Iwanowska was conducted, I am asking Your Most Illustrious and Reverend Excellency to be so kind as to send me a brief but accurate unofficial report on this matter.

I have heard many things about it which are a cause of concern to me. I will tell you frankly that the sentence, issued in the second instance by the Diocese of Mohilow, has more than surprised me; on the force of it that marriage is declared null and void without the Defender of the Marriage Bond presenting an appeal according to the very well known prescriptions contained in Benedict XIV's Bull.

Meanwhile, the aforementioned Princess eagerly hopes to get married again. This would then cause a great occasion for scandal since, according to Holy Canon Law, no marriage should be dissolved unless two identical sentences for its invalidity are issued in the first and second instance.

I ask for your indulgence if necessity causes me to inconvenience most disagreeably Your Most Illustrious and Reverend Excellency, and I hope that you will graciously receive the expression of my respect with which I remain
Your Most Illustrious and Reverend Excellency's
   <most devoted servant>,
<Antonino De Luca,
Archbishop of Tarsus and
Apostolic Nuncio in Vienna>

Nicolaum Wittgenstein et Principissam Carolinam Iwanowska initi penes istam Episcopalem Curiam jamdudum institutus fuerit, rogo Dominationem Vestram Ill[ustrissi]mam et R[everendissi]mam, ut privato modo mihi hac de re accuratam et brevem relationem velit transmittere.

Multa hinc inde audivi, quae me anxium reddunt. Et ingenue fateor haud parvam admirationem mihi intulisse posteriorem in 2^a instantia sententiam ab Archiepiscopali Curia Mohilowiensi prolatam, vi cujus praedictum matrimonium nullum et invalidum declaratur, quin matrimonii defensor appellationem interposuerit juxta praescriptiones notissimae Bullae Benedicti XIV.

Interea superius laudata Principissa quam impense exoptat secundas nuptias inire. Exinde gravis exurgeret occasio scandali, cum juxta S[anc]t[os] Canones nullum matrimonium dissolvendum foret, si saltem duo conformes sententiae in prima et secunda instantia pro invalid<it>ate non starent.

Veniam peto, si necessitate coactus molestus fortasse evaserim Dominationi Vestrae Ill[ustrissi]mae et R[everendissi]mae, et rogo ut meae observantiae sensa excipere humanissime velit, qua cum persisto
D[ominatio]nis V[estr]ae Ill[ustrissi]mae et
   R[everendissi]mae ....

<Antoninus De Luca,
Archiepiscopus Tarsensis,
Nuntius Apostolicus Viennae>

Document No. 33: De Luca to Żyliński, October 20, 1860. Latin. Leaf No. 135.

To: The Most Excellent and Reverend
Monsignor Wenceslas Żyliński,
Archbishop of Mohilow, etc., etc., etc.,
Mohilow

No. 1823/1
Vienna, October 20, 1860
Most Excellent and Reverend Monsignor:

I ask for your forbearance if I must inconvenience you. It is of great importance that I be able to ascertain for sure whether the sentence issued in the second instance in the Diocese of Zhitomir did actually declare the marriage con-

Exc[ellentissi]mo et R[everendissi]mo Domino
Domino Wenceslao Żyliński Archiep[iscop]o
Mohilowiensi etc. etc. etc.
Mohilowium
Mohilow
N. 1823/1
Vindobonae, die 20 Octobris 1860
Excellentissime et R[everendissi]me Domine

Veniam peto si molestiam Excellentiae Vestrae R[everendissi]mae iterum afferre debeam. Mea interest certo rescire an reapse sententia in 2° instantiae gradu prolata penes episcopalem Curiam Zytomiriensem declara-

tracted long ago by Prince Nicholas Wittgenstein and Princess Carolyne Iwanowska valid and legitimate. If this were indeed the case, someone even slightly acquainted with Canon Law will be quite surprised since, after the second sentence issued by the Diocese of Mohilow, that same marriage was declared null and void, and the spouses were immediately given faculty to contract a new marriage. This, without the Defender of the Marriage Bond interposing an appeal according to the very well known Bull of Pope Benedict XIV.

I ask, therefore, out of the goodness of Your Most Reverend Excellency that, in a private and unofficial way, you be so kind as to deal with these doubtful matters in order that accurate information about this very sad business relieve me of my anxiety and succeed in removing an occasion for scandal.

I gladly avail myself of this chance to etc. ...

<Antonino De Luca,
Archbishop of Tarsus and
Apostolic Nuncio in Vienna>

verit validum et legitimum matrimonium inter Principem Nicolaum Wittgenstein et Principissam Carolinam Iwanowska jamdudum initum. Si ita res sese haberet, quisquis vel leviter Canonicarum praescriptionum expers mirabitur[11] sane eo quod post alteram sententiam a Curia Archiepiscopali Mohilowiensi prolatam, idem matrimonium pro nullo et invalido habitum fuerit, et facultas facta conjugibus ad alteras nuptias illico convolandi, quin defensor matrimonii, juxta notissimam Constitutionem Summi Pontificis Benedicti XIV, appellationem interposuerit.

Rogo igitur benignitatem Excellentiae Vestrae R[everendissi]mae, ut privato modo et non officiali via, proposita dubia enucleare velit eum in finem, ut notitia accurata de hoc tristissimo negotio anxietatem animi mei levare et occasionem scandali removere valeat.

Hac utor lubenter occasione, ut etc.

<Antoninus De Luca,
Archiepiscopus Tarsensis,
Nuntius Apostolicus Viennae>

Document No. 34: De Luca to Quaglia, October 24, 1860.
See ASV, CC Doc. No. 46. Doc. No. 28 from this file is enclosed.
See also ASV, CC Doc. No. 47. Italian. Leaf No. 136.

To: The Most Illustrious and Reverend Monsignor <Angelo> Quaglia, Secretary to the Holy Congregation of the Council, etc., etc.,
Rome
No. 1828/1
Vienna, October 24, 1860
Most Illustrious and Reverend Monsignor:

As a follow-up to my previous letter of the 18th of this present month, I feel duty bound to send confidentially to Your Most Illustrious and Reverend Excellency a copy of a letter written by Monsignor the Bishop of Fulda pertaining to the marriage case of Princess Carolyne Wittgenstein. This prelate {justly} shows his righteous indignation for the utterly imprudent action committed by this lady in announcing by telegram the bestowing of an honor upon a member of the clergy—such an honor, according to her, being obtained through her lobbying.

All' Ill[ustrissi]mo e R[everendissi]mo Signore
Monsig[nor] <Angelo> Quaglia
Seg[reta]rio della S[anta] C[ongregazione] del Concilio etc. etc.
Roma
1828/1
Vienna, 24 ottobre 1860
Ill[ustrissi]mo et R[everendissi]mo Signore,

In continuazione della precedente mia lettera de' 18 del corrente mese, mi reco a dovere di comunicare in via riservata a V[ostra] S[ignoria] Ill[ustrissi]ma e R[everendissi]ma la copia di una lettera di M[onsi]g[no]r Vescovo di Fulda relativa alla causa matrimoniale della Principessa Carolina Wittgenstein. Il prelato {giustamente} palesa la sua giusta indignazione per la somma imprudenza commessa dalla suddetta Dama nell'avere annunziato col telegrafo la collazione di un grado onorifico ad un ecclesiastico la qual grazia essa dice essere stata conseguita per le di lei premure.

---

[11]De Luca actually wrote 'miraribur,' which is a *lapsus calumi*.

I beg Your Most Illustrious and Reverend Excellency to take note also, with particular attention, to the warnings sent by this prelate about the absolute necessity to use every possible caution lest {the dignity and} the authority of the Holy See be discredited on account of this matter among the {poor} Catholics of Germany who live in the midst of Protestants {who would gloat a lot about this}.

For the rest, I will await eventual instructions on how to proceed in order that this sad business may be taken care of without causing scandal and without offending the dignity of this Holy Congregation.

With the expression of my particular and respectful esteem, I confirm myself...

<Antonino De Luca,
Archbishop of Tarsus and
Apostolic Nuncio in Vienna>

Prego V[ostra] S[ignoria] Ill[ustrissi]ma e R[everendissi]ma di volere eziandio notare con particolare attenzione le avvertenze esposte dal medesimo prelato intorno all'estrema necessità di adoperare ogni maggior possibile cautela, affinché {la dignità e} l'autorità della S[anta] Sede non soffra per questo riguardo discapito presso i {poveri} cattolici della Germania conviventi co' Protestanti {i quali menerebbero gran trionfo}.

Del resto attenderò le opportune istruzioni sul modo da tenersi, acciocché questo infelice negozio possa aggiustarsi senza scandalo e senza offesa alla dignità di cotesta S[anta] Congregazione.

Con sensi di particolare e rispettosa stima mi pregio di confermarmi .....

<Antonino De Luca,
Arcivescovo di Tarso,
Nunzio Apostolico a Vienna>

Document No. 35: Borowski to De Luca, October 31 (O.S.) = November 12, 1860
(Answer to Document No. 32: De Luca to Borowski, October 19, 1860).
Document No. 36, an Abstract of the Proceedings of Luck-Zhitomir,
is enclosed. Latin. Leaf No. 141. De Luca forwarded a copy of this letter to
Rome (ASV, CC Doc. No. 62).

<To: Monsignor Antonino De Luca,
Archbishop of Tarsus and
Apostolic Nuncio in Vienna>
Zhitomir, October 31 (O.S.), 1860
Most Illustrious and Most Reverend Excellency:

I received Your Excellency's letter from Vienna, dated October 19, 1860, in which you request special information about the manner and outcome of the canon law trial held long ago on the validity or invalidity of the marriage contracted by Prince Nicholas Wittgenstein and Princess Carolyne Iwanowska. You seek confirmation also of the sentence issued in the second instance by the Diocese of Mohilow. Complying with your request, I am sending you a shortened version of those proceedings which I compiled diligently and faithfully from the records of the proceedings up to the sentence of the Consistory of Luck-Zhitomir.

<Domino Antonino De Luca
Archiepiscopo Tarsensi,
Nuncio Apostolico
Viennam>
Illustrissime ac multum Reverendissime
     Domine!

Accepi litteras Excellentiae Vestrae 19 Octobris 1860 Viennae ad me datas, in quibus tum specialis informatio requiritur, qua ratione processus canonicus de validitate aut invaliditate matrimonii inter Principem Nicolaum Wittgenstein et Principessam Carolinam Iwanowska initi jamdudum institutus fuerit; tum certitudo desideratur de sententia Archiepiscopali Curiae Mohileviensis in 2da instantia prolata. Postulationi Excellentiae Vestrae Reverendissimae obsecundando, transmitto brevem relationem supradicti processus, diligenter et fideliter ex causa ipsa extractam, pertingentem usque ad sententiam Luceovien[sis]-Zytomiriensis Consistorii, per memetipsum concinnatam.

As for the question as to what actually was the sentence in the second instance, this can be seen from the report sent to the Consistory of Luck-Zhitomir from that of Mohilow on November 12 of the year 1852, Prot. No. 9415, which is worth quoting verbatim:

"The Metropolitan Archbishop of Mohilow, Ignaz Holowinski, by the injunction sent to the Consistory of Mohilow dated September 8, Prot. No. 2721, upon consideration of the sentence promulgated by the Consistory of Luck-Zhitomir on October 26, 1851, and also of the issues raised by the defenders, of the decision, as if in the second instance, reached by the Consistory of Mohilow in the case pertaining to the validity or invalidity of the marriage of Prince and Princess Wittgenstein, decrees that he has condescended to confirm the opinion in favor of the validity of the marriage presented by Monsignor Laski, presiding over the Consistory, as being in accordance with Church laws. He, moreover, rejects the opinions held by the other members of the Consistory, Monsignor Wrublewski and Fathers Holkiewicz and Kotz, as being in disagreement with those same laws."

The Consistory accepted this decision and ordered its promulgation. There is, therefore, no doubt that the case of attempted divorce between Prince and Princess Wittgenstein was lost in both instances, and their marriage was declared valid and legitimate.

From this it is clear that Princess Wittgenstein is not free from her first marriage bond and cannot, then, contract another marriage.

May Your Reverence and Most Illustrious Excellency kindly wish to accept my respectful esteem in proof of which I profess myself
Your Excellency's
most humble servant,
Caspar Borowski,
Bishop of Luck-Zhitomir.

Quod attinet <ad> q<u>aestionem, quae fuerit sententia in 2da instantia, ex eo perspicitur, quod Consistorio Luceovien[si]-Zytomiriensi per Mohileviense nuntiatum est anno 1852, Novembris 12 die sub N[umero] 9415, quodque describere juvat ad verbum:

"Metropolitanus Archiepiscopus Mohiloviensis Ignatius Holowinski, mandato suo ad Consistorium Mohiloviense dato 8 Septembris sub N[umer]o 2721 decernit: quod, examinatis sententia Consistorii Luceovien[sis]-Zytomiriensis prolata 26 Octobris 1851; animadversionibus defensorum; et decisione Consistorii Mohiloviensis, ceu secundae instantiae, in causa de validitate aut invaliditate matrimonii Principum Wittgenstein confirmare dignatus est opinionem Officialis Consistorii Praelati Laski pro validitate matrimonii, tanquam conformem cum legibus Ecclesiasticis. Opiniones vero aliorum membrorum Consistorii, velut Praelati Wrublewski et sacerdotum Holkiewicz et Kotz improbat, tanquam difformes iisdem legibus."

Hanc decisionem Consistorium sequutum est, et exequendam promulgavit. Nullum igitur dubium est causam attentati divortii Principum Wittgenstein in utraque instantia perditam esse, et matrimonium eorum legitimum firmumque declaratum.

Exinde patet Principissam Wittgenstein non esse liberam a primo vinculo Matrimoniali, neque secundas nuptias inire posse.

Dignetur Vestra Reverentia ac Illustrissima Excellentia benigne excipere meam observantiam, quam testificor profitendo me esse
Excellentiae Vestrae
humillimum famulum
Gaspar Borowski
Ep[isco]pus Luceovien[sis]-Zytomiriensis.
Zytomiriae
die 31 Octobris v<etere> s<tilo>
1860 anni

**Document No. 36: Borowski's Abstract of the Luck-Zhitomir Proceedings
concluded on October 19 (O.S.) = October 31, 1852. Enclosed with
Document No. 35: Borowski to Luca, October 31 (O.S.) = November 12, 1860.
On the verso of the last leaf a note penned by De Luca. Latin. Leaves No. 142–143.
see also ASV, CC Doc. No. 63, a copy sent by De Luca to the Pope,
together with a copy of Doc. No. 35 (ASV, CC Doc. No. 62).**

An abridged account of the case against the validity of the marriage contracted by Carolyne Iwanowska and Prince Nicholas Wittgenstein.

Princess Carolyne Wittgenstein has sued for the annulment of her marriage before the Consistory of Mohilow, on May 4, 1848. In her presentation of the case she states that she was born on January 26, 1819.[12] Her parents were Peter Iwanowsky and Countess Pauline Podowska; after their divorce, which took place soon after, she was brought up in her mother's home until the age of fifteen; in the year 1834 she was asked to marry Prince Nicholas Wittgenstein, but she turned him down; in 1835, however, she was asked by her father to come and stay with him in his property of Bielany in the regional county of Podolia; she was forced to marry Prince Wittgenstein first through persuasion, then through malevolence, confinement in her quarters, harsh words, repulsion, and mean attitude. Because of her intimate affection and reverence for her father she had tried, with tears and entreaties, to avoid such a marriage. Her staying with her father amounted to a cruel torment for seven days; on the seventh day she was summoned to the presence of her father and was angrily upbraided for her obstinacy; he threatened, moreover, to disinherit her if she did not give her consent; wherefore she was moved to declare to her father that she was compelled to consent to his wishes only because of her fear of being poor. Having then been sent back to her mother, she was subjected also to her many efforts to make her fulfill the consent she had given her father, although she had never given it of her own will. Fifteen days before the wedding, she was summoned by her father to his estate in Starostince, in the Parish of Pohrebysze and, in her father's home, not without tears, she was wedded to Prince Nicholas by the local priest on August 26, 1836.

Epitome Causae in qua impugnatur validitas matrimonii inter Carolinam de domo Iwanowska et Nicolaum Principem Wittgenstein initi.

Litem hanc movit Carolina Principissa Wittgenstein accusatione sua ad Consistorium Mohiloviense data 4 Maji an[ni] 1848 in qua enarrat: se natam esse an[ni] 1819 Januarii 26 d[ie] ex parentibus Petro Iwanowski et Paulina Comitissa Podoska; propter eorum divortium mox subsequutum, apud matrem suam adultam fuisse usque ad aetatem 15 annorum; anno 1834 a Principe Nicolao Wittgenstein in matrimonium requisitam restitisse; sed a patre suo an[no] 1835 in bona ejus Bielany in Gubern(i)o Podoliensi sita vocatam; ad matrimonium cum P[rincipe] Wittgenstein ineundum persuasionibus primum, post malevolentia, retentione apud se, verbis asperis, aversione, severo vultu compulsam; se vero praeter amorem intimum et reverentiam erga patrem fletibus et precibus hujusmodi coniugium amoliri fuisse conatam; commorationem ejus apud Patrem per 7 dies crudele tormentum extitisse; 7mo die ad patrem vocatam, ni consentiret, ex ore ejus severo pertinatiae [sic] exprobrationem et comminationes exhaereditationis audivisse; quo fuisse permotam ad declarandum patri se esse ad consentiendum ei compulsam timore paupertatis duntaxat. Tunc reversa ad matrem ab hac etiam multos conatus expertam, ut datum patri consensum perficeret; quem sua sponte nunquam dedisset. Quindecim dies ante nuptias vocatam fuisse a Patre in bona sua Starostince,ibi[que] in Parochia nempe Pohrebyszcensi non sine lacrymis a Parocho in domo patris fuisse copulatam cum Principe N[icolao] Wittgenstein 26 Aug[usti] 1836.

---

[12]There are several errors in this account of the Luck-Zhitomir proceedings for October 1852. Princess Carolyne was born on January 27, 1819 (O.S.); she was only seventeen at the time of her marriage, not eighteen; she was married on April 26, not August 26, 1836; her parents were never divorced; her father died in October, not November 1844.

From the very beginning of her conjugal life she abhorred her husband and lived with him for no other reason than that of not displeasing her father. Although on February 6, 1837, a daughter was born to them who was named at baptism Marie Pauline Antonia, the bond of love was always absent. After her father's death on November 4, 1844, no copulation took place between them.

Having become aware of the Ecclesiastical law, according to which a marriage that was not blessed by one's own priest and was contracted without freely given consent was not valid, she requested that her marriage with Wittgenstein be annulled on the grounds that it was not openly and properly performed, and that there was a lack of consent; but that the daughter born from it be declared lawful in so far as the marriage had been presumed valid.

The Consistory of Mohilow, having heard the case against the validity of this marriage, on May 12 of the same year decided the following: the case should be forwarded to the Archdeacon of Kiev, Prelate and Curate Brink, with the order that, after summoning Princess Wittgenstein to his presence, he should endeavor with religious reasons to bend her toward conjugal love and cohabitation with her husband; should words fail, he should assign her a three days retreat for meditation in his church; should even this have no effect, he should call before him Nicholas Wittgenstein, or one representing him, in order that he answer categorically in writing to the objections presented against the validity of the marriage. Such an answer, together with the material evidence pertaining both to the birth and the union of the two parties in question should be sent to the Consistory. Moreover, the Princess should be requested to choose a place for herself to stay for the duration of the proceedings, either a convent or some respectable home, and evidence of this having been done should be corroborated by the parish priest.

The criteria for the conduct of the trial should be provided by the Bull *Dei miseratione* of Benedict XIV; the Dean of Skvira and Curate of Toporow, Mierzwinski, would be entrusted with the role of Defender of the Marriage Bond. The

A primo statim initio vitae conjugalis abhorruisse maritum, et non nisi ut patri placeret cum eo vixisse. Etsi 6 Februarii 1837 eis fuisset nata filia nominata in baptizmate Maria Paulina Antonina, vinculum tamen amoris in dies fuisse laxius.[12] Post obitum Patris 4 Novembris 1844 jam nullum coitum inter eos locum habuisse.

Cognita lege Ecclesiastica, matrimonium non a proprio Parocho benedictum et absq[ue] libero consensu initum nullum esse; rogare se ut matrimonium suum cum Wittgensteinio, tum ob clandestinitatem, tum ob defectum consensus dissolvatur, filia vero ex eo nata, ceu putative, legitima declaretur.

Consistorium Mohiloviense audita hac matrimonii accusatione, 12 die Maii ejusdem anni statuit: Accusationem istam mittere Archidiacono Kijoviensi Praelato et Curato Brink, eiq[ue] injungere ut, vocata ad se Principissa Wittgenstein, conetur religionis motivis flectere eam ad conjugalem amorem et convictum cum Marito; si verba non proderent, triduanam eidem penes Ecclesiam suam assignaret recollectionem: si et ista effectum non haberet, vocaret ad se Nicolaum Wittgenstein vel ejus procuratorem, qui objectionibus factis validitati matrimonii categorice responderet in scriptis. Tale responsum cum testimoniis matricalibus tum nativitatis tum copulationis litigantium mittere in Consistorium. Praeterea obligare Principissam eligendi sibi commorandi locum, usq[ue] dum lis finiatur, sive in monasterio mulierum, sive in honesta aliqua domo, et quod electum fuerit, testimonio a Parocho subscripto probare.

Pro norma agendi indicare Bullam Benedicti XIV quae incipit *Dei miseratione* et assignare Defensorem matrimonii Decanum Skivirensem, Toporowiensem Curatum Mierzwinski. Qui ambo totum processum legitime

---

[13]*Laxiorem*, is the form in the manuscript. *Laxius* is De Luca's correction in the copy he sent to Rome. See ASV, CC Doc. No. 63.

two of them, once the trial was properly and legally completed, ought to send the case back to the Consistory. The prelate Archdeacon of Kiev, on March 4, 1849, sent to the Consistory the complete results of his investigation, which was marked as Prot. No. 74.

At this point, on March 14 came the petition of Monsignor Wrzeszez, who acted as Carolyne's attorney and, at the same time, that of the Defender of the Marriage Bond, Dean Mierzwinski. Both requested that the case be resolved without delay in accordance with what had been alleged and proved. The Consistory did not have any record of the witnesses' depositions and, to remedy this, sent the case back to the aforesaid Archdeacon.

The latter, given that, at that time, the Archdiaconate of Kiev had been separated from the Diocese of Mohilow and added to the Diocese of Luck-Zhitomir, on August 10, 1850, responded by sending the case, marked Prot. No. 217, to the Consistory of Luck-Zhitomir.

The Consistory of Luck-Zhitomir, having examined the case, found the material evidence pertaining to the birth and union of both parties: Carolyne had been baptized on February 1 in the Church of Monasterzyska; there were then a copy of the pre-nuptial examination of Carolyne and Nicholas Wittgenstein; the Baptism certificate of Marie Pauline Antonia, daughter of the Wittgensteins, taken from the records of the Church of Manowje for February 8, 1837; the summons of Prince Wittgenstein published in the Moscow and St. Petersburg newspapers in 1848 (he did not appear to defend himself in the case); Monsignor Felix Wrzeszez's letter of power of attorney, dated May 30, given him to represent Carolyne; evidence given in Saxony pertaining to a von Rott, citizen of this duchy, about the respectability of his household where Princess Wittgenstein stayed between September 1 and 12, 1848; the oaths of office of both the Defender Mierzwinski and the attorney.

The presentation made by the Defender of the Marriage Bond, dated November 25, 1848, against the evidence brought in favor of the invalidity of this marriage on the basis of the following: 1) the fact that the village of Starostince where the wedding was celebrated was always part of the Parish of Pohrebysze; 2) that Princess

perfectum in Consistorium remittere deberent. Praelatus Archidiaconus Kijoviensis 4 Martii 1849 an[ni] sub N[umero] 74 misit in Consistorium totam suam veritatis indagationem.

Hic et nunc subsecuta erat 14 Martii petitio Procuratoris Carolinae Wrescii (Wrzeszez) et simul Defensoris Matrimonii Decani Mierzwinski, ut causa iuxta allegata et probata absq[ue] mora finiatur. Ast Consistorium non inveniens in causa testium depositiones, ut defectus iste suppleretur, remisit illam dicto Archidiacono.

Qui, quoniam eo tempore Archidiaconatus Kijoviensis ab Archidioecesi Mohiloviensi separatus et Dioecesi Luceorien[si]-Zytomiriensi additus est; remisit hanc Causam in Consistorium Zytomiriense 10 Augusti 1850 sub N[umero] 217.

Consistorium Zytomiriense, examinata Causa, reperit testimonia matricalia de nativitate et copulatione utriusq[ue]: Carolinae 1819 Febr[uarii] 1° die baptizatae in Ecclesia Monastyrzyscensi. Copia examinis antenuptialis Carolinae et Nicolai Wittgenstein; matrica baptizmalis Mariae Paulinae Antoninae filiae Wittgenstein[orum] descripta ex libris Manowiensis Eccl[esiae] 1837 Febr[uarii] 8 d[ie]. Citationes Principis Nicolai per Ephemerides Mosquenses et Petropolitanas factae 1848, (quoniam ipse non comparuit ad defendendam causam). Procuratoris Felicis Wrzeszez instrumentum procurationis sibi commissae per Carolinam 30 Martii. Testimonium in Saxonia, per civem huius regni von Rott datum de honestate domus ejus, in qua commoratur Principissa Wittgenstein 1/12 Septembris 1848. Iuramenti Defensoris Mierzwinski et Procuratoris instrumenta.

Protestatio defensoris 25 Novembris 1848, contra causas pro invaliditate matrimonii adductas, primum ex eo quod Vicus Starostincy, ubi matrimonium benedictum est, semper pertinebat ad parochiam Pohrebyscensem; secundo ex eo quod Principissa Carolina in tali aetate jam erat, ut potuerit nosse coactionem ad ma-

Carolyne had already reached an age in which she could have known that compulsion is an impediment to marriage, and had enough freedom after the wedding to declare immediately to the priest or to someone else close to her that she had been forced to marry against her will; 3) and last, that after her daughter's birth and twelve years of marriage she had not told anyone about being forced to marry against her will, and such compulsion, even if it had indeed taken place, had been extinguished by the subsequent consent and conjugal affection, confirming thus the validity of the marriage. Moreover, in the Princess's case it was not clear that her father had resorted to whipping and made her distraught with fear, but persuaded her only with the argument of wealth that would be increased. He goes on to quote from the Scriptures, *Romans*, Ch. 7, *Corinthians*, Ch. 7, and Jesus Christ's words "What God hath joined, let no man put asunder." He requests then that the integrity of this marriage be upheld and the Princess be forbidden to bring forth whatsoever arguments in favor of its invalidity and that, moreover, she be given an injunction to return to her husband and lead an honest life.

The petition of her attorney, Monsignor Wrzeszez, dated November 26, 1848, in which he declares having accepted both the Commissioner and the Defender.

The appearance on the same day of the Defender in which he states the Commissioner to be acceptable insofar as absolutely not suspect to him. At the same time, on behalf of Prince Nicholas, in order to prove the validity of the marriage, he produces these witnesses: 1) Leo Podowski, 2) Major General Theodor Kalm, 3) Prince Georg Wittgenstein, 4) Mateusz Dlugolentski, 5) Ivan Mieszkowski, 6) Peter Artykowski and 7) Julianna Stolarczuk<owa>, a servant. He adds the questions the witnesses will have to answer; the questions are:

1) That Carolyne, by living a long time with her father in the town of Starostince, without doubt belonged to the Parish of Pohrebysze.

2) That Carolyne's father desired nothing but his daughter's prosperity and the threat to disinherit her did not take place at all.

trimonium impedimentum esse, et libertatis satis habuit post nuptias statim declarandi Parocho sive alicui ex propinquis se fuisse coactam. Tertio denique, ex eo quod post natam filiam et duodecim annos nemini de coactione conquaesta erat, quae coactio etiamsi reapse extitisset, subsequenti consensu et affectu conjugali extinta erat, et validitas matrimonii firmata. Caeterum ex accusatione Principissae non liquet Patrem ejus ad coactionem adhibuisse flagella, perterruisse metu, sed suasisse tantum habita ratione bonorum augendorum. Citat loca Scripturae v[idelicet] *Rom[anos]*, cap[itulum] 7, 1 *Corynth[ios]*, cap[itulum] 7, et verba J[esu] C[hri]sti: *quod Deus conjunxit homo non separet*. Rogat denique ut matrimonium istud integrum servetur, et Principissae vetitum sit quaecumque argumenta pro invalidita<te> adducere, et injunctum ad virum suum reverti et ducere vitam probam.

Procuratoris Wrzesez 26 Novembris 1848 petitio, in qua declarat se habere acceptos et Commissarium et Defensorem.

Manifestatio Defensoris eodem die data in qua acceptum, declarat commissarium et minime sibi suspectum et simul ex parte Nicolai Principis ad probandam validitatem producit testes 1) Leonem Podoski, 2) Generalem-Majorem Theodorum Kalm, 3) Principem Georgium Wittgenstein 4) Matteum Dlugolentski, 5) Joannem Mieszkowski 6) Petrum Artykowski et 7) subditam Juliannam Stolarczuk. Addidit interrogatoria ad quae responsuri sunt isti testes; haec interrogatoria sunt:

1) Quod Carolina longo tempore vivens cum patre in vico Starostincy, absq[ue] dubio ad parochiam Pohrebyszcensem pertinebat.

2) Quod pater Carolinae nihil aliud desiderabat, quam prosperitatem filiae suae si nuberet Principi Wittgenstein, jam vero comminatio exhaereditationis prorsus locum non habebat.

3) That Carolyne, after her marriage, not only did not ever complain to anyone about being forced to marry against her will, but lived with her husband quietly and prosperously.

4) That Carolyne's late father loved her a lot and always dealt with her gently and affectionately.

A declaration of the priest of Pohrebysze, Father Beregowicz, dated November 27, 1848, Prot. No. 83, to the effect that Carolyne, before she got married had lived from the year 1835 with her father in the village of Starostince in the Parish of Pohrebysze; she received her first Holy Communion in the year 1836 in the Church of Pohrebysze, and she was listed as being eighteen years old in the Records for the Parishioners of Pohrebysze for 1836 under No. 1; therefore she was legitimately joined in matrimony with Prince Wittgenstein by her own priest, following three marriage banns, on April 26, 1836.

The declaration to the Committee made by her attorney, Monsignor Wrzeszez, on November 27, in which he refutes the evidence presented by the priest of Pohrebysze and brings forth the argument, presented by Carolyne in her petition, that she stayed in Starostince only for the fifteen days preceding the wedding, and she was summoned there by her father in order for him to exercise more freely his pressures upon her; he declares he is going to prove by means of witnesses that she had no confession in the Church of Pohrebysze other than that preceding the wedding. He claims that the priest of Pohrebysze knew about the compulsion exercised upon her, and that it had been impossible for Carolyne to complain to him lest she be denounced to her father. He, moreover, refutes the Defender as having wrongly presupposed from the very beginning that Carolyne had been a Parishioner in Pohrebysze; secondly, he argues that the young lady had been used from her childhood to revering her father's will and could without any resistance and reaction on her part be ordered against her will to enter the kind of marriage her father desired; he also submits these witnesses for Carolyne's case: 1) Anton Kostenecki, nobleman; 2) Peter Slobodiany; 3) Straton Kurda (they were accepted by the Defender). He presented, moreover, the evidence they had provided, namely:

3) Quod Carolina post matrimonium non solum nemini quaerebatur super coactionem, sed tranquille et prospere cum viro vivebat.

4) Quod defunctus pater Carolinae admodum eam diligebat et semper benigne et amabiliter eam tractabat.

Declaratio Parochi Pohrebyszcensis Beregowicz 27 Novembris 1848 sub N[umero] 83 quod Carolina, antequam nuberet, ab an[no] 1835 habitabat apud Patrem suum in villa Starostincy in Parochia Pohrebyscensi. A[nno] 1836 primam Communionem S[anctam] in Ecclesia Pohzebyscensi suscepit et in Elencho parochianorum Pohrebyscensium descripta 1836 sub N[umero] 1 habens 18 annos: adeoque legitime a proprio parocho copulata est cum Principe Wittgenstein praemissis 3 denunti-ationibus 26 Aprilis 1836 an[ni].

Procuratoris Wreszez declaratio 27 Novembris commissioni data, in qua oppugnat testimonium Parochi Pohrebyscensis et asserit id quod in accusatione per Carolinam data, de ejus tantum per 15 dies commoratione in Villa Starostincy praecedentes nuptias; esse ibi a Patre vocatam ut liberius coactionem suam in ea perficeret. Confessionem non aliam quam antenuptialem in Ecclesia Pohrebyscensi peregisse, id quod per testes se probaturum declarat. Parochum Potirebyscensem coactionem novisse et impossibile Carolinae fuisse conquaeri coram eo, ne accusaretur apud patrem. Oppugnat quoque Defensorem, ostendens quoad primum eum etiam perperam agnoscere Carolinam fuisse parochianam Pohrebyscensem. Quoad secundum, perorat virginem a pueritia assuetam venerari patris voluntatem, potuisse absq[ue] ulla resistentia et vi contra voluntatem suam ad desideratum a patre connubium inclinari; testes etiam in rem Carolinae proponit. 1) Nobilem Antonium Kostenicki 2) Petrum Slobodziany. 3) Stratonem Kurda, quos etiam Defensor approbavit et interrogatoria ad quae responderunt exhibuit:

1) That Carolyne's father was strict and his orders were not to be questioned.

2) That Carolyne, from the moment she met Prince Wittgenstein, was always disinclined toward him and refused with indignation his amorous blandishments.

3) That the Prince, thus rejected by Carolyne, went back to her father who, passing over his daughter's resistance, promised to give her as wife to the Prince.

4) When she received news of his promises, she wept and implored her father not to force her to marry against the inclination of her heart; her father told her sternly that he could not change his mind, for he had already given his word to the Prince; and henceforth his conversation with his daughter became quite harsh.

5) That the father again summoned Carolyne to his presence and, having asked her whether she persisted in her refusal and she entreating him again and again not to force her to marry against her will, became very angry and sent her away saying: "Go to your mother, I shall indeed deprive you of any rights to my inheritance." From that moment on to the time of the wedding she was ever desperate and in tears.

6) That Carolyne never resided in Starostince and was listed as a parishioner in Monasterzyska.

7) That, in her life with her husband following the wedding, she was bound by constant compulsion and her father was afraid that the bond would be broken, which indeed happened after his death. Finally,

8) That among the witnesses introduced by the Defender there was Prince Nicholas' own brother, namely Georg Wittgenstein, who cannot be accepted according to the tenets of Civil Law (which he quotes) ; he therefore dismisses him, while accepting the others.

All the witnesses took their oath and answered to questions in the following manner:

1) Carolyne's subject, that is her servant, Julianna Stolarczuk<owa>, stated that they determined to resort even to fustigation as a means by which Carolyne was finally compelled to marry.

1) Quod pater Carolinae austerus erat et in omnibus praeceptis suis inconcussus.

2) Quod Carolina simul atq[ue] cognovit Principem Wittgenstein semper fuerit ab eo aversa, et ejus erga se amoris blandimenta cum indignatione repellebat.

3) Quod Princeps sic a Carolina alienatus ad patrem ejus se convertit, qui insuper habita renitentia filiae, eam se principi pro uxore daturum promisit.

4) Cujus promissionis dum notitiam accepit, cum lacrymis obtestabatur Patrem ne se contra cordis propensionem nubere cogat. Pater vero dure respondit, quod propositum suum non potest mutare, quoniam Principi jam promisit. Abhinc admodum dura ejus erat cum filia conversatio.

5) Quod Pater iterum vocavit ad se Carolinam, et facta interrogatione num in sua pertinatia persistat, illaq[ue] eum iterum atq[ue] iterum obsecraret ne se cogeret, tunc Pater excanduit eamq[ue] propulsavit dicens: "Perge ad Matrem, ego vero te omnibus haereditatis juribus destituam." Totum abinde tempus usq[ue] ad nuptias in lacrymis et vehementi tristitia transegit.

6) Quod Carolina numquam habitabat in Villa Starostyncz et inter Parochianos Monastyrzyszcenses computabatur.

7) Quod vita ejus post nuptias cum marito, continua coactione vinciebatur, et Pater in metu erat ne disrumperetur istud vinculum, id quod post mortem ejus revera accidit. Denique

8) Quod inter testes a Defensore praesentatos positus est frater germanus Principis Nicolai, nempe Georgius Wittgenstein, qui non potest admitti juxta legem civilem (quae citatur); excipit ergo eum, ceteros vero admittit.

Testes omnes juramentum peregerunt, et ad interrogatoria responderunt:

1°. Subdita seu serva Julianna Stolarczuk fassa est, quod voluerunt addita etiam flagellatione qua Carolina compulsa est ad nuptias.

2) Peter Slobodiany, also her subject, stated like the previous witness that fustigation had been used and that he listened to it through the door.

3) Straton Kurda, a servant of Carolyne's father, answered yes to all the questions.

Likewise, the other witnesses, the servant Antonina Kostenecka and John Mieszkowski, vividly described the harshness of the father and the compulsion against the daughter; they also stated that Carolyne's father never lived permanently in the village of Starostince.

Next follows the testimony of the Lutheran pastor, dated April 26, 1836, about the fact that there are no impediments to the marriage of Prince Wittgenstein. Evidence pertaining to the burial of Leo Podowski which took place on April 1, 1847. Evidence presented about the death of Theodor Kalm. Evidence provided by Carolyne's mother about the compulsion on the part of the father.

After the case was brought before the Consistory of Zhitomir, Carolyne's solicitor pressed insistently for a speedy decision. He complained before the Metropolitan College of the delays in the Consistory of Zhitomir. The College gave orders to accelerate the proceedings. Prince Wittgenstein's solicitor, Peter Rychlinski, sent to the Consistory a letter dated July 1, 1851, giving him power of attorney. On July 8, 1851, the Consistory of Zhitomir appointed Canon Ludkiewicz as the defender in this case and he was sworn in. Having considered the case, he took exception to all the witnesses questioned, both as subjects and servants, and suspected them of having previously arranged their statements, for they use almost the same words and, for the most part, report hearsay. He attacks their depositions and reiterates the recommendations of the first defender in the case. Moreover, he shows that Carolyne's own signature in the records of the premarital examination removes any doubt about the existence of any compulsion, and he clearly shows the futility of the claim of clandestinity. The marriage is therefore valid, and the case is to be concluded by its confirmation.

To such opinion on the part of the Defender, Carolyne's attorney responds, on August 10, by defending the integrity of all the witnesses and by signalling in a long peroration that they had full information of the facts they reported and that it was therefore easy to believe them.

2°. Petrus Slobodiany, item subditus, idem asserebat quod praecedens, etiam flagellationem, quam post ostium audivit.

3°. Strato Kurda servus Patris Carolinae ad omnes interrogationes asserendo respondit.

Item caeteri, serva Antonina Kostenecka, Ioannes Mieszkowski, duritiem Patris, coactionem filiae facunde enarrabant, et asserebant nunquam Patrem Carolinae stabiliter habitasse in Villa Starostince.

Porro sequitur testimonium lutherani pastoris 26 Ap[rilis] 1836 de eo quod nulla adsint impedimenta ad matrimonium Principis Wittgenstein. Testimonium sepulturae Leonis Podoski peractae 1847 Apr[ilis] 1 d[ie]. Testimonium de obitu Theodori Kalm. Testimonium matris Carolinae de coactione ex parte Patris.

Postquam haec causa translata est in Consistorium Zytomiriense, Procurator Carolinae precibus suis instabat ut acceleretur decisio. Coram Collegio Petropolitano accusabat cunctationem Consistorii Zyt[omiriensis]. Collegium jussit accelerare. Procurator Principis Wittgenstein Petrus Rychlinski misit ad Consistorium Zyt[omiriense] 1 Julii 1851 an[ni] litteras procurationis. Consistorium Zyt[omiriense] 8 Julii 1851 pro hac causa designavit Defensorem Can[onicum] Ludkiewicz qui et juramentum perfecit. Ponderata causa, defensor omnes examinatos testes excepit ceu subditos famulos vel suspectos de condicto: iisdem enim fere verbis utuntur, audita plerumque referunt; refutat depositiones et idem quod primus defensor urget; praeterea propriam subscriptionem Carolinae in libro examinis antenuptialis omne submovere dubium de coactione ostendit; futilem esse clandestinitatis objectionem palam facit. Matrimonium itaq[ue] validum, causam finiendam ejusdem confirmatione.

Tali sententiae defensoris Procurator Carolinae 10 Aug[usti] respondit testes omnes probos esse, notitiam eorum quae referunt plene habuisse adeoque facile illis credendum multis verbis innuit.

The Consistory of Zhitomir on August 20 gave the Defender faculty to respond to the solicitor's statement. This he did brilliantly by showing that all seven witnesses, being from the lower classes and domestic servants, could be easily swayed by whatever means but, whether they were subject to hallucination he could not prove with the certainty that is required in marriage cases. Carolyne's solicitor, Wrzeszez, restated what he had previously said. Prince Wittgenstein's attorney declared the Prince had neither seen nor heard anything about his wife being compelled, that her own priest had blessed their union, but it was regrettable that in their married life there was a lack of love on the part of the wife and there was constant discord, and things had become even worse after her father's death. He requested that his wife return to her obligations.

Hence, the Consistory of Luck-Zhitomir—on September 7—ordered the preparation of a special explanation of the whole case and, on October 26, 1851 declared that the marriage of Prince Wittgenstein and Princess Carolyne was valid and not subject to any possibility of divorce. The whole case with this decision was then sent to the Consistory of Mohilow to be dealt with in the second instance. There, after the case was considered and pondered, the sentence of the Consistory of Luck-Zhitomir was in doubt because of differing votes, but it was confirmed by deliberation of the Archbishop of Mohilow, Ignaz Holowinski, on the 19th of November of the year 1852.

Consistorium Zytomiriense 20 Aug[usti] commisit defensori replicationem asserti procuratoris, quod ille praeclare fecit ostendens omnes 7 testes ex infima plebe, servos domesticos, facile quovis flectendos, hallucinationi obnoxios non posse certitudinem suppeditare, quae requiritur in causa matrimoniali. Procurator Carolinae Wreszez idem asserit quod antea. Procurator Principis Wittgenstein declaravit Principem neque vidisse neq[ue] audisse coactionem suae uxoris, parochum quoque proprium matrimonium benedixisse, sed dolendum quod in convictu matrimoniali desiderabatur amor ex parte uxoris, discordiam fuisse continuam, post mortem autem patris rem adhuc pejorem evasisse. Rogat uxorem ad officia sua reverti.

Hinc Consistorium Luceoviense-Zytomiriense 7 Septembris jussit conficere totius causae specialem explanationem; 26 vero Octobris 1851 declaravit: Matrimonium Principis Wittgenstein cum Carolina Iwanowska esse validum nulliq[ue] divortio obnoxium. Totam causam cum sua decisione trasmisit in Consistorium Mohiloviense tanquam ad secundam instantiam. Ubi trutinata et ponderata hac causa, sententia Consistorii Luceovien[sis]-Zytomiriensis disparitate quidem votorum vacillabat, sed Metropolitani Archiepiscopi Mohiloviensis Ignatii Holowinski <deliberatione> confirmata est an[ni] 1852 Mensis Novembris 19 die.

Monsignor the Bishop of Zhitomir. October 31, 1860.
On the Wittgenstein-Iwanowska marriage case.

M[onsi]g[no]r Vescovo di Zytomir, 31 Ott[obr]e 1860.
Su la Causa matrimoniale Wittgenstein Iwanowska.

Document No. 37: Żyliński to De Luca, October 31 (O.S.) = November 12, 1860,
a with note on the verso penned by De Luca (Answer to Document No. 33,
De Luca to Żyliński, October 20, 1860. Latin. Leaves No. 145–146.

To: The Most Excellent and Reverend
Monsignor Antonino De Luca,
Archbishop of Tarsus,
Apostolic Nuncio in Vienna, Austria
St. Petersburg, October 31, 1860 (Old Style)
Most Excellent and Reverend Monsignor:

I wish to comply promptly and zealously with the request made of me in Your Most Reverend Excellency's very kind letter of the 19th of the present month. Therefore, in order to deal with the whole question speedily and to the point, from the proceedings of the marriage case pertaining to Princess Carolyne Wittgenstein, born Iwanowska, which at length and in detail I described in my decree issued on February 24th of this year, and which I exposed also in my letter to Your Most Reverend Excellency dated May 25 of this same year, I decided to repeat briefly the following:

It is a fact that the Consistory of Luck-Zhitomir on November 6, 1851 issued a sentence for the validity of the aforesaid marriage but, on November 13, 1852, in the Consistory of Mohilow, under the Archbishop my predecessor, all the judges, with just one dissenting vote, duly and properly pronounced this marriage null and void. *And this is the judgement in the first instance.* I then, on the force and authority kindly given me, upon request of the petitioner, by the Most Holy Father, for our happiness the present Pope Pius IX, I took up again this case *in appeal* and by a *definitive sentence*, as His Holiness had ordered, I sanctioned the similar sentence on the invalidity of this marriage passed by the judges I delegated to this purpose, whose names are listed in my decree, and declared, therefore, the marriage null and void. *And this is the second sentence.* Note that, according to the Bull of Pope Benedict XIV, here are *two judgements, two sentences*, or *similar and identical decisions*, which moved me to determine and pronounce the dissolution of the marriage bond of Princess Wittgenstein.

Excellentissimo ac R[everendissi]mo D[omi]no D[omi]no Antoni<n>o De Luca
Archiepiscopo Tarsensi,
Nuntio Apostolico,
Viennae in Austria
Excellentissime ac Reverendissime Domine.

Injuncto mihi per literas humanissimas Excellentiae Vestrae Reverendissimae sub d[ie] 19 praesentium, officio, propero ac propenso animo parere volentes, ex processu causae matrimonialis Principissae Carolinae Wittgenstein, de domo Iwanowska, quem disertis verbis ac per singula in decreto 24 d[ie] Februarii currentis anni emanato descripsi, nec non in epistolis meis ad Excellentiam Vestram Reverendissimam 25 Maji ejusdem anni datis exposui, ut paucis rem complectar, haec breviter repetenda duxi:

Reapse Consistorium Luceovio-Zytomirense Anno 1851, Novembris 6 die, pro validitate dicti matrimonii sententiam protulit. Sed in Consistorio Mohiloviensi anno 1852, Novembris 13 die, sub praedecessore meo in Archiepiscopatu, omnes judices, vix uno dissentiente, nullum matrimonium istud rite ac recte pronunciarunt. En *primus instantiae gradus.* Ego dein, vi et praetermissam similem de nullitate dicti matrimonii sententiam Judicum, a me delegatorum et in decreto memoratorum, praesenti 1860 anno 24 d[ie] februarii, auctoritate mihi a S[anctissimo] D[omino] N[ostro] Pio IX Papa feliciter Moderno, ad preces oratricis, benigne concessa, causam istam in *appellationis gradu* reasumpsi et per *definitivam sententiam*, prout Sua Sanctitas jusserat, dijudicavi itemque nullum ac irritum matrimonium declaravi. En *altera sententia.* En juxta Bullam Summi Pontificis Benedicti XIV *duo judicata, duae sententiae* seu *resolutiones* similes et conformes, quae me vinculum matrimonii Principissae Wittgenstein dissolutum censere ac pronunciare permoverunt.

I am very happy to take advantage of this occasion to pay my respects to you, and in so doing I remain
Your Most Reverend Excellency's
very devoted servant,
Wenceslas Żyliński,
Metropolitan Archbishop of Mohilow

Hac occasione lubentissime utor, ut cultum observantiae meae profitear quacum persisto.
Excellentiae Vestrae Reverendissimae
Obsequentissimus famulus
Venceslaus Żyliński
Archiepiscopus Mohilov[iensis] Metrop[olitanus]
1860 Octobris 31 die v<etere> st<ilo>
Petropoli

Monsignor the Archbishop of Mohilow.
October 31 (November 12), 1860.
On the Wittgenstein-Iwanowka marriage.

M[onsi]g[no]r Arciv[escov]o di Mohilow, 31 Ott[obr]e
(12 Nov[embre]) 1860.
Sul matrimonio Wittgenstein-Iwanowska.

Document No. 38: Hohenlohe to De Luca, December 1, 1860, with note penned by De Luca. Italian. Leaves No. 147–148. De Luca will follow Hohenlohe's advice and send copies of Docs. No. 35 and 36 directly to Mons. Stella, the Pope's secretary. See ASV, CC Docs. No. 60, 61, 62, 63.

To: Monsignor De Luca
Apostolic Nuncio,
etc., etc.
Rauden, December 1, 1860
Most Venerable Monsignor:

The day before yesterday I wrote to Your Most Reverend Excellency that my secretary was to arrive on Saturday; instead, he is going to get to Vienna on Sunday, since his stay had to be prolonged a few hours owing to some business.

So Father Marcello Massarenti will show up with this letter, and I place him entirely at your disposal.

If Your Most Reverend Excellency is thinking of sending the papers pertaining to Princess Wittgenstein-Iwanowska, my advice would be to address them directly to the Holy Father, for I have some reasons to think that Cardinal Antonelli does not have very clear ideas about this business.

Father Marcello will deliver your letter for the Holy Father to Monsignor Stella, who can be relied upon to give it to His Holiness. This is at least my suggestion; in your wisdom, you will do as you will deem best.

M[on]s[igno]r Antonino De Luca
Nunzio Ap[osto]lico
etc., etc.
Rauden, 1 dic[embre] 1860
Monsignore Veneratissimo.

L'altro ieri scrissi a V[ostra] E[ccellenza] R[everendissima] che <il> mio segretario ar<r>iverebbe Sab(b)ato, invece arriva Domenica a Vienna, essendosi prolungato per alcuni affari il suo soggiorno di qualche ora.

Si presenterà ora Don Marcello Massarenti con questa mia lettera, e lo metto intieramente a Sua disposizione.

Se manda V[ostra] E[ccellenza] R[everendissima] le carte riguardanti la P[rinci]p[e]ssa Wittgenstein-Iwanowska, Le consiglierei di dirig(g)erle direttamente al S[anto] Padre, perché ho qualche ragione di credere, che il Card[inal] Ant[onelli] non vede perfettamente chiaro in quest'affare.

La lettera al S[anto] Padre Don Marcello la darà a Monsignor Stella, il quale coscienziosamente la consegnerà a S[ua] Santità. Questo è una mia idea, Ella poi nella Sua saviezza farà quel che meglio crederà.

Plate 5.   Cardinal Gustav von Hohenlohe-Schillingsfürst (1823–96), Archbishop of
Edessa. A photograph.

I again pay my respectful homage to you and, in asking you to remember me in your prayers, I have the honor of calling myself
Your Most Reverend Excellency's
most humble, devoted and obliging servant
Gustav von Hohenlohe,
Archibishop of Edessa
Rauden, in the vicinity of Ratibor
December 1, 1860.

Le ripeto i miei profondi ossequi e raccomandandomi alle Sue orazioni ho l'onore di dirmi di V[ostra] E[ccellenza] R[everendissima] um[ilissimo] dev[otissimo] ob[b]l[igatissim]o servo
Gustavo <d'Hohenlohe>
Arciv[escov]o d'Edessa.
Rauden presso Ratibor
1 Dic[embre] 1860.

His Most Reverend Excellency
Monsignor <Antonino> De Luca
Archbishop of Tarsus
Apostolic Nuncio in Vienna

Son Excellence R[e]v[erendissi]me
Monseigneur De Luca
Archevêque de Tarse
Nonce Apostolique à Vienne

Monsignor Hohenlohe. December 1, 1860

M[onsi]g[no]r d'Hohenlohe, 1 Dic[embre] 1860

Document No. 39: Quaglia to De Luca, January 16, 1861, with note on the verso penned by De Luca (Answer to Doc. No 31, De Luca to Quaglia, October 18, 1860; De Luca to Quaglia, October 24, 1860, which enclosed a copy of Doc. No. 28, Kött to De Luca, October 15, 1860. See ASV, CC Doc. No. 47). For the draft of this letter, which contains passages not to be found in the present document, see ASV, CC Doc. No. 68. Italian. Leaves No. 149–150.

To: Monsignor Antonino De Luca,
Archbishop of Tarsus and
Apostolic Nuncio in Vienna
Rome, January 16, 1861
Most Illustrious and Reverend Monsignor:

Following the observations presented by Your Most Illustrious and Reverend Excellency and by Monsignor the Bishop of Fulda in your letters of the 15th and 28th of October of last year, with respect to the sentence of annulment of the marriage of Princess Iwanowska with Prince Wittgenstein, the Holy Father, whom I went to see in order to relate those matters to him, ordered that the question be submitted again to the full Congregation. Having prepared copies of the conclusions, the relative documentation, and the extent of your exposition, the most eminent Fathers, in the general assembly on the 22nd of last December in which *nine* of them participated, having also looked at the intrinsic merit of the case and supplied in this fashion to the absence of the two sentences to the same effect, were again of the opinion that the above mentioned sentence should be carried out, if this was the wish of His Holiness. Having made such a report to the Holy Father, he conde-

Monsig[nor] Antonino De Luca
Arcivescovo di Tarso
Nunzio Apostolico
Vienna
Ill[ustrissi]mo e R[everendissi]mo Signore.

In seguito alle osservazioni fatte dalla Sig[noria] V[ostra] Ill[ustrissi]ma e Rev[erendissi]ma e da Monsig[nor] Vescovo di Fulda con lettere del 15 e 28 Ottobre dello spirato anno relativamente alla esecuzione della sentenza di nullità di matrimonio tra la Principessa Iwanowska ed il Principe Wittgenstein, il S[anto] Padre, cui mi recai a dovere fargliene relazione, ordinò che venisse di nuovo sottoposto l'affare all'esame della piena Congregazione. Redatti pertanto a tale effetto analoghi fogli di deduzioni corredati degli opportuni documenti e di quel tanto che erasi da Lei esposto, gli Em[inentissi]mi Padri, nella generale adunanza dei 22 Decembre ultimo intervenuti nel numero di *Nove*, avendo gustato anche il merito intrinseco della causa, e supplito così alla mancanza delle due sentenze conformi, furono nuovamente di avviso doversi eseguire la menzionata sentenza, ove così piacesse a Sua Santità. Riferita da me in seguito siffatta re-

scended to confirm it and ordered me to write to Your Most Illustrious and Reverend Excellency, which I am doing, in order that you, as is His Holiness' wish, bring all of this directly to the attention of Monsignor the Bishop of Fulda in order that, without setting further obstacles, he should carry out the sentence issued by Monsignor the Archbishop of Mohilow. Since it is also desirable to keep in mind the feared-for consequences that the surprise might cause, it is left to your prudence and to that of Monsignor the Bishop of Fulda to predispose carefully the minds of those most likely to raise questions to receiving with due reverence this declaration of the Holy See.

I must herewith also report to you that your letter, dated December 6, which enclosed the report compiled by Monsignor the Bishop of Zhitomir on the same marriage case as it was brought to judgement in the first instance before that Curia, reached me only after the Congregation's deliberation. In any case, I referred to it in my report to His Holiness, and it was pointed out that the conclusions therein could not have led to issuing a different opinion.

I am counting on your kindness in order to be informed in due time of the effects of the present letter and conclude with the reaffirmation of my singular and respectful esteem.
Your Most Illustrious and Reverend Excellency's most devout and obliging servant,

Angelo Quaglia,
Secretary of the Holy Congregation
of the Council.

Monsignor the Secretary of <the Holy Congregation of> the Council.
January 16, 1861.
He communicates the decision in favor of annulment of the Wittgenstein-Iwanowska's marriage.

lazione al S[anto] Padre, si compiacque confermarla, ed ordinarmi di scrivere a V[ostra] S[ignoria] Ill[ustrissi]ma e R[everendissi]ma, siccome faccio, perché Ella direttamente, come è volere della stessa Santità Sua, deduca tutto ciò a notizia di Monsig[nor] Vescovo di Fulda allo scopo, che dal medesimo venga eseguita la sentenza emanata da M[onsi]g[no]r Arcivescovo di Mohilov, senza frapporre ulteriori ostacoli. E volendosi pure avere un riguardo al temuto pericolo di ammirazione per le conseguenze del fatto, sarà della prudenza ed oculatezza tanto Sua, quanto di Monsig[nor] Vescovo di Fulda, disporre preventivamente gli animi dei più miticolosi ad accogliere col dovuto ossequio questa dichiarazione della S[anta] Sede.

E qui debbo pure significarle che la sua lettera del 6 Decembre decorso, con cui si accompagna il rapporto redatto da Monsig[nor] Vescovo di Zytomir intorno alla stessa causa matrimoniale giudicata in primo grado innanzi a quella Curia, mi pervenne dopo che la Congregazione aveva già pronunziato. Tuttavolta tenni proposito anche del medesimo nella relazione che feci a Sua Santità, e si rilevò che le cose ivi dedotte non avrebbero potuto influire a fare emettere un diverso parere.

Attendendomi dalla sua gentilezza di conoscere a suo tempo il risultato della presente, passo a ripetermi con sensi di distinta e rispettosa stima,
Di V[ostra] S[ignoria] Ill[ustrissi]ma e Rev[erendissi]ma
De[votissi]mo Ob[bligatissi]mo Servo
Angelo Quaglia
Segretario della S[anta] Cong[regazione] del Concilio.
Roma, li 16 Gennaio 1861

M[onsi]g[no]r Segr[etar]io del Concilio, 16 Genn[ai]o, 1861.

Comunica la decisione per lo scioglimento del matrimonio Wittgenstein-Iwanowska.

Document No. 40: De Luca to Kött, February 6, 1861. Latin. Leaf No. 151.

To: His Most Illustrious and Reverend Excellency,
Monsignor Christophe Florenz Kött,
Bishop of Fulda.
Fulda
No. 2060/1
Vienna, February 6, 1861.
Most Illustrious and Reverend Monsignor:

The well known and controversial problem of the marriage contracted some time ago by Prince Nicholas Wittgenstein with Lady Carolyne of the princely Iwanowsky family has again been brought up for review before the Holy Congregation of the Council. On this occasion, newly emerging documents pertaining to this matter have been very carefully examined. Among them there was also a copy of a pertinent letter written to me last October by your Most Illustrious and Reverend Excellency, as well as a copy of a very long letter, also addressed to me, from the most Reverend Bishop of Zhitomir in Russian Poland.

The sentence, that was issued unanimously[14] on the 22nd of last December by the nine cardinals in a general assembly of the Holy Congregation of the Council, declared the aforementioned marriage null and void. The Most Holy Father, our Lord and Liege, approved and ratified that sentence and gave orders to the Reverend Father Secretary of the Holy Congregation that Your Most Illustrious and Reverend Excellency should, through me, be officially informed of it. He ordered, moreover, that, before proceeding to the implementation of this sentence, Your Most Illustrious and Reverend Excellency should employ, with all the prudence and cleverness you are capable of, the necessary delicate precautions to avoid that the minds of the faithful be offended in any way. Therefore, I ask and entreat your Excellency in order that, given the opportunity, you divulge publicly and privately how much diligence has been used by the Holy Congregation of the Council in dealing with this most difficult case which had to be discussed and brought up for judgement so many times after examining documents sought in so many places, which often contradicted one another, and hearing reliable witnesses worthy of faith.

Ill[ustrissi]mo et R[everendissi]mo Domino

Domino Christophoro Florentio Koett
Episcopo Fuldensi
Fuldam
N° 2060/1
Viennae, die VI Februarii, 1861.
Ill[ustrissi]me et R[everendissi]me Domine.

Nota controversia de matrimonio jamdudum inito a Nobili Viro Principe Nicolao Wittgenstein cum nobili Matrona Carolina ex Principibus Iwanowski denuo in examen penes S[anctam] C[ongregationem] Concilii Romae deducta fuit. Hac occasione maturissimo judicio perpensa fuerunt documenta noviter exhibita, quae ad rem respiciunt. Inter caetera etiam exemplar Epistolae a Dominatione Vestra Ill[ustrissi]ma et R[everendissi]ma praeterlapso mense Octobri de hoc argumento mihi inscriptae nec non alterius prolixae Epistolae a R[everendissi]mo Episcopo Zytomiriensi in Polonia Russiaca mihi itidem datae.

Sententia, quae exinde die 22 praeterlapsi mensis Decembris unanimi suffragio novem Purpuratorum Patrum generali conventu ejusdem S[anctae] Cong[regatio]nis adstantium lata fuit, nullum ac invalidum declaravit praedictum matrimonium. Sanctissimus Pater et Dominus Noster {huiusmodi} sententiam probavit et ratam habuit et R[everendo] P[atri] Secretario S[anctae] Congregationis mandavit, ut per me Dominationi Vestrae Ill[ustrissi]mae et R[everendissi]mae officialis notitia comunicaretur. Jussit insuper ut, antequam praedictam sententiam ad effectum reduceret, Dominatio Vestra Ill[ustrissi]ma et R[everendissi]ma, ea qua posset prudentia et dexteritate, exquisitas adhiberet opportunas cautiones ne animi fidelium exinde offendiculi occasionem arriperent. Quapropter rogo et obsecro Dominationem Vestram ut, data opportunitate, propalam et singillatim enarret quanta fuerit adhibita diligentia a S[anta] C[ongregatione] Concilii in hac gravissima causa pluries discutienda et dijudicanda, perspectis documentis undequaque quaesitis et in contrarias partes facientibus et auditis testibus auctoritate et fide pollentibus.

---

[14]The sentence was not actually unanimous. See ASV, CC Doc. 59A, at the end, p. 189.

It follows then that one should stress the care which the Holy Roman Catholic Church employs in supporting and guarding the sanctity of marriage bonds that are sanctioned by divine law. The Church, therefore, never dissolves them and, only in special situations, she declares these bonds to have been null and void from the beginning.

In executing the mandate entrusted to me, I deemed it necessary to tell Your Most Illustrious and Reverend Excellency all these things, and I ask that you be so kind as to inform me in due time of the outcome of this matter.

....

<Antonino De Luca,
Archbishop of Tarsus and
Apostolic Nuncio in Vienna>

Inde pronum est colligere curam qua S[ancta] Romana Catholica Ecclesia sanctitatem vinculi matrimonialis a jure divino sancitam usque fovet et tuetur; ideoque numquam illud dissolvit, sed tantummodo in specialibus casibus declarat nullum ab initio fuisse vinculum.

Haec omnia, mandatis mihi commissis obsequens, Dominationis Vestrae Ill[ustrissi]mae et R[everendisi]mae communicanda censui, rogans ut de exitu rei me, opportuno tempore, certiorem facere humanissime velit.

....

<Antoninus De Luca
Archiepiscopus Tarsensis
Nuntius Apostolicus
Viennae>

Document No. 41: De Luca to Kött, June 5, 1861 (Follow-up to Document No. 40, De Luca to Kött, February 6, 1861). Latin. Leaf No. 152.

To: His Most Illustrious and Reverend Excellency
Monsignor Christophe Florenz Kött,
Bishop of Fulda
Fulda
Fulda file
No. 2259/1
Vienna, June 5, 1861.
Most Illustrious and Reverend Excellency:

As a means of satisfying the request that was made of me by the Holy Congregation of the Council, on the 7th of last February of this year, I sent off to Your Most Illustrious and Reverend Excellency a letter to inform you of the definitive sentence pertaining to the Wittgenstein-Iwanowska marriage as it was issued by said Holy Congregation.

Having received no answer to my letter up to this moment, I beg Your Most Illustrious and Reverend Excellency to let me know whether this aforesaid sentence of the Holy Congregation has been carried out, and Princess Iwanowska

Ill[ustrissi]mo et R[everendissi]mo Domino

Domino Christophoro Florentio Koett
Episcopo Fuldensi
Fuldam
Fulda
No. 2259/1
Viennae die 5 Junii 1861.
Ill[ustrissi]me et R[everendissi]me Domine.

Officio mihi a S[ancta] C[ongregatione] Concilii demandato faciens satis, Epistolam die 7 praeterlapsi Februarii hujus anni Dominationi Vestrae Ill[ustrissi]mae et R[everendissi]mae dedi, eo ut sententiam definitivam a superius laudata S[ancta] Congr[egation]e de matrimonio Wittgenstein-Iwanowska significarem.

Cum nullum responsum hucusque meae Epistolae acceperim, rogo Dominationem Vestra Ill[ustrissi]mam et R[everendissi]mam ut me certiorem facere benignissime velit an praedicta sententia S[anctae] Congregationis ad effectum

has been granted permission to marry again, if she so wishes.

....

<Mons. Antonino De Luca,
Archbishop of Tarsus and
Apostolic Nuncio in Vienna>

fuerit reducta, et Dominae Principissae Iwanowska facultas rite fuerit facta ad alias nuptias convolandi, si ita illi placuerit.

......

<Antoninus De Luca
Archiepiscopus Tarsensis
Nuntius Apostolicus
Viennae>

Document No. 42: De Luca to Cardinal Antonelli, June 9, 1861. A copy of Doc. No. 40 is enclosed. See also ASV, CC Doc. No. 69. Italian. Leaf No. 153.

To: The most Eminent Secretary of State
<Cardinal Giacomo Antonelli>

RE: Letter to the Holy Congregation of the Council

No. 1291
Vienna, June 9, 1861
Most Reverend Eminence:

As part of the venerable despatch of last January 22, I received the letter from the Holy Congregation of the Council. Without delay, on the following February 6, I communicated its contents to Monsignor the Bishop of Fulda according to the orders I had received. I deem it useful to include herewith a copy of my aforementioned letter in order that the Holy Congregation may know the spirit in which it was written.

Up to this day I have not received an answer from that excellent bishop. However, as soon as I received the recent dispatch of last May 25, No. 17558, I reiterated my request for an acknowledgement from him, which I shall immediately convey to the Holy Congregation.

The long silence observed by Monsignor the Bishop of Fulda made me think that he might have sent the necessary information about the outcome of this delicate matter directly through

All'E[minentissi]mo Seg[reta]rio di Stato
<Card. Giacomo Antonelli>

Lettera alla S[anta] C[ongregazione] del Concilio

N. 1291
Vienna, 9 giugno 1861
Em[inen]za R[everendissi]ma.

In seno al ven[erabil]e Dispaccio de' 22 Gennaro p[rossim]o p[assat]o mi giunse la lettera della S[anta] C[ongregazione] del Concilio. Senza frapporre indugio, il dì 6 del susseguente Febbraro ne comunicai il contenuto a Monsig[nor] Vescovo di Fulda conformemente agli ordini a me dati. Stimo opportuno l'annettere qui entro una Copia della predetta mia lettera acciocché la S[anta] Congregazione possa conoscere in quali sensi sia stata scritta.

Insino a questo giorno non ho ricevuto risposta dall'ottimo Prelato. Epperò, ricevuto ch'ebbi il recente Disp[acci]o de' 25 Maggio p[rossim]o p[assat]o, N[umer]o 17558, reiterai le mie istanze per ottenere un riscontro, il quale sarà immediatamente trasmesso alla S[anta] Congregazione.

Il diuturno silenzio osservato da M[onsi]g[no]r Vescovo di Fulda mi faceva supporre che per la via della Nunziatura Apostolica di Monaco avesse rassegnato diretta-

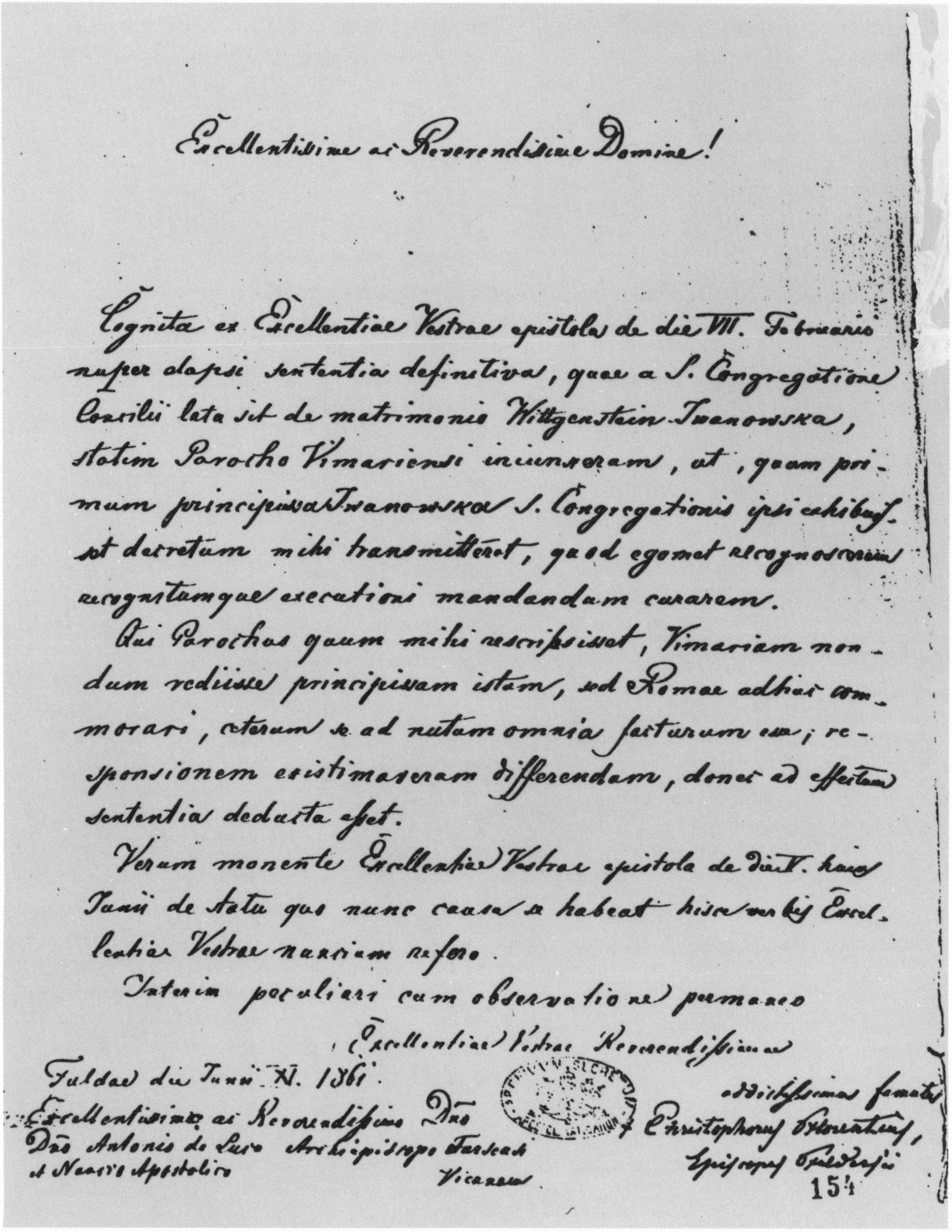

Plate 6. Facsimile of a letter from Bishop Kött to Monsignor De Luca, dated June 11, 1861. "I immediately ordered the Priest in Weimar to send me...the decree of the Holy Congregation..."

the Offices of the Apostolic Nuncio in Munich. I can see now that this supposition was groundless.

<Antonino De Luca,
Archbishop of Tarsus and
Apostolic Nuncio>

_____

To be placed in the file pertaining to the Diocese of Fulda.

mente gli opportuni ragguagli intorno all'esito del delicato affare. Ora vedo che questa supposizione non era fondata.

<Antonino De Luca
Arcivescovo di Tarso
Nunzio Apostolico in Vienna>

_____

Appendice alla Diocesi di Fulda.

Document No. 43: Kött to De Luca, June 11, 1861 (Answers Document No. 40: De Luca to Kött, February 6, 1861 and Document No. 41: De Luca to Kött, June 5, 1861).= Latin. Leaf No. 154.

To: The Most Excellent and Reverend Monsignor
Antonino De Luca,
Archbishop of Tarsus and
Apostolic Nuncio in Vienna
Fulda, June 11, 1861
Most Excellent and Reverend Monsignor!

Having learned from Your Excellency's letter of last February 8 about the definitive sentence issued by the Holy Congregation of the Council on the Wittgenstein-Iwanowska Marriage Case, I immediately ordered the priest in Weimar[15] to send me, as soon as Princess Iwanowska showed it to him, the decree of the Holy Congregation, in order that I could make official verification of it and, having verified its authenticity, I could proceed to its implementation.

When that priest wrote back to me that the Princess in question had not yet returned to Weimar and was even at that time still in Rome, and that, moreover, he would act in everything according to my instructions, I decided to delay my answer until the sentence was carried out.

But, because of Your Excellency's letter of this present June 5, in which you wonder about the present status of the case, I am herewith informing you of what has transpired so far.

In the meantime, with the greatest respect, I remain
Your Most Reverend Excellency's
most devoted servant,
x Christophe Florenz <Kött>,
Bishop of Fulda.

Excellentissimo ac Reverendissimo D[omi]no
D[omi]no Antoni<n>o De Luca
Archiepiscopo Tarsensi
et Nuntio Apostolico
Viennam

Excellentissime ac Reverendissime Domine!

Cognita ex Excellentiae Vestrae Epistola de die VII Februarii nuper elapsi sententia definitiva, quae a S[ancta] congregatione Concilii lata sit de matrimonio Wittgenstein-Iwanowska, statim parocho Vimariensi iniunxeram, ut, quam primum principissa Iwanowska S[anctae] Congregationis ipsi exhibuisset decretum, mihi transmitteret, quod egomet recognoscerem recognitumque executioni mandatum curarem.

Qui Parochus quum mihi rescripsisset Vimariam nondum rediisse principissam istam, sed Romae adhuc commorari, ceterum se ad nutum omnia facturum esse; responsionem existimaveram differendam, donec ad effectum sententia deducta esset.

Verum monente Excellentiae Vestrae epistola de die V hujus Junii de statu quo nunc causa se habeat hisce verbis Excellentiae Vestrae nuntium refero.

Interim peculiari cum observatione permaneo
Excellentiae Vestrae Reverendissimae
addictissimus famulus
x Christophorus Florentius <Koett>,
Episcopus Fuldensis.
Fuldae die Junii XI 1861

_____

[15]The priest in Weimar was Anton Hohmann; see AVR, Doc. No. 4.

Document No. 44: De Luca to Cardinal Antonelli, June 20, 1861 (Follow-up to Document No. 42, De Luca to Cardinal Antonelli, June 9, 1861). A copy of Document No. 43, Kött to De Luca, June 11, 1861 was enclosed (ASV, CC Doc. No. 71), together with a note for Quaglia (ASV, CC Doc. No. 70) not included in this file. Italian. Leaf No. 159.

To: The Most Eminent Secretary of State
<Cardinal Giacomo Antonelli>

———————

Re: Wittgenstein-Iwanowska Marriage Case
No. 1304
Vienna, June 20, 1861
Most Reverend Eminence:

With reference to those matters I had the honor of presenting to Your Most Reverend Eminence in my Memo <No. 1291>,[16] I enclose herewith my answer to Monsignor the Secretary of the Holy Congregation of the Council. It bears a removable seal in order that Your Most Reverend Eminence may peruse its contents.

The answer to my letter of February 7, 1861, to Monsignor the Bishop of Fulda has finally come a little while ago. I am enclosing a copy of it and, as Your Most Reverend Eminence will be able to ascertain for himself upon reading it, it is penned in very dry terms. This is additional evidence from which I can surmise the unpleasant impression produced by the definitive sentence issued by the Holy Congregation of the Council on the aforementioned Bishop and the Catholics in that Diocese.

The annulment of a marriage that lasted many years and was validated by the birth of a child who was the result of it must naturally come as a painful surprise to the Catholics of Central Germany who live in the midst of a Protestant population. I did not omit communicating to the Bishop of Fulda all the arguments presented by Monsignor the Secretary of the Holy Congregation of the Council, and I asked him to use the most diligent care and the greatest caution in implementing the above mentioned sentence and in granting Princess Iwanowska leave to enter a second marriage. I would hope that the feared scandal will be avoided.

All'E[minentissi]mo Seg[reta]rio di Stato
Card. Giacomo Antonelli

———————

Causa Matrimoniale Wittgenstein-Iwanowska
N. 1304
Vienna, 20 Giugno 1861
Em[inen]za R[everendissi]ma.

A tenor di ciò ch'ebbi l'onore di rassegnare all'Em[inen]za V[ost]ra R[everendissi]ma nel mio foglio N[umer]o <1291> compiego qui entro la mia risposta a Mons[i]g[no]r Segretario della S[anta] C[ongregazione] del Concilio. Essa è a sigillo volante, affinché l'Em[inen]za V[ost]ra R[everendissi]ma possa prenderne notizia.

La risposta colla quale finalmente M[onsi]g[no]r Vescovo di Fulda ha, non ha guari, riscontrato la mia lettera de' 7 febbraio 1861, e ch'è qui annessa in copia, è dettata in termini assai secchi, siccome l'Em[inen]za V[ost]ra R[everendissi]ma potrà convincersene dalla lettura di essa. Questo è un nuovo indizio da cui argomento la sinistra impressione prodotta su l'animo del sullodato vescovo e de'Cattolici di quella Diocesi dalla definitiva sentenza della S[anta] C[ongregazione] del Concilio.

Lo scioglimento di un matrimonio durato per molti anni e confermato da prole che n'è stata il frutto, deve naturalmente eccitare dolorosa ammirazione presso i cattolici della Germania centrale che vivono frammisti a' Protestanti. Non lasciai di comunicare al Vescovo di Fulda tutte le ragioni addotte da Mons[i]g[nor] Segretario della S[anta] C[ongregazione] del Concilio, e lo pregai di porre diligentissima cura e la maggior cautela possibile nell'eseguire la sentenza di cui è parola e nel dar licenza alla Principessa Iwanowska di passare a seconde nozze. Voglio sperare che si abbiano ad evitare i temuti scandali.

———————

[16]The protocol number, evident from Doc. No. 42, is left out in De Luca's draft.

....

\<Antonino De Luca,
Archbishop of Tarsus and
Apostolic Nuncio in Vienna\>

_____

To be placed in the file pertaining to the
   Diocese of Fulda.

....

\<Antonino De Luca
Arcivescovo di Tarso
Nunzio Apostolico in Vienna\>

_____

Appendice alla Diocesi di Fulda.

Plate 7. Franz Liszt, circa 1864. A photograph taken shortly before he received the tonsure.

CONGREGAZIONE DEL CONCILIO

Archivio Segreto. Z60: Zitomir

CAUSA MATRIMONII: WITTGENSTEIN—IWANOWSKA
(ZYTOMIRIEN)

––––––––––––––––––––––––

The secret file of the Holy Congregation of the Tridentine
Council, pertaining to the marriage annulment of Princess
Carolyne von Sayn-Wittgenstein (1859–61). Shelf mark Z60,
diocese of Zhitomir in Ukraine.

**Document No. 1. August 2, 1859. Letter from Monsignor Hohenlohe to
Monsignor Quaglia: Okraszewski's appeal to reopen Carolyne's case.
Carolyne's Latin Petition (Doc. No. 2) and Okraszewski's power of attorney
(Doc. No. 3) are enclosed. Italian (2 pages).**

To: Monsignor <Angelo> Quaglia
Secretary of the Holy Congregation
of the Council, etc. etc.
Vatican, August 2, 1859
Most Venerable Monsignor:

I warmly recommend to Your Most Reverend Excellency the bearer of the present letter, Baron Okraszewski,[1] who has already brought to the Holy Father some papers pertaining to the divorce case of Princess Carolyne Iwanowska. The latter was compelled against her will to marry Prince Nicholas von Sayn-Wittgenstein from Russia. I have presented to the Holy Father the enclosed petition in Latin, and he has ordered me to forward it to You, my dear Monsignor, in order that the question be taken up according to the order of the papers His Holiness has already given you and those that the aforementioned Baron is about to bring to You, Most Reverend Excellency; these contain an abstract of the arguments as well as the sentences issued by the Consistories of Mohilow and Luck-Zhitomir.

As for the irregularities that transpired at the Mohilow trial, and about Monsignor Laski's opinion on this case, Baron Okraszewski will be better able to explain these things in person. I hope, therefore, that you will be so gracious as to listen to him. Moreover, you would do me truly a great favor if, as I think, it were possible to hasten the completion of the report for the Holy Father in order that the question be solved as quickly as possible. Baron Okraszewski is here awaiting a decision and does not have much time at his disposal, for he must return to his country and attend to some other business of his own.

I am enclosing a document, written by Princess Carolyne, in which she confers power of attorney on the aforesaid Baron.

Counting on your well known graciousness, I hope you will forgive the trouble I'm causing

Mo[nsi]g[no]r <Angelo> Quaglia,
Segret[ari]o della S[anta] Cong[regazione]
del Concilio, etc. etc.
Vaticano, 2 agosto 1859
Monsignore Veneratissimo.

Rac<c>omando caldamente a V[ostra] E[ccellenza] R[e]v[erendissi]ma il latore della presente, Barone Okraszewski, il quale già ha presentato al Santo Padre delle carte riguardanti la causa del divorzio della Principessa Carolina Iwanowska, la quale dovette sposare per violenza il principe Nicolò di Sayn-Wittgenstein di Russia. Ora io ho presentato al S[anto] Padre l'acclusa istanza in lingua latina, ed il S[anto] Padre mi ha ordinato di inviarla a Lei, Monsignore Carissimo, affinchè si potesse risolvere la domanda in sequela delle carte che Sua Santità già Le ha dato, e delle carte che il suddetto Barone presenterà a V[ostra] E[ccellenza] R[everendissima], carte che sono il ristretto del processo fatto in Russia e che contengono le sentenze motivate dal Concistoro di Mohilow e Lutz-Sitomir (sic).

Sulle mancanze fatte nel processo fatto prima in Mohilow, sull'opinione di M[on]s[i]gn[or] Laski sulla causa suddetta, il Barone Okraszewski Le spiegherà a voce meglio, perciò farà grazia di sentirlo. Più mi pare che se si potesse affrettare la relazione al Santo Padre affinchè si potesse presto sbrigare, sarebbe un vero piacere che mi far(r)ebbe. Il Barone Okraszewski si trova qui aspettando qualche risoluzione e non ha molto tempo a sua disposizione, avendo degli affari suoi nella patria sua a sbrigare.

Le accludo uno scritto della Principessa Carolina nel quale espone l'incarico ch'ella ha dato al sudd[ett]o Barone.

Perdoni colla nota Sua gentilezza l'incomodo che Le do, ma, trattandosi d'un affare interes-

---

[1]The literature has hitherto remained silent about Władislaw Okraszewski's title, although his role as Carolyne's colorful attorney has long been known. According to

the Vatican documents and to his visiting card (Doc. No. 4), Okraszewski lay claim to an aristocratic title that may have gone back to the year 1401, during the period of the union between Poland and Lithuania.

you. It was only because the question is of such importance and does not allow for delays that I was so bold as to inconvenience you. I wish to express to you my great respect and consideration and I confirm myself again

Your Most Reverend Excellency's
most devoted, obliging and affectionate servant,

Gustav von Hohenlohe,
Archbishop of Edessa.

sante e che non permette dilazione, mi sono permesso di incomodarLa e, con alta considerazione e stima, mi ripeto di

Vostra Eccellenza R[e]v[erendissi[ma]
d[e]v[otissi]mo, ob<b>l[igatissi]mo, aff[ezionatissi]mo servo,
Gustavo d'Hohenlohe,
Arciv[escov]o d'Edessa.[2]

Document No. 2. Undated, but August 1859. Carolyne's Petition to Pope Pius IX (Prot. No. 2390). Latin (2 pages).

Erased Note at the top: The decree of August 8, 1859, was issued on the basis of this.
Prot. No. 2390
Copy No. 2.
Most Blessed Father:

Carolyne Iwanowska, a Catholic from the Diocese of Luck-Zhitomir in Russia, prostrated at the feet of Your Holiness, humbly presents the following case. Under compulsion from her own father through intimidation and the gravest threats, she was joined in marriage to Prince Nicholas Wittgenstein, a follower of the pseudo-reformed religion. However, upon the death of her father who had continued to threaten her even after the marriage, she presented to her own Ordinary Office a petition for the annulment of her marriage on account of it being contracted through most grave threats and intimidation.

The case was brought up for judgement but, because the witnesses introduced by the Petitioner lacked the requisites prescribed by law, given that the records do not clearly state that they satisfied the precepts of the Church as to their being of good character etc., the Consistory of that Diocese, on October 26, 1851, resolved, therefore, that the marriage was to be deemed valid.

Having appealed against that decision, the Petitioner obtained that the case be taken up again by the Consistory of the Metropolitan Curia for the whole Russian Empire. The latter provided her with a sentence of annulment of her marriage by reason of it being contracted

{Sub hoc expeditum fuit decretum diei 8 Augusti 1859.}
2390
<Copia> No. 2.
Beatissime Pater.

Karolina Iwanowska Catholica Dioecesis Luk-Zitomir in Russia, ad Pedes Sanctitatis Vestrae provoluta, humiliter exponit quae sequuntur. Metu et minis gravissimis a proprio genitore adacta usque ad aram, matrimonio copulata fuit cum Principe viro Nicolao Wittgenstein pseudo-reformatae religionis addicto. Verum patre vita defuncto, qui etiam post matrimonium minas prosequebatur, Oratrix supplicem dedit libellum proprio Ordinario pro declaratione nullitatis praedicti matrimonii per vim et minas gravissimas contracti.

Caussa inde ad tramites juris confecta est; verum quia testes examinati ex parte Oratricis carebant requisitis a lege, cum ex actis non apparent an praeceptis Ecclesiae satisfecissent, an bonis essent praedicti moribus, etc., ideo a concistorio praedictae Dioecesis sub die 26 Octobris 1851 declaratum fuit Matrimonium pro valido habendum esse.

Itaque factum est ut, per Oratricem instaurata Petitione, iterum proponeretur caussa coram Concistorio Metropolitanae Curiae totius Imperii Russiae; a quo sententiam nullitatis praefati matrimonii veluti ex vi et gravi metu contracti obtinuit. Verum a Vicario Generali de-

[2]Hohenlohe writes fluent but ungrammatical Italian; aside from minor mispellings, his syntax and word order are often awkward.

through violence and grave intimidation. The sentence was not endorsed, however, by the Vicar General of the late Metropolitan, and this was so for the very same reasons stated above, namely, as he wrote himself, that not all the formalities required by the law with regard to the witnesses being examined had been adhered to. As a consequence of this, the case has remained unresolved for many years, thanks to the tricks and deceitful advice of some solicitor.

However, given that, two years ago, Prince Nicholas Wittgenstein contracted a new marriage within the Lutheran faith and, consequently, the situation of the Petitioner having become that much worse, she went to the present Archbishop of Mohilow and requested a definitive sentence of annulment of her marriage to Nicholas Wittgenstein, insofar as it was contracted through violence. She was told by that same Archbishop that her case was presently at the same stage as described above, and that he was not in a position to do anything more about it unless specifically delegated to do so by the Holy Apostolic See. All this clearly transpires from the enclosed information provided by the Archbishop himself.

Having faithfully expounded on these matters, Your most humble Petitioner eagerly entreats Your Holiness to grant the Metropolitan of Mohilow the necessary faculty to take up again the above described case for the annulment of her marriage until a definitive sentence can be provided. That etc.

functi Metropolitani Sententia confirmata non fuit, itaque iisdem de caussis, ut ipsemet scripto tradidit, quia nempe non omnes formalitates a jure requisitae circa testes examinatos impletae fuerint. Sicque ad plures annos, dolo et illusoriis verbis cujusdam procuratoris, caussa insoluta jacit.

Attamen cum duobus ab hinc annis Priceps Nicolaus Wittgenstein ad alias nuptias convolaverit in Lutheranorum Secta et conditio Oratricis eo infelicior evaserit, ideo modernum Archiepiscopum Mohilowiensem adivit pro impetranda absoluta sententia nullitatis praedicti matrimonii ab ipsa cum Nicolao Wittgenstein per vim contracti; ast ab eodem Archiepiscopo edocta fuit presenten suam caussam in supra enunciato statu adhuc jacere; nec posse ab ipso amplius pertractari nisi it<a> a Sancta Sede Apostolica specialiter demandatum fuerit. Haec omnia ex adnexa ejusdem Archiepiscopi informatione liquido apparent.

Hisce igitur fideliter exaratis, enixe postulat humillima Oratrix ut a Sanctitate Vestra tribuatur opportuna facultas Metropolitano Mohilowiensi caussam super praetensa contracti matrimonii nullitate iterum pertractandi usque ad sententiam inclusivam.
Quod <de gratia>, etc.

Document No. 3. Undated. Memorandum. Okraszewski's power of attorney in Carolyne's case. French (1 page) August 1859.

Brief

Monsieur Okraszewski, in his capacity as Princess Carolyne Wittgenstein's solicitor, will present a petition to the Committee on Applications requesting, on the basis of the position taken by the Metropolitan of Russia and expressed to him in a communication dated June 13 (O.S.) /June 25 (N.S.), 1859, that the Roman Court enjoin this same Metropolitan to review the divorce case of the Princess, who protests against the acts of negligence and the irregularities that transpired, without her knowledge, at the proceedings. The Roman Court can either

Résumé

M[onsieu]r Okraszewski présentera comme chargé de pouvoir de la Princesse Carolyne Wittgenstein une pétition à la commission des requêtes à Rome demandant, en vertu de la résolution du Métropolitain de Russie qui lui a été adressée à la date du 13/25 juin 1859, que la cour de Rome enjoigne à ce même Métropolitain de faire réviser le divorce de la Princesse, qui proteste contre les négligences et irrégularités survenues dans la procédure à son insu. La cour de Rome peut: soit demander l'expédition de tous les actes de cette procédure afin de se

request that the records of the case be sent to them in order to convince themselves of the necessity of reopening the case or, trusting in the opinion of the Metropolitan who points out these facts in his communication, it can simply send him, through normal channels, an injunction to this effect. The latter course would have the advantage of saving time as well. Monsieur Okraszewski cannot leave Rome before this injunction is forwarded to Russia.

———

Minsk (written on the verso)

convaincre par elle-même de la nécessité de cette révision, soit, confiante dans l'opinion du Métropolitain qui les signale dans sa résolution, envoyer simplement cette injonction par la voie habituelle, ce qui serait un bienfait comme gain de temps. M[onsieu]r Okraszewski ne pouvant quitter Rome, avant que cette injonction soit expédiée pour la Russie.

———

Minsk

Document No. 4. Okraszewski's visiting card, probably attached to the above. It bears his full name, Władislaw Obminski Okraszewski; above the name there is a round shield divided into four quarters with another small shield in the center. It is surmounted by a crest with a crown. Around the edges of the shield it is possible to read: "Unia Litwyz Polska ... 1401" ("Polish Lithuanian Union ... 1401"). Poland and Lithuania were united at this time, and the card implies that Okraszewski was of aristocratic descent.

Document No. 5. June 13, 1859. Letter. Archbishop Żyliński's to Władislaw Okraszewski (Prot. No. 1146, also 766). Russian (3 pages). Enclosed with Doc. No. 3.

Document No. 6. June 13, 1859. Legal translation of the above approved by the Russian Government (Prot. No. 1146, erased 766). French (3 pages).

Prot. No. 766 (erased in the French translation)
Prot. No. 1146
<Copy> No. 1 (in French Translation only)
Stamp of the Diocese of Mohilow
Translation

From: The Diocesan Archbishop of Mohilow, Metropolitan of all the Roman Catholic Churches of the Empire.

To: Monsieur Władislaw Okraszewski, land-owner and attorney for Princess Carolyne Wittgenstein, born Iwanowska.

St. Petersburg, June 13, 1859.

In your petition, dated the current June 10,<1859>, you state that the Consistory of Luck-Zhitomir, in adjudicating the divorce case pertaining to Princess Carolyne and Prince Nicholas Wittgenstein, declared, in its resolution of

No. 766 (erased)
No. 1146
<Copia> Num. 1
TIMBRE
Traduction.

De l'Archevêque diocésain de Mohilew, Métropolitain de toutes les églises Catholiques Romaines de l'Empire.

A Monsieur le propriétaire Wladislas Okraszewski chargé des pouvoirs de la Princesse Carolyne Wittgenstein née Iwanowska.
St. Petersbourg, 13 juin 1859.

Vous dites dans votre pétition du 10 juin courant que le Consistoire de Luck-Zytomir en jugeant l'affaire de divorce entre la Princesse Carolyne et le Prince Nicolas Wittgenstein, a déclaré dans sa résolution du 26 octobre 1851,

October 26, 1851, that the evidence presented in favor of Princess Carolyne Wittgenstein's petition was deemed unsatisfactory because, during the inquest, there had been negligence in providing indications as to the moral conduct of the witnesses, the parishes to which they belonged, the manner in which they fulfilled their religious duties, and that, for these reasons, basing their position on Canon Law, that Consistory declared this marriage good and valid.

You state moreover that, thereafter, this case was brought, in the second instance, before the Consistory of Mohilow; they, on September 19, 1852, after considering all the relative circumstances, on the basis of the articles of Canon Law applicable in these cases, decreed this marriage null and void; but, at the moment of signing the act, Prelate Laski, expressing his own individual opinion, stated that, since the witnesses had been called to take their oath and give their deposition without all the necessary formalities being satisfied; moreover, since there had been evidence of other improprieties in the course of the hearings, he concurred with the judgement of the Consistory of Luck-Zhitomir. The opinion given by the Prelate Laski was confirmed by the late Metropolitan Holowinski.

Moreover, since the cause of all this was the fact that, at the hearing, the case had been irregularly and negligently handled by the attorneys, you are, therefore, setting for yourself the task of proving the truth of the aforementioned depositions by presenting convincing facts and documents, and you ask me to state the conditions under which the Consistory of Mohilow would review and adjudicate anew this case. You add also that Prince Nicholas Wittgenstein, Princess Carolyne Wittgenstein's husband, married again over two years ago.[3]

In answer to these questions, I wish to inform you that, as in Princess Carolyne's divorce case there have been already two decisions confirmed by my predecessor, the late Metropolitan Holowinski, the one of October 26, 1851, issued by the Consistory of Luck-Zhitomir, and the other of September 19, 1852, issued by the Consistory of Mohilow, I cannot presume to have the right to order a review of this case because of the existing laws on this subject, namely 1) the arti-

que les témoignages présentés en faveur de la demande de la Princesse Carolyne Wittgenstein étaient insuffisants, parce que dans l'enquête on a négligé de donner des indications sur la conduite des témoins, sur les paroisses auxquelles ils appartiennent, sur la manière dont ils remplissent leurs devoirs religieux, et que pour ces causes, se fondant sur des lois canoniques, le dit Consistoire a déclaré ce mariage pour bon et valable; qu'après cela cette affaire passa en seconde instance au Consistoire de Mohilew qui le 19 septembre 1852 considérant toutes les circonstances y relatives, et en vertu des articles du droit canon applicables à ce cas, décréta ce mariage pour nul; mais qu'à la signature de cet acte, le Prélat Laski, exprimant son opinion particulière, dit que les témoins ayant été appelés à prêter serment et à déposer sans avoir accompli toutes les formalités voulues, et qu'ayant trouvé d'autres manques de forme dans l'audition qui en a été faite, ils se ralliait à l'opinion du Consistoire de Luck-Zytomir; laquelle opinion du dit Prélat Laski fut confirmée par feu le Métropolitain Holowinski; qu'en conséquence comme il ressort de tous ces faits que cette affaire a été conduite durant l'enquête sans régularité, et avec négligence de la part des chargés de pouvoir, vous vous engagez à prouver la vérité des témoignages invoqués, par des faits et des documents convaincants, et vous demandez mes ordres pour que cette affaire soit révisée et jugée de nouveau par le Consistoire de Mohilew. Vous ajoutez encore que le Prince Nicolas Wittgenstein, mari de la Princesse Carolyne Wittgenstein dont vous êtes le fondé de pouvoir, a depuis deux ans contracté un nouveau mariage.

En réponse à quoi je vous fais savoir que comme dans l'affaire du divorce de la Princesse Carolyne Wittgenstein, il y a eu déja deux décisions confirmées par l'Evêque mon prédécesseur, feu le Métropolitain Holowinski, l'une du 26 octobre 1851 du Consistoire de Luck-Zytomir, et l'autre du 19 septembre 1852 du Consistoire de Mohilew, je ne me considère pas en droit d'ordonner la révision de cette affaire, à cause des lois existantes à ce sujet, et nommé-

[3]Actually in January 1856.

cles of the Concordate stipulated in 1847 between His Majesty the Emperor of all Russias and His Holiness the Pope, and 2) article 60, Tome 11, of the Russian Legal Code (as issued in 1857).
Signed by the Metropolitan, <Wenceslas> Żyliński

Prot. No. 1237

The Department of Ecclesiastic Affairs and Foreign Cults of the Minister for Internal Affairs certifies the above signature as being that of the Archbishop of Mohilow, Metropolitan of all the Roman Catholic Churches of Russia, Wenceslas Żyliński. June 16, 1859.
Signed by Count Sievres(?), Director.
A. Ivanoff, Section Head

Prot. No. 131

I testify to the authenticity of the signature of the Director of the Department of Ecclesiastic Affairs and Foreign Cults of the Ministry for Internal Affairs, as well as to the correctness of the present French translation.
Weimar, July 3/15 1859
Chargé d'affaires
Baron von Maltitz.
Official Stamps

ment 1° articles du Concordat conclu en 1847 entre Sa Majesté l'Empereur de toutes les Russies et Sa Sainteté le Pape, et 2° de l'article 60, du Tome XI du Code des Lois de la Russie (Edition de 1857).
(Signé) Métropolitain Żyliński

No. 1237
16 juin 1859

Le Département des Affaires ecclésiastiques et Cultes étrangers du Ministère de l'Intérieur atteste la signature ci-dessus de l'Archevêque de Mohilew, Métropolitain de toutes les Eglises Catholiques Romaines de Russie, Wenceslas Żyliński.
(Signé) le Directeur Comte Sièvres.
Chef de Section A. Iwanoff.

N. 31. J'atteste l'authenticité de la signature et du cachet du Département des Affaires ecclésiastiques et des Cultes etrangers du Ministère de l'Intérieur ainsi que l'authenticité de la présente traduction française.
Weimar, ce 3/15 juillet 1859
Le Chargé d'Affaires,
Baron de Maltitz.
Official Stamps

Document No. 7. July 4, 1859. Authentic Copy of the 1852 Mohilow sentence, notarised by the Russian Government, consisting of the majority resolution of the Consistory, the minority opinion of Vicar General Laski, and the formal approval of the latter by Archbishop Holowinski (Prot. No. 11020). Russian (38 pages).

Document No. 8. July 14, 1859. Legal translation of the above done by Okraszewski, with Russian Government approval. French (34 pages).

By order of His Imperial Majesty[4] and according to a resolution passed on November 25, 1852, on a petition by Ivan Gonzaga Pawlichinski, son of Lawrence, State Councillor and solici-

D'après l'ordre de S[a]. M[ajesté] Impériale et d'après une résolution du 25 nov[embre] 1852, sur la requête du chargé de pouvoir de la Princesse Caroline fille de Pierre Wittgenstein,

---

[4]As a citizen of Ukraine, Carolyne was subject to the laws of Russia. Ever since the Concordate of 1847 between Rome and St. Petersburg, all matters pertaining to divorce and the annulment of marriages had to be channelled through the Russian government for final approval by the Tsar. In fact, Roman Catholic clerics were forbidden to communicate

directly with the Holy See on such matters. As an illustration of the bureaucratic jungle in which these cases could become entangled, see ASV, CC, Doc. No. 59, Enclosure No. 3. This protocol caused many delays in the handling of Carolyne's own case.

tor for Princess Carolyne Wittgenstein, daughter of Peter Iwanowsky, the enclosed copy of the decision on the divorce case pertaining to Prince and Princess Wittgenstein, issued by the Consistory of Mohilow on September 19 of the present year and bearing the binding string and seal of the Roman Catholic Archbishop of Mohilow, is hereby released <in an attached appendix of 20 pages> on December 24, 1852, together with a copy of Monsignor Laski's personal position as confirmed by Monsignor Ignaz Holowinski, Archbishop of Mohilow and Metropolitan of all the Roman Catholic Churches of Russia.
The original is signed <in Mohilow on the
    Dnieper> by
Prelate Wrublewski, Assessor
Monsieur Jaroszewicz, Secretary
and Monsieur Romanowicz, Department Head
Place of Seal

Jean fils de Laurent Gonzal Paulichinski (Statskosovietnika), cette copie, ecrit<e> sur le revers de ceci et d'après la ficelle et le sceau de l'Archevêque de Mohiloff Romain Catholique, de la résolution du dit Consistoire donnée le 19 sept[embre] de cet<te> année comme celle de l'opinion particulière du Prélat et Ch. Laski et confirmée par Monseigneur <l'> Archevêque de Mohilow et Métropolitain de toutes les Eglises Catholiques en Russie Chev[alier] Ignace Holowinski, sur l'affaire de divorce des Princes Wittgensteyn ceci est donné le 24 dec[embre] 1852.
L'original est souscrit

Assesseur Prélat Wrublewski
Secrétaire Jarozewicz
Chef de Division Romanowicz
Loco Sigilli

The Sentence of the Consistory of Mohilow.

September 19, 1852. By order of His Imperial Majesty, the Roman Catholic Consistory of Mohilow held a hearing on the following case.

Monsignor Ignaz Holowinski, Archbishop of Mohilow and Metropolitan of all the Roman Catholic Churches in Russia, with a decree issued on May 30 of the past[5] year, Prot. No. 1737, has communicated the decision of the Roman Catholic Consistory of Luck-Zhitomir on the divorce case of Princess Carolyne born Iwanowska and Prince Nicholas, son of Peter Wittgenstein, which was forwarded for His Excellency's decision in the second instance according to the resolution of the Roman Catholic College issued on May 28 of the past[6] year and on the basis of article 14, paragraph 2, letter D of the Concordate of July 22/August 3, 1847. He condescended to order the aforementioned Consistory to examine this case with great attention and to prepare an opinion in accordance with Canon law to be presented to him for his final decision. In proceeding to execute this order, the Consistory of Mohilow, before deliberating on

L'année 1852, le 19 septembre. Sur l'ordre de Sa Majesté Impériale le Consistoire Romain Catholique de Mohilow a écouté:

Mons[eigneur] l'Archevêque de Mohilow Métropolitain de toutes les Eglises Romaines Catholiques en Russie Chev[alier] Ignace Holowinski, avec un ordre du 30 mai cét<te> année, N° 1737, a communiqué la résolution du Consistoire Romain Catholique de Luck-Zytomir sur l'affaire de divorce des Princes Caroline née Iwanowska et Nicolas, fils de Pierre Wittgensteyn, remise à la décision de Monseigneur par la résolution du Collège Catholique Rom[ain] le 28 du mois de mai cet<te> année, comme en seconde instance, et se fondant sur le paragraphe 14, p. 2 lett. D du Concordat du 22 juillet 1847 il a daigné ordonner au dit Consistoire de considérer cette affaire avec une attention toute minutieuse et d'après les lois de l'Eglise constituer son opinion lui sera présentée pour dernière décision. En exécution de quoi le Consistoire de Mohilow, avant de délibérer sur l'affaire l'a envoyée, avec un ordre du 30 juin cet<te> année,

---

[5]The French text erroneously says "this year." Okraszewski's French translation from the Russian contains a large number of mistakes. Wrong words have been corrected, the punctuation adjusted, implausible word order and occasionally been fixed, but we have left his syntax alone. The text has been

checked against the Russian original and occasional mistakes in the transcription of Latin quotations have been corrected. Moreover, phrases omitted in the French translation have been restored in the English translation.
[6]See note 5.

the case, with an injunction dated June 30 of the past year, Prot. No. 4211,[7] submitted it to the opinion of the Defender <of the marriage Bond>, the Reverend Owsiany, Deacon and Professor at the Gymnasium of Mohilow. He responded on July 5,[8] stating in his report to the Consistory that, having carefully examined all the circumstances in the cases and the arguments presented by Princess Wittgenstein in order to obtain the annulment of her marriage to her husband, Nicholas Wittgenstein, he found them as having no value, while the proofs presented by the Defender, the Reverend Ludkiewicz, in favor of the validity of the marriage were, in his opinion, so substantial and strong that he saw no need to corroborate them or to produce additional ones. It was possible, therefore, to rely completely on the opinion issued by the Roman Catholic Consistory of Luck-Zhitomir. Shortly after, the presiding judge, in a note dated August 28, Prot. No. 225, let it be known that the Chairman of the Department for Ecclesiastical Affairs, Count Tolstoy, in virtue of an order of the Associate Minister of the Interior contained in a note dated on the 20th of the same month, had sent him a memorandum from the State Councillor and solicitor of Princess Carolyne Wittgenstein born Iwanowska, requesting his cooperation in seeing that the case be promptly reviewed as the laws demand. This was the reason why the presiding judge, in releasing a copy of this memorandum, asked the Consistory to submit their decision to him in order that it receive prompt legal validation.

The aforementioned memorandum from Monsieur Pawlichinski, the solicitor of the Princess, is reproduced here in outline:

"The Roman Catholic religion regards marriage as a sacrament and considers, therefore, divorce as an impossibility; there are instances, however, where the Church, in accordance with principles in Canon Law, considers marriage as not having taken place and as being invalid. We must count as belonging to this category marriages contracted through violence, that is to say, marriages contracted because of formal constraints imposed on one of the two parties, the constraint being either moral or physical. Under such circumstances, neither the

N° 424, pour être décidée, au défenseur Professeur du Gymnase de Mohilow Diacre Owsiany, qui l'a renvoyée le 5 juin avec un rapport par lequel il fait savoir au Consistoire que lui, en faisant attention avec toute ponctualité aux circonstances de l'affaire et causes présentées par la Princesse Wittgenstein pour obtenir son divorce avec son mari Nicolas Wittgenstein, il trouve comme n'ayant de valeur, et les preuves citées par le défenseur prêtre Lutkiewicz pour légaliser le mariage, sont selon son opinion si valables et fortes qu'il ne voit aucun besoin de les renforcer, ou en produire des nouvelles, ainsi donc il serait relié complètement à l'opinion émise par le Consistoire Romain Catholique de Luck-Zytomir. Après quoi Monsieur le Président, par une transmission du 28 août, N° 225, écrit que Monsieur l'Intendant du Département des affaires ecclésiastiques Comte Tolstoi sur l'ordre de Mons. l'Associé du Ministre des affaires intérieures, par une transmission du 20, a envoyé à Monseigneur un mémoire du chargé de pouvoir (Statskosovietikna) de la Princesse Caroline Wittgenstein née Iwanowska avec demande de sa coopération pour obtenir la prompte prise en considération de la dite affaire d'après les lois. C'est pourquoi M[onsieu]r le Président en donnant copie du dit mémoire prie le Consistoire de faire la décision dépendant de lui pour être référée de suite à la Conférence légale.

Le dit mémoire du Chargé de pouvoir de la Princesse, Pawlichinski, se résume ce qui suit.

"La religion Romaine Catholique en regardant le mariage comme Sacrement considère le divorce comme impossible, mais il y a des cas où l'Eglise se fondant sur les lois canones considère le mariage comme invalide et non avenu. C'est à cette catégorie que l'on doit reporter les mariages contractés de violence, c'est à dire d'après contrainte formelle d'une des parties, d'une manière morale ou bien physique, et, dans ces circonstances citées, ni une longue vie matrimoniale, ni les enfants procréés pendant ce temps ne légalisent un tel mariage (Rein[ffestuel], Lib

---

[7]The French text has No. 424, which is wrong.

[8]The French text has June instead of July.

length of the matrimonial relationship, nor the procreation of children in the course of it can render the marriage legal (Reinffestuel., *Decret.*, Book 1, section 1 par. 3, No. 44; Resp., *Rota Romana*: Decis. 405, par. 9 and 13, part. 18 T. 1; *Begnudes Bassa*, T. 3, p. 87, No. 38; Schmatz Grueber, *loco citato*, No. 393. Barbarossa, voto 1, No. 26, Vol. 21, No. 22, Voto 17, No. 19). On this basis, Princess Carolyne Wittgenstein, upon the death of her father, the landowner Peter Iwanowsky, appealed to the aforementioned Church Consistory to have her marriage to Prince Nicholas Wittgenstein annulled. At the inquiry, on the strength of depositions given <by witnesses> under oath, it was shown that:

1. The Petitioner's parents, being divorced,[9] lived separately, the father in one place, the mother and the daughter in another.

2. Prince Wittgenstein, having twice asked for the hand of Mlle. Iwanowska and being twice denied it, sought to influence her father, an extremely proud man who would not at all countenance any opposition to his will. The latter, considering an alliance with the Wittgenstein family as a personal honor, asked the mother to send their daughter to his place. There, through persuasion, threats and even physical violence, he forced her to marry Prince Wittgenstein whom she could not possibly love since, at that time, she was in love with another man.

3. She always complained to her mother, as well as to people close to her, about the unhappiness awaiting her and, both before and after the marriage, she would break into tears and avoid any contact with her husband.

4. Her father, seeing that his daughter's revulsion for her husband had not diminished with the passing of time, would often say to those who were close to him that he regretted having forced his daughter into a marriage against her will; he had done so in the hope that she would eventually acquiesce to her situation. During the inquest into this divorce case, the petitioner's mother confirmed that the marriage had been contracted because of the force employed on the part of the father and

1, Decret. 1, 3 N.44 Resp. 1 Rota Romana *Decis.* 405, 9 et 13 part. 18 I. 1 Begnudes Bassa I. 3 p. 87 N. 38; Schmatzgrueber loco citato N. 393. Barbarossa voto 1, N. 26, Vol. 21 No. 22 Voto 17 N. 19). Se fondant sur cela la Princesse Caroline Wittgensteyn après la mort de son père propriétaire Pierre Iwanowski eut recours au dit Consistoire Ecclésiastique pour annuler son mariage avec le Major Prince Nicolas Wittgenstein. D'après l'enquête consolidée par des témoins qui ont prêté serment, c'est demontré

1° que les parents de la pétitionnaire étant divorcés vivaient séparément, le père dans une terre, la mère et la fille dans une autre;

2° Que le Prince Nicolas Wittgenstein en demandant la main de la Demoiselle Iwanowska le lui a proposè deux fois, mais ayant été rejeté, il a cherché à influencer son père (homme d'un caractère estrêmement hautain et ne souffrant nul obstacle) qui le regardant comme lui faisant (d')honneur l'alliance de la Famille Wittgenstein demanda à la mère d'envoyer la fille chez lui, et là par les influences morales, par des menaces, et même par des tourments physiques il la força d'épouser le Prince Wittgenstein qu'elle ne pouvait pas aimer, car à cet<te> époque elle aimait un autre.

3° Qu'elle se plaignait toujours si bien à sa mère qu'à tous ceux qui venaient la voir du sort malheureuse qui l'attendait, et que tant avant qu'après le mariage elle fondait en larmes toujours évitant le commerce de son mari.

4° Que son père en voyant que l'éloignement de sa fille contre son mari ne diminuait pas avec le temps, énoncait très souvent à ses proches son repentir d'avoir forcé sa fille à ce mariage contre sa volonté, faite en <l'> espoir qu'elle s'accoutumerait enfin à sa position. Pendent l'enquête de cet<te> affaire de divorce la mère de la pétitionnaire en confirmant que le mariage avait été conclu de force par le père a dit aussí "qu'elle-même ne voulant pas être

---

[9]Carolyne's parents were not divorced but separated.

said, moreover, that, "being herself unwilling to be a witness to her daughter's unhappiness, she had refused to be present at the wedding." Without questioning this testimony, Prince Nicholas Wittgenstein himself said that "his marriage had truly been an unhappy one." Before the case came to a conclusion, the great number of divorces being granted at the time attracted the attention of the government, which found it necessary to point it out to the Primate of the Roman Catholic Church in Russia. Although this action was undertaken merely for the purpose of attracting greater attention to divorce proceedings without any intention of infringing on the Canon laws that regulate the Roman Catholic Church, the Consistories took it as an indirect prohibition and did not, under different pretexts, wish to deliberate on such cases even though they are contemplated, in particular situations, in the laws of all Christian religions and in the Russian Orthodox faith as well. It is in this context that the divorce case of Princess Carolyne, presented as far back as 1848, was submitted for a decision in the first instance to the Roman Catholic Consistory of the Diocese of Luck-Zhitomir. Choosing to ignore both the most obvious evidence of violence and the spirit of Canon Law in such cases, they rejected Princess Wittgenstein's petition on baseless and futile pretexts. Following the established practice, she presented an appeal to the present Consistory. Fearing that her appeal in the second instance might be resolved, under the influence of the same circumstances, in the same manner in which it was dealt with at Luck-Zhitomir—and this would mean the end of all her hopes to obtain a divorce—I enclose here a copy of the original decision reached by the Roman Catholic Consistory of the Diocese of Luck-Zhitomir together with the declaration of the interested parties and the decision of the aforementioned Consistory that considers the marriage of Princess Carolyne Wittgenstein, born Iwanowska, as being good and valid."

The landowner Carolyne Wittgenstein born Iwanowska wrote in the petition she presented to the aforementioned Consistory on May 4, 1848, that

témoin(e) du malheur de sa fille unique n'a pas voulu être présente au mariage. "Ne voulant pas nier les preuves ci-dessous, le Prince Nicolas Wittgenstein dit lui-même "Que son mariage a été réellement très infortuné. "Avant la fin de cette affaire le grand nombre des divorces a attiré l'attention du Gouvernement qui a trouvé nécessaire de le faire remarquer au Chef de l'Eglise Catholique Romaine en Russie. Quoique cette remarque avait pour but seulement d'attirer une attention plus particulière sur le cours des affaires des divorces sans annihiler jamais les lois Canones qui régissent l'Eglise Catholique Romaine, mais les Consistoires en la prenant comme une défense indirecte, sous divers prétextes ne voulait pas délibérer sur <de> semblables affaires, lors quand ces affaires dans certain cas sont permises d'après les lois de l'Eglise de toutes les Religions Chrétiennes, même Grecques-Russes. C'est dans ces circonstances que l'affaire du divorce de la Princesse Caroline Wittgensteyn commencé<e> encore l'année 1848 fut presenté<e> à la Décision de la première instance c'est à dire Luck-Zytomir Cath. Rom. Cons. Ecclés. qui en ne regardant même les preuves les plus décisives de violence, ni l'esprit des lois Canones pour des pareils cas a refusé la demande de la Princesse Wittgensteyn sur des prétextes futiles et sans aucune base, et comme la loi voulait, elle transmit l'affaire pour être déliberée et décidée au présent Cons[istoire]. Craignant que la douzième instance sous l'influence des mêmes circonstances ne décida l'affaire à la manière de Luck-Zytomir, par qui toute possibilité d'avoir le divorce serait anéanti<e>, je joins à ceci la copie de la resolution écoutée en original de la décision de Luck-Zytomir Rom. Cath. Ecclés. Cons. comme de la déclaration des parties intéressées et la décision du dit Consistoire regardant le mariage de la Princesse Caroline Wittgensteyn née Iwanowska comme bon et valable ont ordonné (sic)."

Dans sa pétition remise au dit Consistoire le 4 mai 1848 la propriétaire Caroline Wittgensteyn née Iwanowska écrit

1. She married Prince Wittgenstein, whom she did not love at all, against her will, and was forced to do so by her father.

2. The marriage was celebrated on April 26, 1836, in a Church of Pohrebysze without any knowledge on the part of the competent priest. Since she was then residing with her mother, who was divorced from her father, her parish was that of Monasterszyska. She requested, therefore, that the marriage be invalidated and that the birth of her daughter be declared legitimate as having taken place within a marriage presumed to be valid. In order to establish the truth of the claims made in this petition, the aforementioned Consistory ordered an inquest in loco which was conducted by the Archdeacon of Kiev, Prelate Brink, together with the Defender of the Marriage Bond for this case, the Reverend Skwirsko Lipowiecki Mierzwinski. The inquest being completed, all the documents pertaining to the case were sent for a decision to the Consistory of Luck-Zhitomir on October 26, 1851, and, later, for a decision in the second instance, they were sent also to this Consistory, with a note from the Metropolitan Archbishop Holowinski, dated May 30 of this year, Prot. No. 1737.

One can see that in this case, on the indications provided by the petitioner as well as by the accused, a total of seven witnesses were interrogated under oath according to all the forms prescribed by law. Their depositions were not invalidated by any of the parties involved nor were they deemed suspect. These witnesses provided the following evidence:

1. A servant, Juliana Stolarczukowa, who served from her childhood in the household of the late Monsieur Peter Iwanowsky, waited on his daughter Carolyne and, therefore, knew very well that Princess Carolyne Wittgenstein habitually lived with her mother before she got married. At the time of her visit with her father, she was a witness to many displays of harsh treatment on the part of the Princess's father, for the late Peter Iwanowsky was despotic and severe toward his daughter. Though Prince von Wittgenstein was courting her, she did not love him at all and did not

1° Que ce fut contre sa volonté, et d'après le forcement de son père qu'elle épousa le Prince Wittgenstein qu'elle n'aimait nullement.

2° Que ce mariage a été béni le 26 Avril 1836 dans une Eglise de Pohrebyszeze sans la science du Curé compétent, quand ainsi qu'elle vivait auprès de sa mère divorcée avec son père sa paroisse était Monastiryszeze, elle priait d'invalider ce mariage en prononçant la légalité de la naissance de sa fille comme née *sub figura matrimonii*. Pour établir la vérité des circonstances citées dans cette pétition le dit Consistoire a désigné une erquête sur lieu qui a été dirigée par l'Archidiacre de Kiew, Prélat Brink, en compagnie avec le Défenseur Matrimonial dans cet<te> affaire, Skwirsko Lipowiecki Mierzwinski, et après avoir fini l'enquête tous les documents de cet<te> affaire ont été envoyés en décision au Consistoire de Luck-Zytomir où le 26 octobre 1851 ils ont été décidés, après quoi, en seconde instance, pour être décidé avec une transmission de l'Archevêque Métropolitain Holowinski le 30 mai de cet<te> année, N. 1737, ils ont été transmis dans ce Consistoire.

On voit de cet<te> affaire que sur les designations de la pétitionnaire comme du répondant, on a interrogé les témoins en nombre de sept d'après toutes les formes voulues par les lois sous serment, non invalidés par les parties et non mis en suspicion par elles. Ces témoins ont montré ce qui suit.

1° Une sujette Uliana Stolarczukowa, qui depuis son enfance reste près de la fille Caroline au service du feu M[onsieu]r Pierre Iwanowski et par cette cause elle sait sûrement que quoiqu'elle, Princesse Caroline Wittgensteyn, avant son mariage demeurait habituellement avec sa mère, mais alors de visite de son père le témoin(e) a vu maintes fois les manières rudes que le père de la Princesse employait par la cause que feu Pierre Iwanowski était pour sa fille dur et despotique. Pendant que le Prince de Wittgensteyn lui faisait la cour(t), elle ne l'aimait point, et ne voulait

wish to marry him. When the day of the engagement was set, the elder Iwanowsky called his daughter to his chambers and spoke to her for a long time in a harsh manner and, when his daughter objected to marrying the Prince, he beat her and this is how she was forced to become engaged to the Prince. Afterwards, Monsieur Iwanowsky was always very moody and he would often weep. Some time later, the Princess returned to her mother's home. According to the witness, who was travelling with her in the same coach, the latter kept weeping throughout the whole trip, all the time lamenting the fact that her father was using force on her. After these events, shortly before her mistress's wedding, the witness herself got married to some other servant in the village of Starostince and she was not, therefore, aware of anything else that transpired.

2. Peter Slobodiany, a servant from the village of Starostince, has been for a long time in the service of Monsieur Iwanowsky, landowner, as his personal attendant. His deposition pertaining to the character of his master and the latter's behavior toward his daughter, confirms the statements made by the first witness, Stolarczukowa. He said, moreover, that Monsieur Iwanowsky's daughter Carolyne was never in love with her present husband because she was in love with someone else: this is why, every time Prince Wittgenstein came for a visit, she showed great displeasure. Several times the witness heard her father suggesting to her that she should marry Prince Wittgenstein, and when she eventually expressed her displeasure at the idea and excused herself for not wishing to enter such a marriage, he angrily ordered her to obey his will and, when she still refused, he beat her. The witness himself heard all these things from the next room; finally, Monsieur Iwanowsky opened the door and, threatening to disinherit her, violently threw his daughter out into the very room where the witness happened to be. Mlle. Iwanowska kept weeping and lamenting her unfortunate situation and, afterwards, she never seemed happy and looked pensive all the time. Just before the wedding she cried a lot, and she had to be physically dragged to the ceremony. After the

pas l'épouser. Quand le jour des fiançailles était désigné, le v<i>eil(le) Iwanowski <a> appelé sa fille dans sa chambre et lui a parlé longtemps et âprement et quand sa fille Caroline se refusait d'épouser le Prince, il l'a battue et c'est par cette cause qu'elle était obligée de se fiancer au Prince, mais après cela M[ademoise]lle Iwanowska était toujours très pensive et pleurait souvent, et bientôt après quoi elle se retournait chez sa mère. Quand le témoin(e) qui voyageait pendant dans la même voiture avec sa demoiselle, celle-ci pleurait pendant tout le chemin en accusant son père de la forcer; après cela le temoin avant le mariage de sa maîtresse elle-même se maria à un sujet du village de Starostince et par cette cause elle ne sait plus rien.

2° Pierre Slobodianyi sujet du village de Starostince se trouve depuis longtemps en service du propriétaire Iwanowski comme laquais, et que par rapport du caractère de son maître et ses procédés envers sa fille il a déposé conformément à le prèmièr(e) témoin(e) Stolarczukowa et il a ajouté que la fille de Monsieur Iwanowski, Caroline, n'a jamais aimé son mari actuel par la cause qu'elle a aimé un autre; c'est pourquoi toutes les fois que <le> Prince Wittgensteyn venait elle lui montrait un(e) grand mécontentement. Le déposant a entendu maintes fois comme le père proposait à sa fille d'épouser le Prince Wittgensteyn et, quand elle exprimait tout son mécontentement et s'excusait de ne vouloir pas contracter ce mariage, son père lui <a> ordonné très sérieusement d'exécuter sa volonté et quand elle a pourtant refusé, il la battait ce que le déposant lui-même entendait dans une autre chambre, enfin Iwanowski en ouvrant la porte de sa chambre a jeté sa fille dehors, de fort coup, dans la même chambre ou se trouvait le déposant en menaçant de la déshéritér. La demoi[se]lle Iwanowski a pleuré fortement en accusant sa situation malheureuse et depuis ce temps elle n'était jamais gaie et toujours pensive, avant le mariage même elle pleurait beaucoup, et au mariage même on la présenta de force. Après le mariage, quand la Princesse avec son mari

marriage, when the Princess and her husband went to settle in the village of Woronince, on one of their lands, her father would often come to visit and the witness, as his personal attendant, would accompany him; and several times (especially when the Prince was not present), he saw her complaining to her father about forcing her to marry. Her father would then try to persuade her to ignore the disagreements emerging between her and her husband for, in time, she might become accustomed to him. After Monsieur Iwanowsky died, his daughter separated from her husband and, at that point, their conjugal relation came to an end.

3. The servant Straton Kurda has been, from the time of his infancy, paired with Peter Slobodiany as a personal attendant to Monsieur Iwanowsky; his deposition confirmed on every point that of Peter Slobodiany.

4. The Noble Lady Antonina Kostenecka, interrogated on behalf of the petitioner in the presence of the aforementioned Inquiring Commission, testified that, being employed as governess in the household of Monsieur Iwanowsky, she saw with her own eyes that the late Monsieur Peter Iwanowsky treated his daughter Carolyne in a severe and harsh manner and, when the Princess's mother travelled to go to her daughter's wedding in 1836, before she reached the village of Potok (60 leagues = Km 290), she fell ill and she said to the witness: "I do not really have the courage to attend my daughter's wedding, for I know that she'll be as unhappy as I am, and I do not understand at all why her father is forcing her to do it."[10] All the time before and after the wedding, Carolyne would often cry in despair, lamenting her unfortunate destiny. After the wedding, her life with the Prince was a sequence of disagreements and, under different pretexts, she sought to avoid any conjugal contact with her husband; and this was in spite of her father's strong pressures. After Peter Iwanowsky's death, all conjugal contacts between her and her husband ceased immediately.

5. The Nobleman John Mieszkowski, interrogated on behalf of the respondent and in the presence of the Inquiring Commission testified that: a) Carolyne Iwanowsky never

sont allés pour se fixer à l'une de leur terre<s, le> village de Woronince où le père les fréquentait souvent et le déposant comme laquais était toujours avec <lui>, il a vu que maintes fois, et particulièrement quand le Prince n'y était pas, elle se plaignait à son père de la violence du marriage. Son père la persuadait alors de (ne) dissimuler les mésintelligences surgissantes entr'elle et son mari et qu'avec le temps elle pouvait s'accoutumer à lui. Après la mort du Seigneur Iwanowski sa fille se sépara de son mari et la vie conjugale a cessé depuis lors entr'eux.

3° Le sujet Straton Kurda depuis son enfance il se trouve ensemblé avec Pierre Slobodiani chez le Seigneur Iwanowski comme laquais; il a confirmé en tout point comme le déposant (de) Pierre Slobodiani

4° <La> femme noble Antoinette Kostenetska sur l'interrogatoire qui lui a été présenté du côté de la plaignante et en présence de la dit<e> Commission d'enquête a déposé qu'en étant attachée au service du Seigneur Iwanowski auprès de son ménage a vu de ses propres yeux que feu M[onsieu]r Pierre Iwanowski traitait sa fille Caroline durement et sévèrement et que quand la mère de la Princesse allait pour assister à son mariage en 1836, avant d'y arriver à 60 lieues dans le village Podoli elle tombait malade et elle disait après à la déposante: "Je n'ai pas le courage d'assister au mariage de ma fille, car je sais qu'elle sera aussi malheureuse que moi, et je ne comprends pas pourquoi son père l'y force. Tout le temps avant et après le mariage <elle était> désespérée et pleurait très souvent en se plaignant de son sort malheureuse. Après le mariage sa vie avec le Prince était une suite de mésintelligences; sous divers prétextes elle cherchait à éviter la vie conjugale avec son mari, malgré que son père l'y contraignit fortement. Après la mort de Pierre Iwanowski, du quel <temps> même les apparences de la vie conjugale ont cessées entr'elle et son mari.

5° <Le> gentilhomme Jean Mieszkowski sur l'interrogatoire qui lui a été présenté du côté du répondant et en présence de la Commission d'enquête <a> déposé: a) Caroline

truly resided at Starostince and, therefore, she could not be deemed as belonging to the Parish of Pohrebysze; b) her father, Peter Iwanowsky, was always stern and harsh in dealing with his daughter. From the moment Prince Wittgenstein became acquainted with the Iwanowskys, Carolyne had for him a visible aversion and was not mollified by all his efforts to please her. The witness saw these things with his own eyes and he knows very well that, in response to the prince's twice proffered marriage proposals, he received a formal refusal. Because of this, the prince sought to influence her father, Peter Iwanowsky, who, without even asking his daughter, proceeded to promise her hand to Prince Wittgenstein. Although Carolyne broke into tears and begged her father not to force her into a marriage for which she had no inclination, her father told her that his mind was made up and his resolve unshakable: should she refuse to obey, she could go and stay with her mother and he would disinherit her. Afterwards, Peter Iwanowsky acted coldly and harshly toward his daughter, and she was very sad and would weep a lot, particularly on the eve of her wedding and at the wedding itself; during the ceremony her father never left her side. c) After the wedding, the life of the princess[11] was very unhappy from the start. She could not get used to her husband and found every possible pretext to avoid her conjugal duties; she kept crying and lamenting her fate <every day>. Only her father, Peter Iwanowsky, by visiting them rather often, managed to keep at least the external appearance of their bond. Eventually he told the witness himself: "I am guilty of having forced my daughter into this marriage for, in spite of all Prince Wittgenstein's attentions, she does not love him nor can she love him." After her father's death, even the external appearances were set aside. The witness, who served the Iwanowsky family for over thirty years, personally saw and heard these things.

Iwanowski ne demeurait jamais positivement à Starostince et par cela même elle ne pouvait se compter appartenant à la paroisse de Pohrebiszese; b) Son père Pierre Iwanowski usait toujours de sévérité et brusquerie dans ses rapports avec sa fille. A partir du moment où le Prince Wittgenstein a commencé à faire connaissance avec les Iwanowski, Caroline lui temoignait une aversion visible et elle acceptait tous les efforts du Prince pour lui être agréable avec méconte[nte]ment, ce que le déposant a vu de ses propres yeux et sait suffisamment que le Prince pour réponse à ses propositions de mariage répétées deux fois a reçu un refus formel; c'est par cette cause que le Prince a commencé à influencer le père Pierre Iwanowski qui sans demander <à> sa fille l'a promise en mariage au Wittgensteyn; et quoiqu'elle Caroline priait avec des larmes son père de ne pas la forcer au mariage pour lequel elle n'avait nulle inclination, mais son père lui répondait que sa volonté était stable et inébranlable et que dans le cas où elle ne voudrait nullement obéir, elle pourrait s'en aller chez sa mère, car il la déshéritait. Depuis ce temps Pierre Iwanowski était avec sa fille très froid et plus encore rude, elle s'en lamentait beaucoup, pleurait à grandes larmes, et particulièrement à la veille du mariage aussi bien que dans le moment du mariage même; dans ce moment le père ne s'éloignait d'elle d'un seul pas. c) Après le mariage, et à commencer de la première minute la vie des Princes a été très malheureuse. Elle ne pouvait s'accoutumer à son mari, et elle fuguait sous tout prétexte <ses> devoirs matrimoniaux en gémissant toujours et pleurant sur son sort; seulement son père Pierre Iwanowski la visitant très souvent entretenait au moins le dehors de leur liaison, et enfin il me dit lui-même: "Je suis coupable d'avoir forcé ma fille à ce mariage car malgré tous les soins de la part du Prince Nicolas Wittgensteyn elle ne l'aime ni peut l'aimer." Après la mort de son père même toutes les apparences de leur liaison cessèrent. Le déposant restant plus de 30 ans au service de la famille Iwanowski a vu et entendu lui-même.

---

[10]In the original Russian the sentence is not in quotation marks, and its contents are provided as indirect discourse.

[11]The French text has "princes," whereas the Russian original says "princess."

6. The nobleman Mateusz Dlugolentski was questioned, and he stated that he took the position of overseer in the household of Monsieur Iwanowsky after the marriage of Prince and Princess Wittgenstein. He knows only what he heard. That Princess Carolyne was really forced to marry was confirmed by the fact that her father, Monsieur Iwanowsky, who saw the unfortunate consequences of the violence done to his daughter and regretted that Prince and Princess Wittgenstein did not get along, said to the witness himself: "I cannot forgive myself for forcing my daughter into this marriage for, in spite of all the kindness of the Prince, she is unhappy, does not love him and never has."

7. The officer Peter Artykowski stated under oath that the manners of Monsieur Iwanowsky were very rude in all circumstances, and that he had a difficult and intractable character. The witness was not present at the time when Prince Wittgenstein and Mlle. Carolyne Iwanowsky met, but he knows from his acquaintance with Peter Iwanowsky that, by threatening to disinherit his daughter, the latter managed to force her to get married. In fact, during the years of Prince and Princess Wittgenstein's matrimonial life, Monsieur Iwanowsky often visited his daughter and son-in-law and once, upon returning to Starostince, he was quite depressed and said bitterly: "I cannot forgive myself for having forced my daughter Carolyne to marry Prince Wittgenstein because, in spite of his solicitude, she is unhappy, never loved him and does not love him now." Since the witness was in the service of Monsieur Iwanowsky when the daughter came to visit him in Starostince, he, the witness, saw her always unhappy with her marriage and, after her father's death, all conjugal bonds ceased completely.

The witnesses to the marriage contract, Leon Podowski and Theodor Kalm, were not questioned since they were already dead; moreover, Prince Georg Wittgenstein, being the brother of the accused in the present case, was not permitted to give evidence on the strength of Item 2, Article 2367, Volume 10 of the Imperial Law Code. The Princess's mother, Pauline Iwanowska, solicited to give evidence by the Inquiring Commission, responded in writing by

6° Le Gentilhomme Mathieu Dlugolentski sur un interrogatoire répond qu' il a pris la charge d'intendant chez le Seigneur Iwanowski après le mariage des Princes Wittgenstein et c'est pourquoi il ne sait rien outre ce qu'il a entendu, que la Princesse Caroline avait été réellement forcée au mariage, ce qui a été confirmé par cela que son père Iwanowski a vu les funestes conséquences de la violence faite à sa fille, car les Princes Wittgenstein n'étaient pas d'accord entr'eux, ce qu'il regrettait, et disait au déposant lui-même "ça m'est impardonnable que j'aie forcé ma fille Caroline à ce mariage car, hormis toute la délicatesse du Prince, elle est malheureuse, ne l'aime et ne l'a jamais aimé."

7° <L'> Officier Pierre Artykowski a déposé que les procédés du Seigneur Iwanowski étaient très dures et en toutes circonstances il était d'un caractère grossier et intraitable, lors de la connaissance du Prince Wittgenstein avec Mademoiselle Caroline Iwanowski et leur mariage le déposant n'y a pas été, mais il sait que Pierre Iwanowski par de vues connues de lui en menaçant sa fille da la déshériter la forçait à ce mariage, car du temps de la vie matrimoniale des Princes Wittgenstein, lui Iwanowski visitait souvent sa fille et son gendre et une fois en s'en retournans à Starostince était très fortement chagriné et il disait avec amertume "Ça m'est impardonnable d'avoir forcé ma fille Caroline d'épouser le Prince Nicolas Wittgenstein, car hormis toute sa délicatesse elle est malheureuse, elle ne l'a aimé, et ne l'aime. Pendant que le déposant a été au service du Seigneur Iwanowski, quand sa fille lui faisait visite à Starostince, lui le déposant l'a vu<e> toujours mécontente de son mariage et après la mort de son père toutes les liaisons conjugales cessèrent complètement.

Entre les témoins du contrat du mariage (metríka), Léon Podolski et Théodore Kalm n'ont pas été interrogés à cause de leur mort et le Prince George Wittgenstein n'a pas obtenu la permission de déposer par autorité du Point 2, Art[icle] 2367 du 10me tome des lois de l'empire comme frère du répondant dans cet<te> affaire. La mère de la Princesse, Pauline Iwanowska, sur un interrogatoire de la Commission d'enquête a repondu par écrit "que son

stating that her husband had indeed forced her daughter to marry Prince Nicholas Wittgenstein and had employed all possible means to this effect. He did it because of the prestige that would derive to his family from an alliance with the Wittgenstein line. Her daughter Carolyne was not in the least favorably disposed toward her husband and did not wish to marry him. Since the witness was divorced from her husband, Peter Iwanowsky, she was not able to see him and wrote to him begging him not to force their daughter into such a marriage, but this had no influence on Monsieur Iwanowsky. The latter, after taking his daughter Carolyne to his home in the village of Starostince in order to deprive her of whatever influence her mother could exercise on her, had the wedding performed in Starostince itself. Afterwards, her life was very unhappy and there was incompatibility between the spouses but, owing to her father's strong influence, their conjugal life continued up to the time of his death. Finally, Prince Wittgenstein's solicitor, in his petition dated September 5, 1851, stated that his client's conscience compelled him to admit to the unhappiness of his conjugal life with his wife Carolyne Iwanowska, from whom he received neither love nor affection. He stated, moreover, that their life had been a constant disagreement and their union merely preserved appearances which were kept up only until Monsieur Peter Iwanowsky's death. After that event, his daughter Carolyne left her husband and any contact between them ceased.

As is evident from the testimonies quoted above, the witnesses themselves show, therefore, that Princess Carolyne's marriage took place in circumstances of obvious violence and threats on the part of her father Peter Iwanowsky and, for this reason, this marriage, according to the spirit of Canon Law, was not valid.

"Serious intimidation, unjustifiably inflicted upon an individual who is steadfast in his attitude in order to compel him to marry, causes that marriage to be null and void" (Levya, Examen Episcoporum, Book 1, Chapter 50, item 1 n.d.). "Serious intimidation, such as fear of death, enslavement, beating, imprisonment, exile, carnal violence, loss of part or the whole patrimony, etc. etc., imposed on an individual steadfast in his attitudes and aimed at compelling him to marry as the lesser evil, given that marriage must be an abso-

mari Pierre Iwanowski a réellement forcé sa fille à épouser le prince Nicolas Wittgenstein usant pour cela de tous les moyens sous prétexte de l'honneur qui ressortirait de l'union avec la maison des Princes Wittgensteyn que sa fille Caroline n'avait et n'a la moindre inclination pour son mari et qu'elle ne voulait pas l'épouser, mais que comme la déposante est divorcée avec son mari Pierre Iwanowski, elle ne pouvait le voir, mais elle lui écrivit, en le priant de ne pas forcer sa fille à ce mariage, mais que cela n'avait aucune influence sur lui et que lui, Iwanowski, après avoir pris sa fille Caroline dans sa maison dans le village de Starostince pour l'éloigner de toute l'influence que sa mère pouvait avoir sur elle, là il lui fit épouser le Prince. Depuis ce temps, là sa vie était malheureuse et incompatible mais sur des influences très fortes du père leur liaison conjugale traînait jusqu'à la mort de celui-ci. Enfin le chargé du pouvoir du Prince Nicolas Wittgensteyn dans sa pétition du 5 septembre 1851 dit que son client trouve nécessaire d'après sa conscience d'avouer son chagrin de ce que dans sa vie conjugale avec sa femme Caroline Iwanowski il n'éprouvait d'elle ni amour ni attachement; que leur vie a été une mésintelligence perpétuelle, et que leurs liaison était seulement de forme qui elle-même traînait seulement jusqu'à la mort de M[onsieu]r Pierre Iwanowski après laquelle sa fille Caroline quitta son mari et toutes liaisons cessèrent.

Ainsi d'après les interrogatoires sous serment ci-cités les témoins mêmes démontrent, que le mariage de la Princesse Caroline avait eu lieu avec forte violence, et menaces du père Pierre Iwanowski, par laquelle cause ce mariage d'après l'esprit des lois Canones dès son commencement était invalide.

"Metus gravis iniuste incussus qui cadit in virum constantem ad estorquendum matrimonium facit illus nullum" (Leyva Examen Episcoporum, Lib. 1, Cap. 1, n. D). "Metus gravis cadens in constantem virum et ad matrimonium tamquam ad minus malum promovens, qualis est metus mortis, servitutis, verberum, carceris, exilii, stupri, am(m)issionis bonorum vel majoris partis, etc. etc. et talis metus matrimonium quod maxime liberum esse debet, reddit nullum" (C. 13 et 14, de spons. et matr. Concil. Trid. Sess. 24, Cap. 9 de

lutely free act, causes marriage to be invalidated."
(Chapter 13 and 14, De sponsalibus et matrimonium Concilii Tridentini, *Session 24, Chapter 9,* De Ref. Matr. *where it is so declared at paragraph Cujuscumque). Also Engel,* Corpus Juris Canonici, *Book 10, Item 50: "Upon entering marriage, a certain degree of willingness is not sufficient, it must be complete; therefore, if marriage is contracted through fear, it is, in terms of the same law, null and void." See also Book 3, Item 32, No. 9,* Regula Juris: *"What is invalid from the beginning cannot be validated with the passing of time; therefore, if the <marriage> contract is to be valid, a totally new consent is required."*

After studying the circumstances of this case, the Consistory of Luck-Zhitomir, in its resolution of October 21, rejected the petition presented by Princess Carolyne Wittgenstein for these reasons:

1. Because the Parish of Pohrebysze, where the marriage was celebrated, was deemed appropriate.

2. Because the violence employed toward her in order to compel her to get married is not sufficiently proved.

Regarding the first point, the Consistory of Mohilow is fully in agreement with the decision of the Consistory of Luck-Zhitomir but, with respect to the question of violence, it cannot agree for the following reasons. In the decision of the Consistory of Luck-Zhitomir as it pertains to the issue of violence, the words of the Canonist Sanchez are referred to in order to conclude that the compulsion to marry exercised upon Princess Wittgenstein cannot be said to exist for the reason that the marriage was consummated, a fact that by itself confirms the validity of the marriage even though there was violence in the beginning, to quote: "*If after a marriage was contracted through serious and unjustifiable intimidation, copulation takes place spontaneously and with conjugal affection, that is with feelings appropriate to conjugal status, this marriage is fully validated*" (Sanchez, etc.). Nevertheless, upon consideration of the depositions provided under oath by the witnesses and the declaration of the Petitioner's mother, it is evident that Carolyne Iwanowska, neither before nor after her marriage, acquiesced of her own will and inclination to conjugal life and performed her conjugal

Ref. Matr., et ibi declarat par. cujuscumque). Engel, *Corp. Jur. Canonic. Lib.,* Tit. 10 L: "*In matrimonio non qualiscumque voluntas sufficit, sed omnino requiritur, ideo metu ipso jure nullum est.*" Lib. 3, Tit. 32 n. 9—*Regula Juris: "Quod ab initio non valet tractu temporis convalescere non potest, ergo ad valorem actus, omnino novus consensus requiritur.*" Après avoir comparé les circonstances de cet<te> affaire le Consistoire de Luck-Zytomir par sa décision du 21 octobre refuse à la pétitionnaire Princesse Caroline Wittgensteyn dans son procès

1° Pour cause que la paroisse de Pohrebysze dans laquelle son mariage a été celebré e<s>t décidé<e> comme competent<e>.

2° Que la violence dont on a usé contre elle pour l'obliger au mariage on dit qu'elle n'est pas suffisa<nte>ment prouvée.

Par rapport au premier point le Consistoire de Mohilow est pleinement d'accord avec la décision du Consistoire de Luck-Zytomir, mais en ce qui regarde la violence elle ne peut y adhérer par les raisons suivantes. Dans la décision du Consistoire de Luck-Zytomir, en prononçant sur la violence, il dit d'après les paroles du Canoniste Sanchez que la contrainte de la Princesse Wittgensteyn au mariage ne peut être regardée pour contrainte du moment que les devoirs matrimoniaux ont été accomplis, car par le fait même le mariage a été confirmé, quand même il y avait au commencement violence, c'est à dire: "*Si post matrimonium ex metu gravi iniuste illato contractum habetur copula sponte et affectu maritali id est animo vivendi conjugaliter omnino validatur matrimonium*" (Sanchez, etc.). Mais d'après les dépositions sous serment des témoins et d'après les aveux de la mère de la pétitionnaire <il> est évident que Caroline Wittgensteyn avant et après le mariage à la vie conjugale n'agissait jamais de sa propre volonté et impulsion, mais exécutait les devoirs matrimoniaux s<o>us l'influence imperieuse de la volonté de son père, qui par la vue d'ambition voulait entrer

duties under the imperious influence of her father, who aspired to form an allegiance between his own family and that of the Wittgenstein princes. For this reason, the opinion of the Canonist Sanchez has little value and is not applicable to the present case. Pihring., Book 11, Chapter 1, Section 4, Note 2, states: "*For conjugal cohabitation to be deemed sufficient, conjugal consent on the part of the spouses is required because 1) in ratifying a marriage previously contracted, the spouses should be aware that it was invalid in the first place; nothing in fact is more contrary to consent that being in error; 2) it is required that cohabitation be totally spontaneous in order to remove the original cause of fear since, as long as the cause persists, the fear persists as well.*"

The decision of the Consistory of Luck-Zhitomir is based also on the following reasons:

1. For twelve years after her marriage the Princess never complained about compulsion.

2. She willingly performed her conjugal duties as it is proved by the birth of her daughter.

3. If she had reason to be afraid of her father, she should not, after his death, have lived with her husband another four years. The inquiry shows, however, the contrary; for, as long as her father was alive, daring not to make an official complaint against the strong compulsion used toward her, the Princess nonetheless complained quite often about it in the presence of her relatives; and her father himself confessed to the witnesses referred to above that he had used strong compulsion on his daughter to force her into such a marriage, and he said himself that "she is unhappy because she does not love, nor can she love her husband." Similarly, we have the statement of Prince Wittgenstein to the effect that his wife Carolyne never loved him from the moment they got married and that, following her father's death, she separated from him. The circumstances referred to do not show at all a good conjugal relationship and, even assuming that it was good, given that the Princess did not know that her marriage, insofar as it had been contracted through violence, was not valid, the latter cannot be validated by conjugal relationship (*non est revalidatum*). See *Corpus Juris*, Chapter 10 *De sponsalibus*, Chapter 28 *Consultat*. We cannot

en liaison de famille avec la maison des princes Wittgensteyn c'est pourquoi l'opinion du Canoniste de petite valeur, Sanchez, n' est pas applicable dans le cas actuel. Pihring, Lib. 11, Tit. 1 Sect. 4 Not. 2: "*Ut cohabitatio conjugum sit sufficiens, judicium hujus consensus conjugalis requiritur, 1° ut ratificans matrimonium prius contractum sciat illud fuisse invalidum; nihil enim magis contrarium est consensui quam error; 2° requiritur ut cohabitatio illa sit omnino spontanea ita ut cessaret etiam causa timoris; nam, durante causa metus, durat metus.*"

La décision du Consistoire Luck-Zytomir est basée encore sur ce que

1° La Princesse douze années après son mariage n'a jamais porté plainte(s) pour contrainte;

2° Qu'elle accomplissait les devoirs conjugaux de sa bonne volonté, ce qui est prouvé par la naissance de sa fille;

3° S'il y avait lieu à craindre le père après sa mort elle n'aurait pas vécu avec son mari encore pendant quatre ans. Mais l'enquête démontre au contraire que la Princesse n'osant pendant la vie de son père porter une plainte officiellement contre une forte contrainte qu'on employe contre elle s'en plaignait pourtant à ses parents très souvent car son père lui-même l'avoua aux dits témoins d'avoir accompli sur la personne de sa fille une contrainte très-forte pour la forcer à ce mariage, et il disait lui-même "qu'elle est malheureuse car elle ne l'aime, ni peut aimer son mari." Même de la part du Prince Wittgensteyn on a un aveu que sa femme Caroline ne l'aima pas du moment de son mariage et que tout de suite après la mort de son père Iwanowski elle se séparait de lui. Les circonstances précitées ne démontrent nullement une vie conjugale de bon rapport, qu'en admettant même qu'elle était bonne mais comme la Princesse ne savait pas que son mariage contracté de violence était invalidé par une vie conjugale ne le valide nullement (*Non est revalidatum*1:. *Corp. Jur.*, Cap. X, *de spons*; Cap. 28, *Consultat.*), on ne peut pas compter pour preuve que la Princesse a eu avec son mari une fille, car les règles de l'Eglise dis-

consider as a proof of validity the fact that she had a daughter from her husband, for Canon Law states that "*At any rate, a marriage contracted through violence and intimidation cannot be deemed ratified by long cohabitation if one of the spouses continues to feel under compulsion and seeks constantly to avoid such cohabitation. A marriage contracted through fear is, moreover, invalid even if the woman procreates children, and it is null and void because it was contracted out of reverential fear and because of violent pressures.*" (See *Rota Romana, Decisiones*, 405 No. 9 and 13, part 18, Tome 1, and also Begnudel, *Bassa Tom.* 3, p. 87, No. 38.) That is, the fact that the couple cohabits for a long time does not validate their marriage if it has been contracted through violence and if one of the spouses continues to complain and eventually leaves the other. A forced marriage is invalid even if the woman procreates children. It is equally null and void when the parents persist in demanding it and marriage is eventually contracted out of fear of them.

Within the same decision, it is said that since the mother of the Princess was divorced from the father, even if he really exercised compulsion on their daughter, she could have surely advised her daughter about the ways in which she could obtain the annulment of a marriage contracted under compulsion. Against such a statement, it must be stated that the mother felt obliged to try to reconcile her daughter with her husband rather than provide her with advice on how to obtain a divorce, for such suggestion would be entirely against the law. Finally, as far as the witnesses are concerned, the Consistory of Luck-Zhitomir considered their depositions as insufficient and questionable. These would be open to doubt, since three of the witnesses were in the service of the Princess. On the other hand, since servants are witnesses to anything that happens in a household, they are in a better position than anybody else to know anything that takes place in the premises. Not only does Church <Law> not reject such witnesses, but openly accepts them: "*Moreover, evidence provided by servants is admitted as proof in regard to facts and crimes taking place within the household, since events and crimes taking place in the household cannot be proved by anyone else. Taking the oath removes all suspicions as stated by the Pope in the quoted passage, Par. 4, No. 89*" (Reinffestuel,

ent (*Rota Romana Decis*. 405 N. 9 et 13, pars 18, Tom. 1 et Begnudel *Bassa Tom*. 3, p. 87 N. 38): "*Non tamen ex diuturna conjugum cohabitatione dicitur ratificatum matrimonium vi et metu contractum, ubi alter ex conjugibus semper conquestus est et tandem aufugit. Matrimonium per metum contractum est invalidum etiamsi mulier filios procreavit, nec non ex metu reverentiali et importunis precibus contractum est nullum.*" C'est à dire, par une longue vie matrimoniale des époux le mariage ne se valide pas s'il a été contracté avec violence contraignante et quand un des époux se plaignait souvent et enfin a quitté l'autre. Le mariage contracté de force est invalide quoique la femme eût des enfants. Il est aussi invalide et nul dans le cas où les parents l'exigent incessamment et il est contracté de peur d'eux.

Dans la même décision il est dit que comme la mère de la Princesse était divorcée avec le père, ainsi s'il y avait eu réellement contrainte au mariage, elle aurait assurément conseillé sa fille de quelle manière obtenir l'annulation du mariage contracté de force. Mais contre une telle définition il faut dire que la mère était plutôt obligée de reconcilier sa fille avec son mari que lui suggérer des conseils tendant au divorce; les conseils seraient complétement contre loi. Enfin en ce qui concerne les témoins, le Consistoire de Luck-Zytomir, veut voir les dépositions de ceux-ci non-formelles et douteuses. Douteuses parce que trois de ces témoins sont des sujets de la Princesse. Mais comme les serviteurs sont des témoins de maison qui peuvent mieux que personne savoir toutes les circonstances de la maison, la loi de l'Eglise non seulement ne refuse ces témoins, mais au contraire elle les admet. Reinfestuel Lib. 11 *Decr*., Tit. 20 *de testibus et attestationibus*, 54 n. 127 et 129: "*Insuper domestici testimonium admittitur in probandis factis et delictis domesticis; nam de factis quae domi geruntur per alios probari non possunt. Juramentum tollit omnem suspicionem ut loquitur Pontifex in cit. cum locum, par. 4, n. 89.*" Comme les lois civiles de l'Empire Tom. 15, Art. 1088 (Edit[ion] de l'année 1842), c'est à dire: le serment annule tout soupçon, tout doute au compte

Book 11, Decr., Chapter 20, *De testibus et atte-stationibus*, 54 No. 127 and 129). This notion is also in accordance with Imperial laws; see Tome 15, art. 1088 (as issued in 1842). In other words, the oath annuls all suspicions and doubts with respect to witnesses who are servants. This principle, according to the Reverend Ludkiewicz, Defender of the Marriage Bond, runs against the opinion of the Canonist Pichler, notably where he says that *"servants are not allowed to give evidence in favor of their master unless they have been previously released from their oath of servitude and the case is not in their own interest"* that is to say, literally, that servants are prohibited to give evidence for their masters if they have not been previously freed before they take the oath and if the aforementioned case deals with their own interests. At any rate, this opinion of the canonist, referred to as law in the aforementioned opinion, is improperly quoted here without being applied to the circumstances of the case. In fact, the servants of the Princess, according to the laws of the Empire, could not have pronounced any oath of fealty to their mistress; moreover, the case of annulment of the Princess's marriage in no way can be thought to affect their interests.

In that decision, it is also stated that the testimony of the witnesses is one-sided and unclear insofar as they convey the idea that the Petitioner's father was strict with her and that he used toward his daughter great severity when such behavior was quite usual with the old generation and, in any case, no one would base a petition for divorce on it. Against such a conclusion, the Consistory of Mohilow deems it necessary to explain that they see no obscurity in the depositions of the witnesses, for these depositions do clarify only the evidence, that is to say, the harsh manners of the father toward his daughter and the strong compulsion he employed against her in order to induce her to get married; after all, the father did beat the petitioner and did threaten to disinherit her. In that decision, moreover, the deposition of one of the servants who waited on Monsieur Iwanowsky as a personal attendant has been found suspect since, when Iwanowsky was scolding and chastising his daughter, he was in the anteroom, placed there, as it has been stated, for the specific purpose of being eventually a useful witness for his

des témoins sujets, qui d'après le défenseur Ludkiewicz qui s'appuyait sur l'opinion du Canoniste Pichler et notamment *"Prohibentur testes agere subditi pro domino suo, nisi prius quoad actum praesentem solvantur juramento subjectionis et non agatur de eorum proprio commodo"* c'est à dire, traduisant littéralement "Il est defendu aux sujets de déposer témoignage pour son maître s'il n'est pas auparavant affranchi du serment de sujet, et si dans la dite affaire il a en vue ses propres intérêts; "cependant cet<te> opinion du Canoniste qui est appelée loi dans l'opinion citée, est citée ici injustement et sans se conformer aux details, car les sujets de la Princesse n' avaient aucun serment pour leur maîtresse d'après les lois de l'Empire et l'affaire du divorce de la Princesse ne peut nullement influencer leur propres intérêts.

Dans la décision il est dit encore que les dépositions des témoins ne sont pas claires et <sont> partielles. Sous ce point de vue que le père de la pétitionnaire était pour elle sévère et qu'il, lui, usait avec sa fille une grande sévérité, ces procédés étaient tous habituels chez nos a<nc>êtres et pourtant personne ni basait ni fondait une demande de divorce. Contre une telle conclusion le Consistoire de Mohiloff voit comme nécessaire de répondre que dans les dépositions des témoins on ne voit nulle obscurité, car par ces dépositions on éclairait seulement les témoignages, c'est à dire les procédés durs du père envers sa fille et une forte violence on a employé contre elle pour l'obliger au mariage, car le père a battu la pétitionnaire et l'a menacée de la déshériter. Sur un sujet du Seigneur Iwanowski qui l'a servi comm<e> laquai<s>, et dans la décision on a trouvé sa déposition suspecte par la cause que quand Iwanowski grondait sa fille et la châtiait, lui il se trouvait dans l'antichambre caché comme exprès dans le but d'être à l'avenir un témoin utile à sa maîtresse en cas de besoin.

mistress in case it were needed. But it is impossible to make such an assumption in such a <simple and> normal instance. Quite naturally a servant could have placed himself in the other room as he saw an unpleasant scene emerging between father and daughter. But could he have any thought whatsoever or even foreseen that the Petitioner would definitely marry Prince Wittgenstein, that the two would not get along, and that the whole thing would end in a case for divorce where he would be called to give evidence? Also, according to that decision, the first witness was a woman who was in the service of Mlle. Iwanowska. Being herself unmarried and given her sex and simplicity, she could not understand the cause of her mistress's tears of despair. For this reason, in the opinion of the Defender of the Marriage Bond, the Reverend Ludkiewicz, this chambermaid has been deemed, as stated in that decision, lacking the requisite qualities and her deposition was judged worthless. Since it is not clear from the entire case why and on what grounds this chambermaid has been declared, just because of her sex and her simplicity of mind, as lacking the necessary requisites, it is impossible to agree that her testimony has been of little importance—especially since, during the proceedings, she has neither been disqualified by any of the parties in question nor by the Commission of Enquiry and, moreover, the testimony of this former chambermaid has been supported by the depositions of the other witnesses. Finally, it is stated in that decision that, although the other witnesses were free and of noble origins, since they only reported hearsay about the violence <inflicted upon Princess Wittgenstein>, it is not clear who did so. At any rate, such a decision from the Consistory of Luck-Zhitomir is on every point completely contrary to what transpired at the Inquiry, since three of the witnesses, namely the Noblemen Mieszkowski, Dlugolentski, Artykowski, have testified under oath that it was Monsieur Iwanowsky himself who expressed to them his regret at having forced his daughter, against her will, to marry Prince Wittgenstein. This, therefore, is not hearsay (*ex auditu auditum*), and the fact that the individual himself admitted to it constitutes the best proof (as in Art. 168, Tome 15, of the Civil Law Code, as issued in 1842).

Mais c'est impossible de se faire des soupçon<s> d'un cas si habituel. Très naturellement un laquais pouvait s'être caché dans l'autre chambre en voyant éclater une scène désagréable entre le père et la fille; pouvait-il avoir dans cela une pensée quelconque et prévoir que la pétitionnaire épouserait infaill<ible>ment le Prince de Wittgensteyn, que leur vie ne s'accorderait pas et qu'en résulterait une affaire de divorce dans laquelle il serait appelé à déposer témoignage? Le premier témoin (c'est la decision qui le dit) est une femme qui a été servante chez la demoiselle Iwanowska, elle-même non mariée; d'après son sexe et sa simplicité, elle ne pouvait comprendre quelle était la cause du chagrin et des larmes de sa maîtresse, et pour cette cause, conformément à l'opinion du défenseur Prêtre Ludkiewicz, cette femme de chambre a été reconnue par la décision comme n'ayant de capacité voulue, et sa déposition de peu de valeur. Ce qui est évident après toute la requête est impossible de voir sur quelle base la femme de chambre mentionnée est reconnue d'après son sexe et sa simplicité comment n'ayant pas la capacité voulue et, sur le peu de valeur de son témoignage, on ne peut pas être d'accord d'autant plus que par cette cause elle n'a p[as] été invalidée par les parties ni Commission d'enquête et que d'après les dépositions de l'ex-femme de chambre tous ses témoignages ont été apuyés par les dépositions des témoins suivants. Enfin on dit dans la décision quoique les autres déposant<s> sont des gens libres et d'une provenance noble, néan-moins comme ils ont seulement entendu parler de la violence, mais on ne sait pas de quoi? Cependant une telle décision du Consistoire <de> Luck-Zytomir est complètement, et en tout point contraire à l'enquête, parce que trois parmi les témoins et nommément les gentilhommes Mieszkowski, Dlugolentski, Artykowski ont démontré sous serment que c'est le Seigneur Iwanowski lui-même qui leur a exprimé son repentir d'avoir forcé sa fille contre sa volonté, amour et désir à épouser le Prince Wittgenstein et consequemment ce n'est pas un echo répété (*ex auditu auditum*) mais c'est la même personne dont l'aveu (comme l'Art[icle] 1681 Tom. 15 Edit. 1842 de la loi civile) est la meilleure preuve.

The witness Kostenecka testified that the Princess's mother was, from the beginning, complaining to her about the violence perpetrated on her daughter by Monsieur Iwanowsky; moreover, all the witnesses have testified that, both before and after the wedding ceremony, they actually saw the Princess in tears lamenting her situation. Finally, the petitioner's mother, when questioned by the Commission of Enquiry, responded in writing that her daughter Carolyne had really been forced by her father to marry Prince Wittgenstein; she also said that she did not wish to be present at the ceremony because of the sorrow that this would cause her. As for the conclusion reached by the Consistory of Luck-Zhitomir that the Petitioner's father would not have prevented her from asking for an annulment of her forced marriage (there is no proof of this), this argument is refuted by the fact that, although Monsieur Iwanowsky saw the unfortunate consequences of his violence, he did not permit his daughter to complain officially to anybody (as is shown by witnesses who heard him stating this himself), being himself convinced his daughter would eventually get accustomed to her husband and, moreover, that such compulsion might be held against him in a court of law.

For these reasons the Consistory of Mohilow is of the following opinion:

1. Whereas, in the present case, seven witnesses have already been questioned and, among them, <three peasants and> four noblemen who have been in the service of Monsieur Iwanowsky; and, since these witnesses were constantly attached to his household, they were in a better position to know the compulsion used <by Monsieur Iwanowsky> toward his daughter to force her to marry Prince Wittgenstein; whereas these witnesses have been disqualified neither by the parties involved nor by the Commission of Inquiry and have testified under oath according to all the formalities required by the law, in virtue of Canon Law (see *Corpus Juris, Decret. Papae Alexandri* III, Book XVII, Chapter XII, paragraph 4, No. 89: *Juramentum tollit omnem suspicionem*, i.e., The oath removes all suspicion, and the Laws of the Empire, Tome 10, Article 2402 (1842): "Similar depositions from witnesses are deemed completely believable and totally sufficient.");

Le témoin(e) Kostenetska <a> déposé que la mère de la Princesse se désespérait par devant elle sur la violence faite à sa fille par Iwanowski, et tous les témoins ayant déposé comme témoins oculaires que la Princesse avant et après la cérémonie du mariage se plaignait avec de<s> larmes de son sort; enfin la mère de la pétitionnaire sur un interrogatoire fait par la Commission d'enquête a répondu par écrit que sa fille Caroline réellement a été forcé au mariage avec le Prince Wittgensteyn par son père, auprès de laquelle cérémonie elle-même ne voulait pas être présente à cause de la douleur que ça lui aurait produit. Quand à la conclusion du Consistoire de Luck-Zytomir que le père de la pétitionnaire ne l'aurait empêchée de demander l'annulation de son mariage forcé (on n'a nulle preuve de cela) cela tombe de lui-même car quoique le Seigneur Iwanowski voyait les mauvaises conséquences de sa violence il ne permettait à sa fille de s'en plaindre à quiconque officiellement (comme l'ont déposé les témoins qui l'ont entendu de sa propre bouche) dans la conviction que sa fille s'habituera à son mari, et plus encore que pour violence il pouvait être responsable devant la loi.

C'est pourquoi le consistoire de Mohilow est d'opinion

1° Vu que sur l'affaire présente, qu'on a déjá interrogé sept témoins entre le nombre desquels se trouvent 4 gentilshommes qui ont été au service du S[eigneu]r Iwanowski et comme ces témoins démeurent toujours dans sa maison pouvaient mieux connaître les circonstances détaillées de la violence faite à sa fille dans son mariage avec le Prince Wittgensteyn, et comme ces témoins n'ont pas été invalidés, ni par aucune des parties plaignantes ni par la Commission d'enquête et avec toutes les formalités voulues par la loi, ils ont prêté serment en vertu de la loi Canone (*Corp[us] Juris: Decret[a] Alex[andri] III Pap<a>e* Tit Lib. XVIII cap. XII *Juramentum tollit omnem supicionem* Par. 4 N. 89) que le serment annule tout soupçon et <de> la loi du pays, l'Empire (Tom. 10 Art 2402, Edit. de 1842), <que> les dépositions de semblables témoins <sont> regardés <comme> digne<s> de toute foi et completement suffisante<s>.

2. Whereas the testimony given by witnesses under oath shows that Carolyne Iwanowska contracted marriage not only against her own will, but also "out of reverential fear" because of her father's threats to disinherit her and on account of very strong compulsion inflicted on her, which the Petitioner's father, Monsieur Peter Iwanowsky himself admitted to in a moment of repentance; whereas, as is proved by the witnesses' depositions and by the statement made by Prince Nicholas Wittgenstein himself, from the day of her marriage until her father died, she maintained only external marital relations under pressure from her father and, moreover, after his death her relationship with her husband ceased completely and she left him.

Having considered the Laws of the Church pertaining to marriages contracted through force and against one's will (see *Corpus Iuris, Decret. Papae Alex. III*, First Part, Book 18, Chapter 12, *De sponsalibus et matrimoniis*: namely that *"When there is no consent, as in cases where fear and compulsion are interposed, it is necessary, since the assent of both parties is required, that the grounds for compulsion be removed; for marriage is contracted only by consent and, when a proposal is made, he who is to be so asked must enjoy full security not to have to say, out of fear, that he likes what he actually despises and the result be what is the logical consequence in unwanted nuptials"*); and where there is no good will marriage cannot exist (see Pope Nicholas II, The one and only Chapter, Case 30, Question 11: *"Where there is no consent from both parties, there is no marriage"*), as even the canonists write about compulsion; and whenever it is difficult to prove compulsion it is sufficient to produce witnesses from among one's friends, relatives, or some other persons and, as a last resort, at least one eye-witness. (Reinffestuel, Book 1, Decret., Chapter 40, states: *"Intimidation is proved by the testimony of witnesses, especially insofar as two witnesses testifying about intimidation are much more to be believed when a given situation is also taken into account than a thousand other ones denying that there was intimidation or testifying that the action was undertaken freely and spontaneously."*) The canonist Reinffestuel is, therefore, of the opinion that violence is proved by witnesses of this kind, and it is better to believe two witnesses supporting such a possibility rather

2° Comme de la déposition des témoins jurés on voit que Caroline née Iwanowska non seulement contre sa propre volonté, *ex metu reverentiali*, mais par les menaces de son père qui la menaçait de la déshériter, et par sa contrainte très forte ce qui a été avoué par le père de la pétitionnaire, Pierre Iwanowski, personnellement et dans un moment de repentir et comme dans des dépositions des témoins et de l'aveu du Prince Nicholas Wittgensteyn lui-même il est démontré qu'en comptant du jour de la conclusion de ce mariage elle menait une vie presque célibataire jusqu'à la mort de son père par cause de l'influence exercée sur elle par son père, et après sa mort toutes ses liaisons avec son mari cessèrent et elle le quitta aimer.

Vu les lois de l'Eglise que le mariage conclu à force et sans consentement volontaire (*Corpus Juris, Decret[a] Alex[andri] III Papae*, Tit. 1 Lib. 18 Cap. XII *de Sponsalibus et matrim[onio]*: *"Cum locum non habeat consensus ubi metus et coactio intercedit, necesse est ut ubi assensus cujuscumque requiritur, coactionis materia repellatur; matrimonium autem solo consensu contrahitur et ubi de ipso quaeritur plena debet securitate gaudere ille cujus est animus indagandus, ne per timorem dicat sibi placere quod odit, et sequatur exitus qui de invitis solet nuptiis provenire"*) et ou il n'y a pas de bonne volonté le mariage ne peut pas exister (Nicolaus III Papa, Cap. unic, *caus.* XXX *quest.* 11: *"ubi non est consensus utriusque non est conjugium"*). Même comme le prononce le Canoniste sur la contrainte; comme dans tous les cas c'est bien difficile de prouver la contrainte, ainsi pour prouver, il est assez de produire un témoin de ses amis, parents, ou autre personne et dans le dernier besoin il est suffisant un témoin oculaire (Reinffestuel lib. 1 *decret[a]* Tit. 40: *"Metus probatur per depositionem testium adeo quidem ut magis sit credendum duobus testibus de metu attestantibus una cum existente conjunctura quam mille negantibus seu deponentibus de libera seu spontanea voluntate"*) et le Canoniste Reinffestuel est d'opinion <que> la violence se prouve par les dépositions des témoins de cette manière, il vaut mieux ajouter foi à deux témoins qui prouvent pour le fait qu'à mille autres témoins qui déposeraient contre le forcement et voudrait prouver qu'il y avait bonne volonté et consentement c'est à dire *"cum metus aliunde sit difficilis*

than a thousand others testifying against compulsion and wishing to prove that there has been good will and consent; in other words *"Since intimidation is otherwise difficult to prove, friends and relatives are therefore qualified to testify, and in the final analysis, one direct testimony is sufficient."* A marriage contracted without the consent of one of the two parties is null and void (See *Sacra Rota Romana*, Decision 204, No. 1 part IV Tome 1, Decree 23 No. 1 and 7, Part 12 and Decree 127, No. 3, Part 15), because everything that is done because of fear is null and Canon Law annuls it; see Decree 500, No. 5, Part 15, whereby a marriage contracted through compulsion is also invalid according to natural law. Reinffestuel, Book 1, Decr. Chapter 40, Par. 3 No. 44, Resp. 5. writes: *"A marriage contracted through grave inti,idation unjustly provided is for that very reason null and void."* Marriage contracted through violence and without consent is not validated, therefore, either by a long conjugal life or by the birth of offspring, as long as one of the spouses keeps complaining about it and eventually leaves the other. *"Nor indeed can a marriage contracted through violence and intimidation be ratified by a continuing cohabitation of the spouses, if one of them always feels under compulsion and finally leaves."* (*Rota Romana*, Decis. 405, Nos. 9 and 13, part 18, Section 18, Chapter 1; and Begnudel, Tome 3, page 87, No. 38). Such a law must rigidly be applied in the petitioner's case for she complained to her father of the compulsion exercised on her by him and complained as well to her mother and, after the death of her father, she left her husband; finally, though she had a child, her marriage is null and void just as if her marriage had been contracted only *"through reverential fear"* and after repeated requests, to quote: "

"A marriage contracted through intimidation is invalid even if the woman has a child and it is null, because it is contracted out of reverential fear and because of unwanted requests." Violence on a daughter is not to be seen only as physical violence, but also as "reverential fear," that is to say obedience to her parents, caused by their repeated requests, their anger, and threats in order to make her contract a marriage with an individual she did not love at all; this causes such a marriage to be invalid. Schmaltz Grueber, *loc. cit.*, No. 393, says: *"True is the common opinion that*

probationis et hinc ad testificandum etiam habiles sunt amici, consanguinei et testes singulares, immo sufficit unus testis de visu," le mariage contracté sans le consentement d'une des parties est nul (*Sacra Rota Romana Decisio* 204, N. 1 pars IV tom. 1 Dec. XXIII No. 1 et VII, Part. XII et Dec. CXXVII n. 3 *pars* 15) car tout ce qui a été fait par cause de peur est nul, et les lois Canones l'annulent (*Dec.* 500 N. *pars* 15) le mariage contracté (d') après forcement même d'après la loi de la nature est invalide (Reinfesstuel lib. 1 *Dec.* Tit. XL Par. III n. 44 *Resp.* 5: *"Matrimonium ex gravi metu injuste incusso contractum ipso jure nullum est ac invalidum."*) Le mariage conclu avec violence et sans consentement ne se valide ni par une longue vie matrimoniale, ni par la naissance des enfants, alors quand un des époux s'en plaignait toujours et quitta l'autre enfin: *"Non tamen ex diuturna conjugum cohabitatione dicitur ratificatum matrimonium vi et metu contractum, ubi alter ex conjugibus semper conquestus est et tandem aufugit"* (*Rota Romana*, Dec. 405 n. 9 et 13 *pars* 18, Tit. 1, et Begnudel Tom. III p. 87, N. 38). Cette loi doit être appliquée de toute rigueur au cas de la pétitionnaire qui se plaignait à son père du forcement exercé par lui, et (qu') à sa mère, et enfin après la mort de son père elle quitta le mari et quoiqu'elle eût une fille, son mariage est nul même s'il serait contracté seulement *ex metu reverentiali* et d'après des prières réitérées.

"Matrimonium per metum contractum est invalidum etiamsi mulier filium procreaverit nec non ex metu reverentiali et importunis precibus est nullum." Comme violence pour une fille doit être regardée non seulement le forcement physique, mais aussi *metus reverentialis*, c'est à dire l'obéissance aux parents, leurs prières réitérées, leur colère et menaces pour la faire contracter un mariage avec une personne qu'elle n'aimait pas, c'est pourquoi un tel mariage est invalide. Schmaltz Grueber *loc. cit.* n. 393: *"Communis et vera est illa opinio quod matrimonium sit nullum*

*marriage is not valid if contracted because of rev-
erential fear, and from this it follows that invalid
as well is a marriage contracted by a young lady
with someone she did not like strictly out of reverence toward her parents together with the anticipation of probable indignation, recrimination, harsh
treatment, and similar inconveniences.*" This kind
of "reverential fear" becomes "grave fear" especially in the case of females, that is to say, the
weaker sex, and this is why, in the opinion of the
Canonists, it is considered equivalent to violent
compulsion. (*Collet. Tractat. de met.* Chapter 7
de impedimento; and Schmaltz Grueber, Book 1,
Part 4 *de spons. et matrim.*, No. 41.) Finally, in
addition to what has already been said, it is worth
quoting, on the statement of one belonging to
the Apostolic capital, what the Holy Congregation has decreed in order to reach a decision in
cases of this kind: "*Nevertheless today, according
to the new rules approved by the Council of Trent,
a marriage contracted in a situation that invali-
dates it from the beginning is not validated by subsequent consummation no matter how freely
performed, but a new consent before the Church is
required.*" In other words, without paying attention to all kinds of details, today a new law
passed by the Council of Trent establishes the
principle that a marriage which has not been
validly contracted from the beginning is not validated by a conjugal life, even when consent is
then given to the latter; instead a new vow must
be taken before the Church. (See *Monacelli,
Formularium, for. Ecclesiae*, Section 8, Formula
10, No. 17; also Fagnano, Chapter *de illis*, No. 12
and B, *de desp. impuber.*).

    We reject, therefore, the opinion of the
Defender, Deacon Owsiany, and conclude that
the marriage between Princess Carolyne
Iwanowska and Prince Nicholas Wittgenstein,
having been contracted because of the grave violence exercised by her father and being, therefore, invalid from the beginning (it being
characterised by an unsatisfactory conjugal life of
disagreements, and not validated, moreover, by
the birth of offspring) is null and void. Princess
Carolyne is, therefore, given the faculty to contract, if she so wishes, marriage with an unattached person. Her daughter Marie Pauline
Antonia, insofar as she was born *sub figura matrimonii* (of a marriage that was previously deemed
legal), is considered to have been born legiti-

*si contractum fuit per metum reverentialem; atque
hinc sequitur invalidum esse matrimonium contractum a virgine cum eo quem illa adversabatur
ex mera reverentia in parentes cum indignationis
exprobrationis, durae tractationis et similium in-
commodorum veri simili existimatione con-
juncta.*" Cette sorte de *metus reverentialis*
devient *metus gravis* préeminemment pour les
femmes, c'est à dire le faible sexe, c'est pourquoi
il est regardé comme un forcement violent sur
l'opinion des canonistes. (*Collet. Tractat. de met.*
Cap. VII *de impedimento vi*; et Schmaltz Grueber
lib. 1, Tit. IV *de spons[alibus] et matrim[onio]* n.
41). Enfin pour résumer ce qui avait été dit il
faut encore citer que sur la présentation d'un
des appartenants à la Capitale Apostolique la
Sainte Congrégation a décrété pour décider une
affaire de la substance suivante: "*Nihilominus
hodie Jure novo Concilii Tridentini, matrimonium nulliter a principio contractum non convalidatur per subsequutam copulam quantumvis
libere habitam sed requiritur novus consensus in
facie Ecclesiae*" c'est à dire ne faisant attention à
tout cela d'aujourd'hui une nouvelle loi du Con-
cile Trident[ine] un mariage qui n'a pas été
validement contracté dès le commencement ne
se valide nullement par une vie conjugale si
même elle était de consentement, mais elle
exige un nouveau consentement émis en face de
l'Eglise (Monacell[i] in *Formul[ario] for. Ecclesiae* Tit. VII *for.* X; Fagnan[o] Cap. *de illis* n. 12
et B. *de desp[onsalisbus] imp[uberis]*.

    Par laquelle cause en repoussant l'opinion
du défenseur Diacre Owsiany le mariage de la
Princesse Caroline née Iwanowska avec le
Prince Nicolas Wittgensteyn pour cause de
grande violence exercée par son père et comme
dès son commencement invalidé, et par une vie
conjugale inunanime et courte, ni par les enfants
eus ne se validant pas, se fondant sur l'esprit des
Articles de la loi précitée prononçait cet<te>
union invalide et comme n'ayant pas eu lieu en
laissant à la Princesse Caroline Wittgensteyn le
pouvoir de se marier à une personne libre si elle
le voudrait. Sa fille Marie Pauline Antoinette
comme née *sub figura matrimonii* considerée
comme née legalement en la laissant auprès de
sa mère sous sa tutelle. Comme récompense au

mately and remains under the guardianship of her mother. As a compensation for his labors, Deacon Owsiany, in virtue of the Bull by Benedict XIV, *Dei miseratione*, is assigned 50 silver roubles to be paid by the Petitioner out of her own funds. The Petitioner should also pay 17 silver roubles and ten silver kopecks to the Government Treasury for 57 sheets of unstamped paper used in this case. Copies of the present decree are issued to the two parties involved. The case is to be considered closed, the decree not being executable until it is submitted to Monsignor the Archbishop as from his instructions given on May 30 of last year, Prot. No. 1737.

The original is signed by the President, Prelate Laski, who enclosed his own personal opinion, by the Assessor, Prelate Wrublewski, by the Assessor, Reverend Holkiewicz, by the Reverend Hoe, inspector of monasteries. It is certified by the Legal Secretary, N. Jaroszewicz, and by the Department Head Romanowicz.

On the 8th of October, 1852, Monsignor the Metropolitan Ignaz Holowinski confirmed the opinion of Prelate Laski and rejected the decision of the Consistory.

The truth of this statement is confirmed by the signature of Legal Secretary and Assessor Jaroszewicz.
Checked against the original.
Ivan Romanowicz, Department Head.

D[iac]re Owsiany pour ses péines, en vertu de la Bulle de Pape Benoît XIV qui commence par les mots *Dei miseratione*, désignait 50 Rubles en argent lesquels il est ordonné de recevoir des biens de la pétitionnaire pour son compte. Prendre aussi du dit bien, pour 57 feuilles de papier non-timbré employé pour cette affaire, 17 roubles en argent et 10 Cop. AZ. en argent et les porter dans la Caisse du Gouvernement; et le présent décret donnez en copie à toutes les deux parties plaignantes. Cet<te> affaire sera regardée comme finie, sans l'executer pourtant, mais en la rapportant à Mons[eigneur] en exécution de sa transmission du 30 mai cet<te> année, N° 1737.

L'original est souscrit par le President Prélat Laski avec son opinion particulière.
<L'> assesseur Prelat Wrubleswski
L'assesseur(e) Prêtre Holkiewicz
Visitateur des Monastères Prêtre Hoe.
Consolidé par le Secrétaire N. Jaroszewicz.
Consolidé par le Chef de Table (Kolezhski registrateur) Romanowicz

Le huit octobre 1852 Mons[eigneur] le Métrop[olitain] Ignace Holowinski a confirmé sur l'opinion du Président Prélat Laski en repoussant la décision du Consistoire.

Veritable. Secretaire (Kolezhski) Assesseur Jaroszewicz.

A contrôlé avec l'original. Chef de Division Jean Romanowicz.

The Opinion of the Vicar, President of the Consistory.

September 19, 1852.

The opinion of the president of the Ecclesiastical Roman Catholic Consistory of Mohilow, Prelate Laski, on the case of divorce involving Princess Carolyne born Iwanowska, married to Prince Nicholas Wittgenstein, presented for judgement in the second instance by Monsignor the Metropolitan with a communication dated May 30, 1852, Prot. No. 1737.

Having examined the divorce case pertaining to Princess Carolyne born Iwanowska, and Prince Nicholas Wittgenstein, and having then studied its circumstances, I find the following:

1852 le 19 du mois de septembre.

Opinion du Président du Consistoire Ecclésiastique Romain catholique de Mohilow Prélat Laski sur l'affaire de divorce de la Princesse Caroline née Iwanowska et mariée au Prince Nicolas Wittgensteyn, envoyée avec une transmission de Monseigneur Le Métropolite N. 1737 le 30 mai de l'année 1852 pour être jugée en seconde instance.

Vu l'affaire de divorce de la Princesse Caroline née Iwanowska avec le Prince Nicolas Wittgensteyn et après l'avoir relatée avec ses circonstances je trouve ce qui suit.

Princess Wittgenstein advanced two reasons for annulment: 1) the celebration of her marriage in a church that was not competent to celebrate the wedding, because her own priest had not been informed, i.e. secrecy; and 2) the fact that she was forced to marry, i.e. the impediment of intimidation.

With regard to the first reason, the Princess says that, when her parents separated, she lived with her mother in the Parish of Monastirysze while her father, whom she visited no more than four times a year, normally resided in the village of Starostince in the Parish of Pohrebysze, where she was forced to marry on her father's orders, the marriage being performed by the Curate of this parish, Canon Beregowicz. But, according to the evidence on file, especially the response of the Vicar of the Church of Monastirysze, the Reverend Czerniawski, we can see that Princess Carolyne, born Iwanowska, resided there only until the year 1836, and afterwards, according to the statement of Canon Beregowicz, she resided with her father in the Parish of Pohrebysze throughout 1836. There she made her Easter confession and took also Holy Communion; she was registered as a parishioner in the list of members of the Congregation and was regarded as a member of the congregation of Pohrebysze, where she was married in April 1836, the marriage banns having been previously made. Therefore, the Curate of the Parish of Pohrebysze was legally Princess Carolyne's Curate, insofar as that was her residence.

With regard to the violence done to her, Princess Wittgenstein's marriage was celebrated with all the formalities prescribed by the law, and she underwent a pre-marital examination as is shown in her marriage certificate. As for the argument that the marriage was celebrated without her personal consent and only on account of her being forced to do so by her father, after close scrutiny of the dossier and consideration of the circumstances, in the light of Canon laws and regulations, I find the following:

1. Canon Law absolutely requires that, with regard to witnesses, there must be proof about their religious affiliation, honesty, and irreproachable conduct, whether their reputation is not already tarnished, whether they are rich or poor in order that they not give false evidence in their own interest. See *Corpus Juris Canonici ex*

La Princesse Wittgensteyn produit deux causes d'annulation de son mariage; la célébration du mariage dans une église incompetente sans le savoir de son Curé: *Clandestinitas*, et le forcement: *impedimentum metus*.

Pour répondre à la première de ces causes, la Princesse dit qu'elle, quand ses parents se séparaient, vivait auprès de sa mère dans la Paroisse de Monastirysze, et son père qu'elle ne visitait plus de quatre fois par an demeurait habituellement dans le village de Starostince situé dans la Paroisse de de Pohrebyszeze, où elle était de force mariée par ordre de son père, et le mariage était célébré par le Curé de la dite Paroisse Chanoine Beregowicz. Mais des preuves qui se trouvent au dossier de l'affaire et particulièrement de la réponse du Vicaire de l'Eglise de Monasteryszeze vicaire prêtre Czerniawski, on voit que la Princesse Caroline née Iwanowska seulement jusqu'à l'année 1836, et qu'après cela comme le dit le Chanoine Beregowicz elle demeurait auprès de son père dans la Paroisse de Pohrebyszeze l'année 1836, et elle y accomplissait sa confession Pascale et y prenait la Sainte Communion, était inscrite dans le Registre des Paroissiens, *Status animarum*, elle était regardée comme paroissienne de l'Eglise de Pohrebyszeze, où elle était mariée en Avril 1836, *praecedentibus denunciationibus*. Ainsi le Curé de la Paroisse de Pohrebyszeze était Curé légal de la Princesse Caroline, *quasi domicilii*.

En ce qui regarde le forcement, le mariage de la Princesse Wittgenstein fut célébré avec toutes les formalités voulues par la loi et l'examen accompli comme le prouve <le certificat> (metríka) du mariage. Quant à cela, pour la conclusion de ce mariage qu'il n'y avait pas son consentement personnel et seulement forcement de la part de son père, moi, en considérant le dossier, et rapprochant ces circonstances avec les lois et règlements Canons je trouve ce qui suit.

1° La loi de l'Eglise veut absolument que par rapport aux témoins, on aient des preuves sur leur religion, état, honnêteté, et de conduite irréprochable, si quelqu'un d'eux n'est déjà noté mal, s'il est riche ou pauvre, qu'il ne dépose faussement pour son intérêt. *Corpus Juris Canonici ex concil. Matizenz.* n. 3 fin. e v. 9, 2 et

concil. Maticensi, No. 3 fin. and v. 9. 2 and 3. Diges. "Si testes:" "As for witnesses, one must verify their trustworthiness, status, conduct, and seriousness; therefore, each one must be investigated in person as to whether he is noble or plebeian, whether he leads an honest life untarnished by accusations, whether he has a criminal record and is reprehensible, whether he is rich or poor, for he could easily state anything that could profit him." In the dossier presented to us there is nothing about the witnesses' conduct or their fulfilling their religious obligations; moreover, there is no Police certificate nor any statement from their Curates. We do not know whether they are rich or poor, whether they have a criminal record and, as far as three of the witnesses are concerned, the nobleman Ivan Mieszkowski, Mateusz Dlugolentski, and Antonina Kostenecka, there is no evidence of their age, religion and whether they have ever been indicted. This omission is against civil law as stated in the Imperial Laws, Tome 10, Article 2395,[12] as well as Canon Law, since, in this case, the noble lady Antonina Kostenecka and the peasant Uliana Stolarczukowa have been allowed to testify. See Corpus Juris Canonici, 17, XXXIII, g. 5: "a woman is subject to the authority of her husband and has no prerogatives and indeed cannot say anything or be a witness"; that is to say, a woman who is under the jurisdiction of her husband has no right to make statements or to act as a witness.

2. Some of the witnesses in the dossier based their statements on hearsay, and their depositions cannot, therefore, be accepted as proofs. See Reinffest[uel] Book II, Chapter 20, Paragraph 11, No. 343: "Evidence from hearsay has no value if the witnesses do not provide justification for their information and the evidence they give." There are here some gentlemen testifying to statements that were not made directly by Monsieur Iwanowsky but by others not mentioned here. In the Corpus Juris Canonici, Chapter cum causam, Decret. Gregor., Book 2, Chapter 20, Innocentius III, it is stated as follows: "We prescribe, in the hearing of witnesses that either party wishes to introduce to deal with the main question of the case or as character wit-

3 Digest. "Si testes:" "In testibus fides, dignitas, mores, gravitas examinada sit, ideoque in persona eorum exploranda erunt conditio cujuscumque, utrum quis Decurio an Plebeius sit, an honestae et inculpatae vitae, an vero qui notatus est reprehensibilis, an locuples et egens sit, ut lucri causa quid facile admittat." Dans le dossier ci-présent on ne voit rien sur leur conduite, sur l'accomplissement de leur devoir religieux, on ne voit nul Certificat de la Police, ni du Curé, on ne voit aussi sont-ils pauvres ou riches, ou ne sont ils notés en quelque mauvaise action, et quant à ce qui regarde trois des témoins, comme les gentilhommes Jean Mieszkowski, Mathieu Dlugolentski, et Antoinette Kostenecka il n'est pas démontré même quel âge ils' ont, de quel<le> religion sont-ils, ou n'ont-ils été sous jugement, cet<te> omission est contre la loi même civile comme le dit la loi de l'Empire, Tom. X, Art[icle] 3945, outre cela ont été admis à déposer la femme noble Antoinette Kostenetska et la paysanne Uliana Stolarczukowa contre la loi de l'Eglise, Corpus Juris Canon[ici] 17, XXXIII, g.5: "mulierem constat subjectam esse dominio viri et nullam auctoritatem habere, nec dicere enim potest, nec testis esse," c'est à dire la femme qui est subordonnée à son mari n'a pas le droit ni d'enseigner ni d'être témoin.

2° Quelques uns des témoins dans ce dossier se sont fondés sur quelques circonstances sur des ouï-dire et on ne peut pas recevoir de tel(le)s témoignages comme preuves, Reinffest[uel] lib. II, Tit. 20 par. 11 n. 343: "testimonium de audito alieno non valeat si testes non reddunt causam scientiae seu testimonii sui," il y a ici des témoins gentilshommes qui l'ont entendu non de la propre bouche du Seigneur Iwanowski mais sur des ouïs, ici non mentionnés, Corpus Juris, cum causam, Decret[a] Gregor. lib. 2, Tit. XX, Innocentius III: "Mandamus quatenus recipias testes quos utraque pars tam super principali negotio, quam in personas testium duxerit producendos, ac eos diligenter examinare procures, et de singulis circumstantiis prudenter in-

---

[12]According to the Russian text.

nesses, that you procure to examine them carefully and prudently, inquire about the specific circumstances of the case, namely you should clearly and completely record the place and time, whether the action was seen or heard, whether it is true knowledge or opinion, rumor or certainty."[13]

<3. Canon Law requires a thorough examination of the witnesses; one should inquire about all the circumstances concerning the case, namely what the witness has observed, when and where, whether he has seen the matter himself or has heard it, and from whom; whether he has learned about it by hearsay, or beyond doubt, by conjecture or supposition. In the *Corpus Juris Canonici, cum causam, Decret Gregor.* Book 2, Chapter 20, *Innocentius III*, it is stated as follows: *"We prescribe, in the hearing of witnesses, that either party wishes to introduce to deal with the main question of the case or as character witnesses, that you procure to examine them carefully and prudently, inquire about the specific circumstances of the case, namely you should clearly and completely record the place and time, whether the action was seen or heard, whether it is true knowledge or opinion, rumor or certainty."*> If this is not the case, the deposition has no value; "it follows, therefore," according to Reinffestuel, Book II, Chapter 20, Paragraph XI, page 343, "that hearsay from others has no value." In the present case, the aforementioned law has not been followed, since not all the depositions were detailed and substantial and, as for the third witness, a peasant, his statements are not even recorded. It is said simply that he testified along the same lines as the previous witness, but did he say the same things and what did he say precisely? These things are not mentioned. Moreover, in these witnesses' depositions it is vaguely stated that the father was harsh and severe with his daughter. It is, however, impossible to decide whether this was the result of his natural stern disposition as

quirens de causis videlicet, loco, tempore, visu, auditu, scientia, credulitate, fama et certitudine cuncta plene conscribas."

<3°..

Decret. Gregor. lib. 2, Tit. XX c. *cum causam, Innocent. III: "Mandamus quatenus recipias testes, quos utraque pars tam super principali negotio quam in personas testium duxerit producendos, ac eos diligenter examinare procures et de singulis circumstantiis prudenter inquirens, de causis videlicet, personis, loco, tempore, visu, auditu, scientia, credulitate, fama et certitudine cuncta plene conscribas,"*>[14] en cas contraire le témoignage n'a nulle valeur; *"unde fit,"* ait Reinffestuel, lib. II, tit. 20 par. XI p. 343, *"quod alienum dictum ejus non valeret."* En l'affaire ci-present on n'a pas observé avec ponctualité la loi citée, car toutes les dépositions ne sont pas detaillées et circonstanciées, et le troisieme témoin paysan ses réponses ne sont pas même écrites, et il est dit seulement qu'il a constaté la déposition du premier, mais est-ce réellement la même chose qu'il a dit, et en quoi consiste sa constatation? Il n'est pas démontré. Outre cela dans les dépositions des témoins il est dit vaguement, que le père était avec sa fille brusque et sérieux. Mais si cela provenait de son caractère naturel comme on s'exprime dans le dossier (d'un caractère ambigu), ou de la violence au mariage qu'on voulait exercer contre la fille, il est impossible de la décider, et dans un tel accident il fallait demander <d'> examiner les témoins, *Corpus Juris Can[onici] "cum clamor": "Iterum examinandus est testis, qui obscure deposuit, suppletur ex judicis officio."*

---

[13]It is very likely that this whole quotation, starting with *In the Corpus Juris Canonici,* should be expunged, for it is repeated, more pertinently, in the following paragraph. It would seem there were two errors, one committed by the Russian scribe who inserted the quotation at this point, and one by the French scribe or translator who, realising there was a scribal mistake, avoided duplicating the quotation but made things worse for, in so doing, he omitted to translate the sentence beginning at Point 3.

[14]*Lapsus calami*: a sentence was omitted by the translator or the copyist on account of the same quotation being present in the original Russian. It is also possible, since no new point is being made, that the fault lies in Laski's repetitiveness, and Okraszewski merely attempted to correct it and, in so doing, failed to straighten out the enumeration of the points being made.

stated, somewhat ambiguously, in the dossier, or derived from the violence he wanted to exercise on his daughter to force her into marrying.

On this specific question, it would have been necessary to question witnesses further. According to the *Corpus Juris Canonici*, *"Cum clamor"*: *"A witness who gave vague evidence must be questioned again; as a judge, it is your prerogative to request it."*

4. The deposition of the Princess's mother does not constitute a proof in her daughter's case; see *Corpus Juris Canonici*, paragraph 20: "A father is not a valid witness for the son, nor the son for the father"; and also line 6, Para-xxx graph 34: *"Parents and sons are not to be admitted as witnesses against each other if they do not wish to,"* that is to say that neither the father can provide legal testimony in favor of the son, nor the son for the father. And if they were to testify, neither fathers nor sons can be admitted to testify against each other.

5. Three of the witnesses were servants and one of them a woman; they have testified to the effect that Monsieur Iwanowsky gave his daughter a beating when she refused to contract marriage, but their deposition, since they were serfs, is not legal.

According to Corpus Juris, *Si testes*, 3 *fin. q.u.* and 3 *Digest.*, servants are not allowed to testify either for or against their masters: *"Servants cannot be questioned either in favor of or against their master, but may be questioned about things pertaining to them."* Daune Reiff., Chapter 20 *de testibus et attestationibus*, Par. 1: *"Witnesses are considered according to their condition, sex, and conduct; because of his condition, a servant is often not free from fear of his master and is prone to suppress evidence of the truth; as far as sex is concerned, let it be a man rather than a woman, for women always provide inconsistent evidence and are likely to change their deposition; in terms of conduct, it is important that it be honest and honorable for, if the conduct is not good, the witness cannot be trusted."* In other words, in receiving depositions one must pay attention to the nature, conduct, and condition of the witness, for a serf or a servant, in giving evidence, may alter the truth of his deposition out of fear; by sex he should be a man and not a woman, for the deposition given by a woman is always incon-

4° Le témoignage de la mère de la Princesse ne constitue nulle preuve dans l'affaire de sa fille, *Corpus Juris*, par. XX: *"Testis idoneus pater filio aut filius patri non est"* item l. 6, par. 34: *"Parentes et liberi invicem adversus se nec volentes ad testimonium admittendi sunt;"* c'est à dire comme témoin légal ne peut pas être admis ni le père pour le fils, ni le fils pour le père. Les parents et les enfants mêmes s'ils le rendraient ne peuvent être admis à déposer l'un contre l'autre.

5° Trois des témoins, sujets et serviteurs, et parmi eux une femme, ont deposé que le Seigneur Iwanowski quand sa fille ne voulait pas contracter le mariage, la battait même; mais ces paysans comme gens vulgaires et sujets de la Princesse, la déposition n'est pas légale.

Corp[us] Jur[is] *"Si testes"* 1. III fin. par. n.1 et 3, *Digest.*, Les serviteurs ni pour ni contre leurs maîtres ne peuvent déposer: *"Servi neque pro Domino suo neque adversum dominum, sed pro facto suo interrogari possunt."* Daune Rei[n]ff[estuel], tit. XX de test. et attest., par. 1: *"Testes enim considerantur conditione, natura, et vita : conditione, servus testis non liber saepe metu dominantis testimonium supprimit veritatis; natura sit vir non foemina ; nam varium et mutabile testimonium semper foemina producit; vita, sit innocens et integer actu, nam si vita bona defuerit, fide carebit,"* c'est-à-dire dans le témoignage on doit faire attention au caractère et manière de vivre, état de fortune du témoin car déposant sujet et serviteur peut altérer la vérité de sa déposition par peur; comme <le> sexe du témoin doit être homme et non femme car le témoignage d'une femme est toujours varié et changeant; manière(s) de vivre doit être considerée si honorable et sans tâche car s'il vit mal lui-même on ne peut le croire. C'est par rapport à cela *Corp[us] Jur[is]* 3 *in fin.* par. 2 et 3 *Dig.:*

sistent and changing; the conduct of one's life should be honorable and unimpeachable because, if the witness leads a bad life, he is not believable. It is in relation to these notions that the *Corpus Juris 2, in fin.* 9, 2 and 3 *Dig.* states: "*Those witnesses are not deemed competent who may be ordered to provide testimony,*" or, in other words, we cannot consider those witnesses who could be ordered to testify as reliable. Therefore, Pichler, Book 11, Par. 3, Chapter 8, not without reason concludes that "We must base our judgements on the basis of the reliability of witnesses who are more worthy of faith." If violence was indeed used on the Princess, she would have mentioned it before and after the marriage and would have written about it to her social peers or at least to people worthy of her confidence; therefore, it would not have been impossible for the Princess to find witnesses who, on account of their age and social position, would be more trustworthy (*honestiores*) than servants or serfs. It is true the parties in the case have the right to accept and reject witnesses; nevertheless, there are cases in which such a law is set aside as stated by Reinff., Chapter 20, Paragraph 1, No. 16 and 17. There are people who, on account of their disreputable character, cannot be admitted as witnesses in spite of the wishes of the parties involved because, if they were, this would give offence both to public opinion as well as to the law, and it would be a blow to the dignity of the courts. This happens, for example, when the witnesses themselves have been indicted. The reason for it is that anybody who so wishes can refuse what is in his own interest, but one cannot refuse what is in the public interest. For that reason, one of the parties has the right not to object to the witnesses granted him, except when these witnesses have to be removed on the basis of the accepted rules and the respect due to the law: "*There are situations in which witnesses are deemed incompetent to testify and the parties involved are not allowed to admit them since, in that case, it would be to the detriment of public law and the interest of the commonwealth, and it would offend the dignity of the judges as is the case with witnesses from excommunicated families or some such circumstances*"; No. 21: "*The reason is that someone can, if he so wishes, renounce something introduced to his own advantage, but not something in the public interest*"; *item 51* diligenti,

"*Idonei non videntur esse testes, quibus imperari potest ut testes fiant,*" c'est-à-dire on ne peut pas compter pour témoins légaux aux à qui on peut ordonne<r> d'être témoin. En conséquence de quoi Pichler lib. XI, par. 3 Cap. VIII non sans fondement décide que l'on doit plutôt croire: "*Honestioribus potius testibus credendum et sic judicandum.*" S'il y avait réellement violence pour le mariage exercée contre la Princesse, aussi bien qu'après le mariage elle le dirait ou ecrirait assurement à ses egaux ou au moins aux personnes dignes de foi, ainsi je croirai qu'il ne sera pas impossible à la Princesse de désigner des témoins qui par leur état et position sociale seront plus dignes de foi (*honestiores*) que les serviteurs et les sujets. Il est vrai que les parties en procès ont le droit de désigner et d'invalider les témoins; pourtant il y a des accidents où cette loi est bannie comme le dit Rei[n]ff[estuel, Tit. 20, par. 1 N. 16 et 17. Il se trouve des pareilles personnes qui vu leur indignité ne peuvent pas être admis à être témoins, même sur le désir des parties, par cause que dans le cas contraire l'opinion publique comme la loi seront par cela violentées et la dignité des Tribunaux en sera ebranlée; comme par exemple quand les témoins ont été jugés eux mêmes et la cause en est celle que quiconque le voudra, peut refuser, ce que la loi permet dans son intérêt, mais il ne peut pas refuser ce qui est dans l'intérêt public; c'est pourquoi la partie a pouvoir de ne faire usage invalidement du témoin qui lui est donné par la loi; mais non dans le cas où ces témoins dans l'intérêt public et du respect dû au loi doivent être invalidés: "*Dentur quaedam inhabilitates testium quae per partes remitti non possunt eo quod alioquin l<a>ederetur jus publicum et favor communis Reipublicae, ipsorumque judiciorum decor violaretur uti sit in testibus in familibus (sic) excommunicatis ac hujusmodi*". No. 21: "*Accedit ratio quia potest quis, si vult, renunciare favori pro se introducto, non autem favori publico, (c. 51) diligenti, 12: de foro competen[ti], ac proinde potest etiam pars remittere exceptiones testium in favorem sui introductorum etsi secus sit dicendum de aliis ob favorem publicum seu ex ratione Tribunalium introductis;*" et c'est par cette cause que les femmes et les serviteurs sujets ne doivent pas être admis.

12 de foro competen.: "*Therefore, one of the parties may forgo taking exception to witnesses introduced in his own favor, though it must be said otherwise for other witnesses introduced in the public interest or by a decision of the Court.*" It is for this reason that women and servants must not be admitted.

6. Canon Law states clearly how witnesses are to be questioned: "*In examining witnesses some general and some particular questions must be put to them. General questions are: 1) what are the witness's name, age, and condition and, moreover, whether he is related to the party introducing him or an enemy to the other party. Finally, in case his deposition did not agree with that of the other witnesses, what has he got to say? Does he have a personal interest in the case under debate? Special questions are those pertaining to the facts and circumstances of the case in question*" (Reinff. Book 2, Chapter 20, lines 508-510). But, in the present case, there has been no general questioning of the witnesses (*generalia*) and, as far as particular questions are concerned, the answers were not written down point by point, but in disorder, and it is not clear how the questions were formulated, since they were not recorded together with the answers. The questioning performed by the party of the petitioner tends to be suggestive, i.e., it suggests to the witnesses what they are supposed to state and in what words. This is the case, for example, in point 2. where the witness testified to the fact that, from the time the Princess became acquainted with Prince Wittgenstein, i.e., since the year 1834, the Petitioner never loved him and responded to all his attentions and proposals by displaying quite evident displeasure and told him plainly that she felt no attraction whatsoever toward him and did not wish to be his wife. But, at point 5., the witness states that when Carolyne's father asked her to come to his place for the second time and asked her whether she had reached a decision and was going to fulfill his wishes, she begged him a second time not to force her. At this point, her father became very angry, struck her, and said to her: "Go and live with your mother because I am disinheriting you." Such questioning contravenes the law and the answers to such questions are invalidated. The meaning of "*suggestive questioning*" is explained in the following; see Reinffestuel, Tome 2, Paragraph 17 *de examine testium* No. 516: "*If*

6° Les lois Canones le disent clairement de quelle manière on doit questionner les témoins: "*In examine testium proponantur ipsis interrogatoria, partim generalia, partim specialia. Generalia sunt 1° quo nomine testis vocetur, cujus sit aetatis et conditionis? deinde an sit conjunctus producentis, an inimicus partis adversae? an non cum aliis testibus convenerit quid dicere velit? An non in causa controversa interesse habeat? et specialia quae ex facto controverso ejusque circumstantiis desumuntur.*" (Rei[n]f-[festuel] lib. II, Tit. XX, l. 508-510). Mais dans le dossier présent on <n'>a pas donné un interrogatoire général au témoins (*generalia*) et sur les interrogatoires spéciaux les réponses ne sont pas écrites, spécialement mais sans aucun ordre, c'est pourquoi on ne voit même en quels mots ils ont été faits; l'interrogatoire composé par la partie de la Pétitionnaire est suggestive, c'est-à-dire suggéré ou désignant évidemment aux témoins ce qu'<ils> devaient dire et même les mots, comme par exemple dans le point deux le témoin dépose qu'à compter du temps où la Princesse fit connaissance avec Prince Wittgensteyn, c'est-à-dire depuis l'année 1834, la pétitionnaire ne l'aimait pas et surtout ses soins et propositions elle lui répondait par un mécontentement bien évident et même lui répondait directement qu'elle n'avait pour lui aucun attachement et qu'elle ne voulait pas être sa femme. Et puis dans le point cinq le témoin dépose que quand le père de Caroline l'appela une seconde fois chez lui et lui demanda si elle était decidée et si elle allait accomplir sa volonté, elle le priait alors pour la seconde fois de ne pas la forcer, et qu'alors le père la frappa, étant dans une grande colère et lui dit: "Allez chez votre mère car je vous déshérite. "De telle<s> demande<s> sont contraires à la loi et les réponses données sur des pareilles demandes sont invalides. C'est cela que signifie *Interrogatoria suggestiva* eclairci <en> ce qui suit. Reinffestuel Tom. II par XVII *de examine testium*, n. 516: "*Si judex interroget testem an viderit quod Titius oc-*

the judge is questioning a witness as to whether he actually saw x murdering y on such and such a day and place by going at him with a knife and wounding him in the chest, etc., this kind of questioning is deemed suggestive in that it clearly suggests and indicates to the witness what his answer should be, i.e., 'Yes, I saw x murdering y on such and such a day and place," etc. See, moreover, No. 518: *"Suggestive questioning is to be avoided and is forbidden by law."* As a consequence every decision based on such depositions is not valid. See No. 521:[15] *"Everything that follows from this is null and void."*

7. Finally, Canon Law requires that, when proofs are provided only through depositions which are not confirmed by written documents, the case is not sufficiently proved. See *Corpus Juris Canonici Ex Concilio Maticensi*, Paragraph 30, as above: *"Witnesses alone are not sufficient to provide complete proof unless their testimony is corroborated by other instruments and arguments. It is certain that a case presented on the sole force of depositions and not supported by other proofs is of no consequence."* Besides the depositions, we find no other proof in the dossier.

For this reason, as well as because the witnesses have been admitted and took the oath and were questioned without fulfilling the formalities prescribed by law, their depositions are, therefore, insufficient, though they cannot be invalidated only because they are given under oath; given also the circumstances relative to the marriage of Princess Wittgenstein and especially the fact that the witnesses for the certification of the marriage are people worthy of faith, among whom there is Canon Beregowicz who performed the marriage and who, in his official capacity, was invited by the parties involved to receive the conjugal oath; given also that this priest was the most important participant and a witness above suspicion, and his testimony was supported by other witnesses worthy of faith, I find that a marriage that fulfills all the requirements of the law such as the one contracted by Prince and Princess Wittgenstein cannot be annulled and, for this reason, given a subject as serious as that of the marriage sacrament, I am of the opinion that the marriage of Prince and

ciderit Cajum tali die in tali loco percutiendo ipsum gladio, vulnerando in pectore etc. Hac enim ratione dicitur testis interrogari per suggestionem, suggerendo videlicet seu ipsi indicando quid respondeat, puta, ita vidi quod Titius occiderit Cajum tali die et loco etc. Daune n. 518: *"Interrogatoria suggestiva sunt vitanda et in jure prohibita."* De la sort tout Décret basé sur des témoignages pareils et nuls, N. 521:*"Omniaque inde sequuta ipso jure sunt nulla ac invalida."*

7° Enfin les droits de l'Eglise décident, que quand on produit seulement les témoignages comme preuves non appuyées par des documents et preuves écrites, l'affaire n'est suffisamment prouvée. *Corp[us] Juris Can[onici] Ex Concilio Maticensi ut supra* par. 30: *"Soli testes ad ingenuitatis probationem non sufficiunt nisi instrumentis et argumentis adjuventur sola attestatione prolatam nec aliis legitimis adminiculis causam approbatam nullius esse momenti certum est."* Mais outre les dépositions on ne voit nulle autre preuve dans le dossier.

C'est pour cette cause comme également que les témoins mêmes ont été acceptés à prêter serment et demandés sans avoir pas accompli les formalités voulues par la loi, par quelle cause leurs dépositions sont insuffisantes et (qu')on ne peut les annuler seulement par ce qu'ils sont basées sur le serment, comme aussi vu toutes les circonstances relatives au mariage de la Princesse Wittgensteyn et particulièrement que les témoins de la <certification> (*metrîka*) du mariage sont des personnages dignes de foi, parmi lesquels se trouve le Célébrant de la cérémonie du dit mariage, le Chanoine Beregowicz, qui comme un personnage officiel a été invité par les parties pour recevoir le serment d'une vie conjugale, et comme ce prêtre étant le personnage essentiel appuyé des témoins dignes de foi et lui-même témoin *omni exceptione major*, moi je trouve que le mariage couvert de toutes les formes de la loi comme celui des Princes Wittgensteyn ne peut être annulé, c'est pourquoi dans un sujet aussi grave qu'est le sacrement du mariage je suis d'opinion le mariage des Princes

---

[15]The French text has No. 512.

Princess Wittgenstein must be deemed legal and valid.

The original is signed by Prelate Laski, President of the Consistory.

Wittgensteyn doit être regardé comme légale et valide.

L'original est souscrit Président Prélat Laski.

Decree of Monsignor Archbishop

This opinion is approved by Monsignor Ignaz Holowinski, Metropolitan, on October 8, 1852.

It is undersigned by the Ecclesiastic Secretary of Monsignor the Archbishop of Mohilow, Assessor of the College of the Roman Catholic Church, Prelate Anton Kossowski.
Checked by Legal Secretary Jaroszewicz.

No. 30.
I testify to the authenticity of the present decree.
Weimar, July 2 (O.S.)=July 14, 1859
Signed: Baron Maltitz, Chargé d'affaires
Place of Seal
x Romanowicz, Chief of Division

I have done this translation myself and testify to its accuracy.
Rome, August 3, 1859.

W[ładislaw] Okraszewski
Seal.

Cet<te> opinion est approuvé<e> par Monseigneur le Métropolitain Ignace Holowinski le 8 octobre de l'année 1852 et souscrite par le Secrétaire Ecclésiastique de M[onseigneu]r l'Arch[evêqu]e de Mohilow, Prélat Assesseur du Coll[egium] Rom[anae] Cath[olicae] Ecc[lesiae] Antoine Cosowski.
Contrôlé. Secretaire Jaroscewicz (Kolezhsky Assesseur).
N. 30.
J'atteste l'authenticité du présent acte.
(souscrit) Le chargé d'affaires, Baron Maltitz Weimar, le 2/14 juillet 1859.
Loco Sigilli
x Chef de Division Romanowicz.

J'ai fait cette traduction moi-même et j'en atteste la verbalité.
3 août 1859.
Rom(m)e.
W[ładislaw] Okraszewski
Seal

Document No. 9. Undated, but first week of August 1859. Draft. Memorandum to the Pope from Monsignor Quaglia, Secretary of the Holy Congregation, outlining the merits of the case. Italian (4 pages).

<File>: Diocese of Zhitomir.

Carolyne Iwanowska, a Catholic, claims she married Prince Nicholas Wittgenstein, a Protestant, because of violence and intimidation on the part of her father which continued even after she was married.

After her father's death,[16] Carolyne applied to her own Ordinary Office to have her marriage annulled; but, perhaps because the witnesses called on to testify lacked the requisite qualities, her marriage was declared valid by that Curia. This was in 1851.

Carolina Iwanowska, cattolica, si sposò al Principe Nicola Wittgenstein, protestante, per violenza e timore incussogli dal padre, com'essa asserisce, e perseverante anche durante il matrimonio.

Avvenuta la morte del padre, Carolina fece istanza presso il proprio Ordinariato per la nullità. Ma forse perché i testimoni indotti mancavano delle necessarie qualità, fu nel 1851 il matrimonio ritenuto per valido da quella Curia.

---

[16] Peter Iwanowsky died in 1844. Carolyne started the proceedings to have her marriage annulled in 1848.

She appealed against that sentence before the Consistory of the Metropolitan Diocese of Mohilow: it seems she obtained from it a resolution for the annulment; but this was not endorsed by the Vicar General of the late Metropolitan on account of the same want he noticed in the conduct of the witnesses' examination.

In the meantime, her husband has contracted a second marriage to a member of the Lutheran sect. The lady has presented a petition to the present Archbishop of Mohilow in order to obtain a definitive sentence. He has answered he is unable to deal with this case without a specific authorisation from the Holy See.

It seems the problem is constituted by the question of the Vicar General of the late Archbishop. His is not considered a formal judgement, but a personal statement at best.

With this goal in mind, the lady is petitioning the Holy See to authorise the present Metropolitan, to deal again with her case of annulment until a definitive sentence can be provided.

It seems, moreover, that there have been some intrigues and deceits on the part of the lady's solicitors representing her in that Curia. They did this with the aim of causing some irregularities for the purpose of making the petitioner's goal more difficult to achieve.

From the Archbishop's answer to the lady's original petition to this effect, the above facts are confirmed, and it transpires as well that the obstacle to a further examination of the case on the Archbishop's part arises from an article of the 1847 Concordate with which we are not familiar, but which appears to state that a Metropolitan's final decision on a case is without recourse even in case his judgement is different from that of the judges. Thus, given that there has been a judgement on the case under the late Archbishop, there is in fact a problem.

It would be useful to know the terms of the Concordate in order then to decide whether it is

Appellò innanzi il Concistoro della Curia Metropolitana dal quale sembra ottenesse un opinamento per la nullità; però non venne adottato dal Vicario Gen[era]le del defunto Metropolitano per lo stesso difetto che rimarcò nell'esame dei testimoni.

Intanto l'uomo è passato ad altre nozze nella setta luterana. La donna ha fatto istanza all'odierno arcivescovo di Mohilow per ottenerne una sentenza definitiva; ma ne ha avuto in risposta non potersi in ciò ingerire senza un'autorizzazione particolare dalla S[anta] Sede.

Pare l'ostacolo sia nel fatto del Vicario del defunto Arcivescovo, il quale però non ritiensi un giudicato formale, ma al più per un decreto.

A questo fine la donna fa fervorosa istanza perché dalla S[anta] Sede sia l'odierno Metropolitano abilitato a trattare nuovamente detta causa di nullità fino alla definitiva sentenza.

Pare poi vi sia stato dell'imbroglio ed intrigo per parte dei procuratori della donna presso quella Curia per far nascere delle irregolarità e rendere sempre più difficile l'intento dell'Oratrice.

Da una risposta dell'Arcivescovo stesso sull'interpellanza fattagli dalla donna in proposito vengono constatati i fatti esposti; e rilevasi altresì che l'ostacolo alla ulteriore cognizione dell'affare per parte dell'Arcivescovo nasce da un articolo del Concordato 1847 che non si conosce, dal quale sembra stabilirsi che il giudicato del metropolitano è inappellabile anche nel caso di difformità di giudicati; onde, stante la cognizione della causa avvenuta sotto il passato Arcivescovo, è l'ostacolo di fatto.

Converrebbe conoscere i termini del Concordato per quindi decidere se <si> possa e

possible and proper at least as an instance of complete restitution[17] to agree to the petition.

convenga, almeno in via di restituzione in intiero, annuire alla istanza.

Document No. 10. August 8, 1859. Draft of the Papal Rescript authorising Archbishop Żyliński to review Carolyne's case. In Quaglia's own hand. Latin (1 page).

<File>: Zhitomir
Luck-Zhitomir
Mohilow
Carolyne Iwanowska, Lutheran 1847[18]
Prot. No. 6733/I
From the audience with the Holy Father.
of August 8, 1859

The Most Holy Father kindly agrees to the notion that, whereas there be nothing to the contrary, the present Metropolitan of Mohilow be empowered to take up again this specific case of marriage annulment, review it, and adjudicate it by a definitive sentence according to the level of appeal, having observed otherwise what need be observed especially the Bull *Dei miseratione* issued by the Holy Memory of Benedict XIV. The Archbishop must be notified of this.

Papal Audience

Zytomerien (Luk-Zitomier,

Mokilovo
Carolina Iwanowska, Luterana, 1847)
6733/I
Ex Audientia S[anctis]s[i]mi.
Die 8 Augusti 1859

S[anctis]s[i]mus benigne annuit ut, contrariis quibuscumque non obstantibus, modernus Metropolitanus Mohilowiensis enunciatam causam super nullitate matrimonii reassumere, cognoscere, ac per sententiam definitivam dijudicare valeat in gradu appellationis, servatis ceteroquin de jure servandis, ac praesertim Const[itution]e S[anctae] M[emoriae] Benedicti XIV *Dei miseratione* et notif[icetur] Archiep[iscop]o.

Udienza

Document No. 11. September 1859. Petition by Marie von Sayn-Wittgenstein to Pius IX requesting a declaration of legitimacy (Prot. No. 6733/I), with draft in Quaglia's hand, of papal answer dated September 13, 1859. Latin (2 pages).

<File>: Zhitomir:
Carolyne Iwanowska
Prot. No. 6733/I[wanowska]

To His Holiness
Pope Pius IX.

Most Blessed Father:

Marie von Sayn-Wittgenstein, Princess of the Russian Empire, unmarried, age twenty-three, prostrated at the feet of Your Holiness, states what follows:

Zytomerien
Carolina Iwanowska
6733/I[wanowska]

S[ancti]s[si]mo Domino Nostro
Pio Papae IX

Beatissime Pater.

Maria Princeps Sayn Wittgenstein in Imperio Russiaco, nubilis ann[orum] 23 Catholica, ad Sanctitatis V[estrae] Pedes provoluta humiliter exponit quae sequuntur.

---

[17]The notion of complete restitution (*restitutio in integrum*) is defined, according to Canon Law as follows: "Against a sentence for which there is not the ordinary remedy of appeals or requests to void it, there is the extraordinary remedy of complete restitution within the terms of Canons 1687, 1688, as long as it be certain that there was evident in-

justice in the sentence" (*Codex Juris Canonici Pii X Pontificis Maximi ab eminentissimo Petro Cardinal Gasparri auctus*, Book 4, *De Processibus*, Chapter 15, *Can.* 1905 [Rome: Vatican Press, 1918]).

[18]Added in margin; perhaps a reminder of Carolyne's husband's religious affiliation.

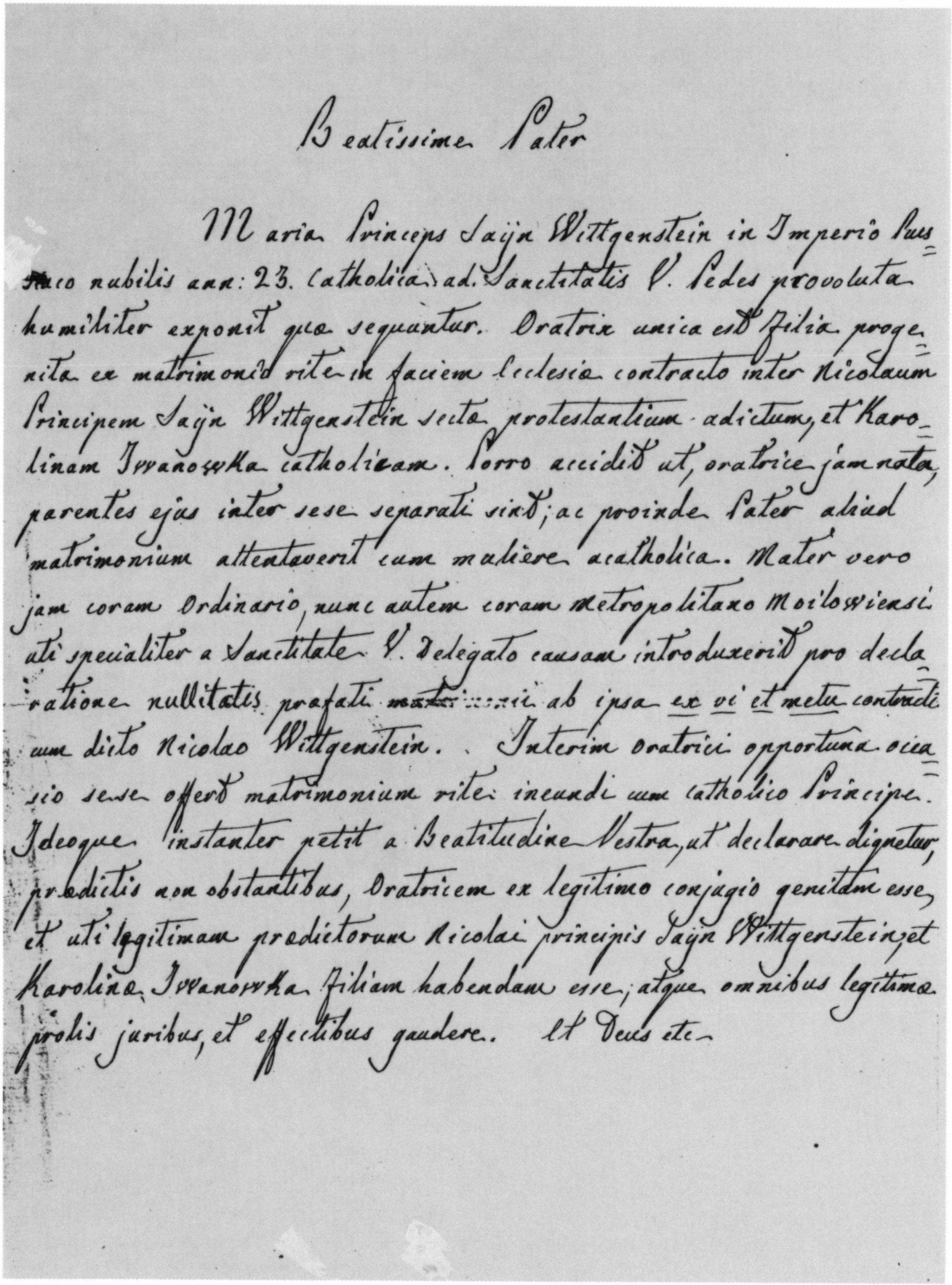

Beatissime Pater

Maria Princeps Sayn Wittgenstein in Imperio Russico nubilis ann: 23. catholica, ad Sanctitatis V. Pedes provoluta humiliter exponit quæ sequuntur. Oratrix unica est filia progenita ex matrimonio rite in faciem Ecclesiæ contracto inter Nicolaum Principem Sayn Wittgenstein sectæ protestantium adictum, et Karolinam Iwanowska catholicam. Porro accidit ut, oratrice jam nata, parentes ejus inter sese separati sint; ac proinde Pater aliud matrimonium attentaverit cum muliere acatholica. Mater vero jam coram Ordinario, nunc autem coram metropolitano Moilowiensi uti specialiter a Sanctitate V. delegato causam introduxerit pro declaratione nullitatis præfati matrimonii ab ipsa ex vi et metu contractæ cum dicto Nicolao Wittgenstein. Interim oratrici opportuna occasio sese offert matrimonium rite ineundi cum catholico Principe. Ideoque instanter petit a Beatitudine Vestra, ut declarare dignetur, prædictis non obstantibus, Oratricem ex legitimo conjugio genitam esse, et uti legitimam prædictorum Nicolai principis Sayn Wittgenstein et Karolinæ Iwanowska filiam habendam esse; atque omnibus legitimæ prolis juribus, et effectibus gaudere. Et Deus etc.

Plate 8. Facsimile of a petition from Princess Marie von Sayn-Wittgenstein to Pius IX, dated September 13, 1859. "She promptly requests Your Beatitude to deign to declare that the Petitioner... enjoys all the rights and privileges pertaining to legitimate offspring." 2 pages.

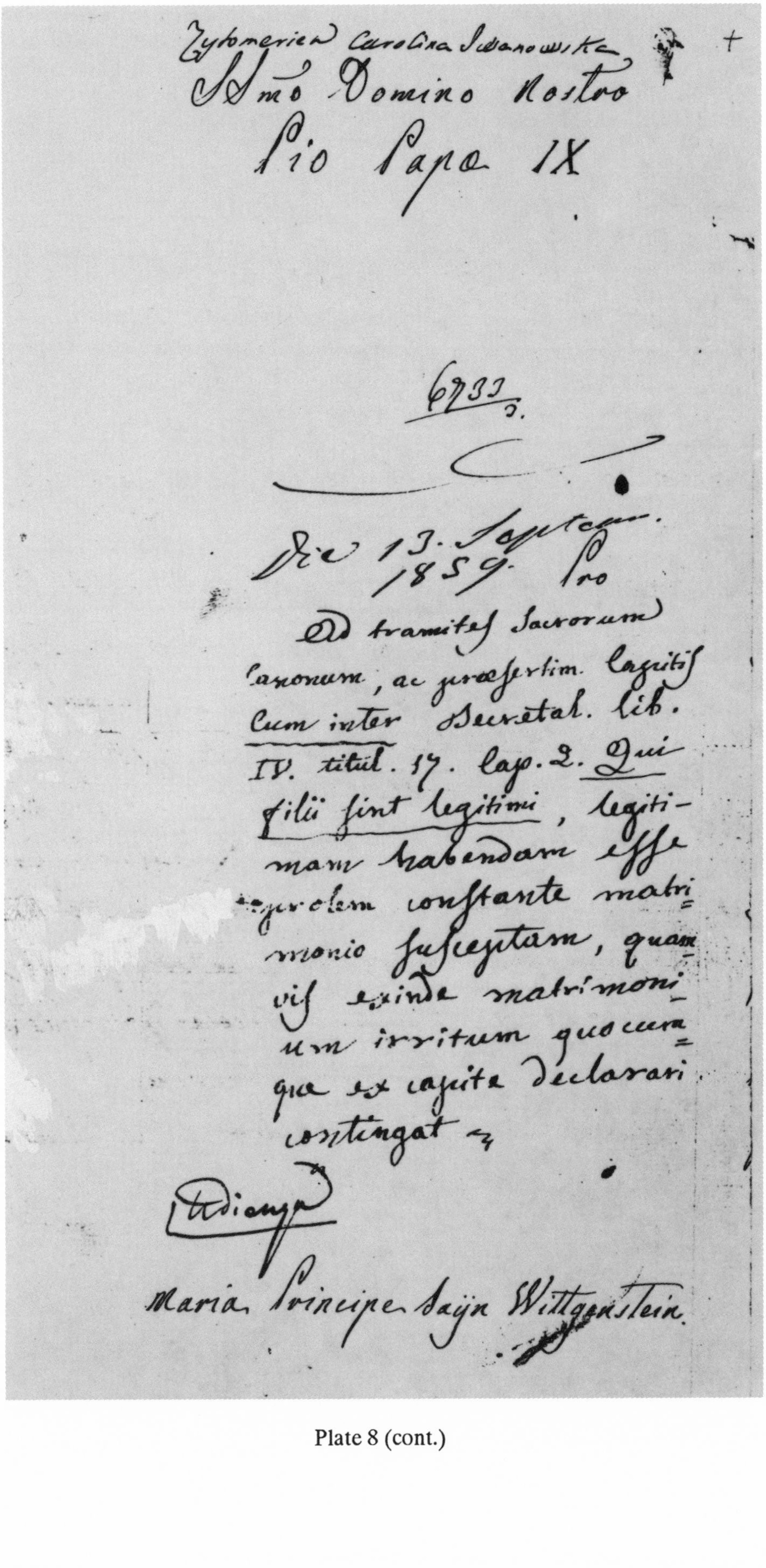

Zytomerien Carolina Iwanowska

Smo Domino Nostro
Pio Papa IX

6933.

Die 13. Septem.
1859. Pro

Ad tramites Sacrorum
Canonum, ac praesertim legitis
Cum inter Decretal. lib.
IV. titul. 17. Cap. 2. Qui
filii sint legitimi, legitimam habendam esse
prolem constante matri
monio suscaptam, quam
vis exinde matrimoni
um irritum quocum
que ex capite declarari
contingat

Adiung

Maria Principe Sayn Wittgenstein.

Plate 8 (cont.)

The Petitioner is the only daughter born of the marriage, rightfully celebrated before the Church, between Prince Nicholas von Sayn-Wittgenstein, Protestant, and Carolyne Iwanowska, Catholic. It then happened that, after the petitioner's birth, her parents separated; later her father was re-married, to a non Catholic lady.

But her mother presented a petition, first before her Ordinary Office, and now before the Metropolitan of Mohilow, especially delegated by Your Holiness, in order to have her marriage to the aforementioned Nicholas Wittgenstein declared null and void by reason of its being contracted through violence and intimidation. In the meantime, the Petitioner is presented with the chance of contracting a rightful marriage with a Catholic Prince. She, therefore, promptly requests Your Beatitude to deign to declare that the Petitioner, in spite of the facts stated above, was born of a legitimate marriage, must be considered the legitimate daughter of the above mentioned Prince Nicholas von Sayn-Wittgenstein and Carolyne Iwanowska, and must enjoy all the rights and privileges pertaining to legitimate offspring. May God etc.

Marie, Princess von Sayn-Wittgenstein

September 13, 1859
On behalf of the Petitioner.

According to Canon Law and especially the chapter *Cum inter, Decretales*, Book 4, Heading 17, Chapter 2, *Which sons are legitimate*, "a son or daughter is to be considered legitimate if born while the marriage lasts, even though the marriage may later be declared invalid for whatever legal reason."[19]

Papal Audience

Oratrix unica est Filia progenita ex matrimonio rite in faciem Ecclesiae contracto inter Nicolaum Principem Sayn Wittgenstein sectae protestantium ad<d>ictum, et Karolinam Iwanowska catholicam. Porro accidit ut, oratrice jam nata, parentes ejus inter sese separati sint; ac proinde Pater aliud matrimonium attentaverit cum muliere acatholica.

Mater vero jam coram Ordinario, nunc autem coram Metropolitano Mo<h>ilowiensi uti specialiter a Sanctitate V[estra] delegato causam introduxerit pro declaratione nullitatis praefati matrimonii ab ipsa *ex vi et metu* contracti cum dicto Nicolao Wittgenstein. Interim Oratrici opportuna occasio sese offert matrimonium rite ineundi cum catholico Principe. Ideoque instanter petit a Beatitudine Vestra ut declarare dignetur, praedictis non obstantibus, Oratricem ex legitimo conjugio genitam esse, et uti legitimam praedictorum Nicolai Principis Sayn Wittgenstein et Karolinae Iwanowska filiam habendam esse, atque omnibus legitimae prolis juribus et effectibus gaudere. Et Deus etc.

Maria, Principe[ssa] Sayn Wittgenstein

Die 13 Septem[bris] 1859
Pro <oratrice>

Ad tramites Sacrorum Canonum, ac praesertim Capitis *Cum inter, Decret[alium]* libr[i] IV, *titul[i]* 17, Cap[itis] 2 *Qui filii sint legitimi*, "legitiman habendam esse prolem constante matrimonio susceptam, quamvis exinde matrimonium irritum quocumque ex capite declarari contingat."

Udienza

---

[19]This statement is the official Vatican response to Marie's petition; it does not mention Cardoni's suggestion (see following Doc. No. 12, 13, 14) that a declaration of legitimacy should be issued by the Archbishop of Mohilow. It is possible, therefore, that the papal pronouncement settled the issue, given that the question is not brought up again in the file. It may also be the case, however, that, for various reasons, it was not pursued any further. The timing of

Princess Marie's petition was significant. By now, she was engaged to Prince Konstantin, the brother of Monsignor Hohenlohe, and their marriage was planned for October 15, 1859, less than five weeks later. It appears that no certificate of legitimacy was ever issued and, when Archbishop Żyliński released his decree of annulment on February 24, 1860 (O.S.), the matter was not addressed.

Document No. 12. September 10, 1859. Letter by Monsignor Cardoni to Quaglia enclosing his legal opinion on Marie's petition. Italian (1 page).

To: The Most Illustrious and Reverend Monsignor Angelo Quaglia, Secretary of the Holy Congregation of the Council The Ecclesiastical Academy, September 10, 1859 Most Venerable Monsignor:

I am sending you the position paper with the vote pertaining to the request presented by Princess Marie Wittgenstein; I have managed to be quite brief, this being a very straightforward matter.

Accept, please, my feelings of the deepest respect and veneration; in expressing them, I have the honor of being

Your most Illustrious and Reverend Excellency's most devoted and obliging servant,

Giuseppe Cardoni, Bishop of Carystos.

Ill[ustriss]imo e R[everendissi]mo Monsignore D[on] Angelo Quaglia, Segr[etario] della S[anta] Cong[regazione] del Concilio Dall'Accad[emia] Eccl[esiastica], 10 settembre 1859 Veneratissimo Monsignore.

Le rimetto la Posizione col Voto relativo all'istanza avanzata dalla Principessa Maria Wittgenstein; ho procurato di esser brevissimo, trattandosi di una cosa assai chiara.

Gradisca li sentimenti del più profondo ossequio e venerazione co'quali ho l'onore di essere

Di V[ostra] S[ignoria] Ill[ustrissi]ma e R[everendissi]ma De[votissi]mo ed Obbl[i]g[atissi]mo Ser[vo] Giuseppe Cardoni, V[escovo] di Caristo

Document No. 13. September 10, 1859. Monsignor Cardoni's expert opinion on the issue of Marie's legitimacy. Latin (5 pages).

<File>: Mohilow
On the question of legitimate birth.

Prince Nicholas von Sayn-Wittgenstein, Protestant, contracted marriage before the Church with Carolyne Iwanowska, Catholic; a daughter named Marie was born of this union. Several years later, after her father's death, Carolyne sued for the annulment of her marriage for the following two reasons: 1) the ceremony was not celebrated by her own priest; 2) she had a reverential fear of her strong-minded and stubborn father. The case being brought before the Ordinary Court, her marriage was declared valid. With respect to the first reason of the alleged annulment, it was found without doubt that the priest before whom the wedding was performed was her own; he was in fact in charge of the Parish of her father's residence where, at the time, Carolyne was living. As to the other reason for annulment, the Ordinary Court decreed that it could not be declared invalid. But now, by

Mohilowiensis.
Super legitimitate natalium.

Nicolaus Princeps Sayn Wittgenstein e Protestantium Secta matrimonium iniit cum Karolina Iwanowska Catholica in facie Ecclesiae, ex quo matrimonio nata est filia nomine Maria. Post plures annos vita functo Carolinae patre, haec litem movit super validitate matrimonii ex duplici capite, tum ex defectu proprii Parochi, tum ex causa metu reverentialis cadentis in fortem et constantem virum. Delata hac causa coram Ordinario Judice, matrimonium fuit validum declaratum; etenim quod primum praetensae nullitatis caput, compertum fuit indubiis argumentis, Parochum coram quo matrimonium contraxerunt proprium fuisse; erat enim Parochus domicilii paterni, quo eo tempore Carolina versabatur. Quoad vero alterum nullitatis caput, censuit idem Ordinarius matrimonium irritum declarari non posse. Nunc vero ex Apostolico Indulto agitur haec causa in gradu

Apostolic concession, the case is being appealed before the Metropolitan of Mohilow. In the meantime, the aforementioned Marie, aged 23 and single, having been offered the possibility of marrying a Catholic prince, promptly requests from the Apostolic See that it deigns to declare that the facts just mentioned do not constitute an obstacle to her being considered a legitimate daughter born of this marriage and enjoying all the rights and privileges of legitimate offspring.

Since, in his graciousness, His Holiness has asked me to issue a judgement on this matter, I'll do so in a few words. There seem to be two questions: 1) whether it be possible to declare Marie to be legitimate; 2) whether it be proper for the Apostolic See to issue such a declaration. It is very well known that, according to Canon Law (See the chapter *Cum inter,* Section "Which sons are to be deemed legitimate"), those children are to be considered legitimate who are born of a marriage even only putatively valid, as long as the marriage was celebrated in public or in Church without anyone objecting, and it was, moreover, celebrated in good faith or in ignorance of an existing impediment, at least on the part of one of the spouses, at the time of the marriage contract or the conception of the offspring. The fact that Marie was born of a marriage putatively valid and performed in front of the Church has been investigated to the point that the invalidity of this marriage could not be proved before the Ordinary Judge. That, indeed, there was no lack of good faith, at least on the part of the woman who was allegedly subjected to intimidation, can be gathered, in general, from the principle according to which, in cases affecting the offspring, good faith is always to be presumed unless it can be proved most clearly that both parents were aware of the impediment. Moreover, it can be presumed specifically from the fact that the marriage was consummated, as is evident from the generation of offspring. Indeed, it must not be presumed, particularly in the case of a Catholic woman, that she was willing to commit the grave sin of consummating a marriage she knew was not valid, for this would amount indeed to fornication. For these reasons, there can be no doubt whatsoever about the legitimacy of Marie, the petitioner in question, even if her parents' marriage were to be declared invalid in the second instance.

appellationis coram Metropolitano Mohilowiensi. Interim praedicta Maria nubilis, et annorum 23, cum nacta fuerit occasionem rite matrimonium ineundi cum Principe Catholico, instanter petit a Sede Apostolica ut declarare dignetur, praedictis non obstantibus, uti legitimam filiam huius matrimonii esse habendam, et omnibus legitimae prolis juribus, et effectibusque gaudere.

Cum ex benignitate Sanctitatis Suae demandatum fuerit hac super re meam aperire sententiam, paucis verbis me expediam. Duo igitur quaerenda videntur. 1° An declarari possit Mariam legitimam esse. 2° Utrum expediat id a Sede Apostolica declarari. Quoad jam notissimum in jure Canonico est (ut in Cap. *Cum inter,* "Qui filii sint legitimi") legitimos filios illos habendos esse, qui nati sunt ex matrimonio etiam putative tantum valido, dummodo publice seu in facie Ecclesiae, et absque contradictione sit initum; et bona fides seu impedimenti ignorantia adfuerit, saltem unius conjugis, tempore contractus matrimonii, seu conceptae prolis. Jam vero quod Maria nata sit ex matrimonio putative valido, et in facie Ecclesiae inito, adeo exploratum est, et coram Ordinario probari nequiverit nullitas hujus matrimonii. Quod autem non defuerit bona fides, saltem ex muliere quae praetenditur metum passa, colligitur, generatim ex eo quod cum agatur de favore prolis semper bona fides praesumenda est, nisi apertissime probetur, utrumque parentum impedimentum cognovisse. Speciatim vero haec praesumptio augetur ex consumatione matrimonii, quae ex ipsa suscepta prole constat. Neque enim praesumi debet praesertim mulierem Catholicam graviter voluisse peccare consumando matrimonium, quod nullum esse sciebat, quod proinde vera fornicatio fuisset. Quam ob rem de legitimitate Mariae Oratricis nullo modo dubitari potest, etsi invalidum in secunda instantia declaretur matrimonium ab ejus parentibus initum.

As to the other question proposed, the Petitioner Marie, in my opinion, has clearly and legally the right to obtain from the Ecclesiastical Authorities a declaration of her legitimacy. Since it is the domain of Ecclesiastical judges to investigate marriage cases, it also pertains to them to investigate whether the above mentioned conditions for considering the offspring to be legitimate do indeed obtain in this particular case. Which authority should she approach in this instance? Since the Apostolic See has entrusted the Metropolitan to deal with this case of alleged nullity, it would be my humble opinion that it might be proper for Marie to present her case for legitimacy to that same Metropolitan. Should, however, the Metropolitan refuse to issue a judgement in his own right and fail to declare her legitimacy, then she should again appeal to this Holy See who, having questioned the Metropolitan on this issue, will decree according to the Law.

I humbly submit the above to the wisdom of His Holiness and, prostrated at his feet, implore His Apostolic Blessing.
Giuseppe Cardoni,
Bishop of Carystos.

Quoad alteram propositam quaestionem, mihi videtur certo jure gaudere Oratrix Maria, ut ab Ecclesiastrica auctoritate sua legitimitas declaretur. Cum enim ad Judices Ecclesiasticos pertineat causas matrimoniales cognoscere, pertinet etiam perpendere, an in casu particulari verificentur conditiones superius recensitae ut filii legitimi habeantur. Quam vero auctoritatem adire debeat? Cum causa praetensae nullitatis matrimonii ad Metropolitanum fuerit demandata a Sede Apostolica, submisso consilio existimarem penes eundem de sua legitimitate Mariam agere oportere. Quod si Metropolita recusaverit suum ferre judicium, et declarare illam legitimam esse, tunc Sanctam hanc Sedem iterum petat, quam de hac re requisito Metropolita de jure decernet.

Haec tamen Sapientiae Sanctitatis Suae humiliter subjicio, ad cujus pedes provolutus Apostolicam benedictionem imploro.
Joseph Cardoni,
Episcopus Carystenus.

Document No. 14. September 1859. Draft. Quaglia's memorandum to the Pope on the merit of Marie's petition, with a report on Cardoni's opinion. Italian (3 pages). For the response to the petition, see end of Doc. No. 11.

<File>: Zhitomir

Monsignor Cardoni has expressed in writing his opinion on the request presented by Princess Marie Wittgenstein to the effect of obtaining a declaration of legitimate birth; the substance of it is that:

1) Her legitimacy cannot be in doubt, on account of well known and established legal principles, even in the event that <her parents'> marriage be declared null and void; this insofar as she was born of parents who appeared to be legitimately married.

2) She has the right to obtain from the ecclesiastical authorities a declaration of legitimate birth; this insofar as, it being a prerogative of ecclesiastical judges to decide on marriage cases, it pertains to them as well to decide if, in a particular case, there are elements to establish the legitimacy of the offspring.

Zitomir.

Mon[si]g[no]r Cardoni ha emesso il suo parere in iscritto sull'istanza avanzata dalla Principessa Maria Wittgenstein all'effetto di ottenere la dichiarazione di legittimità de' suoi natali di cui la somma è

1. Non potersi dubitare della di lei legittimità per le notissime disposizioni di diritto, quand'anche venisse in seguito dichiarato nullo il matrimonio, e ciò perché venne procreata da genitori uniti in figura di matrimonio legittimo.

2. Avere essa diritto che venga dall'ecclesiastica autorità dichiarata la di lei legittimità di natali. Imperciocché spettando ai giudici conoscere le cause matrimoniali, spettar deve anche ad essi l'esaminare se nel caso particolare si verificano gli estremi per ritenere la legittimità della prole.

He is, however, of the opinion that the petitioner must present her appeal for a declaration of legitimacy to the Metropolitan of Mohilow, who has been delegated by the Holy See to review the case for annulment.

But should the Metropolitan refuse to provide a judgement on this issue, then the petitioner herself will have to appeal to the Holy See, who, after previous consultation with the Metropolitan, will decree according to the merit of the case.

Opina però che l'Or[atri]ce debba agire per la sua legittimità presso il Metropolitano al quale è stata dalla S[anta] Sede rimessa la cognizione della causa sulla nullità.

Che se il Metropolitano ricusasse di emettere su ciò il suo giudizio, allora dovrà l'Or[atri]ce stessa rivolgersi alla S[anta] Sede, la quale, inteso prima il Metropolitano, decreterà secondo che esige il caso.

Document No. 15. November 26, 1859. Petition to Quaglia from Ḥohenlohe (Prot. No. 6733/I) to duplicate documents sent to Żyliński that have been lost in the mail. Granted on that date. Italian (2 pages).

<File>: Zhitomir
Carolyne Iwanowska
Prot.No. 6733/I

Zytomerien
Carolina Iwanowska
Prot. No. 6733/I

To His Most Reverend Excellency
Monsignor Angelo Quaglia,
Secretary of the Holy Congregation
of the Council,
etc. etc. etc.
Most Reverend Excellency,

Monsignor Prince von Hohenlohe informs Your Excellency that the papers pertaining to the case of Countess (*sic*) Carolyne Iwanowska, which had been sent to the Metropolitan of all the Russias bearing the date of the past August 18, have been lost. He, therefore, requests the favor that they be duplicated by order of Your Excellency in order that they be mailed again with greater care to ensure that they reach their destination.
For this grace etc. etc. etc.

<Gustav von Hohenlohe>
Archbishop of Edessa

A Sua Eccellenza R[everendissi]ma
Monsignor [Angelo] Quaglia
Segretario della S[anta] Congre[gazione]
del Concilio
etc. etc. etc.
Eccellenza Rev[erendissi]ma,

Monsignor Principe d'Hohenlohe espone all'Eccellenza Vostra essersi smarrite le carte relativamente all'affare della Signora Contessa Carolina Iwanowska, che furono dirette al Metropolita di tutte le Russie sotto la data delli 18 Agosto p[rossimo] p[assato]; per il che supplica la grazia che queste venissero per ordine dell'Eccellenza Vostra rinnovate per quindi farne una più accurata spedizione.

Che della grazia etc. etc. etc.

<Gustavo d'Hohenlohe,
Arcivescovo d'Edessa>

November 26, 1859
Duplicates are to be granted. C.

Die 26 Nov[embris] 1859
Dentur duplicata. C.

Document No. 16. March 1860. Petition. Monsignor Hohenlohe petitions the Pope to move the review of the case to Rome on account of possible bribery in Mohilow. With note on action, in Quaglia's hand, dated March 26, 1860. Latin (4 pages).

To the Most Blessed Father
Pope Pius IX
happily reigning.

Monsignor Gustav von Hohenlohe, Archbishop of Edessa, prostrated at Your Holiness' feet, presents the following:

Before his brother's marriage with Marie von Sayn-Wittgenstein, her mother, Carolyne Iwanowska, Princess von Sayn-Wittgenstein, already for some time separated from her non-Catholic husband in virtue of a civil sentence, obtained in writing from her own daughter, Marie, the promise whereby she would pass on to her mother, out of her own dowry, the conspicuous sum of seventy thousand silver roubles, as they call them, i.e., about eighty thousand scudi. This sum was to be paid to some solicitor (Okraszewski) in order to obtain the annulment of the marriage of her parents, the aforementioned Carolyne and Prince Nicholas von Sayn-Wittgenstein.

And now Your most humble postulant, Gustav Archbishop of Edessa, must relate some very sad news, for the above-mentioned sum in the amount of fifty thousand roubles was to be made available in order to obtain more easily, from the Bishops and the Consistory of Mohilow, a sentence in favor of the annulment of said marriage as being invalidated from the beginning because of violence and intimidation and never validated by subsequent cohabitation and offspring.

Most Blessed Father! In July of last year, that solicitor came to Rome on behalf of the above-mentioned Carolyne and obtained, through the Holy Congregation of the Council, an Apostolic Rescript whereby the Archbishop of Mohilow would be given the faculty to reopen a case already adjudicated in the second instance in favor of the validity of the marriage; to deal with it in the third instance according to the Benedictine *Dei miseratione* to be invoked at all events in substantive matters, and, lastly, to determine its final outcome.

Beatissimo Patri Pio Papae IX
feliciter regnanti.
Beatissime Pater.

Gustavus Hohenlohe Archiepiscopus Edessen[sis] ad pedes Sanctitatis Vestrae humiliter provolutus exponit quae sequuntur.

Ante matrimonium fratris ejus cum Maria de Sayn-Wittgenstein, mater Mariae, Carolina Iwanowska, Princeps de Sayn-Wittgenstein, jam pridem a marito acat<h>olico per sententiam civilem separata, obtinuit ab ipsa filia Maria obligationem in scriptis, qua mediante cederet matri ex bonis suae dotis ingentem summam septuaginta millia—ut ajunt—*roubles argent*, id est circiter octoginta millia scutatorum, quae summa solvenda esset cuidam procuratori (Okraszewski) pro obtinenda solutione matrimonii contracti inter parentes suos, scilicet praedictam Carolinam et Nicolaum Principem de Sayn-Wittgenstein.

Nunc vero humillimus Orator Gustavus Archiep[iscopus] Edessen[sis] in tristissimam devenit notitiam, quod praedicta summa pro quinquaginta <milibus> roublis impendenda erat ad facilius obtinendam favorabilem sententiam Episcoporum et Concistorii Mohilowiensis pro solutione praedicti matrimonii tanquam per vim et metum ab initio irriti, neque per subsequentem cohabitationem et prolem umquam ratificati.

Beatissime pater! Elapso anno mense Julii praedictus procurator, nomine supradictae Carolinae, Romam petiit et obtinuit per S[anctam] Congregationem Concilii Apostolicum rescriptum quo facultas tribuebatur Archiepiscopo Mohilowien[si] reas<s>umendi causam jam in secunda instantia pro validitate matrimonii, de quo in casu, definitam, eamque tertio conficiendi ad tramitem Benedictinae *Dei miseratione* observatae saltem in substantialibus et tandem eam finaliter definiendi.

The postulant is more than certain of the truth of what has been stated, namely that the above-mentioned solicitor is doing his utmost to influence in a surreptitious way the loyalty, sense of justice and the very honesty of those judges who, in the Consistory of Mohilow, will be issuing very soon a sentence on this marriage. He, therefore, entreats Your Holiness to condescend to move the proceedings, already set up before the Consistory of Mohilow, to the Holy Apostolic See for a review and final settlement of the case.

May God etc.

Your most humble postulant,

Gustav von Hohenlohe,

Archbishop of Edessa

At the audience granted by the Most Holy Father on March 26, 1860:

Orders were given to write to the Apostolic Nuncio in Vienna according to the enclosed draft.

Cum vero Oratori certe certius constet de veritate expositorum, et praesertim quod procurator praedictus omnem non moveat lapidem ut fidem, justitiam et honestatem subdole praeoc<c>upet in praedictis judicibus, qui in Concistorio Mohilowien[si] judicum circa praedictum matrimonium quamprimum prolaturi erunt; ideoque enixe postulat a Sanctitate Vestra ut dignetur revocare processum jam confectum apud Concistorium Mohilowiense ad Sanctam sedem Apostolicam pro revisione et causae definitione.

Quod Deus etc.

Humillimus Orator Gustavus Hohenlohe,

Archiep[iscopus] Edessen[sis]

Ex Audientia S[antis]s[i]mi
Die 26 Martii 1860.
Scribatur Nuntio Ap[osto]lico Viennen[si] juxta insertam minutam.

Document No. 17. March 26, 1860. Draft. Memorandum to the Pope on the question of bribery (The date is elicited from Doc. 23). Italian (4 pages).

<File>: Zhitomir

Prince Konstantin von Hohenlohe is married to Marie Iwanowska, daughter of Carolyne, who was separated from her husband, Prince Nicholas von Sayn-Wittgenstein, in virtue of a civil court sentence.

Princess Carolyne is the same one who, having sued for a judgement of nullity of her marriage by reason of violence and intimidation on the part of her father, received, however, from her Ordinary Office, a negative judgement. Having, therefore, presented an appeal to the Metropolitan Consistory, this appeal was rejected by the present Metropolitan on account of a decree issued by the previous Vicar General. It took a rescript, promulgated in the <papal> audience of August 8, 1859, to enable that Metropolitan to reopen and study the case and definitively adjudicate it according to the level of appeal after consideration of what needed consideration and, especially the Benedictine <Dei miseratione>.

Now Prince Konstantin and his wife Marie claim that, before they were married, Marie's mother extracted from her a written promise whereby the daughter was to give the mother, out of her own

Zitomir

Il Principe Costantino d'Hohenlohe si sposò a Maria Iwanowska, figlia di Carolina, la quale con sentenza civile era separata dal suo marito, Principe Nicola de Sayn-Wittgenstein.

La Principessa Carolina è quella stessa la quale avendo intentato giudizio di nullità di matrimonio per aperto timore incussogli dal padre ebbe però da quell'Ordinariato una sentenza contraria; ed avendo quindi appellato al Concistoro Metropolitano, in seguito ad un decreto del cessato Vicario Generale non venne accolto l'appello dall'attuale Metropolita, ed ebbe d'uopo d'un rescritto emanato dalla Udienza degli 8 agosto 1859 mediante il quale veniva abilitato quel metropolitano di riassumere e conoscere qualla causa e giudicarla definitivamente in grado di appello *servatis servandis* e specialmente la Benedettina <*Dei miseratione*>.

Ora i coniugi Costantino e Maria de Hohenlohe rappresentano che prima del loro matrimonio la madre di Maria ottenne da questa una obbligazione in scritto mediante la quale la detta figlia

dowry, a sum of about eighty thousand scudi, which would be entrusted to some solicitor in order to obtain the annulment of the marriage of Marie's parents. Recently these two have learned that, of such a sum, more than fifty thousand scudi[20] will be used to extract more easily, from the Consistory of Mohilow, a favorable sentence of marriage nullity. They remind us also that this same solicitor who is now representing the Princess in the Consistory was the one who obtained from Rome the above-mentioned rescript that permitted the reopening of the case. Since they know very well, on the other hand, that this same solicitor will try the utmost to succeed in his intent by suborning the judges, they request that the trial be recalled from that Curia and the case be judged by the Holy See.

It would not be so bad if this were the whole thing; but, after the rescript of August 8 <1859>, will it be proper for the Holy See to recall the case? Especially if this is to be done on the force of suspicions that may prove without foundation and, in any case, could not be proved.

I would not know, therefore, what weight can possibly be given to this petition.

cedeva alla madre sui beni della sua dote circa 80 mila scudi la quale si sarebbe dovuta sborsare ad un tal Procuratore per ottenere l'annullamento del matrimonio tra i genitori di Maria; e di recente sono venuti a conoscere che di detta somma 50 mila scudi e più dovranno essere impiegati per ottenere più facilmente favorevole sentenza del Concistoro per la nullità del matrimonio. Rammentano che l'istesso Procuratore il quale ora agisce presso quel Concistoro ottenne in Roma il Rescritto di riassunzione sopramenzionato, ed altronde conoscendo essi con ogni certezza che quello stesso Procuratore nulla lascierà intentato per riuscire nell'intento subornando i giudici, domandarebbero che venisse richiamato il processo da quella Curia per esser giudicata la causa dalla S[anta] Sede.

Men male se l'affare fosse integro; ma dopo il decreto degli 8 agosto converrà più alla S[anta] Sede avocare la detta causa? Segnatamente sopra sospetti i quali potrebbero non attuarsi, o non potrebbero provarsi.

Non saprei quindi qual peso possa darsi all'istanza.

Document No. 18. April 4, 1860. Draft letter from Quaglia to De Luca with corrections in Quaglia's own hand (See ASV, NV Document No. 9). Italian (8 pages).

Document No. 19. April 12, 1860. Letter from Archbishop Żyliński to the Pope enclosing a copy of his February 1860 sentence of annulment. Latin (2 pages).

To His Holiness
Pope Pius IX.
St. Petersburg, April 12, 1860 (O.S)

Most Blessed Father!

In keeping with the rescript of the Holy Congregation of the Council, issued on the 8th of August, 1859, I have taken up again the case pertaining to the nullity of the marriage between Carolyne Iwanowska and Prince Nicholas Wittgenstein. I have done so after the case has been

Sanctissimo Domino Domino
Pio Papae IX.
1860 ann[i] Aprilis 12 d[ie] v[etere] s[tilo]
    Petropoli.
Beatissime Pater!

Juxta Rescriptum S[anctae] Congregationis Concilii, sub d[ie] 8 Augusti 1959 anni emanatum, causam super nullitate matrimonii Karolinae Iwanowska cum Principe Nicolao Wittgenstein, post praeviam diligentissimam ejus cognitionem ac perscrutationem a D[ominis] Maximiliano Stanie-

---

[20]This "written promise" has been published in WFL, p. 537. Dated July 15, 1859, it takes the form of a letter from Marie to Baron von Maltitz (Russian ambassador to Weimar) authorizing the release of 70,000 silver roubles to Okraszewski should he obtain the canonical divorce of her mother. By this time, Carolyne had little money of her own.

She had transferred it to her daughter as part of the property settlement she had previously agreed to with her estranged husband. After the marriage of Marie to Hohenlohe's brother Prince Konstantin, in October 1859, the latter reneged on the agreement, and Carolyne had to rely on funds that she and Liszt had invested with his cousin Eduard in Vienna. See WFL, p. 521.

previously examined and studied most diligently by Monsignor Maximilian Staniewski, Bishop of Platen and Suffragan Bishop of Mohilow, Monsignor Andreas Dobszewicz, Provost of Szydlow and Canon of Samogit, and Monsignor Moszezynski, Prelate and Dean of Minsk, all of them men of quite proven virtue and especially delegated by me for this task. After their vote, having heard also the Defender of the Marriage Bond, the Reverend Basil Zottek, Professor at the Roman Catholic Academy, I myself studied the case and, keeping in mind what needed to observed and especially the bull *Dei miseratione* issued by the late Benedict XIV, adjudicated the case and issued a definitive sentence according to the level of appeal. I have given a copy of this decree, issued on February 24, 1860, to the Petitioner and I humbly send another copy to Your Holiness. Prostrated at Your Holiness's feet, with the greatest possible reverence I remain, Most Holy Father,
Your Holiness's most obsequious son,
Wenceslas Żyliński,
Archbishop of Mohilow.

wski Episcopo Plateensi Suffraganeo Mohiloviensi, Andrea Dobszewicz Infulato Praeposito Szytoviensi Canonico Samogitiensi et Domino Moszezynski Praelato Decano Minscensi, viris probatissimae virtutis ad id specialiter a me delegatis, postque prolata ab eis suffragia, nec non audito Defensore matrimonii D[omino] Basilio Zottek Professore Romano-Catholicae Academiae, egomet ipse reassumpsi, cognovi ac per definitivam sententiam in appellationis gradu, servatis servandis, ac praesertim constitutione sac[rae] mem[oriae] Benedicti XIV *Dei miseratione* dijudicavi sententiamque protuli ac oratrici copiam huiusmodi decreti 24 Februarii currentis 1860 anni, extradidi, cujus alteram paginam Sanctitati Vestrae porrigere audeo ac provolutus ad pedes Sanctitatis Vestrae, summa, qua par est, reverentia permaneo, Beatissime Pater,

Santitatis vestrae
Obsequentissimus filius
Venceslaus Żyliński,
Archiepiscopus Mohilov[ensis]

Document No. 20. Enclosed with Doc. No. 19. A copy of Żyliński's decree verified by Monsignor Proniewski (his name is misspelled Prosciewski in copies originating from the one made by Kött). See ASV, NV Doc. No. 6 and ASV, CC Doc. No. 22. The text of the decree is given in ASV, CC Doc. No. 28. In this copy the name of the Archbishop is given in full and is followed by the names and titles of the Revs. Zottek and Proniewski; at the end there is the following note in Proniewski's hand.

For the authenticity of this copy,
Otto Proniewski,
Secretary in Spiritual matters
to His Excellency the Archbishop of
    Mohilow.

Pro vera copia,
Otto Proniewski,
Secretarius in Spiritualibus
Suae Excell[entiae] Archiep[isco]pi
    Mohilov[iensis].

Document No. 21. April 14, 1860. Letter in De Luca's own hand to Quaglia enclosing a copy of Żyliński's decree received from Kött. This letter is not in the ASV, NV file. Italian (1 page).

To: Monsignor Angelo Quaglia,
Secretary of the Holy Congregation of the
    Council, etc., etc., etc.
Rome
Vienna, April 14, 1860

Monsig[no]r <Angelo Quaglia>
Segr[eta]rio della S[anta] C[ongregazione]
del Concilio, etc. etc. etc.
Roma
Vienna, 14 aprile 1860

My Dear and Most Venerable Monsignor:

Almost at the same time as I received your Most Illustrious Excellency's valuable letter, dated the 4th of this month, I received as well the report of Monsignor the Bishop of Fulda on the Wittgenstein-Iwanowska marriage case, with which he enclosed a copy of the sentence of annulment issued this past February by the Metropolitan Diocese of Mohilow.

I answered him suggesting that he should not proceed, for the time being, to the execution of the above-mentioned sentence, and that he should send Your Most Illustrious and Reverend Excellency a similar report, supported by a copy of that same document, and ask for instructions. I also provided reasons to justify the suggested delay.[21]

Indeed, it might have been better to have sent at the right time a note to the Archbishop of Mohilow to prevent the publication of the sentence. But, while I knew that Father <Filippo> M[aria] Guidi had received secret instructions about this, I was at the same time, left officially in complete darkness as to this affair; so I thought I should abstain from taking any steps without first receiving appropriate orders. Having finally received them three days ago, I shall write to that Metropolitan in roughly the same terms contained in Your letter.

In the meantime, I am enclosing a copy of the Decree sent to me by Monsignor the Bishop of Fulda.

With the feelings of my most respectful and high esteem, it pleases me to confirm myself Your Most Illustrious and Reverend Excellency's most devoted, most obliged servant

Antonino <De Luca>,
Archbishop of Tarsus,
Apostolic Nuncio <in Vienna>

Monsig[no]r mio Venerat[issi]mo.

Quasi contemporaneamente alla pregiata lettera di V[ostra] S[ignoria] Ill[ustrissi]ma e R[everendissi]ma de' 4 del corrente mi giungeva il rapporto che M[onsi]g[no]r Vescovo di Fulda mi faceva intorno alla causa matrimoniale Wittgenstein-Iwanowska, trasmettendomi una copia della sentenza di nullità pronunziata nel febbraio p[rossim]o p[assat]o dalla Curia metropolitana di Mohilow.

Io gli risposi inculcandogli di non procedere all'esecuzione della sentenza mentovata più sopra e d'indirizzare a V[ostra] S[ignoria] Ill[ustrissi]ma e R[everendissi]ma un analogo rapporto corredato della copia dello stesso documento per chiedere le opportune istruzioni. Non mancai di allegare le ragioni che giustificano la dilazione da me inculcatagli.

In verità sarebbe stato più opportuno l'indirizzare a suo tempo a M[onsi]g[no]r Arcivescovo di Mohilow per impedire la promulgazione della sentenza. Ma sapendo io che fossero state *secretamente* date al P[adre] M[aria] Guidi istruzioni su l'oggetto, mentre si lasciava questa Nunziatura officialmente nella totale ignoranza dell'affare, ho stimato dovermi astenere da qualsivoglia passo, senza prima ricevere le convenienti commissioni. Giuntemi queste o sono tre giorni, scriverò a quel Metropolitano presso a poco ne' termini contenuti nella di Lei lettera.

Annetto intanto una copia del Decreto trasmessomi da M[onsi]g[no]r Vescovo di Fulda.

Con sensi di ossequiosa e distinta stima mi pregio di confermarmi
Di V[ostra] S[ignoria] Ill[ustrissi]ma e
 R[everendissi]ma
devot[issi]mo obbligat[issi]mo Servitore
Antonino <De Luca>,
Arcivescovo di Tarso,
N[unzio] Ap[ostolic]o

---

[21]It was this letter of De Luca's to Kött that caused the latter to suspend the Russian annulment (see ASV, NV Docs. 8 and 12). One month later, Carolyne left Weimar for Rome in an attempt to have that suspension lifted.

**Document No. 22. Enclosed with Doc. No. 21. De Luca's copy of Żyliński's
decree made from the one sent to him by Kött; See ASV, NV Doc. No. 6;
both these copies provide the wrong spelling (Prosciewski for Proniewski). See ASV,
CC Docs. No. 20 and, for the text, No. 28. Latin (4 pages).**

**Document No. 23. April 30, 1860. Draft. Memorandum from Quaglia to the Pope
suggesting the suspension of the February 1860 sentence and the necessity of an
appeal against it on the part of the Defender. The date is elicited from Doc. No. 25.
Italian (4 pages). Contains references to ASV, NV Docs. No. 9, 13, 15; and
ASV, CC Doc. No. 21.**

<File>: Zhitomir

According to the instructions I received from Your Holiness in the audience of March 26, on the request presented by Monsieur and Madame Hohenlohe, we wrote to the Nuncio in Vienna to the effect that she should write a letter to alert Monsignor the Archbishop of Mohilow to those rumors of corruption to which the judges there might be exposed while dealing with the annulment case brought forth by Princess Carolyne Iwanowska because of the enticements that, they said, were being provided by an agent of the same Princess in order to obtain a favorable decision in her annulment case.

Monsignor Nuncio answers that, almost at the same time he received the letter that was sent to him by order of Your Holiness, the Bishop of Fulda (in whose diocese Madame Iwanowska resides) sent him a copy of the annulment sentence already issued on February 24 by the Curia of Mohilow.

He adds that he immediately intimated to that Bishop that he should not proceed to execute that sentence and added some arguments to justify the ones he was raising. He suggested also that he should make a similar report to the Congregation and enclose that same document.

He then makes some remarks about having been kept in the dark on this subject while he was aware that secret instructions were given to Father Guidi on this matter. He therefore thought he should not take any steps before receiving pertinent instructions.

He says, finally, that he will write immediately to the Metropolitan of Mohilow according to the suggestions provided in the letter we wrote him.

Zitomir.

Secondo le istruzioni ricevute dalla S[anti]tà V[ost]ra nell'Ud[ienz]a del 26 marzo sull'istanza dei Signori Coniugi d'Hohenlohe, si scrisse a M[onsigno]r Nunzio di Vienna perché con sua lettera ponesse in guardia Mons[igno]r Arcivescovo di Mohilow sulle voci di prevaricazione a cui verrebbero esposti quei giudici nella causa di nullità di matrimonio promossa dalla Principessa Carolina Iwanowska, per le arti che dicevano poste in opera da un agente della medesima all'effetto di ottenere una risoluzione a lei propizia nel senso di nullità.

Mons[igno]r Nunzio risponde che, quasi contemporaneamente alla lettera inviatagli per ordine di V[ostra] S[antità], il Vescovo di Fulda (nella cui diocesi sarà la Iwanowska) gli trasmise una copia della sentenza di nullità pronunciata già nel 24 febbraio dalla Curia di Mohilow.

Aggiunge di aver subito fatto sentire a quel vescovo di non procedere alla esecuzione della sentenza adducendo le ragioni giustificanti le ragioni che gl'inculcava; e lo istigava di diri(g)gere alla Congre[gazione] un rapporto analogo corredato dello stesso documento.

Fa poi qualche rimarco sull'essere stato egli tenuto allo scuro su tal argomento mentre conobbe essere state invece date istruzioni segrete al P[adre] Guidi in proposito, onde egli stimò di doversi astenere dal fare alcun passo prima di avere istruzioni.

Dichiara finalmente che andrà subito a scrivere al Metropolitano di Mokilovo nel senso contenuto nella lettera scrittagli.

The sentence issued by the Metropolitan revokes the earlier one which maintained the validity of the marriage.

If the laws of that Empire do not raise any obstacles, the two contradictory resolutions would imply the necessity of an appeal to the Holy See. The Defender of the Marriage Bond in that Metropolitan Diocese should be persuaded to make such an appeal. At the same time, the Bishop of Fulda should be told to suspend the execution of the sentence. Both these things should be accomplished through instructions to be forwarded to the Nuncio.

The rescript of August 8 does not constitute an obstacle to such procedures.

La sentenza del metropolitano è revocatoria della prima che riteneva la validità.

Se non ostano le leggi di quell'impero, la difformità dei giudicati porterebbe la necessità di doversi appellare alla S[anta] Sede. E dovrebbe farsi sentire al difensore del vincolo presso la Curia Metropolitana di appellare. Dovrebbe contemporaneamente farsi sentire al Vescovo di Fulda che sospendesse ogni esecuzione, e proibisse ogni unione. L'uno e l'altro dovrebbe farsi mediante istruzione da inviarsi a M[onsigno]r Nunzio.

Il rescritto degli 8 agosto non forma alcun ostacolo a tale procedura.

Document No. 24. April 1860. Memorandum addressed probably to Cardinal Cagiano de Azevedo, Prefect of the Holy Congregation of the Council, on whether to send orders directly to Kött. Refers to ASV, NV Docs. No. 16 and 17. Italian (2 pages).

From the letter Monsignor the Bishop of Fulda wrote to the Apostolic Nuncio it transpires that, though he awaited the order to delay which was eventually received from the latter, he is, however, in a slightly embarrassing position owing to pressures to bless the marriage coming from the Grand Duke <of Weimar>.[22] So he seems eager to have some document in his hands in order to be able to respond to the pressures made upon him.

So although in the letter written to the Nuncio the latter is requested to transmit to Monsignor of Fulda a formal prohibition from the Holy See, it might not be a bad idea, however, to consult the Holy Father and see whether he might prefer that the order not to proceed with the wedding should be sent directly to him by the Holy Congregation; after all, there is time, since it seems the letter cannot be sent until next Friday.

Dalla lettera di Mons[igno]r Vescovo di Fulda al Nunzio rilevasi che egli, quantunque abbia atteso l'ordine avuto da quest'ultimo di soprass(i)edere, tuttavia si trova in qualche imbarazzo segnatamente per gli officii avuti dal gran Duca di benedire le nuove nozze. Ed egli stesso mostrasi premuroso di avere un qualche documento per schermirsi dalle premure che gli si fanno.

Quindi, quantunque nella lettera scritta al Nunzio gli si dia ingiunzione di trasmettere a Mons[igno]r di Fulda formale inibizione per parte della S[anta] Sede, pure non sarebbe male di sentirci il S[anto] Padre per conoscere se ami che l'ordine inibitorio sia direttamente mandato a quel Prelato dalla S[anta] Congre[gazione]; tanto più che vi è tempo, mentre pare che la lettera non possa partire che Venerdì prossimo.

---

[22]The Grand Duke Carl Alexander, who was of course Liszt's employer, had followed the thirteen-year struggle that Carolyne had waged against the church with close attention. For the past few weeks Liszt had pressed Carl Alexander for his support, and the Grand Duke had made it known to the Bishop of Fulda that it was his royal pleasure to see his distin-guished Kapellmeister marry Carolyne in Fulda Cathedral, which lay in his domains. Carl Alexander also wrote letters in Liszt's behalf to Cardinal Antonelli, and to the Russian ambassador to the Vatican, Count Nicholas Kisseleff. His intervention in Carolyne's case was a source of embarrassment both to Bishop Kött and to Monsignor De Luca.

Document No. 25. April 30, 1860. Papal order to Quaglia to write to De Luca.
See ASV, NV Doc. No. 18.

<File>: Zhitomir
Carolyne Iwanowska
Secret Archive
Prot. No. 1462/4
Papal Audience of April 30, 1860.

We must write to the Apostolic Nuncio
according to the draft enclosed.

Zytomerien
Carolina Iwanowska
Archivio Segreto
1462/4
Ex Audientia S[antis]s[i]mi
Die 30 Aprilis 1860.
Scribatur Nuntio Ap[osto]lico Viennen[si]
iuxta insertam minutam.
Udienza.

Document No. 26. May 3, 1860. Draft of letter by Quaglia to De Luca. For the
text See ASV, NV Doc. No. 18. The second paragraph is reproduced here in full, since
it contains phrases within brackets {} which were erased in the text of
ASV, NV Doc. No. 18.

....

His Holiness approves your warning Monsignor the Bishop of Fulda that he should not proceed with the implementation of the sentence on this marriage case and deems it necessary that you yourself, on behalf of the Holy See, forward without delay to the aforementioned Bishop a formal prohibition to this effect until he receives further instructions from the Holy See, {given that this marriage case must be reviewed in the third instance for the reason that the two judgements rendered so far differ}. At the same time, you are to instruct the Archbishop of Mohilow to suggest to {orders} the Defender of the Marriage Bond in that Curia that he should present to the Holy See an appeal against that last sentence, {as it is rigorously prescribed by the late Benedict XIV in his Bull *Dei miseratione,*} and accordingly forward the records of the proceedings.

....

....

Sua Santità, dopo aver trovato opportuna l'avvertenza da Lei fatta a M[onsigno]r Vescovo di Fulda di non procedere alla esecuzione della sentenza matrimoniale, stima necessario che Ella stessa a nome della S[anta] Sede trasmetta senza ritardo al prelod[at]o Vescovo formale inibizione all' effetto indicato fino a che non riceverà dalla stessa S[anta] Sede ulteriori istruzioni, {dovendo quella questione matrimoniale subire un terzo grado stante la difformità dei due giudicati fin qui emanati}. Con la stessa sollecitudine poi dovrà dare istruzioni a Mons[igno]r Arcivescovo di Molikovo perché informi {ordini} al Difensore del Vincolo matrimoniale presso quella Curia d'interporre ricorso {appello} innanzi alla S[anta] Sede contro l'ultima sentenza, {come viene rigorosamente prescritto dalla S[anta] M[emoria] di Benedetto XIV nella sua Costituzione *Dei miseratione,*} e quindi trasmetta gli atti processuali.

....

Document No. 27. June 3, 1860. Petition by Carolyne to the Pope on removing
the impediments against her new marriage. The case is to be reviewed again.
French (3 pages).

Zhitomir
Carolyne Iwanowska
Secret Archive
Prot. No. 1462/4

Zytomerien
Caroline Iwanowska
Arch[ivi]o Segreto
1462/4

To: His Holiness
Our Most Holy Father
Pope Pius IX

Rome, June 3, 1860

Most Holy Father:

Princess Carolyne von Sayn-Wittgenstein, born Iwanowska, informs Your Holiness that, after her case was reviewed by the Court of the Metropolitan of all the Russias, Monsignor Wenceslas Żyliński, Archbishop of Mohilow, who was granted complete Apostolic powers, she obtained the definitive sentence declaring her marriage to Prince Nicholas von Sayn-Wittgenstein null and void. As a consequence, she obtained at the same time the freedom to enter another union according to Canon Law, as one can see from the enclosed document. Nevertheless, the implementation of this sentence has been suspended, because they say that the Apostolic Nuncio in Vienna has written to Your Holiness on this matter raising some difficulties she is not aware of.

I, therefore, humbly beg Your Holiness to deign to lift me from a condition of very painful anxiety and restore to me the right which I believe is mine. I entreat Your Holiness to consider as well the fact that my case has been submitted to the scrutiny of ecclesiastical courts for over twelve years and, consequently, I pray that you condescend to pronounce on it, as soon as possible, as the infallible oracle to whom I declare my complete submission, for I am and wish to be always, Most Holy Father, your faithful as well as your obedient daughter.

Princess Carolyne von Sayn-Wittgenstein,
born Iwanowska.

_____

June 4, 1860
Let it be received and placed in the file.

A Sa Sainteté
Notre très Saint Père
le Pape Pie IX

Rome, ce 3 juin 1860

Très Saint Père.

La Princesse Carolyne de Sayn-Wittgenstein, née Iwanowska, expose à Votre Sainteté qu'après que sa cause a été traitée au tribunal du Metropolitain de toutes les Russies, Monseigneur Wenceslas Zelinski, Archevêque de Mohilew, muni de pouvoirs apostoliques complets, elle a obtenu la sentence définitive qui déclare la nullité de son mariage avec le Prince Nicolas de Sayn-Wittgenstein en suite de quoi elle a obtenu en même temps la liberté de conclure une autre union selon les lois canoniques, comme on peut le voir dans le document ci-joint. Néanmoins l'exécution de cette faculté s'est trouvée suspendue, parce qu'on dit que le Nonce Apostolique de Vienne a écrit à Votre Sainteté à ce sujet, en soulevant quelques difficultés qu'elle ignore.

Pour cela, je supplie humblement Votre Sainteté de daigner me retirer d'un état d'angoisse fort douloureux, en me donnant le droit, dont je crois être en possession, conjurant en même temps Votre Sainteté de considérer que mon affaire est déjà soumise depuis douze ans à l'examen des tribunaux ecclésiastiques, par conséquent de vouloir bien maintenant, prononcer par elle même, l'oracle infaillible auquel je me déclare parfaitement soumise, étant et voulant toujours être, Très Saint Père, votre fille aussi fidèle qu'obéissante.

La Princesse Carolyne de Sayn-Wittgenstein,
née Iwanowska.

_____

Die 4 Junii 1860
Reassum[atur] et uniatur.

**Document No. 28. Copy of Żyliński's decree made from the official original
dated February 24(O.S.) = March 7 (N.S.), 1860, given by the Archbishop to
Carolyne. Enclosed with Doc. No. 27. Latin (4 pages).**

Abstract
Wenceslas Żyliński,

by grace of God and the Apostolic See
Archbishop of Mohilow, Metropolitan for all the
Roman Catholic Churches in the Russian Empire, Apostolic Delegate for the matters
herewith described:

To each and everyone who will read the
present letters we make it known and testify that
we were lately shown by the Office of the Minister for Internal Affairs of the Russian Empire a
Communication of the Holy Congregation of the
Council issued on August 8, 1859, whereby the
Most Holy Father, kindly condescending to the
prayers of Carolyne Iwanowska, deigned himself
to order that, whereas there be nothing to the
contrary, we take up again the case of the annulment of her marriage to Prince Nicholas Wittgenstein and after studying it, we be empowered
to issue a definitive sentence according to the
level of appeal, provided that in all else we abide
by that which must be considered, particularly
with reference to the Bull *Dei miseratione* issued
by the late Benedict XIV.

After we received this communication with
all due reverence, we proceeded to execute its
commands and entrusted these most distinguished fathers, Monsignor Maximilian
Staniewski, Bishop of Platen, our Assistant;
Monsignor Andreas Dobszewicz, Provost of Szydlow and Canon of Samogit; and Monsignor
Dominic Moszezynski, Prelate Dean of Minsk,
with the task of reviewing and diligently examining the whole case as it was dealt with in the
Consistory of Luck-Zhitomir, and as it was later
reviewed and disposed of again in the Consistory
of Mohilow. First they were to summon, after he
took the customary oath, the Defender of
Marriage Bonds especially chosen by me for this
task in the person of the Reverend Basil Zottek.
Having then gathered the necessary information
about the facts presented, they were to vote
freely and according to their judgement on the
validity or invalidity of that marriage. Having
found, in the course of the proceedings, that:

Extractum
Venceslaus Żyliński,

Dei et Apostolicae Sedis gratia Archiepiscopus Mohyloviensis, Metropolitanus omnium
Romano-Catholicarum in Imperio Rossiaco
Ecclesiarum, ad infra scripta Delegatus Apostolicus.

Universis et singulis praesentes in-
specturis, notum facimus, atque testamur, quali-
ter nuper exhibitum fuerit ex Ministerio
Negotiorum Internorum Imperii Rossiaci Rescriptum S[anctae] Congregationis Concilii sub
d[ie] 8 Augusti 1859 anni emanatum, quo
Sanctissimus Dominus Noster precibus
Karolinae Iwanowska benigne annuens, mandare dignatus est, ut contrariis quibuscumque
non obstantibus, Nos causam super nullitate
matrimonii eius cum Principe Nicolao Wittgenstein reassumere, cognoscere ac per definitivam
sententiam, in appellationis gradu, servatis ceteroquin servandis ac praesertim Constitutione
sa[nctae] mem[oriae] Benedicti XIV, *Dei miseratione*, diiudicare valeamus.

Nos rescripto hoc cum omni, qua decuit,
reverentia recepto, ad executionem eiusdem
procedentes, Perillustribus D[ominis] Maximiliano Staniewski Episcopo Plateensi, Suffraganeo Nostro, Andreae Dobszewicz Infulato
Praeposito Szydloviensi, Canonico Samogitiensi
et Dominico Moszezynski Praelato Decano
Minscensi commisimus, ut Defensore Matrimoni R[everendo] D[omino] Basilio Zottek,
specialiter a Nobis ad id destinato, post praesti-
tum ab ipso consuetum iuramentum, citato,
totam causam, in Luceovio Zytomirensi Consistorio tractatam, atque in Consistorio Mohylo-
viensi examinatam, denuo reassumptam
cognoscant et diligenter examinent, ac sum-
maria informatione de expositis capta, de et
super validitate aut nullitate dicti matrimonii,
libera ac spontanea suffragia sua proferant. Qui
cum in processo constructo reperiissent,

1) Carolyne Iwanowska, Catholic, aged seventeen and a young lady belonging to the nobility, was subjected by her own father to intimidation and grave threats as was proved by witnesses under oath, and that she was then joined in matrimony on April 26, 1836, with Prince Nicholas Wittgenstein, Calvinist; moreover that, in the year 1848, after her father's death, no longer being in fear of being deprived by him of the fruits of his inheritance, she had requested in writing to her own Ordinary Office a declaration to the effect that the aforementioned marriage contract was null and void by cause of violence and threats. The case was dealt with according to the law and, in the first instance, it was brought before the Consistory of Luck-Zhitomir for judgement.

2) The Consistory of Luck-Zhitomir in its deliberations of the 6th of November, 1851, was of the opinion that the witnesses that were called upon to prove that the petitioner was forced to contract marriage through violence and fear, namely the petitioner's mother, a lady-in-waiting, and some of her servants of plebeian birth, rendered any judgement dubious and did not provide sufficient proof, on the strength of the ruling contained in Book 4, Tome 1 of Pichler's Code: "If, after everything is considered, there is still doubt as to whether or not the marriage has been contracted in conditions of such fear that would invalidate it, one must judge in favor of its validity, namely in favor of the sacrament, of the offspring, and the state," declared the marriage was to be deemed valid.

3) The same case being presented in the second instance before the Consistory of Mohilow, it being pertinent that the marriage was contracted initially through intimidation and, even though it is contemplated in common law that, afterwards, through subsequent free and voluntary consummation it can be ratified and validated; nevertheless, at present, according to the new rules established by the Council of Trent, the initial contracting of an invalid marriage is not validated by subsequent consummation no matter how freely performed, and a new consent before the Church is necessary as, in accordance with the declaration of the Holy Congregation, is confirmed by Fagnano in the Monacelli Formularium at Chapter VIII, Formula 10, No. 17; the Judges, therefore, on

1.) Karolinam Iwanowska Catholicam, septemdecim annorum aetatis, nobilem virginem, metu et minis gravissimis a proprio genitore, prout a testibus, interposito iuramento, probatum sit, adactam et matrimonio 26 d[ie] Aprilis 1836 anni coniunctam fuisse cum Principe Nicolao Wittgenstein Calvinianae Sectae addicto, illamque post mortem patris sui 1848 anno non amplius metuentem, quin ab illo praediis bonisque hereditariis privaretur, supplicem dedisse libellum proprio Ordinariatui Loci, pro declaratione nullitatis praedicti matrimonii per vim et minas contracti. Causam inde ad tramites iuris confectam, Consistorio Luceovio-Zytomirensi ex ordine ad diiudicandum oblatam fuisse.

2.) Consitorium Luceovio-Zytomirense 6 d[ie] Novembris 1851 anni censendo, quod testes inducti, prout mater oratricis, famula nobilis et nonnulli ex domesticis eius de plebe, ad probandum, oratricem vi metuque adactam fuisse ad contrahendum matrimonium, dubium facerent iudicium, satisque non probarent, adductis verbis C[odicis] Pichleri Tom[i] I Libr[i] IV: "Si omnibus consideratis manet dubium, an matrimonium tali metu, quod illud redditur invalidum, contractum sit necne? praesumendum est pro valore, scilicet propter favorem sacramenti, prolis imo et rei publicae" declarasse matrimonium illud pro validum habendum.

3.) Proposita eadem causa in secunda instantia, coram Consistorio Mohiloviensi nempe, Iudices, attento quod matrimonium a principio metu contractum, licet iure communi inspecto, per copulam postea libere et voluntarie subsecutam ratificeretur et convalidaretur, nihilominus hodie, iure novo Concilii Tridentini, matrimonium nulliter a principio contractum non convalidetur per subsecutam copulam quantumvis libere habitam, sed requiratur novus consensus in facie Ecclesiae, prout ex declaratione S[anctae] Congregationis firmat Fagnanus apud Monacelli in Formulario Tit[ulum] VIII, For[mulam] X, N[umerum] 17, dictum matrimonium 13 d[ie] Novembris 1852 an invalidum pronuntiasse, uno vix dissentiente Vicario generali, cuius sententiam pro validitate matrimonii su-

November 13, 1852, pronounced the aforesaid marriage invalid, the Vicar General being the only one dissenting. The Archbishop of Mohilow, our fatherly predecessor Ignaz Holowinski, showed his disapproval of the judgement in favor of the annulment brought forth by a clear majority of the judges by ratifying instead the latter's opinion in favor of the validity of this marriage, which rested on the aforementioned declaration of the Consistory of Luck-Zhitomir.

4) Prince Nicholas Wittgenstein, a follower of the Calvinist sect, had already re-married in the year 1857[23] with a lady of the Russian orthodox faith. On the basis of these findings, the above named Judges unanimously decreed Carolyne Iwanowska's marriage to be null and void.

Therefore, after we studied the above proceedings and decrees, checked the laws that were brought to our attention, especially the Chapter *Videtur nobis,* which the petitioners against the marriage placed at the end: "What we read is true, namely that, in criminal cases, the father is not a party in the case of the son, nor is the son in the case of the father. However, in the conjoining or disjoining pertaining to marriage, as a prerogative of marriage itself and as the thing is favorable, this is properly admitted"; and, also the aforementioned declaration of the Holy Congregation reported in Monacelli: "Today, according to the new rules approved by the Council of Trent, a marriage contracted initially in a situation of intimidation must be deemed invalid, and cannot be validated by its subsequent consummation, no matter how freely and willingly performed; a new consent is, therefore, required etc."; and all those other things according to which, in the act of contracting marriage, it is required that there be a true consent and not a simulated one, that it be positive, reciprocal, given in total freedom from threats, violence, or intimidation, and with immunity; having, moreover, heard nothing to the contrary from the Defender of the Marriage Bond, by the apostolic authority invested in us, we deliberated that the marriage of Carolyne Iwanowska to Prince Nicholas Wittgenstein, having been contracted through violence and intimidation, must be definitively deemed, pronounced, and decreed to be and have been, therefore, null, void, and without effect.

---

[23]In fact, it was 1856.

praedictae declarationi Consistorii Luceovio-Zytomirensis innixam, Archiepiscopus Mohyloviensis p[ater] m[eus] Ignatius Holowinski ratam habuerit, reprobato suffragio pro nullitate eius a maiori parte iudicum lato.

4.) Principem Nicolaum Wittgenstein Calvinianae Sectae asseclam iam anno 1857 ad alias nuptias cum virgine Graeco-Rossiacae religionis convolasse; unanimiter matrimonium Karolinae Iwanowska nullum ac invalidum edixerunt.

Idcirco Nos visis actis et decretis suprascriptis ac attentis iuribus coram Nobis exhibitis praesertim cap[itulo] *videtur nobis* qui matr[imonii] accus[atores] pos[uerunt] in fine: "Quod vero legitur, Pater non recipiatur in causa filii nec filius in causa patris in criminalibus causis et contractibus verum est. In matrimonio vero coniungendo et disiungendo, ex ipsius coniugii praerogativa et quia favorabils res est, *congrue* admittuntur" et supracitata declaratione S[anctae] Congregationis apud Monacelli "Hodie iure novo Concilii Tridentini matrimonium nulliter a principio metu contractum non convalidatur per subsecutam copulam quantum vis libere habitam, sed requiritur novus consensus etc." ac omnibus, iuxta quae in contrahentibus matrimonium expostulatur consensus verus, non simulatus, positivus, reciprocus, libertas totalis, a minis, vi et metu immunitas, nec non audito Defensore matrimonii, Auctoritate Apostolica Nobis concessa, matrimonium Karolinae Iwanowska cum Principe Nicolao Wittgenstein per vim et metum contractum adeoque nullum, irritum et invalidum fuisse et esse dicendum, pronunciandum ac definitive sententiandum esse duximus, prout per praesentes, contrariis quibuscumque non obstantibus, quae Sua Sanctitas non obstare voluit, dicimus, pronunciamus, declaramus ac per definitivam sententiam diiudicamus, plenam dictae Karolinae facultatem, ut ad alias nuptias libere ac licite transire valeat, concedendo.
In quorum fidem etc..

Accordingly, by means of the present letters, in the absence of any other impediment which His Holiness thought might be an obstacle, We state, pronounce, declare and, moreover, issue a definitive sentence attributing to the aforesaid Carolyne full faculty to contract a new marriage freely and legitimately.
In proof of the above etc.

Given in St. Petersburg on the 24th day of February of the year 1860.
x Wenceslas, Archbishop.
The Seal of the Archbishop.

I have seen this decree.

Basil Zottek, Defender of the Marriage Bond in the present case.

Otto Proniewski,

Secretary for Spiritual Matters to His Excellency, The Most Reverend and Illustrious Archbishop

Datum Petropoli 1860 anni Mensis Februarii 24 die.
x Venceslaus Archiepiscopus.
Sequitur magnum Sigillum Archiep[iscopi]

Hoc decretum legi

Basilius Zottek Defensor Matrimonii hac in causa.

Otto Proniewski

Secr[etar]ius in Sp[iritua]libus
Suae Excell[entiae] R[everendissi]mi
& Ill[ustrissi]mi Archiep[iscop]i

Approved and validated by the Imperial Minister for Internal Affairs, St. Petersburg, February 27 <O.S.>, 1860.

Approved by the Minister for External Affairs on March 1 <O.S.>, 1860.

There are then other certifying notes by the Chief of Section and the Imperial Legation.[24]

Sequitur Visura et Recognitio Ministri Imperialis Negotiorum Interiorum, Petropoli die 27 Februarii 1860.

Deinde sub die 1ª Martii 1860 apposita est Visura Ministri Negotiorum Exteriorum. Et insuper aliae recognitiones tum Capitis Sectionis, tum Missionis Imperialis.

Document No. 29. July 1860. Princess Carolyne's formal presentation of her case for the Congregation's review as drafted by Okraszewski. Italian (11 pages).

Cases of marriage annulment, like all the other ones that, among Catholics, are within the jurisdiction of the Church, are regulated in Russia by the dispositions of the 1847 Concordate between the Russian Empire and the Holy See. It is to be noted, however, that besides the arti-

Le cause di nullità di matrimonio, come le altre tutte di competenza ecclesiastica tra i Cattolici, sono regolate in Russia dalla disposizione del Concordato del 1847 tra l'impero russo e la S[anta] Sede. E' da notare però che oltre gli articoli contenuti nella primitiva convenzione,

---

[24]Of all the documents in the Vatican archives this one is probably the most important. On the basis of Archbishop Zyliński's decree Carolyne was free to contract another marriage inside the Catholic Church. This was the document with which Okraszewski had returned to Weimar in triumph, in March 1860, his mission as Carolyne's solicitor accom-

plished (see page 11). Although several appeals were made against it by Monsignor Hohenlohe, Monsignor De Luca, and by Bishop Kött, it was formally upheld by the Council of the Holy Congregation on January 8, 1861 (see AVR, Doc. No. 1).

cles contained in the original Concordate, there are others that are fully applicable and are contained in the published collections of imperial laws as an integral part of that same Concordate; these pertain specifically to procedures and practical judicial applications and, above all, to the different levels of jurisdiction to be observed in appeal cases in order that all cases be resolved within the empire.

As is well known, the Church hierarchy is organised in Russia in such a way that there is just one Metropolitan, the Archbishop of Mohilow, while all the other Dioceses are suffraganates. The respective Consistories, when they sit in judgement, are presided over by the Vicar General who has only one vote and a half, while the other three members have one vote each. Their resolutions, even when all the judges are present, including the local bishop, have no force unless they are confirmed by the Bishop himself. An exception is made only for the Archbishop of Mohilow who, as he is considered the Primate for all of Russia and, therefore, resides always in St. Petersburg, does not participate in the deliberations of his own Consistory, since he must sit in judgement at the second or third level of jurisdiction; therefore, the resolutions of the Consistory of Mohilow, when voted on by a majority, are in effect decrees that need not be ratified by the Archbishop.

Such is truly the established hierarchical order that, especially in cases concerning the state, a sentence issued by any one of the suffraganates is appealed before the Consistory of Mohilow which adjudicates, as it has been stated, without the participation of its Archbishop. When the rulings are contradictory, appeals at the third level are brought before the same Metropolitan residing in St. Petersburg where he can consult a College of distinguished members of the clergy as if it were another Consistory. The sentence issued by the Metropolitan in the third instance is *definitive and without recourse*, the losing party being permitted only to appeal to the Holy See.

In order that such forms be universally observed, the imperial laws and legal procedures require the presence at the proceedings of a member of the laity as the Government's delegate, whose task it is to ensure the full observance of those practices. Without his

altri ve ne sono in pienissima osservanza i quali leggonsi stampati nella collezione delle leggi imperiali, come facienti parte integrale dello stesso Concordato; e questi toccano particolarmente la procedura e l'ordine pratico giudiziario, e sopra tutto i vari gradi di giurisdizione per i casi di appello affinché le cause siano terminate nello Impero.

Com'è ben noto, in Russia la Gerarchia ecclesiastica cattolica è così determinata che un solo è il Metropolitano, l'Arcivescovo di Mohilow, di cui sono suffraganee tutte le altre sedi vescovili. I rispettivi Concistori giudicano colla Presidenza del Vicario Generale, il quale ha soltanto un voto e mezzo, mentre gli altri tre componenti non hanno che un semplice voto; questo giudicato però, a Sede piena e presente il Diocesano del luogo, non ha alcuna forza se non è confermato dallo stesso Vescovo. Avvi eccezione pel solo Arcivescovo di Mohilow, il quale, essendo considerato come Primate di tutte le Russie, e perciò risiede costantemente in Pietroburgo, si astiene dall'intervenire al giudicato del suo Concistoro Arcivescovile, dovendo Esso giudicare in secondo o terzo grado di giurisdizione; e quindi il giudicato del Concistoro di Mohilow, emanato a maggioranza di voti ha l'effetto di vera sentenza senza bisogno della ratifica dell'Arcivescovo.

E per verità tale si è l'ordine gerarchico stabilito, massime nelle cause di stato, che dalla sentenza di qualunque dei Suffraganei si porta l'appello al Concistoro Arcivescovile di Mohilow, il quale giudica senza il concorso, com'è detto, del suo Arcivescovo. E nella discrepanza dei giudicati, si dà luogo all'appello in terzo grado avanti il Metropolitano stesso residente in Pietroburgo, ove ha un Collegio di distinti Ecclesiastici cui possa consultare, volendo, quasi fosse un altro Concistoro. La sentenza emanata dal Metropolitano in terza istanza è *definitiva ed inappellabile*, rimanendo soltanto permesso alla parte soccombente il ricorso alla S[anta] Sede.

Ed affinché una tal forma sia osservata egualmente che le leggi e prammatiche dell'Impero, in ogni Concistoro interviene sempre un secolare, come Delegato dal Governo, il quale deve sorvegliare sulla piena osservanza di quelle; e senza la firma e certificato di costui, un atto

certification and signature, no Consistorial decree will be deemed valid and executable.

Given these premises, which are necessary to understand how Ecclesiastical cases are dealt with in Russia, we move on to describe the procedures followed and the resolutions eventually adopted in the case for annulment introduced by Princess Carolyne von Wittgenstein. In this particular case, these procedures were adhered to and the levels of jurisdiction properly observed in complete accordance with what is prescribed by the laws and by the Concordate.

Shortly after the death of her father,[25] who was responsible for the violence and intimidation perpetrated on his daughter in order to induce her to marry Prince Nicholas von Wittgenstein, since there was no longer any cause for any fear of being disinherited, she presented a request for the annulment of her marriage to the Consistory of Mohilow, in whose diocese was situated the parish where the wedding had been performed. Having instituted proper proceedings, the Consistory deliberated in favor of annulment.

However, before the sentence could be issued, the territorial delimitation of the Diocese was modified and, as a consequence, the aforesaid Parish was included in the Diocese of Zhitomir. The Mohilow deliberation was considered as not having taken place and was not, therefore, executable.[26] At this point, having instituted new proceedings, the Consistory of Zhitomir adjudicated the case *in the first instance* of jurisdiction, ruling, however, for the *validity* of the marriage. The reasons for this sentence rested on extrinsic factors pertaining to the character of some of the witnesses who did not document having satisfied their Easter obligation, and on the exclusion of the testimony of the Petitioner's mother and household servants as deemed not qualified to provide testimony in the case.

qualunque del Concistoro non sarebbe riconosciuto per valido ed efficace.

Premesse queste nozioni, necessarie a sapersi per formare un giusto criterio sopra una causa ecclesiastica giudicata in Russia, si viene alla narrazione della procedura tenuta e dei giudicati intervenuti nella causa di nullità del matrimonio della *Principessa Carolina di Wittgenstein*, nella quale a capello sono state osservate le forme le forme enunciate ed esauriti i gradi di giurisdizione nel modo voluto dalle leggi e dal Concordato.

Seguita appena la morte del di Lei padre, autore della violenza e del timore grave incusso alla figlia per indurla al Matrimonio col principe Nicolò de' Wittgenstein, comecché cessata la causa del timore ad evitare la diseredazione, presentò Ella la querela di nullità del suo matrimonio avanti il Concistoro di Mohilow, alla cui Diocesi allora apparteneva la Parrocchia ove il Matrimonio fu celebrato. E, previo un regolare processo, il Concistoro sentenziò per la nullità.

Siccome però, prima che tal sentenza fosse emanata, si era fatto luogo alla circoscrizione della Diocesi, in virtù della quale la detta Parrocchia fu incorporata alla Diocesi di Zitomir, la sentenza di Mohilow si considerò come non avvenuta e quindi di nessuna efficacia. E fu allora che il Concistoro di Zitomir, previo nuovo esame della causa, giudicò *in primo grado* di giurisdizione, ritenendo però la *validità* del matrimonio. I motivi precisi di tal sentenza poggiavano sopra le qualità estrinseche d'alcuni testimoni, i quali non aveano documentato di aver soddisfatto il precetto pasquale, e sulla esclusione della Madre e delle persone domestiche della Attrice, quasi fossero incapaci a testificare.

---

[25] As we have observed elsewhere, Carolyne's father died in 1844; she did not initiate the proceedings for her annulment until 1848, almost a year after she met Liszt. Okraszweski, perhaps taking a hint from an ambiguous sentence in Žylinsky's decree, conveniently telescopes the two events.

[26] Among the many difficulties that Carolyne faced in the succesful pursuit of her case was the little-known problem affecting the parish of Pohrebysze in which she and Nicholas Wittgenstein had been married. Shortly after the preliminary trial in Mohilow, on May 12, 1848 (whose judgement was in her favor), the parish of Pohrebysze was transferred

to Luck-Zhitomir. With a stroke of the pen this parish ceased to exist, and the decision to annul Carolyne's marriage was considered to have no legal standing. The reason for this rigorous interpretation of the law had to do with the Concordate of 1847 between Russia and the Vatican. Under this agreement, the borders of the various dioceses in the Russian Empire were to be re-drawn, a process that eventually overtook Carolyne's petition (or the early stages of it), and for a time left her in limbo. It was shrewd of Okraszewski to bring out this anomaly in his review of the case, because the consistories themselves had always ignored it.

An appeal was then presented to the Consistory of Mohilow which produced an opposite ruling; since they did not consider the exceptions that had been found in the first instance as having any weight according to Canon Law, they resolved, in the second instance of jurisdiction, for the annulment of the marriage. However, since the Vicar General, the only one who had voted against the resolution, had considerable influence upon the Metropolitan who was to give a ruling in the third instance, it so happened that the latter conformed himself to the opinion of his Vicar and to the Zhitomir resolution and ratified, at the third level of jurisdiction, the latter's sentence for precisely the same extrinsic reasons, thus showing his disapproval of the resolution produced by his own Consistory of Mohilow.

Things being so, after a series of political events that personally affected the Princess and that it will not be relevant to mention here, she appealed to the Pontiff and last year in August 1859, she obtained from him, through the office of the Holy Congregation of the Council, the extraordinary faculty whereby the present new Metropolitan of St. Petersburg was delegated to review and definitively adjudicate the Princess's case with the proviso "whereas there be nothing to the contrary" in the observance of the Benedictine Bull *Dei miseratione.*

On the force of this rescript, which was seen and approved beforehand by the Emperor and his Ministers, the Metropolitan set up a Commission composed of three distinguished members of the clergy with the active participation of the Defender of the Marriage Bond, as is required by the above mentioned Benedictine Bull. With the support of the most valid reasons, both intrinsic and extrinsic (there being also a verification of the fulfillment of the Easter precept on the part of the witnesses to whom the Consistory of Zhitomir had taken exception), having properly observed all the legal requirements, they *definitively ruled with apostolic authority* that the marriage was null and void, thereby allowing the Princess freedom to contract a new marriage. The Metropolitan who had been so delegated carefully studied this sentence with respect to its merits and its compliance with the forms of the law and personally sanctioned it.

Venuta la causa in appello al Concistoro di Mohilow, fu questi d'avviso contrario, non riconoscendo per canoniche le eccezioni accampate in prima istanza e perciò *a grande maggioranza* giudicò *in secondo grado* di giurisdizione *per la nullità* del matrimonio. Ma, siccome il Vicario Generale, che era stato *solo* di voto contrario, e esercitava tutta la sua influenza sull'animo del Metropolitano che dovea giudicare in terza istanza, così avvenne che Questi, uniformandosi al voto del suo Vicario e del Concistoro di Zitomir, confermò *in terzo grado* di giurisdizione la sentenza di quello, e precisamente per le stesse estrinseche ragioni, riprovando l'altra emanata dal suo Concistoro di Mohilow.

In questo stato di cose, dopo l'avvenimento di varie vicende politiche influenti nella persona della Principessa, che non è mestier qui ricordare, questa invocò ed ottenne dal Sommo Pontefice per organo della S[anta] Congregazione del Concilio in Agosto dello scorso anno 1859 la facoltà straordinaria, in virtù della quale fu delegato il nuovo attuale Metropolitano di Pietroburgo a rivedere e giudicare *definitivamente* la causa della Principessa colla clausola "contrariis non obstantibus quibuscumque" osservando la Bolla Benedettina *Dei miseratione.*

Il Metropolitano, in virtù di tale rescritto, visto prima ed approvato dall'Imperatore e da' suoi Ministri, deputò una Commissione di tre distinti Ecclesiastici, la quale, coll'intervento del Difensore del Vincolo a forma della citata Benedettina, sull'appoggio di validissime ragioni intrinseche ed estrinseche (verificatosi anche l'adempimento del precetto nei testimoni eccepiti dal Concistoro di Zitomir) colla osservanza di tutte le forme pronunziò *definitivamente, auctoritate apostolica,* per la nullità del matrimonio, concedendo libera facoltà alla Principessa di passare ad altre nozze. Quale sentenza fu dallo stesso Metropolitano delegato attentamente ponderata sul merito e sulle forme, e da lui stesso personalmente confermata.

On the strength of this sentence, which was definitive and without recourse and bore the formal approval and legal authentication of the Imperial Ministers in St. Petersburg—since in the meantime neither the presumed husband, Prince von Wittgenstein, who had remarried in 1857,[27] according to the Schismatic Greek rite, nor the Defender of the Marriage Bond, who more than anyone else had been persuaded of the nullity, had appealed against it, the Princess prepared to get married again in the Diocese of Fulda in Germany, where she had taken refuge after the vexations and persecutions suffered on account of her Catholic faith.

And when everything had been set in preparation for her wedding, Monsignor the Bishop of Fulda took it upon himself to suspend the execution of such an unimpeachable sentence because, it was said, he had received an order to this effect from the Holy See; this was doubtless brought about by intrigues and the worst possible slander. The very notion of such rumours horrified the Princess. How could anyone dare to accuse her of bribing the judges who had been chosen to review her case? This was a most grave accusation that affected, even more than the Princess, the venerable Metropolitan and the Commission he had established by selecting clergymen who were eminent for rank, nobility, merit, and wealth and, therefore, not corrupt and incapable of being corrupted under any circumstance.

But this grievously offends the Princess as well for, having sustained the confiscation of her worldly goods and all kinds of persecutions on account of her steadfast allegiance to Catholicism and the laws of the Church, she must now feel accused of a crime which would belie her religious principles and would make her unspeakably guilty before the sacrosanct laws of the Church.

She cannot but shudder at such vile accusations which were doubtless made up by those who, out of hatred for Catholicism, have been the cause of her previous persecutions and were probably abetted by someone who, out of worldly ambition and for private and personal motives, was interested in preventing her from marrying again. She lays the entire burden of such accusations on the purveyors of intrigues, but must place some responsibility on those people who, even with the best of intentions, did not hesitate to lend credibility to such gross inventions and

Munita di tale sentenza *definitiva ed inappellabile*, corredata di tutte le formalità, legalità e visti dei Ministri Imperiali in Pietroburgo, senzaché né il supposto marito Principe di Wittgenstein, il quale già dal 1857 ha contratto altro matrimonio secondo il rito Greco-scismatico, né il Difensore del Vincolo, più che ogni altro *persuaso della nullità*, ne avesse mosso ricorso od appello, la Principessa pensava a rimaritarsi nella Diocesi di Fulda in Germania ove, per le vessazioni e persecuzioni patite per la sua religione Cattolica, erasi rifuggita.

E mentre tutto era disposto pel suo nuovo matrimonio, Monsignor Vescovo di Fulda credè sospendere gli effetti di tale inattaccabile sentenza per ordine, come si disse, della S[anta] Sede, provocato senza meno dall'intrigo e dalla più acerba calunnia. Al cui vago rumore inorridì la Principessa, come si fosse osato di accusarla di subornazione ai Giudici delegati, trattandosi d'ingiuria gravissima fatta, più che alla Principessa, al venerando Metropolitano ed alla Commissione scelta da lui, composta di ecclesiastici distinti per grado, per nobiltà, per meriti e per ricchezza, e quindi incorrotti ed incorrompibili sotto qualsivoglia riguardo.

Ma il torto è anche gravissimo alla Principessa, la quale, dopo aver sostenuto pel suo inalterabile attaccamento alla Cattolica Religione ed alle leggi della Chiesa l'esilio, la confisca dei beni e vessazioni di ogni sorta, dee sentirsi imputata di un eccesso che smentirebbe la massima sua religiosa e la renderebbe colpevole enormemente in faccia alle leggi sagrosante della Chiesa.

Mentre però non può non fremere a tanta nera calunnia, inventata senza meno da chi è stato la causa delle sue antecedenti persecuzioni, in odio sempre della Religione Cattolica, e fomentata probabilmente da chi ha un qualche interesse ad impedire per umane viste e per fini privati e personali il nuovo suo matrimonio, Ella ne lascia tutto il peso agl'intriganti non senza una qualche responsabilità a coloro che, anche colle migliori intenzioni possibili, hanno creduto di dar credito a tali maligne invenzioni senz'altro effetto che di far

[27]Actually in 1856.

caused a new and heavy handed persecution to fall upon an innocent woman, well noted for her noble birth and religious attitude.

The Princess cannot and will not try to stop those who, to satisfy the wicked, would try to clutch water and air without ever being able to hold in their hands even the minutest evidence of guilt. She is, however, unable to fathom how, on the basis of accusations which are unverifiable and immaterial to the case, some people can wish to invalidate the effects of a solemn and irrevocable sentence which, according to Russian Law and the Concordate, cannot possibly be changed, and wish moreover to impede and further suspend her status as a single woman—a status she finally obtained by pursuing the most lawful and canonical ways and means imaginable, after making many sacrifices and enduring countless deprivations for twelve years.

The Princess will limit herself to pointing out, in the second place, that even if, by the strangest hypothesis, the appointed judges had indeed, as the wicked implied, shown evidence of some human failing, this would not be cause for protesting their resolution, which is fully valid and operative according to the law; nor would this be a reason for stopping and declaring illegal its effects with respect to the Princess, who was granted a sentence that was issued with Apostolic authority according to Canon law and is, therefore, fully executable. In such a circumstance, only the Judges could be deemed responsible and would be punishable for a crime that is solely alleged on the basis of slander.

Indeed, if we consider the intrinsic merits of the case, the violence and intimidation invalidating the marriage have been amply proven by unimpeachable witnesses since, in these instances, Canonical authorities state that blood relations and other household members can provide the best proof, for these things do happen within domestic walls. It has also been amply proven that the lack of consent on the Princess's part not only has never been corrected or replaced by a new consent given before the Church or in any other way, but the impediment was never set aside since an application for annulment was presented as soon as, at her father's death, the cause for the impediment ceased to exist.

If we then consider the form: the Benedictine Bull has been fully observed, given that there have been as well two analogous sentences in favor of

pesare nuovamente la mano con una nuova persecuzione sopra una fem\<m\>ina innocente e distinta pure per nascita e per sentimenti religiosi.

Ma, se da un lato la Principessa non può, né intende impedire che si corra dietro l'acqua che fugge e si batta l'aria senza potere mai stringere in pugno pure un'atomo, per dar solo una soddisfazione iniqua ai malignanti, non sa d'altra parte immaginare perchè sopra una imputazione meramente estrinseca ed impossibile ad appurarsi vogliansi paralizzare gli effetti di un giudicato solenne, irrevocabile, e secondo le leggi Russe consone col Concordato per se stesso irreformabile, coll'impedirsi o sospendere ulteriormente quella libertà di stato che dopo tanti stenti e sacrifici per un decennio patiti è finalmente riuscita a rivendicare coi mezzi e nelle vie le più regolari e canoniche che possano immaginarsi.

E si limita soltanto la Principessa a fare osservare subordinatamente che, ove per stranissima ipotesi si fosse mai verificata secondo il concetto dei maligni una qualche umana fralezza nei Giudici Delegati, non per questo potrebbe essere attaccato il loro giudicato, pienamente regolare ed operativo al cospetto della legge, ovvero esserne meno legali gli effetti rispetto alla persona della Principessa, la quale ha per sè una sentenza canonicamnete proferita *con autorità apostolica* ed in stato di pienissima eseguibilità. Potrebbero tutto al più, nella ipotesi concepita, essere responsabili e punibili le persone dei Giudici per il fallo, che calunniosamente si suppone commesso.

Ed invero, se si considera *il merito intrinseco* della causa, la violenza ed il timore grave annullativo del Matrimonio è provato ampiamente da testimoni inattaccabili, perché in tal genere di cause più provano, giusta i Canonisti, le persone congiunte di sangue e domestiche che non gli estranei, perchè trattasi di cose che avvengono *intra domesticos parietes*. Ed è anche provato largamente che la mancanza del suo consenso non solo non è stata mai corretta e supplita con nuovo consenso né in faccia alla Chiesa né altrimenti, ma neppure fu mai purgato l'impedimento perché il reclamo fu dato tostoché cessò la causa dell'impedimento medesimo colla morte del Padre.

Se poi si riguardano *le forme*, sono state queste pienamente osservate secondo la Benedettina, anche per la concorrenza di due giudicati conformi

annulment, i.e., the 1852 one issued in the second instance by the Consistory of Mohilow, and the other one by the Metropolitan and his Apostolically delegated Commission. The latter, however, would suffice by itself as, normally, marriage cases resolved in terms of nullity or dispensation are adjudicated by the Holy Congregation of the Council in the first and only instance or, sometimes, in the second instance with the revocation of the judgement passed in the first instance. The two resolutions, as customarily provided by the Holy Congregation of the Council (this never occurs in cases of dispensation pertaining to presumably valid marriages, in which case the Congregation renders judgement in the first and only instance) are not contradictory, since it is well known that the decisions of the Congregation, no matter how many times provided, are mere opinions until they are issued as a definitive decree by means of the clause "Amplius, etc.." Indeed, it could not be otherwise since the Judges are always the same and "there cannot be two sentences for the same case."

In any hypothesis, since the question is irrevocably resolved at least according to Russian laws, if we consider as well the political implications of this case: just as it would not be possible, without uselessly offending the Imperial Ministers and the Emperor himself, to reopen the case and assess again its merit and, concurrently, to obtain the documents and the records of the proceedings, the most prudent avenue, given the situation, would be to have the Holy Father sanction the solemn sentence issued, with full consideration and in complete respect of the form, by that distinguished Commission as well as by the Metropolitan himself with Apostolic authority. The concurring of so many favorable elements and circumstances, together with the merits and qualities of the Princess, make her hope that His Holiness will finally deal a blow to the intrigues and conspiracies and will remove all obstacles to the implementation of the effects of the above mentioned sentence by consenting, without further delays, far too damaging in every respect for the Princess, that she contract a new marriage according to Canon Law.

per la nullità, quello cioè del Concistoro di Mohilow dell'anno 1852 *in seconda istanza* e l'altro del Metropolitano e sua Commissione con Autorità Apostolica. Sebbene questo ultimo soltanto sarebbe *per sè solo* sufficiente, come suole accadere delle cause matrimoniali risolute o per titolo di nullità o per dispensa dalla S[anta] Congregazione del Concilio, talora anche *in prima ed unica istanza*, e tal altra *in seconda istanza* colla revoca del giudicato di primo grado. Senzaché possa objettarsi la duplice proposizione, che suol farsi presso la lodata S[anta] Cong[regazio]ne (lo che non accade mai nei casi di dispensa sopra matrimonio rato, ne' quali casi giudica *sempre in prima ed unica istanza),* essendo ben noto che le decisioni di quella S[anta] Cong[regazio]ne, qualunque siane il numero, non sono che *meri opinamenti* finché non siano muniti del decreto definitivo per mezzo della clausola "Amplius." E di fatto non si potrebbe pensarsi diversamente, perché i Giudici sono sempre i medesimi, e "non datur bis in idem".

In qualunque ipotesi poi, essendo la cosa completamente terminata ed irrevocabilmente almeno secondo le leggi Russe, considerata *anche politicamente* la cosa, come non sarebbe possibile non solo di rivenire sul merito, ma neppure di estrarne documenti e processi senza urtare i Ministri Imperiali e lo stesso Imperatore (e ciò senza effetto), sembrerebbe consiglio di prudenza che quand'anche qualche difetto di forma si ravvisasse, o se ne avesse dubbio, il S[anto] Padre sancisse, derogando al bisogno, la sentenza solenne pronunziata con ogni maturità e piena osservanza di forme dalla specchiatissima ed eletta Commissione nonché dallo stesso Metropolitano con Autorità Apostolica. Il concorso di tanti favorevoli elementi e circostanze, e le qualità ed i meriti della Principessa le fanno sperare che Sua Santità si risolva a rompere le fila dell'intrigo, lasciando libera la esecuzione e gli effetti della enunciata sentenza col permetterle senza ulteriore ritardo, per lei troppo pernicioso sotto ogni rispetto, di effettuare canonicamente il nuovo suo matrimonio.

\<File\>: Zhitomir
Carolyne Iwanowska
No: 1462/2
July 4, 1860. To be placed on file.

Zytomerien
Carolina Iwanowska
1462/2
Die 4 Julii 1860. Uniatur

Document No. 30. Undated. Memorandum with comments on Carolyne's presentation of the case. Italian (5 pages).

In the documentation presented, the following facts are put forward:

1. The Petition for annulment was presented to the Consistory of Mohilow in whose Diocese was located, at the time, the Parish where the marriage was celebrated. After a regular trial, that Consistory presented a resolution in favor of annulment. Before the sentence could be issued, however, the territory of the diocese had been redefined so that the aforementioned Parish was incorporated in the Diocese of Zhitomir. The sentence, therefore, was considered as non existent and having no value.

2. Later, after a new trial, the Consistory of Zhitomir ruled according to the first level of jurisdiction and declared the marriage valid.

3. The sentence was appealed before the Consistory of Mohilow, which deliberated in favor of annulment. The Vicar General expressed an opinion contrary to that of the Consistory, however, and both were forwarded in writing to the Archbishop, i.e. both the deliberation of the Consistory and the opinion of the Vicar General which was in favor of validity. The Archbishop approved the latter's opinion.

4. In 1859 a Commission selected by the present Archbishop deliberated in favor of annulment, and their sentence was confirmed by him in virtue of the powers he had received through a rescript from the Holy See.

Of all these actions and judgements, we have on file:

1. The judgement for annulment passed by the Consistory of Mohilow in appeal.

2. The opinion of the Vicar General in favor of validity

3. The approval of the latter by the Archbishop.

All these documents are certified.

From these it emerges (as on page 2) that Consistory was not formally delegated to issue a definitive judgement, but was only charged with providing an opinion which would then be presented to the Archbishop for the definitive decision ("pour dernière decision").

Nei fogli presentati si riportano i seguenti fatti:

1. La querela di nullità del matrimonio fu promossa innanzi il Concistoro di Mohilow alla cui diocesi allora apparteneva la parrocchia ove il matrimonio fu celebrato. E, previo un regolare processo, il Concistoro sentenziò per la nullità. Siccome però, prima che tal sentenza fosse emanata, si era fatto luogo alla circoscrizione della diocesi, in virtù della quale la detta parrocchia fu incorporata alla diocesi di Zitomir, così la sentenza di Mohilow si considerò come non avvenuta e quindi di nessuna efficacia.

2. In seguito di ciò il Concistoro di Zitomir, previo un nuovo esame, giudicò *in primo grado* di giurisdizione e dichiarò *valido* il matrimonio.

3. Fu in grado di appello portata la causa al Concistoro di Mohilow, che emise deliberazione per la nullità. Ma avendo il il Vicario Gen[era]le presidente del Concistoro manifestato una opinione contraria a quella del Concistoro, venne trasmessa all'Arcivescovo l'una e l'altra in scritto, cioè tanto la deliberazione del Concistoro quanto l'opinione del Vicario, che era per la validità, e l'Arcivescovo approvò l'opinione di quest'ultimo.

4. Nel 1859 poi si emise sentenza per la *nullità* da una Commissione deputata dall'odierno Mons[igno]r Arcivescovo e da questo confermata in virtù delle facoltà avute con rescritto della S[anta] Cong[regazio]ne.

Di tutti questi atti e giudicati che si enuciaano esistono in posizione

1. Il giudizio emesso dal Consitoro di Mochilow in grado di appello per la *nullità*,

2. L'opinamento del Vicario Gen[era]le per la *validità*,

3. L'approvazione dell'Arcivescovo di quest'ultimo atto.

E tutti questi atti sono autenticati.

Da essi emerge (come a pag[ina] 2) che quel Concistoro non giudicò definitivamente per *delegazione* dell'Arcivescovo, ma fu incaricato soltanto da questo ad emettere la sua opinione, quale poi doveva presentarsi all'Arcivescovo per la definitiva decisione "pour dernière decision".

This means that the process followed the rules established by the Concordate.

Having agreed with Monsignor Berardi that in order to be able to form a clear idea of the facts under debate, it is necessary to be able to see the documents pertaining to the facts that have been stated, it will be necessary to ask the party in question for:

1. The resolution or sentence issued by the Consistory of Mohilow before the Parish was removed from that Diocese and added to that of Zhitomir.

2. The resolution or sentence issued by the Consistory and Bishop of Zhitomir.

These documents must be authentic.[28]

Dal che si rileva che la cosa procedette e fu trattata a senso del Concordato.

Essendosi quindi concertato con Mons[igno]r Berardi che all'effetto di formarsi un criterio esatto su questo affare occorre avere sott'occhio i documenti relativi ai fatti enunciati, converrà chiedere alla parte

1. L'opinamento o sentenza emessa dal Concistoro di Mohilow prima che la Parrocchia fosse dismembrata ed unita a Zitomir.

2. L'opinamento o sentenza del Concistoro e Vescovo di Zitomir.

Quali documenti dovranno essere autentici.

Document No. 31. July 24, 1860. Letter from the Secretary of State, Cardinal Antonelli, to Monsignor Quaglia, forwarding to him a copy of Żyliński's letter of May 24, which had been sent to Antonelli by De Luca on July 14 (see ASV, NV Doc. No. 24). Italian (2 pages).

From: The Office of the Secretary of State
July 24, 1860
Prot. No. 12754
To: Monsignor <A. Quaglia>
Secretary of the Holy Congregation of the
Council

Monsignor the Nuncio of Vienna, in a letter dated July 14 of this year, Prot. No. 1057, kindly reports that, in conforming to the invitation extended to him by the Secretary of the Holy Congregation of the Council in a letter dated last May 3, he forwarded to Monsignor the Bishop of Fulda and to Monsignor the Archbishop of Mohilow a formal prohibition to proceed to the implementation of the sentence issued by the latter in the marriage case Wittgenstein-Iwanowska. He gave him, moreover, instructions to persuade the Defender of the Marriage Bond to appeal to the Holy See against this latest sentence and asked him to forward the records of the trial. Monsignor the Bishop of Fulda has conformed precisely to the prohibition that he received, but as far as the Archbishop of Mohilow is concerned, he has received his answer through the

Dalla Segreteria di Stato,
24 luglio 1860
12754
Monsig[no]r <Angelo Quaglia>,
Segretario della S[anta] Congregazione
del Concilio

Monsig[no]r Nunzio di Vienna con foglio dei 14 luglio corrente N° 1057 si è dato premura di riferire che conformandosi all'invito fattogli da codesta Segreteria della S[anta] Congregazione del Concilio con la lettera dei 3 maggio p[rossim]o p[assat]o, trasmise a Monsig[no]r Vescovo di Fulda e a Monsig[no]r Arcivescovo di Mohilow formale inibizione di procedere all'esecuzione della sentenza pronunziata da quest'ultimo nella causa matrimoniale Wittgenstein-Iwanowska, e diede pure istruzioni preché s'insinuasse al difensore de' matrimoni il ricorso alla S[anta] Sede contro l'ultima sentenza e trasmettesse gli atti processuali. Che Monsig[no]r Vescovo di Fulda si è esattamente conformato alla ricevuta inibizione, ma che rispetto a Monsig[no]r Arcivescovo di Mohilow gli è giunta col mezzo della Le-

---

[28]As later documents make clear, Carolyne was unable to procure the original copies of these judgements, partly because of the change of jurisdiction for the parish of Pohrebysze in which she had been married, and partly because of the length

of time that had meanwhile elapsed since the 1848 trial. Moreover, she thought it unreasonable to be asked to do so (see, for example, Docs. No. 37 and 38).

Russian legation. Such a letter is hereby forwarded to Monsignor the Secretary of the Holy Congregation of the Council for his information and opportune action.

G[iacomo] C[ardinal] Antonelli

gazione Russa in Vienna la responsiva di lui lettera. Si trasmette pertanto tal lettera a Monsig[no]r Segretario della prelodata S[anta] Congregazione per sua norma e per l'uso opportuno.

G[iacomo] C[ardinal] Antonelli

Document No. 32. Enclosure. Copy of Żyliński's letter to De Luca, dated, May 24 (see ASV, NV, Doc. No. 21). Latin (5 pages). It bears at the top of the first page the note:

Enclosed in the Dispatch from Vienna N. 1057.

Inserto nel Dispaccio di Vienna N. 1057.

Document No. 33. Undated. Memorandum to the Pope on Żyliński's defense, the Concordate, and the status of the case. Responds to Docs. No. 31 and 32. Italian (8 pages).

<File>: Zhitomir

The Office of the Secretary of State has forwarded to us a copy of the answer given by Monsignor the Archbishop of Mohilow to Monsignor the Nuncio in Vienna with respect to the ideas expressed by the latter about the judgement rendered by the Metropolitan Consistory in the Wittgenstein-Iwanowska marriage case.

In his answer, the Archbishop is quite dismayed by the suggestion of corruption of his judges which he considers unjust and unfounded. The judges, among whom is the suffragan bishop, are all, according to him, individuals distinguished for their doctrine, integrity, and piety. They have reviewed the case with absolute circumspection, rigor, and respect for the law, observing in particular the prescriptions of the Benedictine Bull. The Defender is also a distinguished clergyman.

These judges issued a sentence of annulment which the Defender did not wish to appeal.

The Archbishop himself reviewed the work of his judges and, having found it procedurally proper and sufficiently well grounded, issued a sentence for the annulment of the marriage and declared that the lady was free to contract a new marriage, given the existence of two analogous sentences as prescribed by the Benedictine Bull. He believes that such an insulting accusation of corruption of the judges, insofar as it is totally unfounded, is not sufficient ground for a new review of the case.

Zitomir

Dalla Segreteria di stato è stata trasmessa copia della risposta data da Mons[igno]r Arcivescovo di Mokilow a Mons[igno]r Nunzio di Vienna in ordine ai rimarchi fattigli da quello sul giudizio emanato dal Concistoro Metropolitano nella Causa Matrimoniale Wittgenstein-Iwanowska.

In essa risposta l'Arcivescovo si grava non poco della taccia di subornazione ai suoi giudici comecché ingiuriosa ed inesistente. I giudici essere tre Ecclesiastici, fra i quali il suffraganeo, tutti distinti per dottrina, integrità e pietà. Essersi proceduto da essi con tutta regolarità, circospezione e rigore, ed essersi osservate le forme prescritte dalla Benedettina. Il difensore del matrimonio esser pure un ecclesiastico distinto.

Detti giudici avere emanato sentenza di nullità, dalla quale il difensore non ha creduto di appellare.

Egli poi l'Arcivescovo ha voluto richiamare ad esame l'operato dei suoi giudici, ed avendolo trovato regolare ed abbastanza fondato ha emanato la definitiva sentenza per la nullità del matrimonio dichiarando esser la donna libera a passare ad altre nozze stante la uniformità di due sentenze per la nullità conforme prescrive la Benedettina. Crede quindi che una tale ingiuriosa taccia di corruzione de' giudici, comecché destituita di ogni fondamento, non possa essere titolo valido a sottoporre a revisione la questione.

The husband already re-married two years ago in the Lutheran faith.

Earlier we had received a copy of the sentence issued by the Consistory of Mohilow: it does not make clear what is the value of the evidence about violence and intimidation which might have persuaded those judges to rule the marriage null and void.

There is on file a petition from the lady requesting Your Holiness to relieve her from such an abnormal situation grievously affecting her conscience.

Both the Lady and the Archbishop refer to articles in the Concordate, as if to state that the proceeding are in agreement with it. Since the implications of the latter are not known, one would not even know what to think in this respect.

If, however, the Concordate would prove to be irrelevant to the position of the Diocese of Mohilow and of the Lady as well, it would be quite clear that the latest sentence does not have the force of a final judgement.

In fact, if we assume that an annulment case can be finally settled after two analogous sentences and in the event that the Defender refrain from presenting an appeal as prescribed by Benedict XIV and acknowledged by the Archbishop himself, I cannot quite see how, in this case, one can say that there have been two analogous sentences in favor of annulment. After all, the Consistory of Zhitomir ruled for the validity of the marriage. The woman then appealed to the Metropolitan of Mohilow. That Consistory resolved in favor of annulment but, the Vicar General being one of the judges, he voted against, i.e., he voted for validity. The then Archbishop upheld his opinion and refused to approve and confirm the judgement of the Consistory, thus upholding the Sentence issued at Zhitomir.

In virtue of the faculties granted by Your Holiness, that same Consistory, under the present Archbishop, has rendered a judgement of annulment.

Now, considering that the Archbishop is the rightful judge and the members of the Consistory are but consultants, if the first Mohilow sentence was not approved by the then Metropolitan, it cannot be considered a sentence; consequently it could not be said there are two analogous sentences <for annulment>; but there would be rea-

L'uomo è già da due anni passato ad altre nozze nella setta luterana.

In antecedenza erasi trasmessa copia della sentenza proferita dal Concistoro di Mohilow, dalla quale però non riesce desumere il valore delle prove sulla violenza e timore che hanno potuto persuadere quei giudici ad ammettere la nullità.

Esiste pure in posizione una istanza della Donna con la quale supplica V[ostra] S[antità] perché in qualche modo sia liberata da questo stato anormale, esiziale alla di lei coscienza.

Tanto essa quanto l'Arcivescovo fanno menzione degli articoli del Concordato, quasi che l'operato sia in conformità di esso. Ma non conoscendosene il tenore non si saprebbe nemmeno cosa pensare in proposito.

Se però il Concordato non venisse in sussidio della Curia di Mohilow e della donna sarebbe patente che quest'ultima sentenza non può aver forza di re giudicata.

Ed infatti, ritenuto che onde una causa di nullità di matrimonio passi in re giudicata dopo due sentenze conformi qualora il Difensore non creda di appellare, come stabilisce Benedetto XIV e riconosce lo stesso Arcivescovo, non so vedere come nel caso possa dirsi esservi state due sentenze conformi per la nullità. Imperciocché la Curia di Zytomir giudicò per la validità. Allora la donna appellò al Metropolitano di Mohilow. Quel Concistoro pronunciò per la nullità. Ma siccome fra i Giudici vi era anche il vicario Generale il quale fu di parere contrario, cioè per la validità, l'Arcivescovo di quel tempo si attenne alla di lui opinione e non volle approvare e confermare il giudizio del Concistoro, ma riconobbe la sentenza di Zitomir.

In forza poi delle facoltà accordate dalla S[anti]tà V[ost]ra lo stesso Concistoro sotto l'attuale Arcivescovo ha pronunciato per la nullità.

Ora, ritenuto che l'Arcivescovo sia il giudice legittimo, e che i membri del Concistoro non sono che consulenti, se la prima sentenza di Mohilow non venne approvata da quel Metropolitano, non potrà dirsi sentenza, e per conseguenza non si saprebbero combinare le due sentenze conformi, anzi vi sarebbe ragione di

sons to say that there are, indeed, two analogous sentences for validity and only one for annulment.

Therefore, as I said already, unless there is some specific protocol in the Concordate, the Mohilow sentence does not make the lady free to marry again.

The real problem is about what should be done, given that the Defender does not wish to present an appeal and the Curia, otherwise persuaded, will not forward the records.

The lady is in Rome:[29] it would be useful to persuade her that her position is wrong and, by contracting marriage at this point, she would make herself a concubine. We should, then, induce her to request that her case be reviewed by the Holy See.

Would, however, the Imperial Government object to this course of action? Would the Archbishop obey a request to forward the records? These are the questions that must be faced.

ritenere che esistano due sentenze conformi per la validità, ed una per la nullità.

Onde, se, come ho già detto, non avvi qualche disposizione particolare nel Concordato, la donna con la sentenza di Mohilow non può dirsi libera.

La gran difficoltà però sta nel da farsi, mentre il Difensore non vuole appellare, e la curia, persuasa altrimenti, non vorrà mandare gli atti.

La donna è in Roma; converrebbe persuaderla dell'errore e falsa posizione in cui essa è: che contraendo il matrimonio in questo stato di cose commetterebbe un concubinato, e quindi indurla a chiedere la revisione della causa presso la S[anta] Sede.

Ma sarebbe ostacolo il Governo imperiale a questa misura? Obbedirebbe l'Arcivescovo a trasmettere gli atti? Sono queste avvertenze a farsi.

Document No. 34. Undated. An expert opinion on the legal status of the February 1860 sentence of annulment issued by Archbishop Żyliński.
Latin (10 pages).

Zhitomir
Marriage Case

Whatever be may thought about the intrinsic merit of this question, about which no careful opinion can be formed in the absence of the documents of the trial, as far as the extrinsic reasons of the matter are concerned, i.e., the question of the order of judgements about which we must provide an opinion, it is sufficiently clear from what has newly transpired that the case cannot be said or considered to be resolved according to the norms of Benedict XIV's Bull *Dei miseratione*. There, in fact, it is emphatically stated that under no circumstances can the marriage bond be considered dissolved unless two completely similar and analogous judgements, resolutions, or sentences have been issued. Now, in the present case, we have only one sentence for annulment whereas, on the other hand, and this is very much to be stressed, there have been two for the validity of the marriage.

Zytumerien
<Causa> Matrimonii

Quidquid censendum sit de intrinseco huius controversiae merito, super quo tutum efformari nequit judicium deficiente actarum processu, ad extrinsecam rei rationem seu ad iudicii ordinem quod spectat, de quo in praesenti contentione judicandum est, ex noviter deductis satis constare videtur absolutam dici ac retineri non posse causam hanc ad normam Constitutionis Benedicti XIV *Dei miseratione*. Ibi enim disertis verbis edicitur nullo in casu matrimonii vinculum dissolutum censeri nisi duo iudicata vel resolutiones vel sententiae penitus similes et conformes emanaverint. Atqui una tantum in casu habetur pro nullitate matrimonii sententia dum e contra, quod maxime notandum, binae pro validitate fuerunt prolatae.

---

[29]Carolyne arrived in the Eternal City on May 27, 1860. The present (undated) document could not therefore have been drafted before that date.

For one thing, an objection cannot be raised to the effect that the Pope is referring to the ordinary sequence of judgements, and this was not applicable to the present case given that cases of this nature should be reviewed with the goal of complete restitution[30] (as would appear to be the argument in this case, since there were two analogous sentences for validity). The fact is that no exceptions whatsosoever are contemplated in the Benedictine Bull which applies to all cases according to the terms referred to above. Therefore, since two analogous sentences are required even in cases where no sentence for validity has been issued, *a fortiori* it will be necessary that they be required in cases of this sort where the marriage was decreed valid once or twice.

Nor can another objection be raised by citing the instance of this congregation to which marriage cases are deferred in the absence of an intermediate judgement and are resolved on the force of only one sentence. In fact, with the exception of the circumstance in which the Holy Father is advised to grant a dispensation in a situation where marriage has been contracted but not consummated, in which case indeed marriage annulment is settled by only one sentence, a case cannot, however, be settled by only one resolution and, therefore, the Benedictine prescription obtains according to which two sentences or two resolutions are required according to the different merits of each case.

Nor, moreover, does the fact that the Metropolitan of Mohilow issued his judgement as if delegated by the Holy See seem to cause any problem as far as the possibility of an appeal. Apart from the fact that, in the rescript delegating him, the clause "without appeal" was not included, it is certain in any case, that even with this clause, an appeal is possible whenever it is expressly stated by the law. And in this instance, not only is an appeal permitted, but it is prescribed by the Benedictine Bull, because only one sentence, not two, was issued. Since the delegation document contained no express dispensation from this prescription, it follows that the latter must be maintained.

Nec primo objiciendum quod Pontifex loquatur de ordinario judiciorum ordine, et rationem de casu non habuerit, quo in vim restitutionis in integrum (ceu in themate quo duae aderant sententiae pro validitate conformes) de huiusmodi causis cognosci debeat. Nam nulla fit exceptio in Constitutione Benedectina quae in omnes complectitur casus iuxta verba superius citata. Deinde si quidem duae requiruntur sententiae conformes etiam in casu quo nulla prolata pro validitate fuerit sententia, a fortiori id exigi necesse erit in praesenti specie in qua bis et semel validum judicatum fuerat matrimonium.

Nec secundo objiciendum s[it] huius Congregationis exemplum, in qua, cum omisso medio causae matrimoniales ad eam deferuntur, unica absolvuntur sententia. Nam excepto casu quo consulendum sit S[anctissi]mo <Patri> pro dispensatione a matrimonio rato et non consummato, ubi vero de matrimonii nullitate agitur unica quidem sententia, sed non unica resolutione causa absolvi potest, adeoque Benedectina praescriptio obtinet, qua vel duae sententiae vel duae resolutiones, pro casuum diversitate, requiruntur.

Nec denique difficultatem facessere videtur, quod Metropolitanus Mohilowiensis judicaverit tamquam Apostolicae Sedis delegatus, ut adeo appellationi locus esse nequeat. Nam praeterquam quod in rescripto delegationis apposita non fuerit clausula "appellatione remota," compertum praeterea est, non obstante hac clausula, competere appellationem quoties ea in jure sit expresse permissa. Atqui in casu nedum permissa, sed praecepta appellatio est a Constitutione Benedectina, quia non duae sed una tantum sententia pro nullitate emanavit. Cui quidem praescriptioni cum in literis delegationis expresse derogatum non fuerit, consequitur eam servandam esse.

---

[30]Complete restitution is defined, according to Canon Law, as follows: "Against a sentence for which there is not the ordinary remedy ,of appeal or request to void it, there is the extraordinary remedy of complete restitution within the terms of Canons 1687, 1688, as long as as it be certain that there was evident injustice in the sentence issued" (Canon 1905 in *Codex Juris Canonici Pii X Pontificis Maximi ab eminentissimo Petro Card. Gasparri auctus* [Rome: Vatican Press, 1918]).

It is simply not true that, as stated by the other party, two sentences for annulment were issued, one, to be sure, being that provided by the Consistory of Mohilow in the year 1852, the other, the one recently issued by the new Archbishop by delegation of the Holy See. We know for sure that the previous Archbishop did not confirm that sentence, which, therefore, has no value at all since, in virtue of the Concordate, the rendering of judgement pertains solely to the bishop, even though he is bound to seek the opinion of the Consistory; moreover, there is no basis to the claim that, within the Metropolitan See, the Consistory constitutes a Court independent of the Metropolitan.

These things would appear absolutely certain from a legal point of view; it remains to be investigated whether the Concordate between the Holy See and the <Russian> Government on the levels of jurisdiction constitutes an obstacle to a new review of this case. I would observe that the Concordate deals merely with ordinary judgements, but that, in this case, the delegation was provided by the Holy See as an extraordinary remedy, and even under the guise of complete restitution there must be a review, for the case had been closed on account of two analogous sentences for the validity of the marriage. For this reason, the issue has nothing to do with the Concordate.

Things being so, I would advise that a letter be written to the Apostolic Nuncio in order that he may persuade the Archbishop of Mohilow it is absolutely necessary for the Defender to present *ex officio* an appeal and he should induce the latter to do so. The Nuncio should be appraised of the reasons for this decision. Should the Government raise some difficulties about transmitting the records of the trial to the Holy See, the nearest Bishop could be delegated to conduct the review of the case and, if even this is impossible, then the only thing left to protect the dignity of the Holy See would be to beg the Pope to rule on the issue of the lack of a second sentence required by the Benedictine Bull, which would be exceptionally set aside as far as this part is concerned.

Perperam vero duplex sententia pro nullitate lata ex adverso edicitur, altera scilicet a Consitorio Mohilowiensi anno 1852, altera ab novo Archiepiscopo ex S[anctae] Sedis delegatione nuper prolata. Constat enim Archiepiscopum priorem sententiam non confirmasse quae adeo nullius roboris habenda, quia in vim Concordati solius est Episcopi judicium proferre, licet Consistorii consilium exquirere teneatur; nec comprobatur assertum, quod in Metropolitana Sede Consistorium separatum tribunal ab isto Metropolitano constituat.

Haec quidem in jure certissima viderentur; perpendendum tamen an conventio inita inter Gubernium et Apostolicam Sedem super gradibus jurisdictionis huic novae causae revisioni obstaculum paret. Observo autem ea Conventione agi dumtaxat de ordinariis judiciis, delegatio vero facta a S[ancta] Sede in praesenti causa tamquam extraordinarium remedium, ac veluti restitutio in integrum haberi debet, quia ob duas conformes super validitate matrimonii sententias res judicata orta fuerat. Quam ob rem caput iste extraneus a Conventione est. {Ceterum quia aliqua fortasse difficultas ex parte Gubernii posset suboriri, hinc}[31]

Quae cum ita se habeant, scribendum Apostolico Nuntio censerem ut Archiepiscopo Mohilowiensi suadeat necessarium omnino esse ut Defensor ex officio appellationem interponat et eum ad hanc emittendam inducat. Significari autem deberent eidem Nuntio rationes huius resolutionis. Quod si aliqua suboriatur ex parte Gubernii difficultas pro transmissione actorum ad S[anctam] Sedem tunc poterit vicinior Episcopus delegari, et si hoc etiam praepediatur, aliud nihil restat pro S[anctae] Sedis dignitate tuenda agi ut S[anctissi]mo <Patri> supplicetur pro sanatione super alterius sententiae defectu a Benedectina Constitutione requisita, cui Constitutioni hac in parte derogandum foret.

---

[31]Sentence in parenthesis erased in the document; it is an anticipation of ideas expressed in the next paragraph.

Document No. 35. August 1860. Draft Memorandum to the Prefect of the Congregation, Antonio Cagiano de Azevedo, or to the Pope, reviewing the nature of the 1860 Mohilow sentence and the terms of the Russian Concordate.
Italian (8 pages).

<File>: Zhitomir
August 1860.

I have checked the articles of the 1847 Concordate; the regulations that may be applicable to this case are the following:

Art. 13 establishes the Bishop as the only judge and the one responsible for the administration of Church affairs.

Art. 14 lists the situations that must first be decided upon by the Consistory of the Diocese; among these, marriage cases are listed under item E.

Art. 15 states: *"Such affairs are decided by the Bishop after they have been examined by a Consistory, which retains in any case the role of consultation. The Bishop is not really bound to provide the reasons for his decision even in cases in which his opinion differs from that of the Consistory."*

Given such premises, it is a fact that the Consistory of Mohilow "retains only the role of consultation" and, given that the decision of the late Archbishop differed from the Consistory's opinion, the latter cannot be considered a proper sentence. On the contrary, the Bishop being "the only Judge in marriage cases", and having the late Archbishop adjudicated the case in agreement with the Zhitomir resolution, the Mohilow sentence should be considered a second sentence in favor of the validity of the marriage, confirming that of Zhitomir. Therefore, in favor of its nullity there is only the latest sentence by the present Archbishop of Mohilow.

Here, I do not understand how Monsignor the Archbishop can appeal to the Benedictine *Dei miseratione* to support his sentence, which he considers a final decree without appeal, nor can I understand the refusal to appeal on the part of the Defender of the Marriage Bond, while, on the other hand, paragraph 11 is quoted where it is stated that after two sentences annulling a marriage, just as the Defender is not bound to seek an appeal, the spouses, whose marriage has been declared null and void, are free to marry again.

Zitomir.
Agosto 1860.

Ho incontrato gli articoli del Concordato 1847 e le disposizioni che possono riferirsi alla questione sono le seguenti.

All'art[icol]o 13 si stabilisce che il Vescovo è il *solo giudice* ed amministratore degli affari ecclesiastici.

Nell'art[icol]o 14 si enumerano gli affari che debbono prima assoggettarsi alle deliberazioni del Concistoro diocesano; fra i quali sotto la lett[er]a E si riportano *Causae matrimoniales.*

All'art[icol]o 15 si stabilisce: *"Negotia praedicta decernuntur ab Episcopo postquam a Consistorio examinata fuerint, quod tamen consultationis partes tantummodo retinet. Episcopus minime tenetur afferre rationes suae sententiae illis etiam in casibus in quibus ejus opinio ab illa Consistorii discreparet."*

Ciò premesso è un fatto che il fatto del Concistoro di Mohilow *consultationis partes tantummodo retinet*, e che il giudizio dell'Arcivescovo defonto essendo stato contrario all'opinamento del Concistoro, questo non può assolutamente ritenersi per una sentenza. Anzi essendo il solo vescovo *Judex in causis matrimonialibus* ed avendo lo stesso Arcivescovo defonto aderito alla Sentenza di Zitomir, è a ritenersi che il giudizio di Mohilow costituisca un'altra sentenza per la validità del matrimonio confermatoria di quella di Zitomir. Onde per la *nullità* non rimane che la Sentenza ultima emanata dall'attuale Arcivescovo.

E qui non saprei vedere come Mons[igno]r Arcivescovo in sostegno del suo decreto che ritiene per una sentenza inappellabile, non che il rifiuto del difensore del Matrimonio, si appoggi alla Benedettina *Dei miseratione* e riporti il Paragrafo 11 in cui si dispone che dopo due sentenze per la nullità, com'è in libertà il Difensore a non appellare, così possono i coniugi, il cui matrimonio sia dichiarato nullo, passare ad altre nozze.

It is true that, on the whole, the Archbishop's report implies that he, as a consequence of the rescript of August 8, 1859, considers his judgement that of an apostolic delegate and, thus, without appeal, and believes that the word "definitive" in the aforementioned rescript is relevant to this effect. One notes, moreover, that the Archbishop did not consult the regular members of the Consistory, but three individuals delegated by him to study the case. The fact is that there was no intention whatsoever to delegate such a supreme power

1) because in such instances the formula "as a delegate of the Holy See" is customary;

2) because the word "definitive," according to our legal usage, is applicable to any sentence, where one writes "through our definitive sentence."

Indeed, that rescript did nothing but restore to the Archbishop and to his Consistory the faculty of studying and finally adjudicating according to the level of appeal a case that, under his predecessor, had been presumably reviewed by that Consistory but, because of the differing opinion of that Archbishop, did not have any effect, and remained as if suspended. {Indeed the lady in her petition stated}[32] (at that time we did not know the articles of the Concordate).

However things may be, the fact still is that there is only one sentence in favor of the annulment.

It remains to be seen how, if the principle of two analogous sentences is to be upheld, the case might be presented in a third instance.

We know that the Metropolitan can appeal to the Holy See, but can this appeal take place, in the case of the Russian dioceses, without the government interposing any obstacles?

The Concordate does not suggest at all how the levels of jurisdiction are to be established, i.e., whether, in the case of a difference of opinion between the sentence of the suffragan and that of the Metropolitan, another tribunal can be set up to adjudicate in the third instance; or whether the judgement of the Metropolitan is to be considered without appeal.

Vero è che dal tutt'insieme del rapporto dell'Arcivescovo si rileva che egli, in sequela del rescritto 8 Agosto 1859, ritiene aver giudicato come delegato Apostolico ed *inappellabilmente* come crede che importi la parola apposta a detto rescritto *definitivam,* e si rileva altresì dal non essersi l'Arcivescovo <servito> dei membri ordinari del Concistoro, ma di tre individui specialmente da lui deputati a conoscere la questione. Ma in fatto si è che né s'intese, né si volle accordare tale delegazione suprema

1°. perchè in simili casi suol adoperarsi la clausola "tamquam delegatus S[anctae] Sedis,"

2° perché la parola definitiva secondo il nostro uso forense suole applicarsi a qualunque sentenza dicendosi "per hanc nostram definitivam etc."

In effetto quel rescritto non faceva che redintegrare l'Arcivescovo e suo concistoro nella facoltà di poter conoscere e definitivamente giudicare in grado di appello una causa che sotto il suo antecessore dicevasi conosciuta da quel concistoro, ma che pel contrario pensare dell'Arcivescovo era rimasta senza effetto, e come in sospeso (allora non si conoscevano gli articoli del Concordato).

Checché sia di ciò, il risultato però è sempre questo, che cioè una sola sentenza si ha per la nullità.

Rimarrebbe quindi a vedersi se volendosi tener ferma la massima delle due sentenze per la cosa giudicata, come possa ottenersi un terzo grado.

Si sa che dal Metropolita si appella alla S[anta] Sede. Ma per le Diocesi di Russia potrebbe ciò aver luogo senza ostacoli per parte di quel governo?

Dal Concordato non si rileva affatto come siano stabiliti i gradi di giurisdizione, se cioè nel caso di difformità di giudicati fra la sentenza del suffraganeato e quella del Metropolita sia designato un altro tribunale che vegga in terzo grado; oppure se il giudicato del Metropolitano si ritenga per inappellabile.

---

[32]Sentence in parenthesis erased in the document.

It would not be easy to have a clear idea of the substantial merit of the case in the absence of the records of the trial. One can only point out that the late Archbishop of Mohilow did not wish to endorse the resolution of his Consistory because the witnesses that had been called to testify were said to be wanting with respect to some formalities prescribed by the law and, among other things, because the petitioner's mother, too, had been called to testify, which was not thought to be admissible.

As a consequence of this, serious thought must be given as to the best way of proceeding with this case. In case the opinion of the Congregation were to be sought, there is the question whether this should be done in secret in order to avoid the insistence of the woman being present and her agent, etc.

Sull'intrinseco della causa non si saprebbe dare alcun ragguaglio, mentre non si ha il processo. Solo si rileva che il defonto Arcivescovo di Mohilow non volle aderire all'opinamento del suo Concistoro perchè i testimoni deponenti della violenza e timore dicevansi mancanti di alcune formalità volute dalla legge, e, fra le altre, perché era stata ammessa a deporre la madre della reclamante, che si riteneva inammissibile.

Dopo ciò sarà seriamente a pensarsi qual partito convenga adottare. Nel caso si credesse interpellare la Cong[regazio]ne sarà a domandarsi se ciò abbia a farsi *sub secreto*, per evitare l'insistenza della donna presente e di lei agente, etc.

Document No. 36. August 22, 1860. Monsignor de Ferrari's letter to Quaglia, enclosing the Princess's answer to a request for additional documentation. See Doc. No. 30. Italian (1 page).

To: Monsignor Angelo Quaglia,
Secretary of [the Holy Congregation]
of the Council.
(f)
Vatican, August 22, 1860

I brought to Her Highness, Princess Carolyne von Sayn-Wittgenstein, the answer that was agreed upon in our conversation about her case. She gave me the enclosed document and asked me to send it to Your Most Illustrious Excellency. As I perform this duty, I am asking you to give the document the consideration it deserves.

I take advantage of this opportunity to express my veneration for you, while declaring myself
Your Illustrious Excellency's
most devoted and obliging servant,
Father Giacinto de Ferrari,
deputy advisor.

Monsignor Don Angelo Quaglia
Segretario [della Santa Congregazione]
del Concilio.
(f)
Vaticano, 22 Agosto 1860

Avendo io portata a Sua Altezza la Principessa Carolina de Sayn-Wittgenstein la risposta convenuta nel nostro colloquio circa la causa di Lei, ne ebbi l'accluso foglio, che mi pregò trasmettere a V[ostra] S[ignoria] Ill[ustrissi]ma. Adempio pertanto a tal commissione, e la prego ad averne quella considerazione che merita.

Con tale opportunità mi allieto di poterle attestare la mia venerazione onde mi dichiaro

di V[ostra] S[ignoria] Illust[rissi]ma
d[evotissi]mo e obb[ligatissimo ser[vo]
P[adre] Giacinto De Ferrari,
del[egatus] Consultor.

Document No. 37. August 1860. Enclosed with Doc. No. 36. Carolyne's answer to a request for additional documentation.

Monsignor Secretary of the <Holy Congregation of the> Council has requested, as a basis for the considerations of fact and law already presented, authentic copies of the first sentence of the Consistory of Mohilow and of the one issued by the Consistory of Zhitomir. The Princess, however, besides not being in a position to provide them for reasons that will be presented below, does not think she should let herself be subjected to requests that have been suggested by those whose aim is to prevent the implementation of a solemn and definitive sentence or, at least, to delay the solution of her case for less than reasonable purposes. As far as she is concerned, the definitive sentence issued *with apostolic authority* by the Metropolitan of all Russias is sufficient.

It would be a ridiculous thing to seek an *authentic* copy of the sentence of annulment of her marriage pronounced by the Consistory of Mohilow before the case was dealt with by that of Zhitomir. Such a sentence had no legal status and was ignored by the imperial laws because it was brought forward at the time when, owing to the restructuring of the Diocese, the parish where the wedding had been performed had already been attached to the Diocese of Zhitomir. For this reason, this sentence was not considered as having been issued and was therefore deemed non existent before the law. How then could one obtain an authentic copy of an act that has no legal status, especially in Russia where, in order to obtain an authentic copy of any document, one inevitably needs the formal permission of the Government and its Ministers? A *private, informal* copy might perhaps be found among the personal papers of the Secretary of that Consistory, but what legal proof would it provide even if it could be found and obtained? The substantive arguments in that sentence are identically reiterated in the other Sentence issued in the second instance by that same Consistory in 1852, after the resolution of the Consistory of Zhitomir. This second sentence is already on file with the Holy Congregation of the Council. It would be superfluous to look for it when an equivalent document is already enclosed with the petition.

As for the sentence issued in 1851 by the Consistory of Zhitomir, either the Holy Congregation has already on file an authentic complete copy of it, or it can deduce the substance of both

Al fronte delle premesse considerazioni di fatto e di diritto sonosi richieste da Monsignor Segretario del Concilio alla Principessa le copie autentiche della prima sentenza del Concistoro di Mohilow e dell'altra emanata dal Concistoro di Zitomir. Ma la Principessa, oltreché sarebbe nell'assoluta impossibilità di somministrarle per quel che se ne accennerà più sotto, non crede doversi affatto prestare a cotali inchieste, suggerite da chi ha lo scopo di stornare la esecuzione di un giudicato solenne e definitivo od almeno di mandar per le lunghe la cosa con fini men che ragionevoli, bastando a Lei la sentenza definitiva emanata *con autorità Apostolica* dal Metropolitano di tutte le Russie.

Della sentenza pronunziata per la nullità del Matrimonio dal Concistoro di Mohilow prima di quello di Zitomir sarebbe cosa ridicola il cercarne copia *autentica*, trattandosi di sentenza disconosciuta e messa nel nulla dalle leggi imperiali, perché proferita quando, per la nuova circoscrizione della Diocesi, la parrochia ove fu celebrato il matrimonio era già stata applicata alla Diocesi di Zitomir, per cui tal sentenza si riputò come non avvenuta, e quindi inesistente in faccia alla legge. Come dunque aver copia autentica di un atto che legalmente non esiste, massime in Russia, ove per avere una copia autentica di un atto qualunque si richiede inevitabilmente il permesso formale del Governo e de' suoi Ministri? Una copia *privata* ed *informe* forse potrebbe trovarsi tra le carte private del Cancelliere di quel Concistoro, ma qual prova questa fornirebbe, se pur potesse rinvenirsi ed ottenersi? I fondamenti e le ragioni poi di quella sentenza sono identicamente esposti nell'altra sentenza dello stesso Concistoro proferita *in seconda istanza* nel 1852, dopo il giudicato cioè del Concistoro di Zitomir, e questa seconda sentenza del Concistoro di Mohilow esiste già negli atti della S[anta] C[ongregazione] del Concilio, per cui la ricerca sarebbe superflua avendosi un atto equipollente in posizione.

Relativamente poi alla sentenza emanata nel 1851 dal Concistoro di Zitomir, negli atti della S[anta] Cong[regazio]ne o esiste già la copia autentica nel suo intero tenore, o per lo meno se

the issues that were to be considered and the resolution (that upheld the validity of the marriage) with its specific arguments indicated by the Princess in her presentation of the case written in Italian and already on file, and stated again in the Sentence issued in the second instance by the Consistory of Mohilow. Such a request is, therefore, out of place, and it appears to aim only at delaying the decision requested by the Princess for no other purpose than to work to her detriment and help the triumph of the wicked. It will be pointed out, moreover, that it might not even be possible to obtain from the Ministers an authentic copy of the Zhitomir sentence since they would consider the sentence of annulment as concluding the case and would not, therefore, allow the releasing of either an abstract or an authentic copy of this or any other document pertaining to the proceedings, if they only suspected that Rome might wish to rescind a sentence that was issued in full observance of the forms and regulations in effect in Russia. It would be an insult as well to the Metropolitan himself, as if there could be any doubts about the propriety of the sentence, which was definitively issued *with apostolic authority* by the Commission he delegated for this purpose, and which he himself scrupulously examined and confirmed.

ne ha la sostanza sia dei considerandi sia della dispositiva (che ritenne valido il matrimonio) coi suoi rispettivi fondamenti indicati dalla Principessa nei suoi fogli italiani, negli atti e nella sentenza del Concistoro di Mohilow in seconda istanza. Talché la richiesta è inopportuna, e non sembra mirare che a dilazionare inutilmente la risolutiva provocata dalla Principessa col solo di Lei pregiudizio e col trionfo dei maligni. Si fa poi notare subordinatamente che anche della sentenza di Zitomir una copia autentica probabilmente senza effetto si cercherebbe dai Ministri Imperiali, i quali riguardando come cosa terminata il giudizio di nullità non permetterebbero estratto o copia autentica né di questo né di altri atti relativi al giudizio medesimo al solo sospetto che in Roma si volesse censurare una sentenza proferita colla piena osservanza delle forme e leggi Russe; e sarebbe un'offesa che si farebbe allo stesso Metropolitano, come se si dubitasse ancora della giustizia della sentenza emanata *con autorità apostolica* in senso definitivo dalla Commissione da Esso deputata e da Lui stesso scrupolosamente esaminata e confermata.

Document No. 38. August 1860. Memorandum, probably addressed to Cagiano de Azevedo. Comments on Doc. No. 37 and the enclosure of a copy of the Princess's presentation of her case (Copy of Doc. No. 29) and a copy of Doc. No. 37 without the introductory paragraph. Italian (4 pages).

<File>: Zhitomir

Having informed Princess Wittgenstein's agent that you requested an authentic copy of the first Mohilow resolution and sentence and a copy of the Zhitomir sentence, the aforementioned Princess has sent a document whereby she declares

1) It is impossible to obtain the first document since that sentence, having been pronounced at the moment of the diocesan territorial reorganisation, is not recognised and is, therefore, ignored by the imperial laws; even if it existed, it would not be possible to obtain a legal copy from the government, for the latter does not recognise it. A private copy, in draft form, might possibly be found among the papers of the Secretary of the Consistory, but it would not

Zitomir

Avendo fatto conoscere all'agente della Principessa Wittgenstein che la S. V. voleva si esibisse copia autentica del primo giudicato e sentenza di Mohilow, e della sentenza di Zitomir; la prelod[at]a Principessa ha fatto tenere un foglio col quale dichiara

1. Essere impossibile avere il primo documento, mentre quella sentenza pronunciata nel momento della separazione territoriale viene disconosciuta e messa nel nulla dalle leggi imperiali; e seppure esistesse non sarebbe possibile averne copia autentica da quel governo che la ritiene per nulla. Una copia privata ed informe forse potrebbe trovarsi fra le carte private del Cancelliere di quel Concistoro, ma essa non costituirebbe

provide a valid proof. She states, however, that the substance and the arguments of that sentence are identical to the ones presented in the other sentence issued in the second instance by that same Consistory in 1852, after the sentence from Zhitomir.

As for the other document, the sentence from Zhitomir, this one, at least for the substance of the considerations and dispositions, is faithfully reproduced in the sentence in the second instance of the Consistory of Mohilow; she thinks, therefore, that to insist that these documents be exhibited is useless and superfluous besides being impossible, for it would not be easy to obtain from that government an authentic copy of the Zhitomir sentence, because the case is considered by the government as closed in virtue of the sentence issued by the Archbishop of Mohilow on the strength of the rescript from the Holy See.

She requests finally that all impediments be removed from the implementation of the last sentence, suspended on account of false and slanderous accusations.

In the eventuality that during the Audience this business might be taken up, I am sending you the position paper with the outline of the Princess's new presentation.

alcuna prova. Dice però che i fondamenti e le ragioni di quella sentenza sono identicamente esposte nell' altra sentenza proferita dallo stesso Concistoro in seconda istanza nel 1852, dopo cioè la sentenza di Zitomir.

In quanto poi all'altro documento, cioè alla sentenza di Zitomir, questa in quanto almeno alla sostanza sia dei considerando, sia della dispositiva è riportata fedelmente dalla sentenza del Concistoro di Mohilow in seconda istanza, onde l'insistere sulla esibita di tali documenti reputa cosa inutile e superflua, oltrecché impossibile, mentre non sarebbe neppure facile ad aversi da quel governo copia autentica della sentenza di Zitomir, dopo che colla sentenza proferita dall' Archiv[escov]o in virtù del rescritto della S[anta] Sede si considera dal medesimo governo come affare compiuto.

Chiede infine che sia tolto ogni ostacolo alla esecuzione dell'ultima sentenza sospesa per una falsa e calunniosa imputazione.

Nella possibilità che nell'Ud[ienz]a sia abbia a parlare di quest'affare le rimetto la posizione col ristretto sul nuovo esposto della Principessa.

Document No. 39. Enclosure. Copy of Doc. No. 29. Italian (9 pages).

Document No. 40. Enclosure. Copy of Doc. No. 37. Italian (3 pages). The first paragraph is omitted and replaced by a single, more businesslike line at the beginning of the second paragraph, where the main clause of the first sentence is also toned down.

Authentic copies of two sentences are requested. But it would be unfortunately impossible to obtain an authentic copy etc.

Si richiedono copie autentiche di due sentenze. Ma della sentenza pronunziata . . . sarebbe cosa per mala ventura impossibile...

Document No. 41. September 2, 1860. Letter in De Luca's hand to Hohenlohe suggesting that Quaglia should request the records of the 1860 Mohilow Proceedings and order the Bishop of Fulda to suspend the wedding. With a note in Latin, in Quaglia's hand, dated September 24, about writing to De Luca in terms of the resolution passed by the Congregation on September 22 and approved by the Pope. Italian (2 pages).

<File>: Zhitomir
Carolyne Iwanowska
Secret Archive

Zytomerien
Carolina Iwanowska
Archivio Segreto

_____   _____

To: His Most Reverend Excellency
Monsignor Gustav, Prince von Hohenlohe
<Archbishop of Edessa>
etc. etc. etc.
Rome
Vienna, September 2, 1860
My Most Venerated Monsignor:

I feel it is my duty to acknowledge your kind letter, dated the 11th of this past August, which reached me by way of Salzburg with a considerable delay. I must also ask you to endeavor to persuade that most excellent Monsignor Secretary of the Holy Congregation of the Council that he should seek the necessary authorisation to order Monsignor the Archbishop of Mohilow to forward to Rome the records of the proceedings of the Wittgenstein-Iwanowska case and formally enjoin, moreover, Monsignor the Bishop of Fulda not to bless the second matrimonial union of the aforementioned Princess. Since I am far away from those regions, I may not be in a position to know what is happening in Russia or in Weimar. In affairs of such a delicate nature it is necessary to adopt the legal means prescribed in the Holy Canons.

So that I may know how to proceed, I shall await information as to the whereabouts of the Princess and the decisions she may have reached before leaving Rome.

With the expression of my particular respect and esteem, it behooves me, My Most Venerated Monsignor, to confirm that I remain
Your most devoted and obliging servant,
Antonino <De Luca>
Archbishop of Tarsus
Apostolic Nuncio <in Vienna>

Monsignor <Gustav> von Hohenlohe presents his compliments to Monsignor <Angelo> Quaglia and sends him this letter from Monsignor Nuncio in Vienna.

From the Audience with the Most Holy Father of September 24, 1860.
We must write to the Apostolic Nuncio in Vienna according to the inserted draft.
See the resolution at the bottom of the confidential documents in print.

A Sua Eccellenza R[everendissi]ma
Mons[i]g[no]r Gustavo de' P[rinci]pi Hohenlohe

etc. etc. etc.
Roma
Vienna, 2 Settembre 1860
Monsig[no]r mio Venerat[issi]mo

Mi reco a dovere di riscontrare la cortese Sua lettera degli 11 del p[rossim]o p[assat]o Agosto a me trasmessa con notevole ritardo da Salisburgo. Debbo però pregarla di voler impiegare i Suoi valevoli uffici presso cotesto ottimo Monsig[nor] Segretario della S[anta] C[ongregazione] del Concilio acciocché colla debita autorizzazione intimi a M[onsi]g[no]r Arciv[escov]o di Mohilow di trasmettere a Roma gli atti del processo Wittgenstein-Iwanowska e inoltre mandi a M[onsi]g[no]r Vescovo di Fulda formale inibizione di benedire le seconde nozze della prelodata Principessa. Io posso, perché lontano da' luoghi, ignorare quel che possa accadere sia in Russia come eziandio in Weimar. In affari di sì delicata natura è mestieri di adoperare gli espedienti prescritti da' S[an]t[i] Canoni, e per via legale.

Attenderò per mia regola un ulteriore cenno per sapere ove si trovi la Sig[no]ra Principessa e le determinazioni da lei prese prima di partirsi da Roma.

Con sensi di particolare e rispettosa stima mi pregio di confermarmi
di Lei, Monsig[nor] mio Venerat[issi]mo
devot[issi]mo obblig[atissi]mo Servitore
Ant[onino] <De Luca>
Arciv[escov]o di Tarso
N[unzio] Ap[ostolic]o

M[onsi]g[no]r d'Hohenlohe presenta i suoi complimenti a M[onsi]g[no]r Quaglia e gli manda questa lettera di M[onsi]g[no]r Nunzio di Vienna.

Ex Audientia S[anctissi]mi <Patris>
Die 24 Septembris 1860.
Scribatur Nuntio Ap[osto]lico Viennen[si] iuxta insertam minutam.
Resolutionem vide in calce folii restrictus typis editi.

Per comando della Santità di NOSTRO SIGNORE si sottopone al giudizio degli EE. PP. della S. Congregazione dell' Concilio la presente questione con la legge del Segreto Pontificio.

ZITOMIR

MATRIMONIALE

22. Settembre 1860.

La Principessa Carolina Iwanowska cattolica della diocesi di Luck-Zitomyr in Russia nell'anno 1836. contrasse matrimonio col Principe Nicola Wittgenstein di religione riformata. Dopo dodici anni di unione conjugale, da cui si ebbe prole, cioè nell'anno 1848, avvenuta la morte del genitore della Principessa Carolina, questa diresse istanza all' Ordinariato del luogo affinchè fosse dichiarato nullo il suo matrimonio, che asseriva contratto *per vim et metum* incussole dal detto suo genitore. Compilatosi il processo la causa venne discussa e definita per la *validità* del matrimonio dal Concistoro di Zitomir con sentenza del giorno 6. Novembre 1854.

La Principessa Carolina però nelle sue deduzioni (Alleg. num. I) narra che un altro giudizio e sentenza per la *nullità* aveva avuto luogo in antecedenza innanzi al Concistoro di Mokilow : sentenza per altro che si considerò come non avvenuta, perchè pronunciata dopo che la parocchia in cui fu celebrato il matrimonio, in forza della nuova circoscrizione della diocesi era stata separata dall' Archidiocesi di Mokilow ed unita a quella di Zitomir.

Interpostosi dalla stessa Principessa appello dal giudicato di Zitomir, la causa fu proposta avanti il Concistoro di Mokilow; il quale fu di contrario parere, ritenendo la *nullità* del matrimonio: Ma avendo il Vicario Generale Presidente del Concistoro manifestato il suo voto difforme da quello degli altri giudici concistoriali, il

1

Plate 9. Printed documentation for the meeting of the Holy Congregation of Cardinals, dated September 22, 1860, which upheld the sentence in favor of annulment. "Pontifical secrecy is required."

Document No. 42. September 22, 1860. Printed documentation for the meeting of the Holy Congregation of Cardinals, dated September 22, 1860, consisting of the following documents enumerated in alphabetical order:

A) Statement of the case and the eventual decision of the Congregation, recorded in Quaglia's hand, to uphold the Mohilow sentence. Italian (6 pages).

By order of His Holiness, our Lord, the present question is submitted to the judgement of the Most Eminent Fathers of the Holy Congregation of the Council. *Pontifical Secrecy is required.*

\<File\>: Zhitomir
Marriage Case
September 22, 1860

Princess Carolyne Iwanowska, a Catholic from the Diocese of Luck-Zhitomir in Russia, contracted marriage, in the year 1836 with Prince Nicholas Wittgenstein, a Protestant. In the year 1848, after twelve years of conjugal union and the birth of a child, Princess Carolyne's father being now dead, she applied to the local Ordinary office for the annulment of her marriage, which she claimed had been contracted through violence and intimidation engendered by her own father. The case was presented before the Consistory of Zhitomir which, on November 6, 1851, issued a sentence in favor of the validity of that marriage.

In her presentation of the case (See Enclosure No. 1), Princess Carolyne states that the case had been previously discussed at the Consistory of Mohilow, which had issued a sentence in favor of the annulment. This sentence, however, was considered as not being issued, because it had been brought forth after the parish where the marriage had been celebrated had been removed from the Archdiocese of Mohilow and incorporated into the Diocese of Zhitomir.

Having presented an appeal against the Zhitomir judgement, the case was reviewed by the Consistory of Mohilow, which expressed a different opinion and resolved in favor of the nullity of the marriage. However, the Vicar General, who was presiding over the Consistory, voted against the resolution of the other judges in the Consistory, and the Metropolitan upheld the opinion of his Vicar, thus confirming the Zhitomir sentence. The resolution of the Consistory, together with the opinion of the Vicar and the decree issued by the Metropolitan in 1852, are to be found in Enclosure No. 2.

Per comando della Santità di Nostro Signore si sottopone al giudizio degli E[minentissimi] P[adri] della S[anta] Congregazione del(l') Concilio la presente questione con la legge del *Segreto Pontificio.*
Zitomir
\<Causa\> Matrimoniale
22 Settembre 1860

La Principessa Carolina Iwanowska cattolica della diocesi di Luck-Zitomir in Russia nell'anno 1836 contrasse matrimonio col Principe Nicola Wittgenstein di religione riformata. Dopo dodici anni di unione conjugale, da cui si ebbe prole, cioè nell'anno 1848, avvenuta la morte del genitore della Principessa Carolina, questa diresse istanza all'Ordinariato del luogo affinché fosse dichiarato nullo il suo matrimonio, che appariva contratto *per vim et metum* incussole dal detto suo genitore. Compilatosi il processo la causa venne discussa e definita per la validità del matrimonio dal Concistoro di Zitomir con sentenza del giorno 6 novembre 1851.

La Principessa Carolina però nelle sue deduzioni *(Alleg[ato] Num[ero] 1)* narra che un altro giudizio e sentenza per la nullità aveva avuto luogo in antecedenza innanzi al Concistoro di Mokilow: sentenza per altro che si considerò come non avvenuta, perché pronunciata dopo che la parrocchia in cui fu celebrato il matrimonio, in forza della nuova circoscrizione della diocesi, era stata separata dall'Archidiocesi di Mokilow ed unita a quella di Zitomir.

Interpostosi dalla stessa Principessa appello dal giudicato di Zitomir, la causa fu proposta avanti il Concistoro di Mokilow; il quale fu di contrario parere, ritenendo la nullità del matrimonio. Ma avendo il Vicario Generale Presidente del Concistoro manifestato il suo voto difforme da quello degli altri giudici concistoriali, il metropolitano, attenendosi al parere del suo Vicario confermò la Sentenza di Zitomir. Tanto l'opinamento del detto Concistoro, quanto il parere del Vicario, ed il decreto del Metropolitano emanati nel 1852 sono a vedersi nell'*All[egato] Num[ero] 2.*

After several years of silence, in June 1859 to be precise, the Princess, through the offices of a solicitor representing her, approached the new Archbishop of Mohilow, requesting that he take up again the case which, on account of the differences of opinion among the members of the Consistory during the tenure of the late Archbishop, she considered not to have been definitely resolved. The response of Monsignor Archbishop, whereby he informed the petitioner that, in view of the judgement rendered under his predecessor, he thought he was not in a position to review again this case unless especially empowered by the Holy See to do so, is to be found in Enclosure No. 3. At this point, Princess Carolyne appealed to His Holiness and addressed to him a petition which is found in Enclosure No. 4. To that petition, by an order of His Holiness himself, this Holy Congregation responded with the following rescript: "*August 8, 1859. The Most Holy Father kindly agrees to the notion that, whereas there be nothing to the contrary, the present Metropolitan of Mohilow be empowered to take up again this specific case of marriage annulment, review it, and adjudicate it by a definitive sentence according to the level of appeal, having observed otherwise what needs be observed, especially the Bull* Dei miseratione *issued by the Holy Memory of Benedict XIV. The Archbishop will be so notified.*" On the strength of this decree, the Archbishop of Mohilow delegated three respectable members of the High Clergy not connected with the Consistorial Court to review and adjudicate the case with the assistance of a Defender of the Marriage Bond, especially chosen for this purpose.

In the meantime, toward the end of the month of March, an important personage[33] informed the Holy Father there were serious reasons to believe that Princess Carolyne was endeavoring to corrupt those judges with huge sums of money and a request was made, for this reason, that the proceedings should be stopped and moved to Rome, where the case would be reviewed by the Holy See. His Holiness decided against accepting such a request, both because it was not proper to do so in the light of the fact that the rescript mentioned above had been issued and, though it was possible that the Princess had every intention to suborn those

Dopo il silenzio di più anni, e precisamente nel giugno 1859, la Principessa per mezzo di un suo agente si rivolse al nuovo Arcivescovo di Mokilow affinché venisse da esso riassunta la questione, che, per la difformità dei pareri fra i membri del concistoro sotto l'Arcivescovo defonto, riteneva come non regolarmente definita. La risposta di Monsig[nor] Arcivescovo, colla quale significava al postulante che, dopo il giudicato avvenuto sotto il suo Antecessore, non si credeva in facoltà di conoscere nuovamente la questione, a meno che non ne venisse specialmente autorizzato dalla S[anta] Sede, è a vedersi nell' *Allegato Num[ero] 3*. Fu allora che la Principessa Carolina si rivolse alla Santità di N[ostro] S[ignore] colle preci che si leggono nell'*Allegato Num[ero] 4*, sulle quali, per ordine della stessa S[antità] fu da questa S[anta] Congregazione emesso il seguente rescritto: "*Die 8 Augusti 1859. S[anctissimus] benigne annuit ut contrariis quibuscumque non obstantibus, modernus Metropolitanus Mokylowiensis enunciatam causam super nullitate matrimonii reassumere, cognoscere, ac per sententiam definitivam judicare valeat in gradu appellationis servatis ceteroquin de jure servandis, ac praesertim Constitutione S[anctae] M[emoriae] Benedicti XIV Dei miseratione; et notificetur Archiepiscopo*"; e in virtù di questo decreto l'Arcivescovo di Mohilow commise l'esame e giudizio della causa a tre rispettabili Ecclesiastici estranei al tribunale concistoriale, colla deputazione ed assistenza del Difensore di officio.

Intanto, sul declinare del mese di marzo di quest'anno fu da ragguardevole personaggio rappresentato al S[anto] Padre esservi fondato sospetto a credere che la principessa Carolina si adoperasse di corrompere con ingenti somme di denaro quei Giudici; ed imploravasi a tale effetto l'avocazione della causa alla S[anta] Sede. Ma Sua Santità non credette di accogliere questa dimanda, sia perché non trattavasi di cosa integra, stante il rescritto sopra riportato, sia perché, quantunque fosse possibile nella Principessa l'intendimento di subornare quei giudici, non ne seguiva però che potesse ritenersi come un fatto la loro prevaricazione, e d'al-

---

[33]Monsignor Gustav von Hohenlohe. See his Petition, ASV, CC, Doc. No. 16.

judges, it did not follow that they were in fact being corrupted and, finally, this suspicion was not corroborated by any document whatsoever. His Holiness, believing that these concerns should not be entirely dismissed, ordered us to write to Monsignor Nuncio in Vienna to the effect that he should inform the Archbishop of Mohilow about what had transpired regarding the presumed machinations on the part of the Princess and alert him to that possibility.

However, already in the previous February, the Commission so delegated had issued a sentence in favor of annulment and this sentence had been sanctioned by the Archbishop. Furthermore, after the legal requirements had been fulfilled, it had been forwarded to the interested party. In due time, we received a copy of it from the Archbishop himself (see Enclosure No. 5). The intervention of the Nuncio being now useless, by order of His Holiness Himself, we wrote again to the latter that he should send the Bishop of Fulda, in whose Diocese the Princess was residing at this time, a formal order to suspend the execution of the sentence until he received new instructions from the Holy See. The Nuncio was also told to instruct Monsignor the Archbishop of Mohilow to suggest to the Defender of the Marriage Bond in that Diocese that he should appeal against the last sentence before the Holy See. Monsignor Nuncio faithfully executed the instructions he received and, consequently, Monsignor the Bishop of Fulda abstained from implementing the aforementioned sentence. The reaction of the Metropolitan of Mohilow can be seen in his answer to Monsignor Nuncio in Enclosure No. 6.

After learning that the sentence was not being executed by express order of the Holy See, the Princess, who was already planning to remarry, came immediately to Rome to request from the Pontiff himself the removal of the interposed impediment. But the Holy Father (though no proof had been brought forth to corroborate the presumed attempted corruption) did not assent to her request. There were now new questions arising from the order and level of judgements produced in this case and, from their review, it did not appear that two analogous sentences in favor of the nullity of that marriage had been produced. The Princess was informed of the problem and produced the above-mentioned

tronde nemmeno il sospetto veniva convalidato da un qualche documento. Tuttavolta stimandosi dalla Santità Sua doversi tenere in qualche conto siffatte apprensioni, ordinò scriversi a Monsig[nor] Nunzio di Vienna (il che fu adempiuto con lettera del 4 aprile) affinché portasse a cognizione di Monsig[nor] Arcivescovo di Mohilow quanto erasi dedotto in ordine alle asserte machinazioni della principessa, per porlo in guardia sulle medesime.

Senonché fin dal febbraio precedente quel tribunale commissario aveva proferito sua sentenza per la nullità del matrimonio; sentenza che venne approvata dall'Arcivescovo, e che previe le debite legalità si spedì e ne fu fatta consegna alla parte. Di questa se n'ebbe a suo tempo copia trasmessa dallo stesso Arcivescovo (*Alleg[ato] Num[ero] 5*). Resa così inutile la prat(t)ica di Monsig[nor] Nunzio, si tornò per comando della stessa Santità Sua a scrivere al medesimo, perché formalmente inibisse a Monsig[nor] Vescovo di Fulda, nella cui diocesi trovavasi domiciliata la Principessa, di dare esecuzione alla menzionata sentenza fino a nuove disposizioni della S[anta] Sede. Gli s'ingiungeva ancora di dare istruzioni a Monsignor Vescovo di Mohilow perché insinuasse al Difensore del Vincolo matrimoniale presso quella Curia d'interporre appello innanzi alla S[anta] Sede contro l'ultima sentenza. Monsignor Nunzio eseguì accuratamente le ricevute ingiunzioni; in seguito di che Monsignor Vescovo di Fulda si astenne fin qui dal dare esecuzione alla detta Sentenza. Quale poi ne sia stato l'esito presso il Metropolitano di Mohilow si raccoglie dalla sua risposta a Monsig[nor] Nunzio (*Alleg[ato] Num[ero] 6*).

Pertanto la Principessa, nel proposito in cui già era di passare ad altre nozze, avendo conosciuto che per divieto fatto dalla S[anta] Sede non si dava esecuzione alla Sentenza, recossi a Roma istantemente reclamando presso il Trono Pontificio la remozione dell'apposto impedimento. Il S[anto] Padre però (non ostante che non si producessero prove di sorta per avvalorare il concepito sospetto della tentata corruzione) non stimò di annuire; imperocché si accampavano nuove difficoltà tratte dall'ordine dei giudizi occorsi in questa causa, dal cui esame sembrava potersi ritenere non concorrere nel caso due sentenze conformi per la nullità. Questa difficoltà venne partecipata alla Principessa, dalla quale si ebbero le di sopra

statement which is available in Enclosure No. 1. The examination of the latter led to the discovery, as it was stated earlier, that there had been another sentence issued by the Consistory of Mohilow before the one from Zhitomir; neither of these, moreover, was available for the record. By order of the Holy Father, the Princess was then asked to produce them. Unable do so, the Princess produced, instead, the document enclosed as No. 7.

The Holy Father, therefore, before coming to any decision on this case that is not without difficulties, has ordered that the question be examined by Your Most Reverend Eminences for an opinion on its merits.

The main thing to be considered here pertains to the value of the different sentences and judgements that have been given in favor of annulment. Since two analogous sentences to this effect are required by law for a marriage to be declared null and void, it remains to be seen whether there have been two such sentences in this case. It is also useful to keep in mind the dispositions of the Concordate made in 1847 between the Holy See and the Emperor of Russia and presently in effect. There, after Article 13, which states that the Bishop is the sole judge and the one solely responsible for the conduct of Church affairs, Article 14 lists the matters that must first be deliberated upon by the Consistory of the Diocese; among these, at Section E, are listed Marriage Cases. Art. 15 then says that *"Such affairs are decided by the Bishop after they have been examined by the Consistory; the latter retains merely a consultative role. The Bishop is not at all bound to explain the reasons of his decision, even in those cases where his opinion happens to differ from that of the Consistory."*

From the above dispositions, it would follow that the 1852 sentence of the Consistory of Mohilow cannot be seen as being in favor of annulment, because it was not sanctioned by the Archbishop. This applies even less to the first sentence allegedly issued by the Consistory of Mohilow. After all, even if we disregard the fact that there is no record of it whatsoever, this sentence was not considered at all by that Ordinary Office and was perceived as if it had not been issued by reason of the aforementioned restructuring of the Diocese. Therefore, in favor of an-

mezionate deduzioni riportate coll'*Allegato Num[ero] 1*. Essendosi poi dall'esame di queste rilevato che un'altra sentenza per la nullità era stata, come si asseriva, pronunciata, anteriormente a quella di Zitomir, dal Concistoro di Mohilow, delle quali due sentenze non si aveva copia in atti; per ordine del S[anto] Padre fu significato alla Principessa di farne produzione. In evasione di tale richiesta si ebbe si ebbe dalla medesima il foglio *Alleg[ato] Num[ero] 7*.

Quindi il S[anto] Padre prima di prendere una determinazione qualunque in un affare non scevro di difficoltà ha ordinato che il caso si sottoponga all'esame delle Eminenze Loro Reverendissime per un parere in proposito.

La principale osservazione che a fare si presenta nell'attuale controversia sembra potersi riferire al valore delle diverse sentenze od opinamenti per la nullità esternati; poiché ritenuto che per disposizione di diritto si richieggano due sentenze conformi all'effetto che sia dichiarato nullo un matrimonio, resta in fatto a vedersi se queste due sentenze abbiano avuto luogo nel presente caso. Giova poi qui riferire le disposizioni del vigente concordato conchiuso nel 1847 fra la S[anta] Sede e l'Imperatore di tutte le Russie. Ivi, dopo essersi detto all'art[icolo] 13 che il Vescovo è il solo giudice ed amministratore degli affari ecclesiastici, all'art[icolo] 14 si enumerano gli affari che debbono prima assoggettarsi alle deliberazioni del Concistoro diocesano; fra i quali sotto la lett[era] E si riportano le *Causae matrimoniales*. All'art[icolo] 15 poi si dispone così: *"Negotia praedicta decernuntur ab Episcopo postquam a Consistorio examinata fuerint; quod tamen consultationis partes tantummodo retinet. Episcopus minime tenetur afferre rationes suae sententiae, illis etiam in casibus in quibus ejus opinio ab illa Consistorii discreparet."*

Dalle premesse disposizioni ne seguirebbe non potersi avere a calcolo per la nullità del matrimonio la sentenza emanata nel 1852 dal Concistoro di Mohilow, poiché non fu confermata dall'Arcivescovo. Molto meno poi potrebbe aversi in considerazione la prima sentenza, che si asserisce pronunciata dallo stesso Concistoro di Mohilow, per la ragione che, prescindendo dall'osservare non essersi di essa prodotto documento alcuno, non fu neppure attesa da quell'Ordinariato e si considerò come non avvenuta a cagione della soprammenzionata di-

nulment, we would have only the last sentence issued by the present Archbishop on the force of the aforementioned rescript of the Holy Congregation.

But, whatever the questions emerging from the sequence of judgements, these would appear to be irrelevant in the face of the fact that the Archbishop, in virtue of the rescript issued on August 8, 1859[34], deemed himself to be officially delegated by the Holy See and, therefore, authorised to review, study, and adjudicate this case in a definitive way. This, in his own opinion, would not have been in his ordinary jurisdictional mandate, since his predecessor had already passed judgement on this matter. That this is indeed the case results, moreover, from his entrusting the judicial review not to the ordinary Consistory, but to three judges especially chosen.

Should Your Eminences feel that a ruling for annulment cannot rest securely on only one sentence, whatever its value, it would be necessary to propose what remedies might be adopted in this situation. In this connection, consideration must be given, therefore, to the Archbishop's statements in Enclosure No. 6 and to the Princess's observations (see Enclosure No. 1) as to the problems that would be raised by a new trial.

As for the rest, Your Eminences should determine whether the alleged first sentence from Mohilow and the 1852 resolution of the Consistory, both in favor of annulment but without credibility in strict legal terms, could be used as supporting evidence for the last sentence in order the better to appreciate its validity and justice. To this effect, a careful examination of the arguments presented herewith in Enclosures No. 2 and 5 might be useful.

Therefore, etc.

The First Judgement of the Holy Congregation of the Council

The Holy Congregation resolved that letters be sent to Monsignor the Nuncio in Vienna to the effect of ordering Monsignor the Bishop of Fulda to proceed to the execution of the sentence in favor of annulment issued by the Archbishop of Mohilow.

smembrazione. Onde non rimarrebbe nel senso della nullità che l'ultima sentenza proferita dall'odierno Arcivescovo in seguito al decreto della S[anta] Congregazione, riportato di sopra.

Però qualunque difficoltà che emerge dall'ordine dei giudizi sembrerebbe venir tolta di mezzo dall'altra osservazione, che cioè l'Arcivescovo appoggiato al rescritto degli 8 agosto 1849 ritennesi abilitato a riassumere, conoscere, e definitivamente giudicare la causa come delegato della S[anta] Sede; ciò che, secondo il suo parere, non avrebbe potuto eseguire in forza dell'ordinaria sua giurisdizione, dopo che il suo Antecessore vi aveva già pronunciato. La qual cosa si arguisce ancora dall'avere egli commesso l'esame ed il giudizio della causa non al Concistoro ordinario, ma a tre giudici specialmente deputati.

Quante volte però sembrasse alle Eminenze Loro di non poter essere tranquilli sopra una sola Sentenza, qualunque ne sia il valore, all'effetto che sia dichiarato nullo il matrimonio, rimarrebbe a vedersi qual rimedio convenga adottare nel caso. Intorno a che va ponderato quanto espone l'Arcivescovo nell'*Allegato Num[ero] 1* sulle difficoltà che involgerebbe un nuovo giudizio.

Del resto veggano l'Eminenze Loro se tanto l'asserta prima sentenza di Mohilow, quanto l'opinamento del Concistoro del 1852 nel senso della nullità, sebbene non attendibili a stretto diritto, possano venire in sussidio dell'ultima sentenza perché ne sia apprezzato il valore e la giustizia; al che potrà anche influire un accurato esame degli argomenti che si adducono *hinc inde* negli *Alleg[ati] Numero 2* e *Num[ero] 5*.

Laonde ec<c>.

Il primo giudizio della Santa Congregazione del Concilio

La S[anta] Cong[regazion]e opinò che si debba scrivere a M[onsigno]r Nunzio di Vienna affinché ordini a M[onsigno]r Vescovo di Fulda di dare esecuzione alla sentenza emanata per la nullità del matrimonio dall'Arcivescovo di Mohilow.

---

[34]In the printed original, the year is wrongly given as 1849.

Those present were the Most Eminent Cardinals <Antonio> Cagiano <de Azevedo>, Prefect of the Congregation, <Gerolamo> D'Andrea, <Pietro> Marini, <Giuseppe> Bofondi, <Pietro de> Silvestri, <Teodulfo> Mertel, who all agreed to this resolution with the exception of the aforementioned Mertel, who felt that the rescript <of August 8, 1859>, issued after an audience with the Holy Father, authorised the Archbishop to adjudicate only according to the second degree of jurisdiction.

At the audience given on the 24th of the current month of September, this resolution was presented to the Holy Father, who deigned to confirm it.

Intervennero gli E[minentissi]mi <Antonio Maria> Cagiano <de Azevedo> Prefetto, <Girolamo> D'Andrea, <Pietro> Marini, <Giuseppe> Bofondi, <Pietro de> Silvestri, <Teodulfo> Mertel, i quali convennero in questa risoluzione, ad eccezione del prelodato E[minentissi]mo Mertel, che opinava essersi col rescritto emanato dalla udienza del S[anto] Padre autorizzato l'Arcivesc[ov]o a giudicare soltanto in secondo grado di giurisdizione.

Nella udienza del 24 settembre corr[en]te fu riferito tale opinamento al S[anto] Padre che si degnò confermarlo.

B) Enclosure No. 1. Printed transcription of ASV, CC Doc. No. 29, Carolyne's presentation of her case for upholding the 1860 Mohilow sentence issued by Żyliński. Italian (6 pages).

C) Enclosure No. 2. Printed transcription of ASV, CC Doc. No. 8, the French translation, done by Okraszewski of the 1852 Sentence issued at Mohilow, with Monsignor Laski's minority position which was upheld by Archbishop Holowinski. French (24 pages). Okraszewski's statement about the accuracy of the translation is not reproduced.

D) Enclosure No. 3. Printed transcription of ASV, CC Doc. No. 6, the French translation of Żyliński's letter to Okraszewski, dated June 13, 1859. French (2 pages).

E) Enclosure No. 4. Printed transcription of ASV, CC Doc. No. 2, Carolyne's 1859 Petition to the Vatican to authorise the Archbishop of Mohilow to reopen her case. Latin (2 pages).

F) Enclosure No. 5. Printed transcription of Żyliński's Mohilow sentence, dated February 1860. See ASV, CC Docs. No. 20, 21, and 28. See the latter for the complete text. See also ASV, NV Doc. No. 6. This copy derives from De Luca's copy (Doc. No. 21), in turn made from ASV, VN Doc. No. 6, where Proniewski's name is spelled Prosciewski. Latin (3 pages).

G) Enclosure No. 6. Printed transcription of ASV, CC Doc. No. 32; see Żyliński's letter of May 24, 1860, to De Luca protesting against the accusation of bribery (ASV, NV Doc. No. 21). Latin (3 Pages).

H) Enclosure No. 7. Printed transcription of ASV, CC Doc. No. 40, a slight variation of ASV, CC Doc. No. 37: Carolyne's response to the Congregation's request for authentic copies of the sentences of Mohilow (1851) and Zhitomir (1851). Italian (2 pages).

Document No. 43. September 25, 1860. Draft of letter from Quaglia to De Luca, informing him of the decision of the Congregation. See ASV, NV Doc. No. 25. Italian (2 pages).

Document No. 44. September 28, 1860. Carlo Modesti, a Roman attorney, petitions on Carolyne's behalf for the return of the original of the 1860 Mohilow sentence. Granted by Quaglia on the same day. Italian (2 pages).

To his Most Reverend Excellency
Monsignor <Angelo Quaglia>,
Secretary of the Holy Congregation of the
  Council
Most Reverend Excellency:

    The undersigned Carlo Modesti, Attorney at law, especially delegated by Her Highness, Princess Carolyne Iwanowska, entreats Your Most Reverend Excellency to endeavor to have the original of the sentence pronounced by the Metropolitan of Mohilow as Apostolic delegate, which is presently kept on file, returned to him.
Carlo Modesti,
Attorney at law,

    For this grace etc. on behalf etc.

September 28, 1860
The document has been surrendered as
  requested, etc.

    The sentence referred to in the present instance has been received by the undersigned and given to the Princess, who is its rightful owner.
September 28, 1860

Carlo Modesti, Attorney at law

A Sua Eccellenza R[everendissi]ma
Monsignore <Angelo Quaglia>,
Segretario <della Santa Congregazione>
del Concilio
Eccellenza R[everendissi]ma

    L'Avv[ocat]o Carlo Modesti, incaricato specialmente da S[ua] Altezza la Sig[no]ra Principessa Carolina Iwanowska, prega la Eccellenza Vostra R[everendissi]ma a fargli restituire la sentenza autentica pronunziata dal Metropolitano di Mohilow come Delegato Apostolico, trovandosi quella in atti.
L'Avv[ocat]o Carlo Modesti
nel nome etc.
Che [della grazia etc.]

Die 28 Sept[em]bris 1860
Juxta preces relicta acceptilatione(sic)

    La sentenza, di cui si parla nella istanza, è stata ritirata dal sottoscritto e consegnata alla S[igno]ra Principessa, cui quella appartiene.
Li 28 Settembre 1860
C[arlo] Avv[ocat]o Modesti

Document No. 45. October 18, 1860. Letter from De Luca to Quaglia, raising questions about the September 22 decision of the Congregation. For the text, see De Luca's draft in ASV, NV Doc. No. 31. Italian (2 pages). It bears the Prot. No. 1819/1, and it is signed as follows:

Your most devoted and obliged servant,
Antonino <De Luca>, Archbishop of Tarsus,
  Apostolic Nuncio.

devot[issi]mo obblig[atissi]mo Servitore,
  Ant[onino], Arciv[escov]o di Tarso,
  N[unzio] Ap[ostoli]co.

**Document No. 46. October 24, 1860. Letter from De Luca to Quaglia enclosing
a copy of Kött's letter of October 15, 1860. See De Luca's draft in ASV, NV, Doc.
No. 34. Italian (2 pages). It is signed as follows:**

Your Most Illustrious and Reverend
    Excellency's most devoted and obliged
    servant,
Antonino <De Luca>, Archbishop of Tarsus,
    Apostolic Nuncio.

Di Vostra Signoria Illustrissima e
    Rev[erendissi]ma devot[issi]mo
    obblig[atissi]mo Servitore
Ant[onino] <DeLuca, Arciv[escov]o di Tarso,
    N[unzio] Ap[ostolico]

**Document No. 47. Enclosure. Copy of Kött's letter to De Luca, dated October
15, 1860. See ASV, NV Doc. No. 28. Latin (2 pages).**

**Document No. 48. December 2, 1860. Memorandum. Caterini, the new Prefect
of the Congregation, writes to Monsignor Berardi requesting documents from
the Office of the Secretary of State. Italian (1 page).**

To: Monsignor Giuseppe Berardi,
Substitute in the Office of
The Secretary of State
<Rome,> December 2, 1860

Mons[igno]r Giuseppe Berardi,
Sostituto della Seg[rete]ria di Stato

2 Dec. 1860

The better to understand certain matters,
the Holy Congregation of the Council needs a
copy of the Dispatch of July 2 1848, prot. No.
6437/6 {addressed to the Russian Embassy}, with
which the Holy See approved the proposals
made by the Russians with respect to the levels
of jurisdiction to be observed in ecclesiastical
matters.

A piena cognizione di cose occorre alla
S[anta] Congregazione del Concilio una copia
del Dispaccio dei 2 luglio 1848, No. 6437/6
{diretto all'Ambasciata Russa} col quale vennero approvate dalla S[anta] Sede le pro-
posizioni fatte dalla Russia sui gradi di
giurisdizione giudiziaria da osservarsi nelle materie ecclesiastiche.

It is for this reason that the undersigned
Cardinal, Prefect of that same Holy Congregation <of the Council>, turns to you, Most Illustrious and Reverend Monsignor, and requests
that you be so gracious as to send it to him.

Egli è perciò che il sott[oscritt]o Card[inal]
Prefetto della med[esima] S[anta] Cong[re-
gazio]ne si rivolge alla S[ignoria] V[ostra]
Ill[ustrissi]ma e R[everendissi]ma colla preghiera
di fargliene la trasmissione.

Certain that in your kindness you will favor
him, he goes on to declare himself, with the expression of singular esteem,
<Yours...>
<Prospero Cardinal Caterini,
Prefect of the Holy Congregation of the
    Council>

Sicuro di essere favorito dalla di Lei gentilezza passa a dichiararsi con sensi di stima distinta...

<Prospero Cardinal Caterini,
Prefetto della Santa Congregazione del
    Concilio>

Document No. 49. December 3, 1860. Berardi responds to Caterini. Italian (1 page). The documents originally enclosed are not in the file, but they are reproduced in ASV, CC Docs. No. 59C, D, and E.

From the Office of the Secretary of State
To the Most Eminent Cardinal
<Prospero> Caterini,
Prefect of the Holy Congregation of the Council
December 3, 1860.

Quickly responding to your Most Reverend Eminence's venerable note dated yesterday, the undersigned Substitute in the Office of the Secretary of State has the honor of enclosing the requested copy of the Dispatch, dated July 2, 1848, Prot. No. 6437/6, pertaining to the approval on the part of the Holy See of the Russian Government's proposals on the levels of jurisdiction to be observed in ecclesiastical matters.

Since the enclosed document refers to communications made by that Government in the dispatch signed by His lordship, Count de Nesselrode, a copy of which is already in Your Eminence's possession, the writer suggests that you keep in mind that document in order to understand fully the Dispatch, a copy of which is now being sent to you.

Bowing to kiss Your Holy Purple, with the expression of the deepest reverence, I sign myself
Your Most Reverend Eminence's
most devoted, humble, and obliging servant,

Giuseppe Berardi
Enclosure

E[minentissi]mo Sig. Cardinale <Prospero> Caterini
Prefetto della S[anta] C[ongregazione] del Concilio
Dalla Segreteria di Stato, 3 Decembre 1860.

In pronto riscontro al venerato foglio di Vostra Eminenza R[everendissi]ma in data di ieri il sottoscritto Sostituto della Segreteria di Stato ha l'onore di compiegarle la richiesta copia del Dispaccio dei 2 luglio 1848 N. 6437/6 relativo all' approvazione per parte della S[anta] Sede delle proposte del Governo Russo sui gradi di giurisdizione da osservarsi nelle materie ecclesiastiche.

Riferendosi poi l'accluso foglio alle Comunicazioni fatte dal Governo medesimo col Disp[accio] del Sig[nor] Conte di Nesselrode, la di cui copia già si possiede dall' E[minenza] V[ostra], lo scrivente La prega a voler avere presente quel documento a piena intelligenza del Disp[accio] di cui ora si dà copia.

Inchinato al bacio della S[anta] Porpora con sensi di profondissimo ossequio si rassegna

Dell'Eminenza V[ostra] R[everendissi]ma
De[votissi]mo U[milissi]mo Ob[li]g[atissi]mo Servitore
Gius[eppe] Berardi
(con inserto)

Document No. 50. December 3, 1860. Draft. Memorandum from Caterini to Quaglia about the documentation necessary for the December 22 meeting of the Congregation. Italian (1 page). The enclosed documentation, not kept in the file, was reproduced in ASV, CC, Docs. No. 59B, C, and D.

<Rome,> December 3, 1860
Marriage case

It is necessary to prepare a brief report for the first meeting of the Congregation, which will include, however, a supplementary summary.

We shall put in the Summary the complete texts of the Russian Note and the Dispatch from the Secretary of State, herewith enclosed, as well as a memorandum containing observations which Monsignor Secretary <of the Congregation>

3 dec[embre] 1860
Matrimonii

E' necessario di preparare una breve relazione per la prima Congregazione, fornita però di sommario addizionale.

Nel Sommario si porrà per extensum la Nota Russa ed il Dispaccio della Seg[rete]ria di Stato qui annessi.

might wish to examine, correct, delete, or even appropriate.

To expedite this matter, it will be better to make use of the printing press, but it is understood that the Pontifical secret is to be enforced.
<Prospero Cardinal Caterini, Prefect of the Holy Congregation of the Council>

Ed anche il foglio di osservazioni, che Mon[signo]r Seg[reta]rio potrebbe esaminare, correggere, cancellare, etc. ed anche far proprio.

Per sollecitare sarà meglio di fare uso della stampa, ma sempre *col segreto Pontificio*.

<Prospero Cardinal Caterini, Prefetto della Santa Congregazione del Concilio>

Document No. 51. December 10, 1860. Draft of memorandum from Quaglia to Cardinals D'Andrea, Silvestri, Marini, and Mertel on whether they intend to be present at the December 22 meeting of the Congregation and whether they still have the printed documentation for the September 22 meeting. Italian (2 pages).

To: Cardinal <Gerolamo> D'Andrea
Cardinal <Pietro de> Silvestri
Cardinal <Pietro> Marini
Cardinal <Teodulfo> Mertel
From the Office of the Secretary
of the Holy Congregation of the Council.
<The Vatican,> December 10, 1860

I, the undersigned Secretary of the Holy Congregation of the Council, take the liberty to ask Your Most Reverend Eminence to deign yourself to let me know as soon as possible whether you still have with you the printed documentation concerning the marriage case from the Diocese of Zhitomir. The latter, by order of the Holy Father, was reviewed by the Holy Congregation in the General Assembly recently held on September 22.

I should like also to take advantage of this occasion, as I bow to kiss the hem of Your Most Reverend Eminence's Holy Purple, to express again to you my feelings of the greatest esteem and deepest respect.
<Angelo Quaglia,
Secretary of the Holy Congregation of the
    Council>

Sig[no]r Card[inal]e <Gerolamo> D'Andrea
    Sig[no]r Card[inal]e <Pietro de> Silvestri
    Sig[no]r Card[inal]e <Pietro> Marini
    Sig[no]r Card[inal]e <Teodulfo> Mertel
Dalla Segreteria della Santa Congregazione
del Concilio
Li 10 Decembre 1860

Il sottoscritto Segretario della S[anta] C[ongregazione] del Concilio si permette pregare L'Em[inen]za V[ost]ra R[everendissi]ma ad avere la degnazione di significargli con qualche sollecitudine se tuttora si ritrovi presso di Lei la posizione a stampa concernente la causa *Zytomirien: Matrimonii* che per ordine del S[anto] Padre venne sottoposta all'esame del S[anto] Consesso nella Congregazione generale dei <22> Settembre p[rossi]mo passato.

Profitta lo stesso scrivente di questo incontro per rinnovarle i sensi della più alta stima e particolare rispetto nell'atto che bacia il lembo della S[anta] Porpora dell'Em[inen]za V[ost]ra R[everendissi]ma
<Angelo Quaglia,
Segretario della Santa Congregazione
del Concilio>

Document No. 52. December 10, 1860. Draft of memorandum from Quaglia to Cardinal Milesi for the same reasons presented in ASV, CC, Doc. No. 51. Italian (2 pages).

To: Cardinal <Giuseppe> Milesi
From the Office of the Secretary
of the Holy Congregation of the Council.
<The Vatican,> December 10, 1860

Sig[no]r Cardinal <Giuseppe> Milesi
Dalla Segretreria della S[Anta] C[ongregazione]
del Concilio
li 10 Decembre 1860

I, the undersigned Secretary of the Holy Congregation of the Council, take the liberty to ask Your Most Reverend Eminence to deign yourself to let me know as soon as possible whether you still have with you the printed documentation concerning the marriage case from the Diocese of Zhitomir. The latter, by order of the Holy Father, was reviewed by the Holy Congregation of the Council this past September. Should you still have those papers and were unable to come to the meeting of the Congregation of this month, please return them to me.

I take advantage of this occasion to express again to you my highest esteem and particular respect.

Your Most Reverend Eminence's

....

<Angelo Quaglia,
Secretary of the Holy Congregation of the
 Council>

Il Sottoscritto Segre[ta]rio della S[anta] C[ongregazione] del Concilio si permette di pregare V[ost]ra Em[inen]za R[everendissi]ma ad avere la degnazione di significargli con qualche sollecitudine se tuttora si ritrovi presso di lei la posizione a stampa concernente la causa *Zytomirien: Matrimonii*, che fu proposta per ordine del S[anto] Padre nella Cong[regazio]ne del decorso settembre; e nel caso affermativo compiacersi di ritornargliela qualora non potesse intervenire nella prossima Cong[regazio]ne del mese corrente.

Profitta lo Scrivente stesso di quest'incontro per rinnovarle i sensi della più alta stima e particolare rispetto.

Dell'Em[inen]za V[ost]ra R[everendissi]ma

....

<Angelo Quaglia,
Segretario della Santa Congregazione del
 Concilio>

**Document No. 53. December 10, 1860. Draft memorandum from Quaglia to
Cardinal Villecourt along the same lines as ASV, CC, Docs. No. 51 and 52.
Italian (2 pages).**

To: Cardinal <Clément> Villecourt
From the Office of the Secretary
of the Holy Congregation of the Council.
<The Vatican,> December 10, 1860

I, the undersigned Secretary of the Holy Congregation of the Council, take the liberty to ask Your Most Reverend Eminence to deign yourself to return to me as soon as possible the printed documentation pertaining to the marriage case from the Diocese of Zhitomir. The documents were forwarded to you, with the prescription of secrecy, for discussion at the general meeting of last September. I am making such a request in the eventuality that you may be unable to attend the next general meeting this month.

I take advantage of this occasion to express again to you, as I bow to kiss your holy purple, my feelings of the highest esteem and particular respect.

Your Most Reverend Eminence's

....

<Angelo Quaglia,
 Secretary of the Holy Congregation of the
 Council>

Sig[no]r Card[inal]e <Clément> Villecourt
Dalla Segreteria della S[anta] C[ongregazione]
del <Concilio>
li 10 Decembre 1860

Il Sottoscritto Segretario della S[anta] C[ongregazione] del Concilio si permette pregare l'Em[inen]za v[ost]ra R[everendissi]ma ad avere la degnazione di ritornargli con qualche sollecitudine la posizione a stampa concernente la causa *Zytomirien: Matrimonii* che Le venne distribuita con la legge del Segreto per la Cong[regazio]ne Gen[era]le del<lo> scorso settembre, quante volte[35] però l'Em[inen]za V[ost]ra non creda intervenire alla prossima Congre[gazio]ne di questo mese.

Profitta lo scrivente di quest'incontro per rinnovarle i sensi della più alta stima e particolare rispetto nell'atto che le bacia la S[anta] Porpora.

Dell'Em[inen]za V[ost]ra R[everendissi]ma

......

<Angelo Quaglia,
Segretario della Santa Congregazione del
 Concilio>

---

[35]Obviously a *lapsus calami*; instead of "quante volte," the writer meant to say "qualora."

Document No. 54. December 10, 1860. Memorandum from Quaglia to Cardinal Bofondi, with the latter's answer on the same sheet. Italian (1 page).

To: Cardinal <Giuseppe> Bofondi
From the Office of the Secretary
of the Holy Congregation of the Council.
<The Vatican,> December 10, 1860

I, the undersigned Secretary of the Holy Congregation of the Council, take the liberty to ask Your Most Reverend Eminence to deign yourself to let me know, as soon as possible, whether the printed documentation concerning the marriage case from the Diocese of Zhitomir is still in your possession. By order of the Holy Father, this case was reviewed by the Holy Congregation at the General Assembly recently held on September 22.

I take advantage of this occasion to express again to you, as I bow to kiss the hem of your holy purple, my feelings of the highest consideration and particular respect.
Your Most Reverend Eminence's
most humble, devoted and obliging servant

Angelo Quaglia, etc.

Sig[no]r Cardinale <Giuseppe> Bofondi
Dalla Segreteria della S[anta]
Cong[regazio]ne del Concilio
li 10 Decembre 1860

Il Sottoscritto Segretario della S[anta] Cong[regazio]ne del Concilio si permette pregare L'Em[inen]za V[ost]ra R[everendissi]ma ad avere la degnazione di significargli con qualche sollecitudine, se tuttora si ritrovi presso di lei la posizione a stampa concernente la Causa *Zytomirien: Matrimonii*, che, per ordine del S[anto] Padre venne sottoposta all'esame del S[anto] Consesso nella Cong[regazio]ne Generale dei 22 settembre prossimo passato.

Profitta lo Scrivente stesso di questo incontro per rinnovarle i sensi della più alta stima e particolare rispetto nell'atto che Le bacia il lembo della S[anta] Porpora.

Di V[ost]ra Em[inen]za R[everendissi]ma
U[milissi]mo D[evotissi]mo ed Obb[ligatissi]mo
   Servitore
Angelo Quaglia, etc.

<Bofondi's answer to Quaglia's inquiry on the same page.>

I returned the documentation you mention to our excellent Monsignor Secretary the very morning the case was discussed. I checked, to be sure, the dossier concerning the Congregation, and I did not find any papers pertaining to that case.

I avail myself of this occasion to confirm to my dear Monsignor my most sincere assurance of the highest esteem and to reiterate again my being
Your most devoted and obliging servant,
Giuseppe Cardinal Bofondi

La posizione di cui si tratta venne da me restituita all'ottimo Monsig[no]r Segretario nella mattina stessa in cui si propose la Causa. Esaminato difatti il mazzo di quella Congregazione, non ho trovato alcuna carta relativa alla detta causa.

Approfitto di quest'occasione per confermare a Monsig[no]r Mio le assicurazioni più sincere della distinta mia stima e per ripetermi
Dev[otissi]mo Obb[ligatissi]mo Servitore
G[iuseppe] Card[inal] Bofondi

Document No. 55. December 11, 1860. Cardinal Mertel's answer to ASV, CC Doc. No. 51. Italian (1 page).

To: Monsignor Angelo Quaglia,
Secretary of the Holy Congregation of the
   Council
Ruffo Palace, December 11, 1860

Monsig[nor] Angelo Quaglia
Segretario della S[anta] Cong[regazio]ne
del Concilio
Palazzo Ruffo, 11 Dicembre 1860

Most Illustrious and Reverend Monsignor:

Some time ago, together with other papers, I destroyed the printed documentation pertaining to the marriage case from Zhitomir that you request of me in Your Most Illustrious and Reverend Excellency's much honored note.

With the expression of my greatest esteem, it is a pleasure to confirm myself
Your Most Illustrious and Reverend Excellency's most devoted servant,
Teodulfo Cardinal Mertel.

Ill[ustrissi]mo e R[everendissi]mo Sig[no]re.

Le stampe relative alla causa *Zytomirien: Matrimonii*, di cui V[ostra] S[ignoria] Ill[ustrissi]ma e R[everendissi]ma mi fa richiesta col preg[iatissi]mo foglio del 10 corr[ent]e furono da me lacerate tempo fa insieme ad altre carte.
Con piena stima mi pregio confermarmi
Di V[ostra] S[ignoria] Ill[ustrissi]ma e
     R[everendissi]ma
De[votissi]mo Servitore
T[eodulfo] Card[inal] Mertel

Document No. 56. December 11, 1860. Note providing Cardinal Milesi's answer to ASV, CC, Doc. No. 52. Italian (1 page).

December 11, <1860>

Cardinal <Giuseppe> Milesi wishes to inform Monsignor Quaglia that he still has the printed documentation pertaining to the marriage case from Zhitomir and intends to attend the next meeting of the Congregation of the Council.

11 Dicembre

Il Cardinal <Giuseppe> Milesi fa sapere a Mons[igno]r Quaglia che la stampa della causa Zytomirien/Matrimonii è presso di lui, e che intende d'intervenire alla pross[ima] Cong[regazio]ne del Concilio

Document No. 57. Cardinal de Silvestri's answer to ASV, CC, Doc. No. 51. Italian (1 page).

To: Monsignor Angelo Quaglia
Secretary of the Holy Congregation of the
     Council, etc., etc., etc.
Rome, December 12, 1860

I, the undersigned Cardinal, hasten to inform Your Most Illustrious and Reverend Excellency that the printed documentation concerning the marriage case from Zhitomir, presented for discussion in the Holy Congregation on September 22, is still in my possession.

I take advantage of this occasion to renew the expression of my particular esteem and consideration and, as I bow to kiss your hands with true affection, I remain,
Your Most Illustrious and Reverend Excellency's truest servant,

Pietro, Cardinal de Silvestri

Mons[igno]r <Angelo> Quaglia
Seg[reta]rio della S[anta] Cong[regazio]ne
del Concilio etc. etc. etc.
Roma 12 Dicembre 1860

Lo Scrivente Cardinale si fa premura di significare alla S[ignoria] V[ostra] Ill[ustrissi]ma e R[everendissi]ma che la posizione a stampa concernente la causa *Zytomirien: Matrimonii* sottoposta all'esame della S[anta] Congregazione del giorno 22 Settembre si trova tuttora presso il sottoscritto.

Profitta chi scrive di questo incontro per rinnovarLe i sensi di particolare stima e considerazione con cui Le bacia di vero cuore le mani e si rassegna
Di V[ost]ra S[ignoria] Ill[ustrissi]ma e
     R[everendissi]ma
Servitor Vero,
P<ietro> Card[inal] de Silvestri

Document No. 58. December 21, 1860. Note by Cardinal Cagiano De Azevedo to Quaglia about the meeting of December 22. Italian (1 page).

To: The Most reverend and Illustrious

    Monsignor Angelo Quaglia

    Secretary of the Holy Congregation of the Council

<The Vatican,> December 21, 1860

My Most Esteemed Monsignor:

    Being deeply involved in Holy Penance, I have not been able to study all the cases that tomorrow will be brought before the Holy Congregation of the Council. But I have studied the one with the *Pontifical Secret*. Now I would ask as a favor, should you obtain permission to do so from the Prefect, that you present this case last since I shall come in rather late in order to gain the time to complete the rescripts from tonight's audience.

With the expression of my customary highest
    esteem, I am

Your Servant,

Antonio <Maria> Cardinal Cagiano <de
    Azevedo>

All'Ill[ustrissi]mo e R[everendissi]mo Sig[nor]
Mons[igno]r <Angelo> Quaglia
Seg[retari]o <della Santa Congregazione> del
    Concilio
<Vaticano,> li 21 D[icem]bre 1860
Mons[ignor]e Mio Sti[matisssi]mo

    Le gravissime occupazioni della S[anta] Penit[enz]a non mi han permesso di studiare tutte le cause che domani si propongono innanzi la S[anta] C[ongregazione] del Concilio. Ho studiato bensì quella col *Segreto Pontificio*. Ora la prego, ottenutone il permesso dall'E[minentissi]mo Prefetto, proporla in ultimo, venendo io più tardi per aver tempo a terminare i rescritti dell'udienza di questa sera.

Sono colla solita perfetta stima
Suo
Servitor V[er]o
Ant[onio] <Maria> Card[inal] Cagiano <de
    Azevedo>

Document No. 59. December 22, 1860. Printed documentation for the meeting of the Holy Congregation of the Council, consisting of

A) Position Paper about the case together with the decision in Carolyne's favor and the voting record, written in Quaglia's hand. Italian (4 pages).

Diocese of Zhitomir
Marriage Case
December 22, 1860

    By order of His Holiness, Our Lord, and with the requirement of Pontifical Secrecy, the present case was presented to the Congregation on a separate document on the 22nd of September of the present year, now coming to the end.

Zytumerien
Matrimonii
Die 22 Decembris 1860

    Per ordine della Santità di Nostro Signore, e con legge del Segreto Pontificio si propose in foglio separato la presente controversia nella Congregazione tenuta a dì 22 settembre dello spirante anno.

After examining the question, Your Eminences deliberated that there was no impediment to the execution, on the part of Monsignor the Bishop of Fulda, of the sentence issued by the Mohilow Commission, which declared the marriage contracted by Princess Carolyne Iwanowska with Prince Nicholas Wittgenstein to be null and void.

His Holiness, Our Lord, in the audience granted on the 24th of last month, was informed of the decision of the Holy Congregation and the Holy Father deigned to approve it and ordered that, through the offices of Monsignor Nuncio in Vienna, the aforementioned Monsignor Bishop of Fulda be notified of it. This was done in a letter dated the following day.

After the autumn holidays, however, we received two dispatches from Monsignor Nuncio; in the first of them, in answer to the communication received, he said he felt compelled, on account of the gravity of the matter, to voice some considerations on this question. He says specifically:

"I am not aware of the details of the momentous trial whose outcome was a declaration to the effect that the marriage of Prince Wittgenstein and Princess Iwanowska was null and void. I and many others only know that the sentence issued in the first instance by Diocese of Zhitomir had been in favor of the validity of this marriage.

"At a first glance, therefore, it would seem that the prerequisites established in the Bull *Dei miseratione*, which requires that there be at least two analogous sentences in order to proceed to the dissolution of the marriage bond, have not been observed.

"Let us add, moreover, the fact that the Princess would be making use of the permission to marry again she has now been granted by marrying Monsieur Liszt, a Hungarian very well known in his country. Now it was precisely in Hungary that there were, and perhaps even now there are, such scandalous instances of sentences of annulment all too easily granted by those

Le Eminenze Loro preso ad esame l'affare furono di avviso nulla ostare a che la Sentenza pronunciata dalla Commissione di Mohilow, con cui si dichiarava la nullità del Matrimonio contratto dalla Principessa Carolina Iwanowska col Principe Nicola Wittgenstein, si rendesse esecutoria da Monsig[nor] Vescovo di Fulda.

L'opinamento del S[anto] Consesso fu portato a cognizione della Santità di N[ostro] S[ignore] nell'udienza del giorno 24 dello scorso mese, ed il S[anto] Padre si degnò approvarlo, ordinando che per mezzo di Monsig[nor] Nunzio di Vienna se ne desse partecipazione al prelodato Monsig[nor] Vecovo di Fulda, come fu eseguito con lettera in data del giorno sussequente.

Per altro dopo le ferie autunnali si sono ricevuti due dispacci da parte di Monsig[nor] Nunzio, nel primo dei quali, in risposta alla partecipazione avuta, dice reputarsi obbligato a comunicare alcune riflessioni in proposito, attesa la gravità dell'affare.

Egli così si esprime: "A me sono ignote le particolarità dell'importante processo, il cui risultato si fu la dichiarazione di nullità del matrimonio tra il Principe Wittgenstein e la Principessa Iwanowska. Soltanto si conosce da me, e da moltissimi altri, che la Sentenza nella prima istanza presso la Curia Vescovile di Zytomir era stata favorevole alla validità del medesimo matrimonio.

A prima vista adunque sembrerebbe che in quest'affare non si fosse strettamente osservata la regola prescritta nella Bolla *Dei miseratione*, la quale esige almeno due sentenze conformi per lo scioglimento del vincolo matrimoniale.

Si aggiunga l'avvertenza che la Signora Principessa farebbe uso della facoltà concessa di passare a seconde nozze collo sposare il Sig[nor] Liszt, ungherese notissimo nella sua patria. Ora per l'appunto nell'Ungheria accadevano e forse non sono ancora cessati gli scandali di Sentenze pronunciate dalle Curie Vescovili che sciogievano con grande facilità il vincolo matrimo-

Dioceses on the strength of the argument of violence and intimidation that the Holy Congregation of the Inquisition felt compelled, at the time, to send to those bishops special instructions from Rome on how to proceed in problematic cases of this sort.

"One can well imagine the unfavorable impression these bishops will receive from this permission to marry again granted to Princess Carolyne Iwanowska."

In consideration of these factors, Monsignor Nuncio requested that these notions be humbly brought to the attention of His Holiness and that pertinent instructions be sent directly to the Bishop of Fulda; he would be prepared to transmit them to him.

In the second dispatch, he forwarded *confidentially* a letter pertaining to this case that was sent to him by Monsignor the Bishop of Fulda; therein he requested that we "take note also, with particular attention, of the warnings sent by this prelate about the absolute necessity of using every possible caution lest, on this account, the authority of the Holy See be discredited among the Catholics of Germany who live surrounded by Protestants." He concluded that he would be awaiting, at any rate, "eventual instructions on how to proceed in order that this sad business be disposed of without causing scandal and without offending the dignity of this Holy Congregation."

In the aforementioned letter from Monsignor the Bishop of Fulda, the latter, aroused by a telegram from the Princess who was informing him of the favorable outcome of her case, says as follows:

"I cannot truly believe that, in Rome, men endowed with so much prudence and integrity could approve something that is not quite consistent with the law and is such that, at this unfortunate time, it may just provide the occasion, as far as our enemies and the heretics are concerned, to question somehow the firm determination to uphold the indissolubility of the marriage sacrament that the Holy Apostolic See exhibited for so many centuries. The gravity of the case requires, therefore, that everything be reviewed accurately, and I'll be quite happy to take advantage of Your Excellency's humaneness and send to Vienna that letter as soon as I receive it, in order that Your

niale *ex capite vis et metus*, tanto che la S[anta] Congregazione dell'Inquisizione da Roma ha dovuto inviare a quei Vescovi una speciale istruzione sul modo di procedere in somiglianti difficilissime cause.

"Si può ben immaginare l'impressione che i predetti Vescovi risentiranno dalla licenza accordata alla Principessa Carolina Iwanowska di passare a seconde nozze."

In conseguenza delle anzidette cose Monsignor Nunzio si faceva a pregare che si umiliassero alla Santità di N[ostro] S[ignore] le precedenti osservazioni; e che le analoghe istruzioni fossero inviate direttamente a Monsignor Vescovo di Fulda esibendosi egli pronto a farne la trasmissione.

Coll'altro dispaccio rimetteva *riservatamente* una lettera di Monsignor Vescovo di Fulda a lui diretta, relativa a questa causa, con preghiera "di voler notare con particolare attenzione le avvertenze esposte dal medesimo prelato intorno all'estrema necessità di adoperare ogni maggior possibile cautela affinché l'autorità della S[anta] Sede non soffra per questo riguardo discapito presso i Cattolici della Germania conviventi co' protestanti;" e conchiudeva che del resto avrebbe atteso " le opportune istruzioni sul modo da tenersi, acciocché questo infelice negozio possa aggiustarsi senza scandalo e senza offesa alla dignità di questa S[anta] Congregazione."

Nella suddetta lettera poi Monsignor Vescovo di Fulda prendendo motivo da un telegramma speditogli dalla Principessa a fine di partecipargli la favorevole risoluzione ottenuta si esprime in questi termini:

"Vix vel ne vix quidem credere possum Romae a Viris tanta prudentia et integritate praeditis quidquam fieri, quod cum jure non bene cohaereat, quoque specie tenus hominibus inimicis aut Haereticis occasio forte praebeatur notissimae illi per saecula Sanctae Sedis Apostolicae in tuenda Sacramenti indissolubilitate firmitati hoc funestissimo tempore vel aliquid detrahendi. Unde causae gravitas postulat ut omnia accurate discutiantur, lubentissimeque Excellentiae Vestrae humanitate usurus litteras, ubi primum accepero, Viennam transmittam, ut Excellentia Vestra instrumenti genuinitatem et veritatem pro

Excellency may duly verify the authenticity and truth of that document and most graciously communicate to me what you think should be done."

Given these questions, we deemed it necessary to consult the Pope on what needed to be done to bring this issue to a conclusion. The Holy Father was appraised of the situation, and the aforementioned observations were submitted to him. His Holiness ordered that the issue be submitted again to the scrutiny of the Holy Congregation and that the proviso of Pontifical Secrecy be maintained.

As Your Eminences are again requested to issue an opinion on the matter, you will be able to review the question on the basis of the documentation previously received; besides that, additional notions and a summary are provided here to facilitate your examination.

Therefore, etc.

The Second Judgement of the Holy Congregation of the Council

The Holy Congregation, in answer to the above, resolved that *"The Sentence of the Archbishop of Mohilow be executed."*

Of the Most Eminent Cardinals of the Congregation present, their Eminences <Antonio> Cagiano <de Azevedo>, <Gerolamo> D'Andrea, <Giuseppe> Milesi <Pironi Ferretti>, <Pietro> Marini, and <Pietro de> Silvestri fully agreed with the resolution.

His Eminence <Giuseppe> Bofondi expressed some difficulties, but he, too, agreed.

His Eminence <Prospero> Caterini, Prefect, expressed disagreement on the basis of the considerations presented in the printed documentation for this second review of the question.

His Eminence <Vincenzo> Santucci remained in doubt.

His Eminence <Teodulfo> Mertel persisted in the opinion expressed in the previous resolution.

The Holy Father, after receiving a precise and detailed report, upheld the vote of the majority and confirmed the above stated resolution in the audience of January 7, 1861.

munere suo recognoscat, et quid censeat agendum, gratiosissime mecum communicet."

In questo stato di cose si stimò necessario d'interpellare nuovamente l'Oracolo Pontificio su ciò che avesse a farsi per terminare questa pendenza. Se ne fece quindi relazione al S[anto] Padre, Cui si sottoposero le suddette osservazioni; e Sua Santità ordinò che l'affare di nuovo si proponesse all'esame della S[anta] Congregazione ferma rimanendo la legge del *segreto*.

Essendo pertanto le E[minenze] L[oro] invitate nuovamente a dare un parere in proposito, sono pregate di riassumere la storia di questa controversia dai precedenti fogli; ai quali si aggiungono qui annessi alcuni altri fogli di osservazioni corredate di un Sommario addizionale per facilitarne l'esame.
Laonde etc.

Il Secondo Giudizio della Santa Congregazione del Concilio

La S[anta] Congregazione opinò rispondere *"Sententiam Archiep[iscop]i Mohilowiensis esse exequendam."*

Degli E[minentissi]mi Cardinali intervenuti alla Cong[regazion]e gli E[minentissi]mi <Antonio> Cagiano <de Azevedo>, <Gerolamo> D'Andrea, <Giuseppe> Milesi, <Pietro> Marini e <Pietro de> Sivestri convennero pienamente nella risoluzione.

L'E[minentissi]mo <Giuseppe> Bofondi esternò qualche difficoltà, e quindi convenne ancor esso.

L'E[minentissi]mo <Prospero> Caterini, Prefetto, fu di contrario parere riportandosi alle riflessioni nei fogli stampati per questa seconda proposizione.

L'E[minentissi]mo <Vincenzo> Santucci rimase dubitativo.

L'E[minentissi]mo <Teodulfo> Mertel persisteva nel parere esternato nella precedente risoluzione.

Il S[anto] Padre, a cui nella udienza del 7 gennaro 1861 ne fu fatta esatta e dettagliata relazione, attenendosi alla maggioranza dei voti, confermò la sudd[et]ta risoluzione.

B) Enclosure No. 1. Printed observations on the merit of the case.
Italian (8 pages).

Diocese of Zhitomir
Marriage Case
Observations to facilitate the examination of the present case.
ON THE MERIT OF THIS CASE.

The records of the trial held in Zhitomir about the nullity of the marriage in question are not available.

Therefore we have no knowledge of the proofs presented in favor of nullity. We do not know whether a Defender of the Marriage Bond was nominated. We ignore whether the petitioning Princess was subjected to the usual interrogations to check her assertions against the depositions of the witnesses. We do not even know whether the Prince, a party most interested in this case, was summoned and what he may have said. According to the resolution passed by the Consistory of Mohilow in 1852, it seems that only witnesses produced by the Princess were questioned and it is not known how the questioning was conducted and whether objections were raised to questions leading the witnesses. It does not seem that there was a public interrogation of those present at the wedding, like the parson himself and those serving officially as witnesses at the wedding. These people could have testified as to whether the Princess was sad or happy. The same applies to those people who, in the course of those twelve years, would have been frequent visitors and would visit the home of the couple as guests or would come on the occasion of christenings. They could have produced information as to whether or not the violence and intimidation continued after the wedding.

Even the sentence issued at Zhitomir in the first instance is not available; it could have clarified some questions in the absence of the records of the trial.

Assuming that the fear did cease after the marriage, and that it gave way to acceptance of the circumstances with free cohabitation and normal and spontaneous conjugal habits, would it have been necessary in this case to contract a new marriage before a priest and witnesses? The Consistory, relying on the authority of Monacelli, who in turn quotes Fagnano, issued in 1852 an affirmative opinion. Now what Monacelli wrote is true, but not

Zytumerien
<Causa> Matrimonii

Foglio di osservazioni per facilitare l'esame della presente Causa.
SUL MERITO.

Manca in Posizione il Processo compilato in Zytomir sulla nullità del matrimonio di cui si tratta.

Quindi s'ignorano le prove addotte per la nullità del matrimonio. Non si sa se vi sia stata la deputazione del Difensore del matrimonio. Se la Principessa attrice sia stata assog<g>ettata ai consueti interrogatori per confrontare i suoi detti colle deposizioni dei Testimonj. Nemmeno si conosce se il principe, parte interessatissima, sia stato chiamato in giudizio, e che cosa abbia risposto. A quanto disse il Concistoro di Mohilow nel suo opinamento del 1852, pare che siano stati sottoposti ad esame i Testimonj soltanto indotti dalla Principessa, né se ne conosce con precisione il tenore, né se sussista l'eccezione delle domande sug<g>estive. Non pare che siano state esaminate almeno d'officio le persone intervenute agli sponsali, né il Parroco, né i Testimonj presenti alla celebrazione del matrimonio, i quali avrebbero potuto testificare sulla giocondità o mestizia della Principessa. Anche le persone che nel decorso del dodicennio, ovvero all'occasione dei battesimi o d'inviti, frequentarono la casa degli sposi, potevano somministrare notizie per conoscere se la violenza ed il timore durò(sic) anche dopo le nozze.

Manca perfino la sentenza di prima istanza emanata dalla Curia di Zitomir, la quale nella mancanza del Processo avrebbe potuto spargere maggior lume.

Posto che il timore dopo il matrimonio fosse cessato, e fosse succeduta la connivenza, la libera coabitazione, lo spontaneo uso coniugale, sarebbe stato necessario di contrarre di nuovo il matrimonio avanti il Parroco e Testimonj? L'opinamento del Concistoro esternato nel 1852 fu per l'affermativa appoggiandosi all'autorità del Monacelli, il quale cita il Fagnano. Ora è vero quanto scrisse il Monacelli; ma egli non fu del tutto esatto. Il Fa-

totally accurate. Fagnano, in his commentary to the Chapter *Is qui fidem, de sponsal.*, No. 14, makes a distinction between a situation in which violence and intimidation are publicly known and one in which violence and intimidation are hidden and private. He writes: "*If a marriage contracted before the Church was not valid on account of intimidation and the impediment was not known, then it could become validated by the mutual consent of the spouses as formally declared by Pius V. Now, the Bishop of Geraci doubted that a marriage could be deemed valid today, the form prescribed by the Council of Trent not being otherwise observed, if such a marriage, contracted and consummated in fear, though the form stipulated by the Council of Trent may have been respected in all other matters, was later made whole by the mutual consent of the spouses and their spontaneous cohabitation. Cardinal Carafa noted that, if the impediment of fear was not known, there would be no necessity to contract another marriage with a new ceremony, since that was ritually performed in the first contract. But if the impediment was evident and known, the vows should be repeated in order to preserve the form of the Tridentine Council.*" Pirhing., Decretales, Book 4, Chapter 1, section 4, No. 123, agrees: "*A marriage contracted because of grave intimidation is confirmed by subsequent copulation practiced without any more fear, completely freely and out of marital affection ... And it is also true that, after the Council of Trent, if the marriage had been contracted through intimidation before a priest and witnesses who were not aware of the hidden impediment, it was then validated by subsequent spontaneous copulation once the fear was removed.*" This was also stated in a document from this Holy Congregation, Diocese of Ceneda, dated April 10, 1723, at the paragraph *Exclusa* where it is stated that "*There is no necessity to renew one's consent before a priest and witnesses according to the form prescribed by the Council because, when the impediment is hidden but the form of the Council has been preserved, even though the marriage is invalidated from the start, it is not necessary to repeat the marriage vows to validate it.*" Also in the marriage case of the Diocese of Luni and Sarzana, dated September 17, 1795, at paragraph Uno, we read: "*In one instance only, an invalid marriage can become valid through consummation and other subsequent actions, if the case for invalidity is brought about by a hidden lack of consent, for the Church cannot deliberate on what*

gnano, nel suo commento al Cap[itolo] *Is qui fidem, de sponsal[ibus]* No. 14, distingue il caso della violenza e del timore pubblico e manifesto dall'altro del timore o violenza incussa occultamente. Ecco le di lui parole: "*Si matrimonium in facie Ecclesiae contractum esset nullum ex causa metus, et impedimentum esset occultum, tunc mutuo consensu conjugum convalesceret ex declaratione Pii V. Dubitavit namque Episcopus Hieracen[sis] si matrimonium contractum et consummatum fuerit per metum, servata in caeteris forma Tridentini Concilii, et postea conjugum mutuo consensu et spontanea cohabitatione convaluerit, an hodie illud censeatur validum non aliter servata forma Concilii Tridentini? Card[inal] Carafa haec adnotavit: si impedimentum ex metu praesupposito occultum sit, non esse opus iterum contrahere repetitis solemnitatibus alias rite adhibitis in primo contractu. Si autem impedimentum esset manifestum, matrimonium de novo contrahendum esse servata forma Concilii Tridentini.*" Ne conviene anche il Pihring., lib. 4. Decret *tit. 1 sect. 4 n. 123*: "*Matrimonium metu gravi contractum confirmatur per sequentem copulam, deposito metu, omnino libere et affectu maritali habitam... Idque etiam verum est post Concilium Tridentinum, si prius matrimonium coram Parocho et testibus ignorantibus occultum impedimentum incussi metus legitime contractum fuit, et deposito metu per subsequentem spontaneam copulam ratificatum fuit.*" E fu anche notato nel foglio di questa S[anta] C[ongregazione] nella *Caeneten. 10* aprile *1723*, par. *Exclusa*, ivi "*Exclusa necessitate renovandi consensum ad formam Concilii coram parocho et testibus, quia quando impedimentum est occultum, et in matrimonio licet nulliter a principio contracto servata est forma Concilii, non est opus pro revalidatione iterum contrahere repetitis solemnitatibus.*" E nella *Lunen. Sarzanen. Matrimonii 17 Sept. 1795* al par.*Uno* si legge: "*Uno casu matrimonium nullum convalescere potest per consummationem aliosque subsequentes actus, si res sit de nullitate ex defectu consensus occulto, nam de occultis non judicat Ecclesia. Ubi vero de nullitate agitur ex defectu publico ..... conveniunt Doctores omnes, novum omnino praestandum esse consensum novamque requiri praesentiam Parochi et testium.*"

is hidden. But if a case for invalidity is made because of a public lack of consent ... all the authorities agree that an entirely new consent must be provided, and the presence of a priest and witnesses is required again."

In the present case, assuming the gravity of the intimidation at the moment of celebrating the wedding, was the fear and, therefore, the lack of consent known or was it hidden? If hidden, did it stop because of a cohabitation that lasted twelve years and involved conjugal acts? The Princess states that her fear and revulsion persisted as long as her father was alive. But, since the fifth, sixth, and seventh witnesses (See Summary 2, page 7) declared that her father used to say that he had committed an unpardonable deed in forcing his daughter to marry, it would be possible to infer that he had ceased to impose any fear in her. And, supposing that, afterwards, the cohabitation with her husband and the performance of conjugal duties had been free and characterised by conjugal affection, would this be sufficient to validate the marriage? One would need to know, moreover, whether the Princess was aware that her marriage was not valid, but, on this question, there is no evidence, either in favor or against.

EXTRINSIC FACTORS PERTAINING TO THIS CASE.

Benedict XIV, in his widely known Bull *Dei miseratione*, expressly requires two analogous sentences stating that a marriage is null and void; moreover, before the two parties can be permitted to contract another marriage, the sentences must not have been appealed by either of the two interested parties or by the Defender of the marriage bond.

Are there, in the present case, two such analogous sentences?

It is doubtless clear that the Zhitomir sentence declared that the marriage was valid.

What can one say of the one pronounced in the second instance by the Archbishopric of Mohilow in 1852? Obviously the Princess deemed it contrary to her interests and took it to be a confirmation of the first; thus, she presented an appeal, as far as it is known, and kept her peace until 1859. Then she started again an action and, through her agent, she requested the new Archbishop to review and judge her case again. But the new Metropolitan of Mohilow, on June 13,

Nel caso presente supposta la gravità del timore nell'atto della celebrazione del matrimonio, il timore ed il dissenso fu palese ovvero occulto? Se occulto, questo cessò colla coabitazione continuata per dodici anni e con gli atti conjugali? La Principessa afferma che il timore e il dissenso continuò finché visse il Padre: ma avendo il 5°, 6° e 7° testimonio (Somm[ario] 2, pag[ina] 7) deposto che il Padre diceva di aver commesso un fallo imperdonabile coll'aver forzato la figlia al matrimonio, si potrebbe congetturare che avesse cessato d'incuterle alcun timore. E nella supposizione che di poi la convivenza col marito e la prestazione degli ossequj matrimoniali fosse stata libera e con affetto coniugale, basterebbe per dirsi convalidato il matrimonio? Bisognerebbe anche sapere se la Principessa conosceva la nullità del suo matrimonio: su ciò peraltro non si hanno argomenti né favorevoli né contrarii.

SULL'ESTRINSECO.

Benedetto XIV nella sua notissima Costituzione *Dei miseratione* vuole espressamente due sentenze conformi che dichiarino nullo il matrimonio, e che niuna delle parti interessate, e nemmeno il Difensore del matrimonio abbia interposto l'appello, pria che le parti possano passare a seconde nozze.

Nel presente caso si hanno due sentenze conformi?

E' indubitato, e non si controverte che la sentenza di Zytomir dichiarò valido il matrimonio.

Che dovrà dirsi di quella pronunciata in grado di appelo dalla Curia Arcivescovile di Mohilow nel 1852? La Principessa la reputò a se contraria e quindi confermatoria della prima, per cui non appellò, per quanto sembra, e si pose in silenzio fino al 1859. Finalmente si scosse, e per mezzo del suo Agente, si rivolse al nuovo Arcivescovo dimandando che la causa fosse riveduta e giudicata di nuovo: ma il nuovo Metropolitano di Mohilow ai 13 giugno 1859

1859 (see Summary No. 3), responded that it was not within his faculties to deal with the case, since "there have already been two decisions confirmed by the Bishop, my predecessor."

Nevertheless the Princess, or better her Solicitor, now states that the 1852 sentence is not a confirmation of that of Zhitomir, but actually rescinds it. In her Petition (Summary No. 4) she takes it for granted that, in 1852, the Consistory of Mohilow *"granted her a sentence in favor of annulment of her marriage insofar as it was contracted through violence and grave intimidation."* However, she hastens to add that "the sentence was not confirmed by the Vicar General of the late Metropolitan." Now the Vicar General was a member of the Consistory as a consultant. How then could he confirm or rescind? Even in her Presentation of the case (Summary No. 1), she pretends that the 1852 sentence pronounced her marriage to be null and void, so that sentence together with the other, issued in the present year 1860 in favor of annulment, would provide the two analogous sentences prescribed by the Benedictine Bull. (See the aforementioned Summary, pages 5, paragraph 6 *Se poi*). As a corroboration of this interpretation, her Solicitor states unequivocally that the Archbishop of Mohilow is the Primate of all Russia, and that, therefore, the Consistory of Mohilow decides in the second instance without the presence of the Archbishop, and, finally, that the Archbishop, as the Primate, decides in the third instance. This whole argument is set up for the sole purpose of allowing him to conclude that since in 1852, the majority of the Consistory of Mohilow voted for annulment with the sole exception of the Vicar General presiding over the Consistory, the latter having expressed an opinion in favor of the validity of the marriage, one should not attribute any importance to the fact that the Metropolitan approved the opinion of the Vicar General, but should pay attention only to the vote of the majority of the members of the Consistory. In this guise, then, the sentence of 1852 could be seen as one rescinding the one of Zhitomir.

To correct this distortion of facts and ideas, one can observe that

1. The Holy See attributes to the Archbishop of Mohilow neither the title nor the function of Primate, nor does the Archbishop himself appropriate it.

(Somm[ario] N. 3) rispose che non era sua facoltà di occuparsene perchè "il y a eu déjà deux décisions confirmées par l'Evêque mon prédécesseur."

Ciò non ostante, ora la Principessa, o meglio, il suo Difensore sostiene che la sentenza del 1852 non sia una confermatoria di quella di Zytomir, ma una revocatoria. Difatti nella Supplica (Somm[ario] N. 4) pone per indubitato ch'essa dal Concistoro di Mohilow nel 1852 *"sententiam nullitatis praefati matrimonii veluti ex vi et gravi metu contracti obtinuit"* sebbene aggiunga che *"a Vicario Generali defuncti Metropolitani confirmata non fuit."* Il Vicario Generale faceva parte del Concistoro, e perciò aveva il voto consultivo. Come dunque poteva confermare o revocare? Anche nel foglio delle sue deduzioni (Som[mario] N. 1) pretende che la sentenza del 1852 abbia pronunciato la nullità del matrimonio, qual sentenza unita all'altra emanata nel corrente anno 1860 per la nullità formerebbero le due conformi prescritte dalla Benedettina (cit. Som. pag. 5 par. 6 *Se poi*). A corroborare questo suo divisamento il Difensore dà per certo che l'Arcivescovo di Mohilow sia il *Primate* di tutte le Russie: che quindi il Concistoro di Mohilow giudichi da sé solo e senza l'Arcivescovo in grado di appello: e che l'Arcivescovo come Primate giudichi in terzo grado. Tutta questa macchina è fabbricata onde poter conchiudere che siccome la maggior parte del Concistoro di Mohilow nel 1852 opinò per la nullità ad esclusione del Vicario Generale Presidente del Concistoro, il quale espresse il suo sentimento per la validità del matrimonio, così non si debba valutare l'atto del Metropolitano che approvò il parere del Vicario Generale, ma soltanto la maggioranza dei Componenti il Concistoro, cosicché il giudicato del 1852 revocherebbe la sentenza <di> Zytomir.

A rettificare questo stravolgimento di vocaboli e d'idee si osserva

1. Che la S[anta] Sede non attribuisce all'Arcivescovo di Mohilow né il titolo né il grado di Primate, e che nemmeno lo stesso Arcivescovo se lo appropria.

2. The Archbishop decides in the second instance on cases previously adjudicated by his Suffragans (see Additional Summary, No. 1, Paragraph *La première*).

3. Therefore, cases at the third level of appeal are not brought before the Archbishop, but before the Holy See as prescribed by the normal dispositions of Canon Law and by the articles of the Concordate with the Holy See approved as early as July 2, 1848 (See the aforementioned Additional Summary at paragraph *Reste*), as is evident from the Dispatch from the Office of the Secretary of State (Additional Summary No. 2).

4. "*The Bishop is the sole judge and administrator of the ecclesiastical affairs of his Diocese, etc.*" This is stated in the articles agreed to by the Holy See and the Emperor of Russia; see specifically article 13, published in the collection *Acta Pii IX Pontificis Maximi, page 119. This principle, with respect to marriage cases, conforms fully to the deliberations of the Council of Trent, session 24, de reformationibus*, Chapter 25, where it is established that "reviews of marriage cases will be within the sole jurisdiction of the Bishop."

5. If article 14 of the Concordate, as stated in paragraph 2, prescribes that, among other things, "*marriage questions pertaining to proving marriage validity, certifications of birth, etc., must be subjected to the deliberations of Diocesan Consistories*," it is also beyond dispute, according to article 15, page 123, that "*these questions are decided by the Bishop after they have been examined by the Consistory which has, therefore, only a consultative role*"; moreover, "*the Bishop is not at all required to give reasons for his own deliberations, even in those cases where his opinion differs from that of the Consistory*" so that the judgement of the Bishop is the relevant ele-ment and provides the definitive sentence even when all the members of the diocesan Consistory hold an opposite view.

In view of these general and specific legal principles, it becomes clear that the Solicitor for the Princess, in Summary No. 1, pages 2 and 3, was quite wrong in arguing that, in 1852, the Consistory of Mohilow was in fact the judge in the second instance of appeal, and that the Metropolitan, in following the contrary opinion of the Vicar General, came to judge the case in the third instance. It is true that, in 1852, the case

2. Che l'Arcivescovo giudica in secondo grado le cause preventivamente giudicate dai suoi suffraganei (Somm[ario] add[izionale] N. 1, par. *La première*).

3. Che quindi in terza istanza le cause non sono deferite all'Arcivescovo, ma bensì alla S[anta] Sede a forma delle comuni disposizioni canoniche e degli articoli convenuti colla S[anta] Sede fin dal 2 luglio 1848 (Somm[ario], par. *Reste*) e Dispaccio della Segreteria di Stato (Somm[ario] add[izionale] N. 2).

4. Che "*Episcopus est solus judex et administrator negotiorum Ecclesiasticorum suae Diocesis etc.*" giusta gli articoli convenuti tra la S[anta] sede e l'Imperatore delle Russie all'articolo XII riportati nella Raccolta intitolata *Acta Pii IX P[ontificis] M[aximi] pag. 119. Lo che quanto alle cause matrimoniali è pienamente conforme al Concilio di Trento, il quale alla sess. 24 de reform.*, cap. 25 stabilisce che "*causae matrimoniales.... Episcopi tantum examini et jurisdictioni relinquantur.*"

5. Che se all'art[icolo] 14 di detta Convenzione viene prescritto "*subjici debent deliberationibus Consistorii Dioecesani* (fra gli altri affari anche) *causae matrimoniales, probationis legitimitatis matrimoniorum, acta nativitatis etc.*" come al par. 2, è peraltro anche indubitato a forma dell'art[icolo] 15 pag. 123 che "*praedicta negotia decernuntur ab Episcopo postquam a Consistorio examinata fuerunt, quod tamen consultationis partes tantummodo retinet;*" che anzi, "*Episcopus minime tenetur afferre rationes suae sententiae, illis etiam in casibus, in quibus ejus opinio ab illa Consistorii discreparet*" talché il giudizio del Vescovo è quello che prevale e costituisce la sentenza definitiva ancorché tutti li componenti il Concistoro Diocesano fossero di contrario avviso.

Presso questi principj di diritto comune e particolare apparisce manifestamente quanto male a proposito il Difensore della Principessa nel *Somm[ario] n. 1 pag. 2 et 3* pretenda che il Concistoro di Mohilow fosse nel 1852 il vero giudice di appello in secondo grado, e che il Metropolitano seguendo il parere contrario del Presidente dello stesso Concistoro venisse a *giudicare in terza istanza*. E' vero che nel 1852 por-

being brought before the Archbishop "as if in the second instance," he delegated dealing with it to the Consistory as one can read in the sentence report (Summary No. 2); it is also certain, however, that the Consistory was not called upon to adjudicate, but to express "its opinion," and with the stated reservation that such an opinion be presented to him for his final decision. Nor could it be otherwise since, as observed above, the members of the Consistory are not the judges in a case, but act as advisors to the Bishop. The Bishop is the sole judge; he is bound to consult with the Consistory, but is not bound to follow their advice, and can, therefore, even pronounce a sentence contrary to their opinion. This is indeed what happened in 1852, for the Archbishop, rather than abiding by the opinion in favor of annulment issued by the majority of the members of the Consistory, followed the opinion of the President of the Consistory who expressed himself in favor of validity.[36] By approving it, he came to issue a definitive sentence in the second instance in favor of validity.

If this be the case, and there is hardly any room for doubt, it follows that the sentence under discussion was a confirmation of the first. Therefore, there were two analogous sentences for the validity of the marriage; it could actually be said that the issue was judicially settled, since it does not appear that the Princess requested an appeal and, even less, that she presented one, since she kept her peace from 1852 to 1859.

At any rate, the fact is that the Princess succeeded in getting her case reviewed and definitively adjudicated by the New Archbishop of Mohilow. It is also a fact that the Archbishop, on February 24, 1860, pronounced his definitive sentence in full agreement with the wishes of the Princess. It remains to be seen, now, what might be the best course to follow, i.e., whether the case should be reopened in order to obtain another sentence on it, or the execution of the last sentence could and should be permitted.

tata la causa avanti l'Arcivesco *comme en seconde istance*, egli rimise l'affare al Concistoro come si legge nella narrativa della Sentenza (Somm[ario] N. 2): è peraltro anche certo che la remissione fu fatta al Concistoro non perché giudicasse, ma sibbene perché esternasse *son opinion*, e con l'espressa riserva che siffatto opinamento *lui sera présentée pour dernière décision*. Né poteva esser diversamente, giacché come si è di sopra osservato i membri componenti il Concistoro non sono i giudici delle cause, ma soltanto i consiglieri del vescovo. Il Vescovo é *solus judex*: egli è tenuto a consultare il Concistoro, ma non è tenuto a seguirne il consiglio, e quindi può pronunciare una sentenza anche contraria all'opinamento del Concistoro. E così difatti accadde nel 1852, dappoiché l'Arcivescovo anziché seguire l'opinamento della maggior parte dei membri del Concistoro Diocesano che stavano per la nullità del matrimonio, abbracciò il parere del Presidente del Concistoro, il quale opinò per la <validità>, ed approvandolo, venne a pronunciare la sua sentenza definitiva in secondo grado di giurisdizione a favore della validità.

Se ciò sussiste, come pare non possa dubitarsene, ne siegue che la sentenza in discorso fu confermatoria della prima, talché si ebbero due sentenze conformi per la validità del matrimonio: anzi potrebbe dirsi, si ebbe la cosa giudicata, giacché non co<n>sta che la Principessa interponesse l'appello, e molto meno che lo proseguisse, avendo dal 1852 al 1859 usato un perfetto silenzio.

Comunque però ciò sia, sta in fatto che la Principessa ottenne che la sua causa fosse riassunta e giudicata definitivamente dal novello Arcivescovo di Mohilow: sta anche in fatto che l'Arcivescovo li 24 febbraro anno 1860 pronunciò la sua sentenza definitiva pienamente favorevole ai desideri della Principessa. Ora resta a vedersi qual partito convenga prendere, vale a dire se debbasi di nuovo esaminare la causa per avere un'altra sentenza in merito, ovvero si possa e si debba permettere l'esecuzione dell'ultima sentenza.

---

[36]Nullity, not validity, is in the original, but it is an obvious *lapsus calami*.

The advocate for the Princess argues that the last sentence, insofar as it has been issued by a Judge delegated by the Holy See cannot, for this very reason, be appealed and can, therefore, be executed.

It would seem, however, that he may have been wrong both legally and factually. Factually, 1) because the Judge pronounced his definitive sentence within the terms of the mandate received, but did not claim the authority to issue a verdict without appeal; 2) because the rescript stating his mandate did not include the clause "*without appeal,*" as would have been necessary in order that the delegated Judge's sentence could become a sentence without appeal. Legally, moreover, because, even if the rescript delegating that Archbishop had contained the clause "without appeal," the husband, had he been involved in the case, would have had the right to appeal, and this would apply as well to the Defender of the marriage bond who should actually have done so. In fact, in his commentary to the Chapter *Pastoralis de Appellat.,* after observing that, in ecclesiastical matters, only the Pope can give someone the faculty to judge without appeal, Fagnano stipulates at No. 1 and following that, nevertheless, an appeal is permitted in some cases. He says: "*By the clause 'without appeal,' any appeal is formally forbidden which is not expressly permitted by law.*" Reiffenstuel, *Decretales,* Book 2, Chapter 28, No. 288, writes: "*There are many instances in which the law clearly permits appeals in spite of the clause 'without appeal'*". Similarly Schmatzgrüber., *Jus Canonicum, de appell.* Chapter 28, No. 29, says that "*the question in No. 3 as to whether appeals are deemed to be forbidden when the Pope delegates a case with the clause 'without appeal' can be answered by saying that this clause removes all appeals, even legitimate ones, unless these are especiallystated and permitted by law... There are many instances of this kind. Therefore, in every case where the law so specifies there is the possibility to appeal.*"

Now, if we presuppose that only the last sentence is in favor of marriage invalidity, it can be appealed. Actually, the Defender of the marriage bond must, at any rate, present an appeal according to the Benedictine *Dei Miseratione.* The latter, at Chapter 8, prescribes that: "*If (for the first time) a verdict is rendered against the validity of a marriage,*

Il Difensore della Principessa sostiene che l'ultima sentenza come emanata da un giudice abilitato dalla S[anta] Sede a giudicare, sia per questo *inappellabile*, e quindi senz'altro in istato di esecuzione.

Se non che parrebbe che il medesimo abbia errato in fatto e in diritto. *In fatto* 1. perché il giudice pronunciò la sua sentenza *definitiva* a forma della commissione ricevuta, ma non si arrogò l'autorità di giudicare *inappellabilmente*; 2. perché nel rescritto di commissione non vi fu apposta la clausola *remota appellatione*, come sarebbe stato necessario ad oggetto che la sentenza del Giudice commissario avesse potuto formare una sentenza inappellabile. *In diritto* poi, giacché fatta anche l'ipotesi che il rescritto di commissione fosse stato munito della clausola *remota appellatione*, nel caso presente avrebbe potuto appellare l'uomo se fosse stato in causa, a avrebbe dovuto d'officio appellare il Difensore del matrimonio. Ed infatti il Fagnano nel commento al cap[itolo] *Pastoralis de appellat.*, dopo di aver osservato che nelle materie ecclesiastiche il solo Sommo Pontefice può commettere il giudizio colla clausola remota appellatione, insegna al N. 1 e seq. che, ciò non ostante, in alcuni casi è permessa l'appellazione. Eccone le parole: "*Per clausulam appellatione remota omnis appellatio prohibetur, quae a jure non est expresse permissa.*" Ed il Reiffenst[uel] lib. 2 *Decret.* tit. 28 N.288 scrive: "*Plures sunt casus, in quibus jure expresse concedente licitum est appellare, haud ostante clausula illa: appellatione remota.*" Similmente Schmatzg[rüber] Jus Can.,de appellat[ione] tit. 28 al N. 29: "*Quaeritur 3. qualis appellatio censeatur esse prohibita quando supremus Princeps causam delegat cum clausula: appellatione remota?*" risponde "*dicendum per huiusmodi clausulam removere appellationes etiam justas, nisi specialiter sint expressae et permissae a jure... Tales autem casus plures inveniuntur. Denique in omni casu, in quo jura simpliciter concedunt appellari posse.*"

Ora partendo dall'ipotesi che l'ultima sentenza soltanto sia per la nullità del matrimonio, la medesima è appellabile, anzi il Difensore del matrimonio deve onninamente interporre l'appello a senso della Benedettina *Dei miseratione* ove al paragrafo 8 si prescrive "*Sin autem contra matrimonii validitatem sententia* (cioè la prima

the Defender must formally present an appeal, within the legally specified time, to the superior court...for we are not at all willing (Paragraph 16) to accept that in any case the marriage bond be deemed dissolved, unless two clearly similar, analogous judgements, resolutions, or sentences have been issued, which neither of the parties involved nor the Defender have any reason to appeal." Indeed, sometimes three analogous sentences in favor of annulment are required, the Pope allowing the party upholding the validity as well as the Defender to appeal the second analogous sentence in favor of annulment. Indeed we read at Par. 11: "For even if the other party appeals the second sentence, or things are such that the Defender cannot, against his conscience, think of acquiescing to it, or the sentence appears to him clearly wrong and not valid; or even if the judgement in the third instance goes against the preceding sentence issued in the second instance in favor of nullity, we wish the case to be reviewed in the third and even the fourth instance, both husband and wife in the meantime being formally forbidden to contract a new marriage." It is, therefore, evident that the definitive sentence issued by the present Archbishop, even if it had been issued with the clause "without appeal," would be subject to appeal because it is the only one of this kind, whereas the Pontiff requires at least two absolutely analogous ones before the spouses can be permitted to contract a new marriage. In the present case, moreover, it is rather remarkable that the two preceding sentences, which presumably upheld the marriage validity, might be rescinded by one sentence only.

These arguments openly show how wise it was to advise the Archbishop of Mohilow, through the offices of the Nuncio in Vienna, that the Defender of the Marriage Bond should present an appeal to the Holy See against the latest sentence. It is very unfortunate that the suggestion was not accepted, since "the Defender of the marriage bond decided to acquiesce to such a sentence" (Summary No. 6, Par. 2). These are the words of Monsignor the Archbishop of Mohilow, who writes without providing any reason for this strange behavior, especially considering the advice he received.

If, therefore, the arguments presented so far by the Princess were deemed insufficient for the present purpose, it would seem convenient to proceed in this direction and write again to the Archbishop of Mohilow that he should persuade

volta) feratur, Defensor inter legitima tempora appellabit... ex officio ad superiorem judicem.... nolentes omnino (paragrafo 16) ut ullo in casu matrimonii vinculum dissolutum censeatur, nisi duo judicata, vel resolutiones, vel sententiae penitus similes et conformes, a quibus neque pars, neque Defensor matrimonii crediderit appellandum, emanaverint." Anzi tal volta si richiedono tre sentenze conformi sulla nullità, lasciando il Pontefice in libertà la parte che sostiene la validità, ed anche il Difensore del matrimonio, di appellare dalla seconda conforme sulla nullità. Ed invero al paragrafo 11 si legge: "Quod si a secunda sententia super nullitate vel altera pars appellaverit, vel hujusmodi sit ut ei, salva conscientia, Defensor matrimonii acquiescendum non putaverit vel quia sibi videtur manifeste injusta vel invalida, vel quia fuerit lata in tertia instantia, et sit revocatoria alterius praecedentis super validitate in secunda instantia emanatae, volumus ut firma remanente utrique coniugi prohibitione ad alias transeundi nuptias.... causa in tertia vel quarta instantia cognoscatur." E' pertanto evidente che la sentenza definitiva emanata dall'attuale Arcivescovo, ancorché fosse munita della clausola appellatione remota, sarebbe appellabile perché unica, mentre il Pontefice ne vuole almeno due del tutto conformi pria che i coniugi possano passare ad altre nozze. Nel caso presente poi è assai rimarchevole che le due precedenti sentenze avrebbero riconosciuto la validità del matrimonio, le quali verrebbero revocate da una sola sentenza.

Da questa narrativa emerge con quanta sapienza per mezzo di Monsig[nor] Nunzio di Vienna si facesse sentire a Monsig[nor] Arcivescovo di Mohilow, acciò inducesse il Difensore del matrimonio ad interporre appello alla S[anta] Sede contro l'ultima sentenza. Disgraziatamente l'insinuazione non fu secondata perché "defensor matrimonii hujusmodi sententiae acquiescendum putaverit" (Somm[ario] N. 6 paragrafo 2) come scrive Monsig[nor] Arcivescovo di Mohilow senza rendere alcuna ragione di sì strano operare specialmente dopo l'eccitamento ricevuto.

Se pertanto ciò che finora ha dedotto la Principessa non venisse giudicato sufficiente al presente scopo, sembrerebbe opportuno di coltivare la via già aperta, scrivendo di nuovo all'Arcivescovo di Mohilow, affinché induca il

the Defender of the marriage bond to present an appeal to the Holy See. This letter should, however, come from the Holy Congregation <of the Council>, and it should explain clearly to both of them that it is not possible, with only once sentence no matter how impartial and well motivated, to dissolve a marriage that has been consummated and was contracted twenty-four years ago, and this after twelve years of silence on the part of the Princess.

Should this attempt succeed, the result would not only be the positive advantage of referring the appeal to Rome, where a marriage case would be thoroughly and properly reviewed, but we would obtain the transfer of all the documentation pertaining to both the latest Proceedings and the first sentence. Moreover, we would definitely be in a better position as far as knowing the merit of this delicate case.

Difensore del matrimonio ad interporre l'appello alla S[anta] Sede, mediante però una lettera di Congregazione motivata ed atta a far conoscere all'uno e all'altro che non si può con una sentenza, ancorché imparziale ed emessa con maturità di consiglio, sciogliere un matrimonio consumato, e contratto or sono ventiquattro anni, e dopo dodici anni di silenzio serbato dalla Principessa.

Riuscendo felicemente questo nuovo tentativo, si otterrebbe non solo il vantaggio che venisse deferito a Roma l'appello e quivi con ogni regolarità giudicata una causa matrimoniale, ma ancora si otterrebbe il trasporto di tutti gli atti inclusivamente al Processo ed alla prima sentenza, e quindi si potrebbe conoscer meglio il merito di questa scabrosa pendenza.

C) Enclosure No. 2. Additional Summary: No. 1. The Russian proposal on the levels of jurisdiction. French (2 pages).

ADDITIONAL SUMMARY
No. 1

A NOTE FROM THE RUSSIAN AMBASSADOR CONTAINING THE PROPOSALS ON THE LEVELS OF JURISDICTION.

Among the issues still to be settled, one of the most important, in our considered opinion, is the question of jurisdiction in marriage and ecclesiastical cases. These are mentioned in article 6 of the second protocol signed in Rome on August 3, 1847. We propose, therefore, to the Pontifical Government that this question be resolved before any other. We shall begin by stating that, as no objection has been raised regarding the organisation of the first and second levels of jurisdiction, we are prepared to adopt the terms in which this organisation has been formulated and accepted by both parties. The terms are as follows:

"The first level of jurisdiction pertains to the Bishop of the local Diocese. The second one pertains to the Metropolitan Archbishop, if the case to be reviewed has been dealt with in another diocese. If the case has been dealt with in the Archdiocese itself, then the appeal in the second instance, which should customarily be

SOMMARIO ADDIZIONALE
Num[ero] 1

NOTA DELL'AMBASCIATORE DI RUSSIA CON LE PROPOSTE SUI GRADI DI GIURISDIZIONE.

Au nombre des points demeurés en suspens, nous n'hésitons pas à considérer comme un de<s> plus importants, celui de la jurisdiction des causes matrimoniales et ecclésiastiques, tel qu'il a été mentionné à l'Article 6 du second protocole, signé a Rome le 3 août 1847. Aussi proposons-nous au Gouvernement Pontifical de régler ce point préalablement à tout autre. Nous commencerons par déclarer que comme aucune objection n'à été élevée pour ce qui concerne l'organisation de la première et seconde instance nous somme<s> préts à adopter les termes, dans lesquels cette organisation a été formulée et acceptée de part et d'autre. Ces termes sont les suivants:

"La première instance est celle de l'Evêque dioecésain. La seconde est celle de l'Archevêque Métropolitain, si la cause à réviser provient d'un autre diocèse. Si la cause appartient à l'Archidiocèse, alors le jugement en seconde instance, canoniquement dévolu dans ce cas au S[ain]t Siège par l'effet d'une concession

brought to the Holy See, in virtue of a concession from the latter and in consideration of the distances involved, shall be delegated to the nearest Bishop, acting in the second instance for a period that shall not exceed five years. It is understood nonetheless that, in both instances, the assistance and participation of the Defender of the Marriage Bond shall be required as part of the proceedings and deliberations and that he shall have the right, according to the terms of the Bull *Dei miseratione* issued by Benedict XIV, to present an appeal whenever a ruling in favor of marriage annulment is issued. Such a disposition will apply not only to the adjudication of all marriage cases, but to all other cases decided in the first instance by the metropolitan court for which the right of appeal is contemplated."

What remains to be established is an agreement about the third instance of appeal. We think that the simplest and most practical way to solve this question, in a mutually satisfying manner and in a way that will avoid the numerous problems it has raised, is to renounce, as far as we are concerned, the idea of establishing a tribunal in the third instance in our land and admit a direct appeal to the Holy See for all cases adjudicated in the second instance. This is to be done through the mediation of the Imperial Legation in Rome. Since appeals beyond the third instance are always, according to Canon Law, dealt with in Rome, it will be understood that such appeals will be possible after adjudication in the second instance. It is true that, as a result of this agreement, the appealing parties will encounter an additional difficulty, but this does not deter us from concurring fully with the views and intentions of the Holy Father about the goal of impeding rather than abetting scandalous cases of dissolution of marriage. We are certain in advance that the Holy See will be in full agreement with this point of view. I ask Your Eminence to submit this proposal to the Pontifical Cabinet and to inform us of the reception it will meet with.

The Holy See completely agreed to the proposal of the Russian Government with a Note dated July 2, 1848, Prot. No. 6437/6, which follows.

de sa part et par égard pour les distances, serait délégué à l'Evêque le plus voisin de la seconde instance, pour un temps limité qui ne pourrait dépasser cinq années; en admettant toutefois et pour les deux instances l'assistance de l'intervention des défenseurs du mariage à la procédure et au jugement avec le droit d'appeler contre celui-ci lorqu'il est admis en faveur de la nullité du lien, en vertu de la constitution de Benot XIV, *Dei miseratione*. Cette disposition s'étendrait, outre le Jugement des affaires matrimoniales, à toutes autres causes jugées en première instance par le tribunal métropolitain et pour lesquelles existe le droit d'appel."

Reste à s'entendre sur le troisième instance. Nous pensons que le moyen le plus simple et le plus pratique de résoudre cette question, d'une manière mutuellement satisfaisante et d'éviter les nombreux embarras, qu'elle a soulevés, serait de renoncer de notre coté à l'établissement d'une troisième instance chez nous et admettre l'appel direct au S[aint] Siège pour toutes les causes jugées en seconde instance, lesquelles passeraient par la voie régulière de la Mission de l'Empereur à Rome. Comme après la troisième instance il y aurait selon la loi canonique toujours appel à Rome, il serait entendu que cet appel trouverait son application dès la seconde instance. Il est vrai qu'il résulterait de cette marche une difficulté de plus pour les parties appelantes, mais cette considération saurait d'autant moins nous arrêter que nous entrons complètement dans les vues et les intentions du S[ain]t Père, pour entraver et non pour <encourager> les scandaleux procès en dissolution du mariage. Sous ce rapport le suffrage du S[ain]t Siège nous est donc certainement acquis d'avance. J'engage V[otre] E[minence] à soumettre cette proposition au Cabinet Pontifical et de nous faire connaitre l'accueil qu'elle aura rencontré de sa part.

La S[anta] Sede accolse interamente l'Offerta del Governo Russo con Nota dei 2 luglio 1848, N. 6437/6 che segue.

D) Enclosure No. 3. The Vatican's acceptance of the Russian proposal on jurisdiction in ecclesiastical cases. Italian (3 pages).

No. 2

To: the Right Honorable Count de Bouteneff, Envoy Extraordinary and Minister Plenipotentiary of His Majesty the Emperor of All Russias and King of Poland
July 2, 1848.

I, the undersigned Cardinal Secretary of State, hasten to respond to the official Note with which it pleased Your Lordship to communicate to me the contents of a Dispatch that was forwarded to you by the Right Honorable Count de Nesselrode on April 19 of this year pertaining to an agreement, proposed by His Majesty the Emperor of Russia and King of Poland, on two questions not yet settled between the Holy See and the Imperial Government. One of these pertains to the procedure to be followed in the conduct of Marriage and other Ecclesiastical cases.

His Holiness has received such a communication with particular and heartening satisfaction and could not help recognising in it a new confirmation of the determination, on the part of His Majesty the Emperor, to do the utmost to fulfill the heartfelt aspirations and the repeated appeals of the Holy See to resolve the various questions, still pending in the Concordate between the Holy See and the Imperial Government, which constitute the protocol of the articles not agreed to.

With regard to Pontifical agreement with the two aforementioned questions, His Holiness condescended to order the undersigned Cardinal Secretary of State to express to Your Excellency his complete approval and Pontifical confirmation of what has been proposed with respect to the procedures to be followed in marriage and other ecclesiastical cases. Specifically, after cases are dealt with in the second instance by the Dioceses of the respective Metropolitans, higher level appeals must be always referred to this Apostolic See. It is proposed, moreover, that His Holiness delegate, for a determined period of time not to exceed five years, to the two Bishops most closely situated with respect to the Metropolitan Sees the authority to render judgement in the second instance on marriage and other ecclesiastical cases resolved in the first in-

Num[ero] 2

Sig[nor] Conte de Bouteneff Inviato Straordinario e Ministro Plenipotenziario di S[ua] M[aestà] l'Imperatore delle Russie e Re di Polonia.
2 luglio 1848

Il sottoscritto Card[inal] Segretario di Stato si affretta a dare un riscontro all'officiale comunicazione che a V[ostra] E[ccellenza] è piaciuto di fargli di un Disp[accio] direttole dal Sig[nor] Conte di Nesselrode in data dei 19 aprile di questo anno, relativo ad un accomodamento proposto da S[ua] M[aestà] l'Imp[eratore] di Russia e Re di Polonia sopra due dei punti non ancora convenuti fra la S[anta] Sede e l'Imperiale Governo. Uno di questi riguarda la procedura per le cause matrimoniali ed altre ecclesiastiche etc.

La Santità di N[ostro] S[ignore] con particolare soddisfazione del suo cuore ha preso notizia di siffatta comunicazione, e non ha potuto a meno di non ravvisarvi un nuovo argomento della decisa volontà di S[ua] M[aestà] l'Imperatore di adoperarsi con ogni premura affinché abbiano il bramato compimento i vivi desideri e le ripetute domande della S[anta] Sede sopra i vari punti dei quali è rimasta in sospeso la trattativa fra la stessa S[anta] Sede e l'Imperiale Governo e che formano il protocollo degli Articoli non convenuti.

Perciò poi che riguarda la Pontificia adesione ai due punti in discorso, Sua Santità si è degnata ordinare al sottoscritto Card[inal] Segretario di Stato di esprimere a Vostra Eccellenza la sua piena approvazione e pontificia conferma a quanto viene indicato in ordine alla procedura delle cause matrimoniali ed altre ecclesiastiche, le quali dopo la seconda istanza sperimentata nelle Curie dei rispettivi Metropolitani, dovranno costantemente esser portate per le ulteriori rispettive istanze a questa Sede Apostolica. Si propone poi la stessa Santità Sua di autorizzare ad un tempo determinato *non ultra quinquennium* i due Vescovi viciniori alle Sedi *Metropolitane affinché possano ex delegata potestate* giudicare in seconda istanza le cause matrimoniali ed altre ecclesiatiche giudicate in prima dalle rispettive Curie Arcive-

stance by the respective Archdioceses. The Right Honourable Count de Nesselrode, in his dispatch to Your Excellency, indicated the way to be followed in the referral to the Holy See of the cases already adjudicated in the second instance, this being through the Imperial Legation established here in Rome. With reference to this point, the undersigned Cardinal cannot help pointing out to Your Excellency that this question pertains to the first article of the second protocol still pending. On this point as well as the others, His Holiness awaits from the Emperor, in his fairness, His Majesty's agreement to the proposals already presented by His Plenipotentiary to the Holy See, etc.

In asking that it please Your Excellency to forward to His Imperial Majesty the aforementioned agreement, which I, the undersigned Cardinal, am honored to communicate to you by order of His Holiness through this present responsive Note, I wish to express to you again my feelings of the greatest respect.

scovili. Il Sig[nor] Conte di Nesselrode nel precitato suo Dispaccio a Vo[stra] Eccellenza ha indicato il mezzo da tenersi nella trasmissione alla S[anta] Sede delle cause già giudicate in seconda istanza, quello cioè della Legazione Imperiale stabilita qui in Roma. In proposito di ciò il sottoscritto Cardinale non può dispensarsi dal fare osservare a V[ostra] E[ccellenza] che l'indicato argomento è riferibile al primo degli articoli del secondo protocollo rimasti in sospeso, nel quale non meno che sugli altri, la Santità Sua attende dall'equità dell'Imperatore la Sovrana adesione alle proposte già fatte dal Suo Pontificio Plenipotenziario etc.

Lo scrivente Cardinale, nel pregare V[ostra] E[ccellenza] a voler far giungere a S[ua] M[aestà] Imperiale quanto egli ha avuto l'onore di manifestarle per ordine di Sua Santità colla presente Nota responsiva, le rinnova i sensi della più distinta considerazione.

E) Enclosure No. 4. French (1 page).

No. 3

A Communication from the Russian Government to the Bishops of the Empire.
Article 14. Paragraph concerning Bishops.

Following the signing and ratification of the stipulations agreed with the Roman Court, by means of the present Act, in virtue of a special arrangement with the aforementioned Court, the following principle has been established for the review of marriage cases and other ecclesiastical questions. The first level of ecclesiastical jurisdiction for cases in this category will be constituted by the local Diocesan Bishops and, within the Archdiocese, by the Archbishop, together with their respective Consistories, in conformity with the regulations established for this purpose by Article 15 of this Concordate. The second level of jurisdiction for cases decided in the first instance by the Bishops will be constituted by the Archbishop and, with respect to cases adjudicated in the first instance by the Archbishop himself, by the Bishop of one of the Dioceses closest to the Archbishop, previously designated by the Pope. Should there be a divergence in the judgements rendered in the first two levels of ecclesi-

Num[ero] 3

Comunicazione fatta dal Governo Russo ai Vescovi dell'Impero.
Art[icle] 14, paragraphe concernant les Evêques.

Après la signature et la ratification des stipulations convenues avec la Cour de Rome par le présent acte, en vertu d'un arrangement spécial avec la d[ite] Cour, la marche suivante a été arrêtée pour la connaissance des causes matrimoniales et autres affaires ecclésiastiques. La première instance de juridiction ecclésiastique pour les affaires de cette catégorie sera formée par les Evêques diocésains locaux, et dans le diocèse Archiépiscopal par l'Archevêque avec leurs Consistoires respectifs conformément aux règles établies à ce subjet par l'Art. XV, de cette Convention: la seconde instance pour les affaires jugées en première instance par les Evêques, sera formée par l'Archevêque, et quant aux affaires jugées en première instance par l'Archevêque lui-même par l'Evêque d'un des diocèses les plus voisins de l'Archi-Evêche désigné préalablement par le Pape; s'il y a divergence entre les arrêtés des deux premières instances de juridiction ecclésiastique, ainsi que

astical jurisdiction, or should there be need for an appeal to complain or protest against the verdict received, the review of marriage cases is the prerogative of the Holy See in Rome.

dans le cas d'Apel(le), de plainte ou de protestation, la connaissance des affaires matrimoniales appartient au St. Siège de Rome.

Document No. 60. December 26, 1860. The Pope's secretary, Monsignor Stella, sends De Luca's letter of December 6 (not in ASV, NV) to Quaglia. It encloses Borowski's letter of October 30, as well as his resume of the Zhitomir trial of 1851. Italian (1 page).

From the Vatican, December 26, 1860.
Most Venerable Monsignor:

By order of the Holy Father I am sending you the enclosed information provided by the Bishop of Zhitomir, together with the accompanying letter by Monsignor Nuncio in Vienna.

On this occasion, Most Venerable Monsignor, I have the pleasure to confirm myself, with the expression of my singular reverence and esteem,
Your most devoted and obliging servant,
Giuseppe Stella

Vaticano, 26 dicembre 1860.
Monsig[nore] Veneratissimo.

D'ordine del S[anto] Padre invio a Lei l'acclusa informazione del Vescovo di Zytomir, ed infine la lettera di M[onsigno]r Nunzio di Vienna con cui Egli l'ha accompagnata.

In questo incontro ho il piacere di confermarmi con sentimenti di particolare stima ed ossequio
Di Lei Veneratis[sim]o Monsignore
Dev[otissi]mo Servitore Obb[ligatissi]mo
Giuseppe Stella

Document No. 61. December 6, 1860. De Luca's letter, in his own hand, to Monsignor Stella. Italian (1 page).

To: The Most Illustrious and Reverend
 Monsignor Giuseppe Stella,
Secret Attendant to His Holiness
etc., etc., etc.
Rome
Vienna, December 6, 1860
My Most Venerable Monsignor:

I think I must take advantage of Your Most Illustrious and Reverend Excellency's extreme courtesy and ask you to present to His Holiness the herewith enclosed copy of a letter, addressed to me, from Monsignor the Bishop of Zhitomir in Wolinia, pertaining to the well-known marriage case Wittgenstein-Iwanowska. It seems quite evident and beyond doubt that, in case this marriage were to be declared null and void, the prescriptions formulated in Benedict XIV's Bull *Dei miseratione* would not be observed. According to them, the annulling of a marriage requires two analogous sentences. In this case instead, the sentences, issued in 1849 and 1852, were in favor of the marriage bond.

Ill[ustrissi]mo e R[everendissi]mo Signore
Mons[ignor] Giuseppe Stella
Camerier Segreto della Santità
di N[ostro] S[ignore] etc. etc. etc.
Roma
Vienna, 6 dicembre 1860
Monsig[no]r mio Veneratissimo.

Stimo dover profittare della somma cortesia di V[ostra] S[ignoria] Ill[ustrissi]ma e R[everendissi]ma per pregarla di volere rassegnare alla Santità di N[ostro] S[ignore] la qui compiegata copia della lettera a me indirizzata da M[onsi]g[no]r Vescovo di Zytomir nella Wolinia intorno alla nota Causa matrimoniale Wittgenstein-Iwanowska. Pare cosa indubitata e manifesta che dichiarandosi nullo e invalido questo matrimonio non si osserverebbe il prescritto della Bolla di Benedetto XIV *Dei miseratione*, secondo la quale si richiedono due sentenze conformi ad invalidarlo. Laddove nel caso nostro le sentenze di 1 e 2ª istanza nel 1849 e 1852 sono state favorevoli al vincolo matrimoniale.

Should such a marriage be annulled, all the good Catholics in these parts would be greatly shocked and surprised.

I avail myself of this occasion to wish Your Most illustrious and Reverend Excellency great happiness and divine rewards during the next Christmas festivities. I wish as well to confirm the devotion and affectionate esteem which I have held for you for a long time, and I remain

Your Most Illustrious and Reverend Excellency's most devoted and obliging servant,
Antonino <De Luca>,
Archbishop of Tarsus
Apostolic Nuncio

Grande sarebbe invero l'ammirazione di tutti i buoni fedeli in queste parti se vedessero disciolto un tal matrimonio.

Profitto di questa occasione per augurare a V[ostra] S[ignoria] Ill[ustrissi]ma e R[everendissi]ma felicissime e piene di celesti consolazioni le prossime S[anti]s[sime] feste natalizie, e per reiterarle gli attestati della mia antica servitù ed affettuosa stima con che mi pregio di confermarmi
Di V[ostra] S[ignoria] Ill[ustrissi]ma e R[everendissi]ma
devot[issi]mo obblig[atissi]mo servitore
Ant[onino] <De Luca> Arcivescovo di Tarso
N[unzio] Ap[ostolic]o

Document No. 62. Enclosure. Copy of Borowski's letter, dated October 30, 1860. (De Luca's mistake: the original is dated unequivocally October 31, 1860.) See ASV, NV, Doc. No. 35, Latin (2 pages). The text is preceded by the following note in De Luca's own hand:

Copy of the letter written by Monsignor the Bishop of Zhitomir in Wolinia, pertaining to the marriage of Princess Iwanowska and Prince Nicholas Wittgenstein.

Copia di lettera di M[onsi]g[no]r Vescovo di Zytomir nella Wolinia sul matrimonio della Principessa Iwanowska col Principe Nicolò Wittgenstein.

Document No. 63. Enclosure. Copy of Borowski's resume of the Zhitomir Proceedings of 1851. See ASV, NV, Doc. No. 36. Latin (6 pages).

Document No. 64. Undated. Memorandum from Quaglia to the Pope about De Luca's and Kött's concern about repercussions in Germany, should Liszt and Carolyne be married there. Suggestions about performing their marriage in Vienna or in Rome.[37] Italian (5 pages).

<File>: Diocese of Zhitomir

This past September <1860>, after briefing Your Holiness about the outcome of the review of Princess Iwanowska's marriage case that was conducted by the <Holy> Congregation <of the Council>, in accordance with the Pontifical pronouncement, we wrote a letter to Monsignor Nuncio in Vienna[38] informing him that, after the question had been examined, it was recognised that

Zitomir

Nel settembre scorso, dopo avere dato discarico alla S[anti]tà V[ost]ra del risultato che ottenne presso la Cong[regazio]ne la questione matrimoniale della Principessa Iwanowska, e coerentemente all'Oracolo Pontificio, si scrisse lettera a Mons[igno]r Nunzio di Vienna partecipandogli che in seguito ad esame preso della questione essendosi riconosciuto non potersi i-

---

[37]Written after De Luca's letter of October 24, containing Kött's letter of October 15 and some time before Quaglia's letter to De Luca dated January 16, 1861 (see ASV, NV, Doc. No. 39). It refers to the Congregation's second deliberation on Carolyne's case of December 22, 1860, not

mentioned here. In all probability, the memo dates before the December 22 deliberation of the Congregation whose position paper refers to the same documents.
[38]See ASV, NV, Doc. No. 25, September 25, 1860.

the implementation of the Mohilow sentence, which had been suspended by the Bishop of Fulda, could not be stopped. He was then instructed to write to that Bishop to the effect that he could proceed to said implementation and allow the above-mentioned Princess to contract a new marriage.

On October 18, <1860>, Monsignor Nuncio wrote back[39] that, while he was not informed of the details of the proceedings, it seemed to him that, in the absence of two analogous sentences, the procedures prescribed by the Benedictine Bull had not been observed. He added that, on account of the scandals taking place in Hungary on account of the easy manner in which marriages were annulled on the basis of violence and intimidation, he thought that this pronouncement would produce a very negative impression on those Bishops. He begged me to make Your Holiness aware of these implications and suggested that the Bishop of Fulda should receive direct instructions on this matter, while he declared himself willing to forward them to him.

On the 24 of the same month, he wrote another letter,[40] which enclosed the original of a letter addressed to him by the Bishop of Fulda,[41] in which the latter expressed to Monsignor Nuncio his surprise at receiving a telegram from the Princess, informing him of the successful outcome achieved in her case and requesting him to write a letter of recommendation for a Priest from the town of Weimar, for whom she reportedly obtained from Your Holiness the title of Honorary Gentleman of Papal Chambers. He was astonished that either fact could be true, particularly the outcome of the marriage case which he said will constitute a bad precedent in those areas which are predominantly Protestant, and said that, as soon as he received the document from Rome, he would send it to him to make sure of its legal value and would await his instructions.

At this point, Monsignor Nuncio himself awaits instructions on how to proceed in order that this unfortunate affair be settled without scandal and without adverse consequences for the Holy See.

The Princess is still in Rome. It might be useful if we wrote a Latin letter to Monsignor Bishop that would be forwarded to him by Monsignor Nun-

nibire l'esecuzione della sentenza di Mohilovo rimasta sospesa presso il Vescovo di Fulda, partecipasse a questo prelato potersi da esso procedere alla detta esecuzione e permettere che l'anzidetta Principessa passasse ad altre nozze.

In data 18 ottobre Mons[igno]r Nunzio rispondeva che, non essendo a lui noti i particolari del processo, sembravagli per lo meno che in tale affare non si fossero osservate le forme prescritte dalla Benedettina stante la mancanza di due sentenze conformi. Aggiungeva che non essendo ancora cessati gli scandali nell'Ungheria per la facilità nelle curie di sciogliere i matrimoni *ob vim et metum* prevedeva la sinistra sensazione che avrebbe prodotto nei vescovi una tale licenza. Pregava quindi che si rappresentasse tutto questo alla S[antità] V[ost]ra e che fossero inviate direttamente a Mons[igno]r Vescovo di Fulda le analoghe istruzioni dichiarandosi pronto a farne egli la trasmissione.

In data 24 dello stesso mese inviava altra lettera compiegandovi un<a> autografa di Mons[igno]r Vescovo di Fulda nella quale questi esprime la sua sorpresa a Mons[igno]r Nunzio per aver ricevuto un telegramma dalla Principessa col quale gli partecipa il buon risultato che ha ottenuto la sua causa e lo prega di una commendatizia per un tal Parroco della Città di Weimar a cui avrebbe essa ottenuto dalla S[antità] V[ostra] di esser nominato *cameriere d'onore*. Fa le sue meraviglie per l'una e l'altra cosa e segnatamente per l'esito della causa matrimoniale che dice di cattivo esempio in quei luoghi ove abbondano Protestanti e lo avverte che appena avrà partecipazione da Roma gli trasmetterà il documento per cerziorarsi della legalità ed attenderà da lui istruzioni.

Dopo di che Mons[igno]r Nunzio aspetta anch'esso istruzioni sul modo da tenersi acciocché questo infelice negozio possa aggiustarsi senza scandalo e senza offesa alla S[anta] Sede.

La Principessa è ancora in Roma. Parrebbe potesse scriversi una lettera latina a M[onsigno]r Vescovo da trasmettere per mezzo di

---

[39]See ASV, NV, Doc. No. 31, October 18, 1860.
[40]See ASV, NV, Doc. No. 34, October 24, 1860.

[41]See ASV, NV, Doc. No. 28, October 15, 1860.

cio. In it, we should summarise the reasons for the position adopted by the Holy See on this question, and provide justifications for the decision touching upon the extrinsic as well as the intrinsic elements of the question. We could add that, should there be fear of possible scandals on account of the wedding being performed in that region, the Nuncio himself, upon being presented with the documents certifying the Princess's single status, could be delegated to perform, with all possible secrecy, the canonic wedding. Another possibility would be to tell Monsignor Bishop to send us the aforementioned sentence, together with a certificate of single status on the part of the would-be bride and groom covering the length of their residence in that diocese and perform the marriage here in Rome. Your Holiness will decide what is best.

Mons[igno]r Nunzio, nella quale sommariamente si avesse ragione della condotta tenuta dalla S[anta] Sede su tale affare, e si giustificasse il suo giudizio toccando tanto l'estrinseco quanto l'intrinseco della questione. Dopo di che si aggiungesse che, ove siano a temersi scandali per la celebrazione del matrimonio in quelle contrade, potrebbe delegarsi lo stesso nunzio a celebrare il matrimonio con ogni riservatezza previi i documenti di stato libero; oppure potrebbe avvertirsi Mons[igno]r Vescovo a trasmettere la detta sentenza con una testimoniale autentica di stato libero de' contraenti pel tempo di loro dimora in quella diocesi, e fare il matrimonio qui in Roma.
Deciderà però meglio V[ostra] S[antità].

Document No. 65. Undated, but probably from the Spring of 1861 (see note to ASV, CC Doc. 66. Memorandum in Quaglia's own hand to Caterini, with comments in margin by the latter presenting the draft of the Congregation's final decision, originally dated January 8, 1861.

<To: Monsignor Prospero Caterini>

I would ask Your Most Reverend Eminence to examine the enclosed draft of the decree pertaining to the familiar case of Princess Iwanowska.

In my opinion it would be better to leave out the last section where the Bishop of Fulda is given the task of implementing the aforementioned decree.

I concur.

Last night I went to see the Most Eminent <Cardinal Giacomo> Antonelli to give him personally the letter we agreed about and, unable to see him, I left it with his attendant in order that, as soon as the meeting of the Council of Ministers was over, he could give it immediately to him.

That's fine.

A Monsignor Prospero Caterini>

Prego l'Em[inenz]a V[ostra] Re[verendissi]ma di esaminare l'acclusa minuta di decreto relativo alla consaputa causa della Principessa Iwanowska.

A me sembra più opportuno di tralasciare l'ultima parte in cui si commette al Vescovo di Fulda l'esecuzione del sudd[ett]o decreto.

Ne convengo.

Ieri sera mi recai dall' Em[inentissi]oAntonelli per consegnargli la consaputa lettera e, non avendolo potuto vedere, la lasciai al di lui caudatario acciò, terminato appena il consiglio dei ministri, la ricapitasse in mani del prelodato Em[inentissim]o.

Va bene.

Document No. 66. January 8, 1861. See AVR, Doc. No. 1. This draft, enclosed with ASV, CC Doc. No. 65, contains at the end a deleted passage (translated below) that was not included in the final document kept in the Vicariato file and contains the decree of the Holy Congregation of the Council dated January 8, 1861, after the Pope's approval on January 7.[42] Latin (4 pages).

....and ordered that the Bishop of Fulda should be formally notified of it for the pertinent legal effects.

And for this reason the same Holy Congregation <of the Council> ordered the Bishop of Fulda to endeavor to proceed to the implementation of the above stated resolution, observing in every respect its spirit and letter and ensuring throughout that it be done according to the rules.

....confirmavit, {eamque notificari Ep[iscop]o Fuldensi pro respectivo juris effectu mandavit.

Proptereaque eadem S[ancta] Congregatio commisit Ep[iscop]o Fuldensi ut ad exequutionem superius descriptae resolutionis ejusdemque forma et tenore in omnibus et per omnia adamussim servatis gratis devenire possit et valeat}.

Document No. 67. January 7, 1861. Papal authorisation to write to De Luca. Latin (1 page).

Secret Archive
Audience
As ordered at the Papal Audience of
January 7, 1861,
we are to write to the Apostolic Nuncio
according to the draft enclosed.

Archivio Segreto.
Udienza
Ex Audientia S[anti]s[si]mi
Die 7 Januarii 1861
Scribatur Nuntio Ap[osto]lico Viennen[si] juxta insertam minutam.

Document No. 68. Draft of the January 16, 1861, letter to De Luca. See ASV, NV Doc. No. 39. The draft was originally written on the 13th, and the date was subsequently penned over to read January 16, after the text was presented for approval to the Pope on January 14. The draft, in the hand of one of Quaglia's scribes (not the same who wrote the actual letter in the ASV, NV file), contains corrections and insertions in Quaglia's own hand and notes to the extent that these were suggested by the Pope himself. Italian (4 pages).

To: Monsignor Antonino De Luca
Archbishop of Tarsus
Apostolic Nuncio in Vienna
January 13 (corrected to read 16), 1861
Most Illustrious and Reverend Monsignor:

Following the observations presented by Your Most Illustrious and Reverend Excellency

Monsig[nor] Antonino De Luca
Arcivescovo di Tarso
Nunzio Apostolico in Vienna
Roma, li 16 gennajo 1861
Ill[ustrissi]mo e R[everendissi]mo Signore.

In seguito alle osservazioni fatte dalla Sig[noria] V[ostra] Ill[ustrissi]ma e Rev[e-

[42]The deletion by Quaglia of this paragraph from the final version of the document would suggest that, while the document was written originally on January 8, the paragraph was deleted at a later date when the Vatican, as a result of De Luca's letters, no longer wished the marriage to be performed in Fulda. This was already tentatively suggested in ASV, CC Doc. No. 64, and agreed to in No. 65. Moreover,

the document finally issued to Carolyne, while bearing the same January date, must have been issued to her at a much later date, possibly in June. This is confirmed by Liszt, who, in a letter written to her on March 27, 1861, refers to the fact that she had not yet received that document (see LLB, Vol. V, p. 146). The wedding plans did not begin in earnest until early October 1861.

and by Monsignor the Bishop of Fulda in your letters of the 15th and 20th of October[43] of last year, with respect to the sentence of annulment of the marriage of Princess Iwanowska with Prince Wittgenstein, the Holy Father, whom I went to see in order to relate those matters to him, ordered that the question be submitted again to the full Congregation. Having prepared for this purpose a set of statements pertinent to the case, accompanied by the relevant documentation and the extent of your exposition, the Most Eminent Fathers, in the general assembly of the 22nd of last December, **which nine of them attended, having looked also at the intrinsic merit of the case and supplied thus to the absence of two analogous sentences** (N.B.: *This phrase was suggested by the Holy Father when this draft was presented to him at the audience granted on January 14, 1861*), were again {as a majority} of the opinion that the above-mentioned sentence should be carried out subject to the approval of His Holiness. Having subsequently reported this resolution to the Holy Father, he condescended to confirm it and ordered me to write to Your Most Illustrious and Reverend Excellency, and I do this now so that you, according to the wishes of His Holiness himself, may bring all these things to the attention of Monsignor the Bishop of Fulda in order that, **without interposing further obstacles**, he should {promptly} carry out the sentence issued by Monsignor the Archbishop of Mohilow. **And since it is also desirable to pay attention to the feared-for consequences that the surprise might cause, predisposing the minds of the most doubtful to receive, with due reverence, this declaration of the Holy See is left to your prudence as well as to that of Monsignor the Bishop of Fulda** (N.B.: *The contents of this sentence were suggested by the Holy Father*).

I must herewith also report to you that your letter, dated December 6 and enclosing the report compiled by Monsignor the Bishop of Zhitomir about this same marriage case, as it was adjudicated in the first instance by that Curia, reached me only after the Congregation's deliberation. In any case, I referred to it in my re-

rendissi]ma e da Monsig[nor] Vescovo di Fulda con lettere del 15 e 28 Ottobre dello spirato anno relativamente alla esecuzione della sentenza di nullità di matrimonio tra la Principessa Iwanowska ed il Principe Wittgenstein, il S[anto] Padre, cui mi recai a dovere fargliene relazione, ordinò che venisse di nuovo sottoposto l'affare all'esame della piena Congregazione. Redatti pertanto a tale effetto analoghi fogli di deduzioni corredati degli opportuni documenti e di quel tanto che erasi da Lei esposto, gli Em[inentissi]mi Padri, nella generale adunanza dei 22 Decembre ultimo **intervenuti nel numero di Nove, avendo gustato anche il merito intrinseco della causa, e supplito cosí alla mancanza delle due sentenze conformi** [N.B. *Le qui aggiunte espressioni furono suggerite dal S[anto] Padre, a cui nella udienza del 14 gennaro 1861, si sottopose questa minuta]*[44], furono nuovamente di avviso doversi eseguire la menzionata sentenza, ove cosí piacesse a Sua Santità. Riferita da me in seguito siffatta relazione al S[anto] Padre, si compiacque confermarla, ed ordinarmi di scrivere a V[ostra] S[ignoria] Ill[ustrissi]ma e R[everendissi]ma, siccome faccio, perché Ella direttamente, come è volere della stessa Santità Sua, deduca tutto ciò a notizia di Monsig[nor] Vescovo di Fulda allo scopo, che dal medesimo venga {con la debita prontezza} eseguita la sentenza emanata da M[onsi]g[no]r Arcivescovo di Mohilov, **senza frapporre ulteriori ostacoli. E volendosi pure avere un riguardo al temuto pericolo di ammirazione per le conseguenze del fatto, sarà della prudenza ed oculatezza tanto Sua, quanto di Monsig[nor] Vescovo di Fulda, disporre preventivamente gli animi dei più miticolosi ad accogliere col dovuto ossequio questa dichiarazione della S[anta] Sede** (N.B. *Il contenuto in questo periodo fu suggerito dal S[anto] Padre*).

E qui debbo pure significarle che la sua lettera del 6 Decembre decorso, con cui si accompagna il rapporto redatto da Monsig[mor] Vescovo di Zytomir intorno alla stessa causa matrimoniale giudicata in primo grado innanzi a quella Curia, mi pervenne dopo che la Congregazione aveva già pronunziato. Tuttavolta tenni

---

[43]Actually October 24.

[44]The sentence originally read: "....degli opportuni documenti e di quel tanto che erasi da lei dedotto, nella generale

adunanza dei 22 decembre ultimo, gli Em[inentissim]i Padri a pluralità di suffragi furono nuovamente d'avviso doversi eseguire...."

port to His Holiness, and it was pointed out that the conclusions therein contained could not have led to issuing a different opinion.

I am counting on your kindness as to being informed in due time of the effects of the present letter and go on to reaffirm my particular and respectful esteem.
Your Most Illustrious and Reverend Excellency's
<most devoted and obliging servant

Angelo Quaglia,
Secretary of the Holy Congregation
of the Council>

proposito anche del medesimo nella relazione che feci a Sua Santità, e si rilevò che le cose ivi dedotte non avrebbero potuto influire a fare emettere un diverso parere.

Attendendomi dalla sua gentilezza di conoscere a suo tempo il risultato della presente, passo a ripetermi con sensi di distinta e rispettosa stima,
Di V[ostra] S[ignoria] Ill[ustrissi]ma e
    R[everendissi]ma
<De[votissi]mo Ob[bligatissi]mo Servo
Angelo Quaglia
Segretario della S[anta] Cong[regazione] del
    Concilio.>

Document No. 69. Unsigned copy of De Luca's letter to Kött, dated February 6, 1861 (see ASV, NV Doc. No. 40), sent by De Luca to Antonelli in his dispatch No. 1291 (see ASV, NV Doc. No. 42). Latin (3 pages). It bears the following annotations:

Insert in the Dispatch from Vienna No. 1291

Copy
No. 2060/1

Inserto nel Disp[accio] di Vienna N[umer]o 1291
Copia
No. 2060/1

Document No. 70. De Luca's Letter to Quaglia, dated June 22, 1861, not included in the ASV, NV file and originally enclosed with ASV, NV Doc. 44, a letter to Antonelli (Dispatch No. 1304) whose draft date was June 20, 1861. Italian (1 page).

To: The Most Illustrious and Reverend
Monsignor Angelo Quaglia,
Secretary of the Holy Congregation
of the Council, etc., etc.
Rome
(with enclosure)
No. 2283/1
Vienna, June 22, 1861
Most Illustrious and Reverend Monsignor:

Enclosed with this note, Your Most Illustrious and Reverend Excellency will find the answer I recently received from Monsignor the Bishop of Fulda to my letter to him of February 7, 1861, pertaining to the well-known marriage case Wittgenstein-Iwanowska. I do not need to point out that I had then communicated to the aforementioned Bishop the prescriptions contained in Your Most Illustrious and Reverend Excellency's letter of last January 15.[45] I hope that the Office of the Secretary of State may

Ill[ustrissi]mo e R[everendissi]mo Signore
Monsignor Angelo Quaglia
Segretario della S[anta] C[ongregazione]
del Concilio ecc. ecc. Roma

(con inserto)
N. 2283/1
Vienna, li 22 giugno 1861
Illustrissimo e Reverendissimo Signore.

In seno al presente foglio Vostra Signoria Illustrissima e Reverendissima troverà la risposta che or di recente mi ha fatta M[onsi]g[no]r Vescovo di Fulda in riscontro alla mia lettera de' 7 febbraro 1861 intorno al noto processo matrimoniale Wittgenstein-Iwanowska. Non mi occorre notare che allora comunicai al prelodato M[onsi]g[no]r Vescovo le avvertenze contenute nel foglio di Vostra Signoria Illustrissima e Reverendissima de' 15 gennaio p[rossim]o p[assat]o. Spero che dalla Segreteria di Stato Le sarà stata

---

[45]Actually January 16.

have forwarded to you a copy of my above mentioned letter which I sent a few days ago.

It is with pleasure that I avail myself of this occasion to reiterate to Your Most Illustrious and Reverend Excellency the protestations of my singular and respectful esteem and, on this note, I have the honor to confirm myself
Your Most illustrious and Reverend Excellency's most devoted and obliging servant,

Antonino <De Luca>
Archbishop of Tarsus,
Apostolic Nuncio

consegnata la copia dell'anzidetta mia lettera da me già trasmessa or sono pochi giorni innanzi.

Colgo con piacere quest'occasione per reiterare a Vostra Signoria Illustrissima e Reverendissima le proteste della distinta e rispettosa stima, con la quale mi pregio di confermarmi

Di Vostra Signoria Illustrissima e
R[everendissi]ma
devot[issi]mo obblig[atissi]mo servitore
Ant[onino] <De Luca>
Arcivescovo di Tarso,
N[unzio] Ap[ostolic]o

Document No. 71. Enclosure in the Dispatch from Vienna No. 1304. De Luca's Copy of Kött's letter to him, dated June 11, 1861. See ASV, NV, Doc. No. 43. Latin (1 page).

Document No. 72. Monsignor Hohenlohe's letter to Caterini indicating new evidence in favor of the validity of Carolyne's marriage, with a note about its inclusion in the Secret Archive's file. Italian (3 pages).

To: the Most Eminent Cardinal
Monsignor <Prospero> Caterini
Prefect of the Holy Congregation of the Council

etc., etc., etc.
The Vatican, October 18, 1861
Most Eminent Prince:

My conscience and sense of duty compel me to ask Your Most Reverend Eminence to deign yourself to grant an audience to the bearers of this letter, the most Reverend Father Semenenko from the Church of San Claudio dei Polacchi <in Rome> and His Lordship Count Potoczki,[46] both of whom are known in Poland as well as in Rome for their piety and integrity.

They are to speak about a very troublesome marriage case concerning a Princess Wittgenstein Iwanowska, and they wish to forestall a grave scandal. Trusting that you will consent to do this favor, as I bow with the greatest respect to kiss Your Most Reverend Eminence's Holy Purple, I have the great honor of signing myself

E[minentissi]mo Signor Cardinale <Prospero> Caterini
<Prefetto della Santa Congregazione del Concilio>
etc. etc. etc.
Vaticano, 18 ottobre 1861
Eminentissimo Principe.

Per dovere di coscienza mi vedo obbligato di pregare Vostra Eminenza Reverendissima di voler ricevere e sentire i latori di questa lettera, il R[e]v[erendissi]mo Padre Semenenko di S[an] Claudio de' Polacchi <in Roma> ed il Signor Conte Potoczki, ambedue conosciuti in Polonia ed a Roma per la loro pietà ed onestà.

Hanno da parlare sopra un gravissimo affare matrimoniale di una P[rinci]p[e]ssa Wittgenstein Iwanowska, onde impedire un grave scandalo. Sicuro che vorrà fare questo favore, ho l'alto onore di rassegnarmi, col più profondo rispetto inchinato al bacio della Sagra (sic) Porpora di Vostra Eminenza R[e]v[erendissi]ma,

---

[46]Hohenlohe's spelling of this name should be probaly changed to Podowski, which would make this gentleman a relative of Carolyne's on her mother's side. Father Peter Semenenko was a Polish priest attached to the Church of San

Claudio dei Polacchi, better known as Chiesa della Resurrezione, located in Via San Sebastianello, not far from the Spanish Steps.

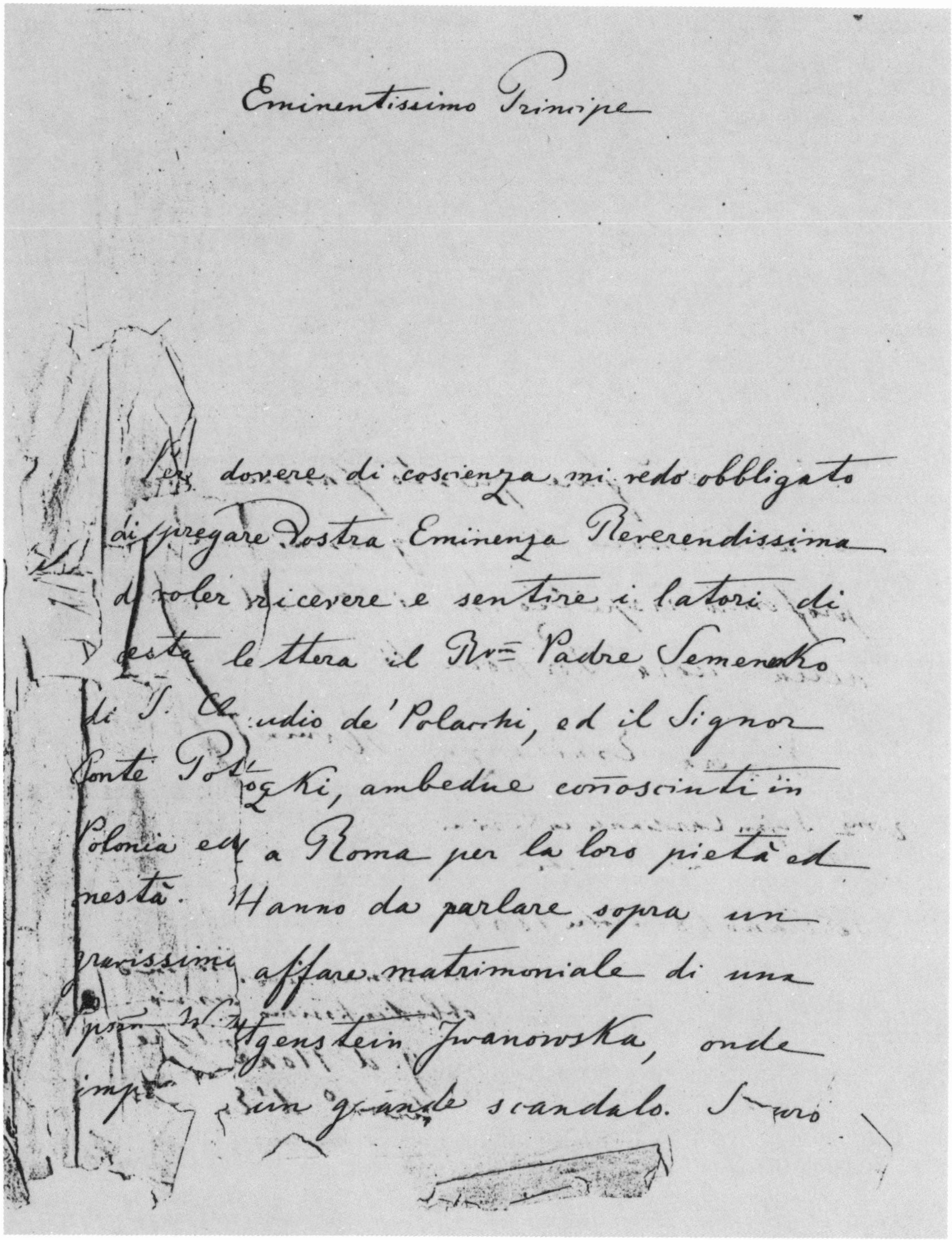

Eminentissimo Principe

Per dovere di coscienza mi vedo obbligato
di pregare Vostra Eminenza Reverendissima
di voler ricevere e sentire i latori di
[illegible]esta lettera il Rev.mo Padre Semenenko
di S. Cl[illegible]udio de' Polacchi, ed il Signor
Conte Potoçki, ambedue conosciuti in
Polonia ed a Roma per la loro pietà ed
[illegible]nestà. Hanno da parlare sopra un
[illegible]ravissimo affare matrimoniale di una
[illegible]pessa W[illegible]ttgenstein Iwanowska, onde
impe[illegible] un grande scandalo. I loro

Plate 10. Facsimile of a letter from Monsignor Hohenlohe to Cardinal Caterini, dated October 18, 1861: "...to forestall a great scandal."

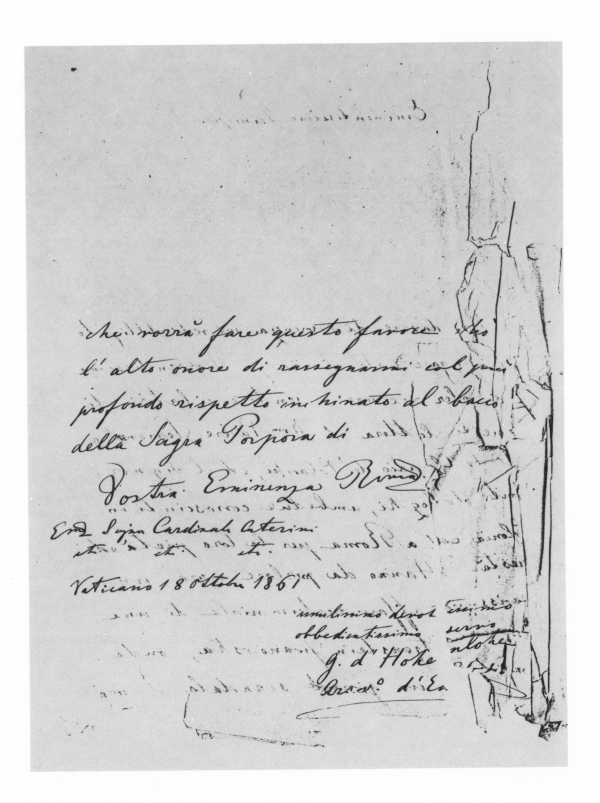

che vorrà fare questo favore che

l'alto onore di rassegnarmi col più

profondo rispetto inchinato al bacio

della Sagra Porpora di

Vostra Eminenza Rma

Emo Sigr Cardinale Caterini

Vaticano 18 Ottobre 1867

umilissimo devot

obbedientissimo servo

G. d'Hohe

Plate 10 (cont.)

Your humblest, most devoted and obedient
    servant,
Gustav von Hohenlohe,
Archbishop of Edessa

umilissimo, devotissimo, obbedientissimo servo

G<ustavo> d'Hohenlohe,
Arciv[escov]o d'Edessa

(overleaf)
Zhitomir
Carolyne Iwanowska
1462/4
November 12, 1861
To be placed in the file
61

Zytomerien
Carolina Iwano<w>ska
1462/4
Die 12 Nov[embre] 1861
uniatur
61

Document No. 73. An article from a newspaper referring to the strange outcome of Carolyne's efforts to obtain an annulment in order to marry Liszt.

From LA NAZIONE, a political daily. Florence.
Year 3, No. 338
Wednesday, December 4, 1861
OTHER EVENTS.
— . . . .
— . . . .

— The *Gazetta del Popolo* expresses surprise at the fact that a lawsuit against the *Commerce* has not been advancing at all since last August and wishes to know the reason of our silence. We have said nothing about it for one reason only, that we are so used to such petty cases that they do not cause us to be surprised anymore. As long as the music makers remain the same, the music will never change.

— Liszt, already celebrated for his pianistic talents, is acquiring a different kind of notoriety as a consequence of the problems he has encountered in trying to celebrate his nuptials with Princess Wittgenstein. This lady's husband is still alive, and yet, so many years after that wedding was celebrated, the Roman Court declared that marriage null and void. In the wake of appeals made with the typical persistence and cleverness that characterize a woman in love, and thanks to the notorious penchant of the Curia for bowing low before titles and gold, Rome allowed the Princess to marry a second time. Just as the preparations for the wedding had been completed and the bride and groom had come to Rome, they were formally prohibited from getting married. Prince von Hohenlohe, a relative of the Princess, managed to obtain the veto. This proves that the Prince must be richer than Liszt and Madame Wittgenstein!!

LA NAZIONE, Giornale politico quotidiano
Mercoledì, 4 dicembre 1861
Anno Terzo - Num[ero] 33 8
FATTI DIVERSI.
— . . . .
— . . . .

— La Gazzetta del Popolo fa le meraviglie perché un processo contro il Commercio dorme dall'agosto in poi: e ci chiede il perché del nostro silenzio. Noi non abbiamo detto nulla per una sola ragione, perché ormai a questi casetti ci siamo abituati tanto, che non ci recano più sorpresa. Fino a che i maestri di Cappella saranno gli stessi, la musica non muterà mai.

— Liszt già celebre per il suo talento di pianista va acquistando un'altra celebrità al seguito delle difficoltà che incontra per celebrare il suo matrimonio con la principessa Wittgenstein. Vive tuttora il marito di questa principessa; ma dopo lunghi anni di quel primo connubio, la Corte di Roma dichiarò nullo quel matrimonio, ed al seguito di pratiche fatte con la persistenza e l'intelligenza che caratterizza la donna innamorata, e grazie ancora alla nota arrendevolezza di quella Curia ai titoli e all'oro, Roma permise che la Principessa convolasse a seconde nozze. Fatti i preparativi per la festa nuziale, e giunti a Roma gli sposi, è stata intimata loro formale inibizione di contrar matrimonio. Il Principe di Hohenlohe, parente della Principessa, ha ottenuto questo veto. Questo prova che il Principe deve essere più ricco di Liszt e della Wittgenstein!!

ARCHIVIO STORICO DEL VICARIATO DI ROMA
L/41, FILE NO. 4477

————————————————

From the Archive of the Vicariato di Roma, in St. John Lateran.
Some documents pertaining to the marriage of Liszt and
Princess Carolyne von Sayn-Wittgenstein, 1861.
Shelf mark N. 4477, L/41.

Plate 11. Pope Pius IX, a photograph.

**Document No. 1. Certified copy of the final judgement of the Holy Congregation of the
Council (December 22, 1860), dated January 8, 1861, which upholds their earlier
decision of September 22, 1860; and the Russian annulment issued by Archbishop
Wenceslas Żyliński's on February 24 (O.S.), 1860 (see ASV, NV Document No. 6, and
ASV CC Docs. No. 20 and 22; see No. 28 for the text). For a paragraph not included
here, see the draft of this document in ASV CC Doc. No. 65). Enclosed with Doc. 2.
Latin (2 pages).**

January 8, 1861.

On the 22nd of September, 1860, by order of
Pope Pius IX, the Holy Congregation of the most
eminent Cardinals of the Holy Roman Church, in-
terpreters of the Council of Trent, gathered in
General Assembly and conducted a review of the
various and conflicting decisions provided by the
Consistories of Luck-Zhitomir and Mohilow in the
case of annulment of the marriage contracted, with
the alleged invalidating impediment of violence and
intimidation (*assertum vis et metus dirimens impedimentum*),[1] by Princess Carolyne Iwanowska,
Catholic, and Prince Nicholas Wittgenstein, non-
Catholic. This was specifically done in order to establish whether there was anything preventing the
carrying out of the last decision of the Archbishop
of Mohilow in favor of the annulment of the
marriage which was issued on February 24, 1860, on
the strength of special faculties given him by a rescript of His Holiness on August 8, 1859. After a
thorough examination of all things pertinent both
to the propriety of the decision and the intrinsic
merit of the case, the same Holy Congregation concluded that there was nothing preventing the carrying out of the aforesaid decision of the Archbishop
of Mohilow, and ordered that the Bishop of Fulda
be notified of this resolution. Because of peculiar
circumstances, he had been previously given orders
to deny Princess Carolyne, who lived in his diocese,
permission to contract another marriage until the
Holy See decided otherwise. Having reported on
the above to the Holy Father at an audience on the
24th of the aforesaid month and year, His Holiness
condescended to approve and confirm the decision
of the Holy Congregation.

Die 8 Januarii 1861.

S[ancta] Congregatio Eminentissimorum
S[anctae] R[omanae] E[cclesiae] Cardinalium Concilii Tridentini Interpretum de mandato
S[anctissi]mi D[omi]ni Nostri Pii Papae IX, die 22
Septembris 1860, in Generali habito Conventu examen instituit super variis iisque difformibus senten-
tiis editis a Consistoriis Zitumirien[si] et Mokil-
owien[si] in causa nullitatis matrimonii inter Carolinam Iwanowska Principissam Catholicam et Nicolaum Wittgenstein Principem Acatholicum ob
assertum vis et metus dirimens impedimentum,
praesertim vero ut decerneretur an aliquid obstaret
quominus exequutioni esset committenda postrema
sententia ab Archiepiscopo Mokilowiensi edita pro
nullitate matrimonii die 24 mensis Februarii 1860 in
vim specialium facultatum eidem tributarum rescripto S[anctissi]mi D[omi]ni Nostri diei 8 Augusti
1859. Et rebus omnibus mature perpensis tum ad
iudicii ordinem tum etiam ad intrinsecum causae
meritum pertinentibus, eadem S[ancta] Congregatio censuit rescribendum nihil impedimento esse
exequutioni praefatae sententiae Archiepiscopi
Mokilowiensis; et hujusmodi resolutionem, ad effectum supradictae exequutionis, notificari mandavit Episcopo Fulden[si], cui antea ob peculiares
circumstantias litterae datae fuerant eum in finem,
ut Principissae Carolinae, quae in eius Diocesi
domicilium agebat, licentiam denegaret alias ineundi nuptias usquedum a S[ancta] Sede aliter non
provideretur. Factaque de praemissis relatione
S[anctissi]mo D[omi]no Nostro in audientia diei 24
praedicti mensis, et anni, Sanctitas Sua resolutionem S[anctae] Congregationis benigne ap-
probare, ac confirmare dignata est.

---

[1]According to Canon Law, a *dirimens impedimentum* or invalidating impediment is one which "seriously prevents contracting marriage and, if contracted, makes it invalid. Even if
the impediment affects only one of the two parties, it causes
marriage to be illicit and invalid" (*Codex Juris Canonici*,
Book III, Chapter II, par. 1036).

Since the execution of the aforementioned sentence was left suspended because of unforeseen developments, His Holiness thought of expediting matters and order the same Holy Congregation to conduct a new review of the whole case. Therefore, in a General Assembly on December 22 of the same year, the most eminent fathers, having debated all that was pertinent according to the law and according to the facts so far presented, having considered, moreover, all the other concomitant things pertaining to the facts, concluded that the judgement issued by the Archbishop of Mohilow on February 24, 1860, was to be executed. His Holiness in his benevolence approved and confirmed this resolution in the audience of January 7, 1861.

Originally signed by Prospero Cardinal Caterini, Prefect, and Angelo Quaglia, Secretary.
Seal
The above fully conforms to the signed original with which it was compared.
Monsignor Bernardino Maggi, Deputy[2]

Cum vero ob nonnullas exortas difficultates exequutio praedictae resolutionis in suspenso relicta fuisset, expedire visum fuit S[anctissi]mo D[omi]no Nostro rem omnem ejusdem S[anctae] Congregationis examini iterum committere. Ideoque in Generalibus Comitiis diei 22 Decembris ejusdem anni, Emi[nentissimi] Patres, ratione habita ad ea omnia quae in jure ac in facto hinc inde noviter deducta fuerunt aliisque omnibus concomitantibus rerum adjunctis maturiori consilio perpensis, rescribendum censuerunt sententiam Archiopiscopi Mokilowiensis diei 24 Februarii 1860 esse exequendam; quam resolutionem Sanctitas Sua in audientia diei 7 Januarii 1861 benigne pariter approbavit et confirmavit.

P[rospero] Card[inal] Caterini, Praef[ectus]
A[ngelo] Quaglia, Secretarius
Loco Signi
Concordat cum originali subscripto exhibito.

Bernardinus Can[onicus] Maggi deput[atus]

Document No. 2. Princess Carolyne's and Liszt's marriage application, addressed to Pope Pius IX and dated September 18, 1861, referred by the Holy Congregation of the Holy Office to the the Vicar General of Rome. Italian with Latin notes (3 pages).

Presented on behalf of the Petitioner
To His Holiness
Happily Reigning,
Pope Pius IX

Blessed Father,
 Franz, son of the late Adam Liszt, a Catholic from Hungary, aged 50 years, desiring to contract matrimony in Rome, presents a Certificate of Baptism and a certificate of single status from 1848 to the present and, for the previous period, he is presenting a certificate from his future bride stating that he received confirmation in 1829. He requests Your Holiness to admit such documents and dispense with any other certificate.

Per gli Entroscritti Oratoris
Alla Santità di Nostro Signore
Pio IX felicemente regnante

Beatissimo Padre,
 Francesco del fu Adamo Liszt, Cattolico di Ungheria di anni 50, volendo contrarre matrimonio in Roma esibisce la fede di Battesimo e stato libero dal 1848 fino al presente, e per l'epoca anteriore presenta l'attestato della sua futura sposa da cui si rilieva che fu confermato nel 1829. Supplica V[ostra] S[antità] ad ammettere cotali documenti dispensandolo da ogni altra fede.

---

[2]With this decree in hand, which was sanctioned by Pius IX himself, Liszt and Carolyne were free to marry, and they began to assemble the documents required for their wedding. The various depositions and papers which follow are to be found in their marriage file, and they are proof positive of Liszt's intention to marry Carolyne—the popular literature on this topic notwithstanding. Much of their correspondence during the year 1861 is taken up with the question of where the marriage should take place—Weimar and Fulda being mentioned as possibilities. In the end, the marriage was planned to take place in Rome, on October 22, Liszt's fiftieth birthday.

Carolyne, daughter of the late Prince Peter Iwanowsky, a Catholic, aged 42, who, in 1836, had been forced to marry Prince Nicholas Wittgenstein, a scismatic, in the Metropolitan Bishopric of Mohilow, having legally petitioned for the annulment of that marriage as it was contracted *per vim et metum* [through force and intimidation] and the case being accordingly decided on February 24, 1860, to the effect that her marriage was declared annulled, has been certified as being single. On January 7, 1861, this resolution having been presented to the Holy Congregation of the Council, she obtained the *exequatur* [authorisation to proceed] with the Pontiff's approval as it transpires from the original document, which is submitted with the intention to retrieve it after releasing a certified copy of it. She begs Your Holiness, therefore, to admit this authoritative certificate and to dispense her from exhibiting the certificates of Baptism, Confirmation, and Single Status from the time of that decision to the present in order to be able to marry the aforementioned Liszt.

Carolina del fu Pietro de' Principi Iawanowska (sic), cattolica di anni 42, essendo stata costretta a sposare nel 1836 il Principe Nicolò Wittgenstein, scismatico, nella Curia Metropolitana di Mohylow, introdusse legalmente causa di nullità di quel matrimonio contratto *per vim et metum* e ne ebbe analoga sentenza a dì 24 Febraro 1860, nella quale, dichiarato nullo quel matrimonio, ottenne il documento di Libertà. Quindi portata questa risoluzione nella S[anta] C[ongregazione] del Concilio con approvazione pontificia ne ottenne l'*exequatur* a dì 7 Gennaro 1861 come risulta dall'autentico documento che esibisce con animo di ritirarlo rilasciandone copia. Prega perciò V[ostra] S[antità] di ammetterle questo autorevole attestato dispensandola dall' esibire le fedi di Battesimo, Cresima, e di stato libero da quella decisione fino al presente, onde potersi legittimamente congiungere col suddetto Liszt. Che <della grazia ecc.>

Wednesday, September 18, 1861.

Upon request of the Petitioner, the Holy Congregation of the Holy Office, on condition that there be no canonic impediment, forwards the petitioner's request to the Most Eminent and Reverend Cardinal Vicar of the City for his decision.
Signed, for the Reverend Angelo Argenti..., by
  Giovenale Pelami

Free for what pertains to the petitioner's request; for the agent, one scudo.

The documents indicated above are admitted according to the requests and dispositions of the petitioner;...
G. Angelini for the authorizing official.
Monsignor Bernardino Maggi, Deputy

Fer[iis] IV. 18 Septembris 1861.

Sacra Congregatio S[ancti] Officii, dummodo nullum obstet canonicum impedimentum, remisit Oratoris instantiam arbitrio E[minentissi]mi et R[everendissi]mi D[o]m[in]i Cardinalis Urbis Vicarii.
Pro D[omi]no Angelo Argenti S. R...... et ...
Juvenalis Pelami sub[scrip]tus

Quae ad i[instantiam] O[ratoris] gratis; pro agente scut. unum

Admittantur indicata documenta juxta preces et oratoris ad jussu,
.... comminatis .....
G. Angelini Pro Vicesg[erente]
B[ernardinus] Can[onicus] Maggi Deput[atus]

Document No. 3. Copy of Liszt's Baptism Certificate, dated May 22, 1848
(enclosed with Doc. 2). Latin (1 page).

IDENTICAL COPY OF AN ENTRY IN THE BAPTISMAL RECORDS OF THE PARISH OF LÓK IN THE DIOCESE OF RAAB.

Year, Month and Day of the Baptism:
October 23, 1811

Name of the Child:
Franz
Place of Residence:
Doborján
Name and Surname of the Parents and their Occupation:
Adam Liszt, Overseer of sheep in the employ of Prince Eszterhazy, and Maria Anna Lager.
Name and Surname of the God-parents:
Franz Zambothy and Julianna Szalay.

Priest performing the Baptism:
Father G. Mersits, Chaplain of Lók.

Observations:

I testify that this Document, faithfully copied and stamped with the Parish Seal, agrees word for word with the Entry in the Baptismal Records of the Parish of Lók, and I vouch for it with my own signature.
Giuseppe Colasanti, Freiherr Baumgartner von Baumgarten,
Parish Priest of Lók
Signed at Lók on the 22nd of May, 1848.[3]
[Illegible Parish Seal]

EXTRACTUS E MATRICULA BAPTISATORUM PAROCHIAE LOÖKENSIS IN DIOCESI IAURINENSI.

Annus Mensis et Dies Baptismi:
Annus Millesimus Octingentesimus Undecimus (1811)
Mensis Octobris
Vigesima Tertia <Dies>
Nomen Infantis:
Franciscus
Locus Domicilii:
Doborjan
Nomen et Cognomen Parentum et eorum Conditio:
Liszt Adamus, Ovium Rationista Principis Eszterhazy et Lager Maria - Anna.
Nomen et Cognomen Patrinorum:
Zambothy Franciscus et
Szalay Julianna.
Baptisans:
R[everendus] D[ominus] Mersits G. Capellanus Loökensis.
Animadversio:

Praeinsertum Extractum fideliter desumptum, Sigilloque Parochiali munitum, cum Matricula Baptisatorum Parochiae Loökensis de verbo ad verbum concordare, in fidem propria manu subscriptus attestor.
Josephus Calasanctius Liber Baro Baumgartner de Baumgarten,
Parochus Loökensis
Signato Loök die 22° Maii 1848.
[Illegible Parish Seal]

Document No. 4. A Deposition from Father Anton Hohmann, the Roman
Catholic Priest from Liszt's Parish in Weimar, certifying the latter's unmarried
status since 1848; dated July 18, 1861.[4] Latin with notes in German (2 pages).

Weimar, July 18, 1861

I hereby testify to the following: that the illustrious Monsieur Franz Liszt, Doctor of Philosophy, born in Hungary, aged 49 years and nine

Weimar die 18 Julii 1861

Tenore presentium testor illustrissimum Dominum Franciscum Liszt, Doctorem Philos[ophiae], natum in Hungaria, nunc in

---

[3]Although the village of Lók was then in Hungary, it is today in the Austrian Burgenland. Its German name is Unterfrauenhaid.

[4]For further information about this document, see Liszt's letter of June 27, 1861, in LLB, Vol. 5, pp. 188-194.

months, from the year 1848, when he set up his residence in Weimar, to the present day, at which time he still resides in that same town where he has lived continually for 13 years, has been always and is still single, is not bound in any way, and is not held by any canonic impediment, as far as it is known, that may prevent him, therefore, from contracting marriage with an unattached woman. I testify, moreover, that the aforesaid Monsieur Liszt, a Catholic, has always given evidence of piety and of a good Christian life and has not omitted to fulfil the duties that Our Holy Mother Church prescribes to a Catholic man. Nothing contrary to the above has come to the attention of myself, the undersigned priest.

A. Hohmann,
Catholic Priest in the City of Weimar.
[SEAL OF THE PARISH CHURCH IN WEIMAR—BAPTISMS]

The above, written by the parson of Weimar, A. Hohmann, and signed in his own hand, bears the seal of the parish. This we confirm by placing our seal.
Fulda, July 29, 1861.
Chapter of the Cathedral of Fulda,
F. Hohmann[5]
[SEAL]

The authenticity of the above signature of the Episcopal Chapter of Fulda, as well as the competency of the parish Office for issuing the above document, are confirmed herewith.
Weimar, August 5, 1861
Grand Ducal Commission
for the Catholic Churches and Schools of Saxony.
Signed: Schmidt

The binding competency of the Grand Ducal Commission for Catholic Churches and Schools in this place for issuing the present document, as well as the authenticity of the signature and seal, are hereby certified.

Weimar August 5, 1861
Grand Ducal State Ministry of Saxony,
Department of the Grand Ducal Household and Foreign Affairs.
Signed: Watzdorf

aetate annorum quadraginta novem novemque mensium constitutum, ab anno 1848, quo domicilium fixit in civitate Weimar usque ad presentem diem, qua adhuc in eadem moratur ibique continuo per tredecim annos permansit, in statu libero semper fuisse et esse, nulloque vinculo teneri vel impedimento canonico irretiri, quod sciatur, quominus matrimonium cum libera possit inire. Insuper testor, praefatum D[omi]num Liszt, catholicum religione, semper pietatis et vitae bene christianae praebuisse argumenta nec omisisse catholici viri officia, quae S[ancta] Mater Ecclesia praescribit, adimplere. De eo quid in contrarium nil mihi parocho infra scripto innotuit.

A. Hohmann,
p. t. Parochus catholicus civitatis Weimar.
[SIGILLum ECCLesiae PAROCHialis VIMARIAE - BAPTismata]

Quae supra leguntur, a parocho Weimariensi A. Hohmann manu propria scripta, subscripta, quoque sigillo parochiali munita esse, hisce testamur apposito nostro sigillo.
Fuldae, die 29 Julii 1861.
Capitulum Eccl[esiae] Cathedr[alis] Fuldensis,
F. Hohmann
[SEAL OF FULDA]

Die Aechtheit vorstehender Unterschrift des bischöflichen Domkapitels zu Fulda sowie die Zuständigkeit des Pfarramts zur Austellung obigen Zeugnisses wird hierdurch bezeugt.
Weimar den 5. August 1861
Großherzogliche Sächsische Immediat-Commission
für das Katholische Kirchen- und Schulwesen.
Schmidt

Die verhaftungsmäßige Kompetenz der Großherzoglichen Immediat-Commission für das Katholische Kirchen- und Schulwesen hier zur Austellung des vorstehenden Zeugnisses, sowie die Aechtheit der Unterschrift und des Siegels werden andurch beglaubigt.
Weimar am 5. August 1861
Großherzoglich Sächsisches Staats-Ministerium,
Departement des Großherzoglich[e]n Hauses und der auswärtigen Angelegenheiten.
Watzdorf

---

[5]F. Hohmann of Fulda was the brother of A. Hohmann of the parish of Weimar.

Document No. 5. A deposition from Carolyne testifying to Liszt's unmarried status up to the year 1848, dated September 18, 1861. (Enclosed with Document No. 2). Italian (1 page).

I, the undersigned, testify on my honor and conscience to the truth that Monsieur Franz Liszt, son of the late Adam, born in Hungary in 1811 and brought to Paris in 1820 while still in his infancy, received there his confirmation in 1829 and resided there until 1838, when he went to Italy. Afterwards, having completed some voyages to the main capitals of Europe for the purpose of instruction, he established his residence in Weimar in 1848, attached to the court of the Grand Duke. There he has continued to reside and is still residing at present, conducting himself always as a true Christian Catholic. I can also testify with full and certain knowledge that, from the time of his birth to the present, he has remained unattached, never having entered any bond or taken any pledge that may prevent him from marrying according to the Catholic rite. This I can establish on the basis of the acquaintance I have had and even now have with him and his family. On my word, etc.

Rome, this 18th of September, 1861.
Princess Carolyne von Sayn-Wittgenstein born Iwanowska[6]
[Seal]

Io sottoscritta attesto nel mio onore e coscienza per la verità che il Signor Francesco Liszt, figlio del fu Adamo, nato in Ungheria nel 1811, sin dalla infanzia recato a Parigi nel 1820, ivi nel 1829 fu cresimato e vi rimase sino all'anno 1838, d'onde in questa epoca venne in Italia e poscia, fatti dei viaggi istruttivi nelle principali Capitali d'Europa, si ridusse nel 1848 a Weymar attaccato alla Corte di quel Granduca, ove sempre rimasto e vi rimane tuttora, vivendo sempre da vero cristiano cattolico. E posso anche attestare con piena e certa scienza che il medesimo si è sempre dalla sua nascita sino al giorno presente conservato libero, non avendo mai contratto alcun vincolo od impegno che possa impedirgli di contrarre matrimonio secondo il rito cattolico. E tutto ciò mi co<n>sta dalle relazioni che ho avuto ed ho tuttora con esso e colla di lui famiglia. In fede etc.

Roma, questo giorno 18 Settembre 1861.
Principessa Carolyna di Sayn-Wittgenstein, N[ata] Iwanowska
[Seal]

Document No. 6. A request in Notary Erasmo Ciccolini's hand to waive the reading of the marriage banns, probably included with Documents No. 7 and 8. Italian (2 pages).

The following is presented, on behalf of the Petitioners, by Erasmo Ciccolini, Notary.

To His Most Reverend Excellency the Monsignor Vicar General of Rome

Most Reverend Excellency:

Commander[7] Franz Liszt, son of the late Adam, having come to Rome for the purpose of

Per gli entro[scri]tti Or[atoris] Not[aio] <Erasmo> Ciccolini

A Sua Ec[cell]enza Re[verendissi]ma Mons[ignor] Vic[ario] G[enerale] di Roma

Ec[cell]enza Rev[erendissi]ma.

Il Commendatore Francesco Liszt, figlio della bo[na] me[moria] Adamo, venuto in Roma

---

[6]The factual errors in this sworn statement would have rendered it suspect in law. Thus, Liszt was brought to Paris in 1823, not 1820; he resided there until 1835, not 1838; his "voyages" to the main capitals of Europe were hardly "for the purpose of instruction"; and in September 1861, Liszt no longer resided in Weimar, having closed down the Altenburg on Carolyne's own instructions the previous month. It remains only to observe that the Princess appears to have been

surprisingly ill-informed about the details of Liszt's earlier years.

[7]On May 31, 1861, Liszt had been named Commander of the Legion of Honor by Napoleon III. Previously, on October 29, 1859, he had also been named Commander of the Order of St. Gregory the Great by Pope Pius IX (see ASV, SS Docs. No. 1, 2, 3).

entering into matrimony (*ad effectum nubendi*), and Lady Carolyne, Princess of Sayn-Wittgenstein, born Iwanowska, daughter of the late Peter from the parish of St. James in Avgustivka, Your Most Reverend Excellency's humblest petitioners, wishing to join in holy matrimony in haste and secrecy on account of just and legitimate reasons presented verbally, beseech you to exert yourself in order to exempt them from the three customary publications.

October 20, 1861
For the granting,
G. Angelini, signing for authorising official[8]

ad effectum nubendi, e Donna Carolina Principessa di S[ayn] Wittgenstein nata Iwanowska, figlia della bo[na] me[moria] Pietro della Cura di S[an] Giacomo in Augusta, or[atori] umi[lissimi] dell'E[ccellenza] V[ostra] R[everendissima], bramando unirsi in S[anto] Matrimonio con sollecitudine, e segrettezza per giuste, e legittime cause esposte a voce, La pregano a degnarsi dispensarli, dalle tre consuete pubblicazioni. Ch[e della grazia ecc.]

20 Octobris 1861
Pro Gratia
G. Angelini, Pro Vicesgerente

Document No. 7. An instrument of interrogation bearing the names of Liszt and Carolyne, dated October 20, 1861, in which the penalties for bearing false witness are set forth. Pertaining to Document No. 8. Latin (2 pages).[9]

No. 4477
QUESTIONING TO BE CARRIED OUT

in the examination of those witnesses who are convened in the chambers of the most reverend and eminent Cardinal Vicar of the City, for the purpose of contracting marriage; witnesses have to be warned from the outset of the gravity of oaths, particularly terrifying in such a matter, because both the Divine and the human Majesties are offended, because of the importance and solemnity of what is involved, and because those who provide false testimony are sentenced to prison.
Day: October 20, 1861
Pertaining to: Franz Liszt and Carolyne
    Iwanowska

N. 4477
INTERROGATORIA FACIENDA

pro examine illorum Testium, qui inducuntur pro contrahendis Matrimoniis in Curia E[minentissi]mi et R[everendissi]mi Domini Card[inalis] Urbis Vicarii, et in primis monendi erunt Examinandi de gravitate juramenti in hoc praesertim negotio pertimescendi, in quo Divina simul, et humana Majestas laeditur, ob rei de qua tractatur, importantiam, et gravitatem, et quod imminet poena Triremium, deponenti falsum.

Die: 20 Ottobre 1861
Pro: Francesco Liszt e Carolina Iawanowska
    (sic)

---

[8]Liszt got to Rome on October 20, 1861, and for the first time learned that the banns had not yet been read. This application to have them waived talks of "just and legitimate reasons" for the marriage to take place in haste and secrecy, and it was made within hours of Liszt's arrival in the Eternal City. We surmise that Carolyne had already learned of Hohenlohe's intention to bring forward witnesses to testify against her and have the marriage stopped. A public reading of the banns, of course, would have alerted Hohenlohe to the time and place. In the end he discovered these things anyway and caused the ceremony to be halted shortly before it was to take place. (See ASV, CC, Doc. No. 72).
[9]The specific guidelines for the interrogation of couples are omitted here.

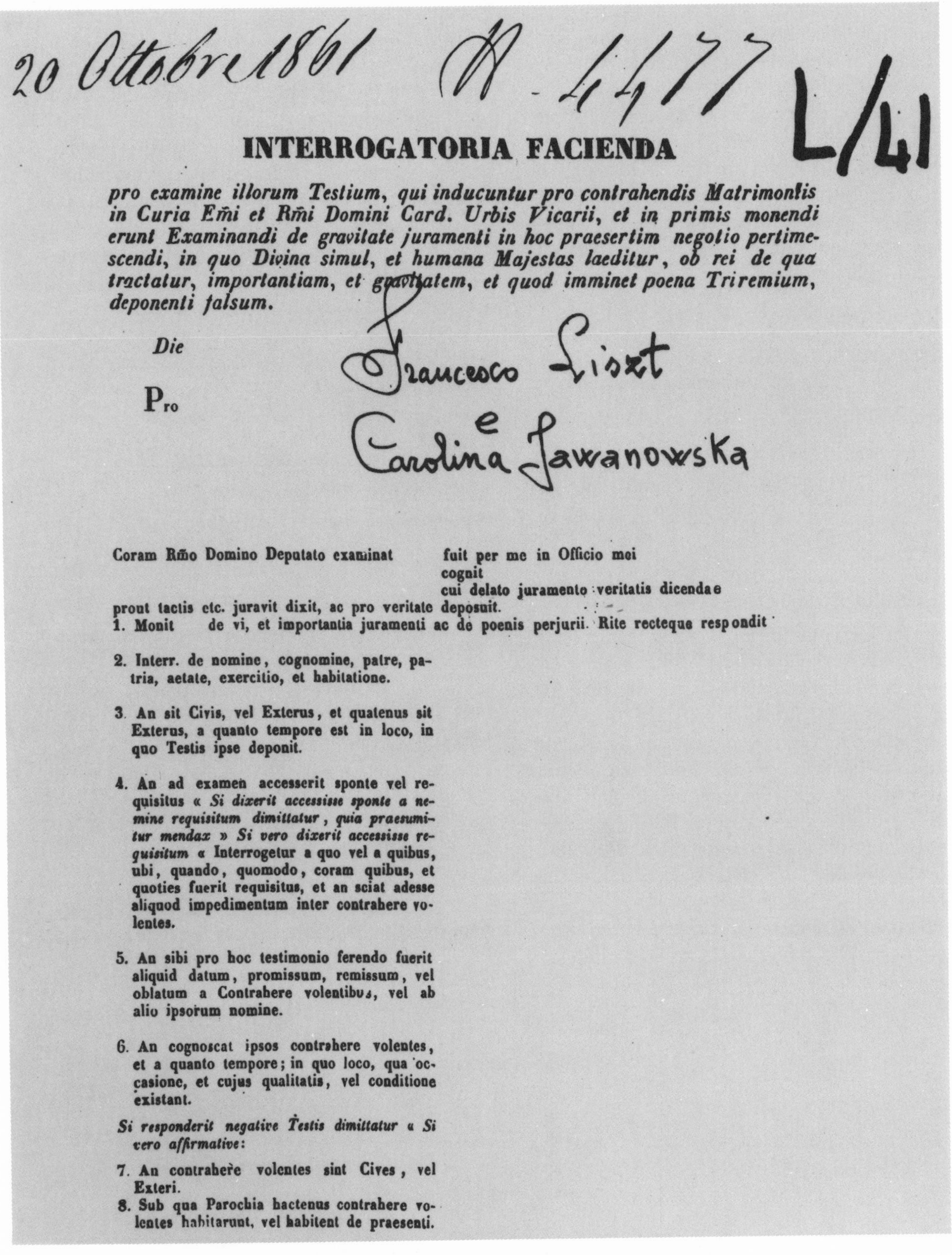

INTERROGATORIA FACIENDA

pro examine illorum Testium, qui inducuntur pro contrahendis Matrimoniis in Curia Emi et Rmi Domini Card. Urbis Vicarii, et in primis monendi erunt Examinandi de gravitate juramenti in hoc praesertim negotio pertimescendi, in quo Divina simul, et humana Majestas laeditur, ob rei de qua tractatur, importantiam, et gravitatem, et quod imminet poena Triremium, deponenti falsum.

Die

Pro

Francesco Liszt

e

Carolina Jawanowska

Coram Rmo Domino Deputato examinat   fuit per me in Officio mei
                                              cognit
                                              cui delato juramento veritatis dicendae
prout tactis etc. juravit dixit, ac pro veritate deposuit.
1. Monit   de vi, et importantia juramenti ac de poenis perjurii. Rite recteque respondit

2. Interr. de nomine, cognomine, patre, patria, aetate, exercitio, et habitatione.

3. An sit Civis, vel Exterus, et quatenus sit Exterus, a quanto tempore est in loco, in quo Testis ipse deponit.

4. An ad examen accesserit sponte vel requisitus « *Si dixerit accessisse sponte a nemine requisitum dimittatur, quia praesumitur mendax* » *Si vero dixerit accessisse requisitum* « Interrogetur a quo vel a quibus, ubi, quando, quomodo, coram quibus, et quoties fuerit requisitus, et an sciat adesse aliquod impedimentum inter contrahere volentes.

5. An sibi pro hoc testimonio ferendo fuerit aliquid datum, promissum, remissum, vel oblatum a Contrahere volentibus, vel ab alio ipsorum nomine.

6. An cognoscat ipsos contrahere volentes, et a quanto tempore; in quo loco, qua occasione, et cujus qualitatis, vel conditione existant.

Si responderit negative Testis dimittatur « Si vero affirmative:

7. An contrahere volentes sint Cives, vel Exteri.
8. Sub qua Parochia hactenus contrahere volentes habitarunt, vel habitent de praesenti.

Plate 12. An instrument of interrogation bearing the names of Liszt and Carolyne, dated October 20, 1861, in which the penalties for bearing false witness are set forth.

Document No. 8. A joint deposition from Liszt and Carolyne, written in the hand of Notary Erasmo Ciccolini, testifying to the fact that they were both single, dated October 20, 1861. Enclosed with Document No. 6. Italian (1 page).

In the Name of God.

Rome, October 20, 1861

In the personal presence of the Most Reverend Deputy in charge of Marriages, the Most Illustrious Commander Franz Liszt, Chamberlain of the Grand Ducal Court of Weimar, son of the late Adam, presently in Rome for the purpose of contracting marriage, and Her Highness Lady Carolyne Iwanowska, Princess von Sayn-Wittgenstein, daughter of the late Peter, spontaneously ratify the contents of the present document drawn up on their request after the order of the Holy Office following the Executive Decree of His Excellency the Lord Cardinal Vicar, and swear, with their hand on the Holy Gospels, to be single, not to have taken respectively wife or husband, become a Priest or Monk or a Nun, contracted impediments, become wedded, or promised marriage to others to whom they may now be bound, not even to relatives by blood in the first degree, from the unmarrying age to the present as far as the Most Illustrious Commander Liszt is concerned, and from the Judgement declaring her first marriage null and void to the present as far as Her Highness Lady Carolyne is concerned. The aforementioned Illustrious Commander swears also to have received confirmation in Paris in the year 1829 in the church of St. Vincent de Paul.

After receiving previous warning as to the force of oaths and as to the sentences meted out to those who are polygamous and perjurers, they have signed below

F. Liszt

Princess Carolyne von Sayn-Wittgenstein,

born Iwanowska

The above-mentioned made their oath in the presence of myself, Monsignor Bernardino Maggi, Deputy.[10]

Nel Nome di Dio.

Roma, 20 ottobre 1861

Avanti al Rev[erend]o Sig[nor] Deputato a Matrimoni personalmente costituito, l'Ill[ustrissi]mo Sig[nor] Commendatore Francesco Liszt, Ciamberlano della Corte Granducale de Weiymar, figlio della bo[na] me[moria] Adamo, venuto in Roma *ad effectum nubendi*, e Sua Altezza Donna Carolina Iwanowska, Principessa di S[ayn] Wittgenstein, figlia della bo[na] me[moria] Pietro, spontaneamente ratificando l'esposto nella presente memoria come che tutta a di loro istanza, in sequela del Rescritto del S[anto] O[ffizio] e susseguente Decreto esecutoriale di S[ua] E[minenza] R[everendissima] Sig[nor] Card[inal] Vicario, giurano toccando il S[anto] Evangelo di esser liberi, non essersi ammogliato, o maritata, fatti prete o frate, Monaca, né aver contratto impedimenti, sponsali, o dato parola di matrimonio ad altri, cui ora siano tenuti, e nemmeno a Consanguinei rispettivi in primo grado, dalla innubile età fino al presente in quanto all'Ill[ustrissi]mo Sig. Commendatore Liszt, e dalla Sentenza che ha dichiarato nullo il primo Matrimonio fino al presente <in> rapporto a S[ua] A[ltezza] Donna Carolina. Giura inoltre il lodato Ill[ustrissi]mo Sig[nor] C[ommendato]re di esser stato confirmato in Parigi nell' anno 1829 nella Chiesa di S. Vincenzo di Paola.

Tutto ciò previa ammonizione sulla forza del giuramento e comminaz[ione] della pena contro i Poligami e Spergiuri e si sono sottoscritti

F. Liszt

Pr[incipe]ssa Carolyna di Sayn-Wittgenstein

nata Iwanowska

Supradicti jurarunt coram me.

Bernardinus Can[onicus] Maggi deput[atus].

---

[10]This document is of more than passing interest. It is the only known occasion on which Liszt himself swore before witnesses that it was his solemn intention to marry Princess Carolyne. Both Liszt and Carolyne were cautioned as to the gravity of the oaths they were making. The penalties for perjury were severe, and not only included excommunication but a long term in prison as well. It is in this context that the charges of bribery and corruption brought by Hohenlohe have to be viewed. Had he been correct, and had he been able to prove that he was correct, Carolyne would undoubtedly have found herself in the gravest legal and spiritual crisis of her life.

Document No. 9. A bill signed by Notary Erasmo Ciccolini for services and the writing of instruments required for getting married. Italian (1 page).

Executive decrees	20.	Decreti esecut[orii]		20.
Dispensing oath of single status for both, and Confirmation for the man	50.	Giuram[ento] di <stato> libero, entram[bi], e Cres[ima], Uomo		50.
Dispensation from banns	30.	Dispensa pub[blicazioni]		30.
Monsignor Vice-Gerente	20.	M[onsignor] Viceg[erente]		20.
Deputy	2.10.	V[ice] Deputato		2.10.
Interrogation	32	Processetto		32
Janitor	05.	Bidello		05.
	3.67			3.67

File: 4477			4477		
V.	.30		V.	.30	
D.	2.10		D.	2.10	
C.	1.12		C.	1.12	
P.	------		P.	____	
b.	.15		b.	.15	
	3.67			3.67	

Forms	1.12	Cance[lleria]		1.12
Copying	10.00	Ricopia[tura]		10.00
	11.12			11.12

Erasmo Ciccolini, Notary   Not. <Erasmo> Ciccolini

A FEW CONTEMPORARY DOCUMENTS PERTAINING TO LISZT AND CAROLYNE IN THE ARCHIVES OF THE SECRETARY OF STATE OF THE HOLY SEE (1859–60).

Plate 13. Cardinal Giacomo Antonelli, Secretary of State to the Vatican.
A photograph.

Document No. 1. ASV, SS 1859: Rubric 220, fasc. 3, leaves No. 140- 141. Liszt's letter of thanks to Antonelli upon being informed that the Holy See has made him a Commander of the Order of St. Gregory the Great. French (2 pages).

220/3

Weimar, August 25, 1859.

Your Eminence:

It is with feelings of the most sincere gratitude that I wish to express to Your Eminence my most respectful thanks for your letter through which you wished to honor me; it is, moreover, a most valuable proof of the favor with which you look upon my modest merits.

The high distinction His Holiness the Pope deigns to bestow on me by conferring on me, thanks to your benevolent intercession, the rank of Commander of the Order of St. Gregory the Great, imposes even more urgently upon me the obligation to bear witness to the world my filial devotion to the most august and revered Spiritual Head of our Holy Religion.

May I be so bold as to beg your Eminence to place at the feet of His Holiness the homage of my humble gratitude, together with the vow I am making to endeavor, with the utmost zeal, to make myself ever more worthy of His complete approbation.

With the deepest respect, I have the honor of being

Your Eminence's most humble and obedient servant,

F. Liszt

220/3

Weymar, 25 Août 1859.

Votre Eminence.

C'est avec le sentiment de le plus sincère reconnaissance que je viens exprimer à Votre Eminence mes très respecteuse remerciment pour la lettre dont elle veut bien m'honore, et qui m'est une preuve si prècieuse de la grâce avec laquelle elle prend en considèration mes faibles mérites.

La haut distinction que la Sainteté le Pape daigne m'accorder sur votre bienvéillante intercession en me confèrant le grade de commandeur de l'ordre de S[an] Gregorio Magno, m'impose plus directement encore l'obligation de rendre tèmoignage au monde de ma filiale dèvotion envers le très auguste et très venéré Chef de notre Sainte Religion.

J'ose prier Votre Eminence de mèttre aux pieds de la Sainteté l'hommage de mon humble gratitude en même temps que le voeu que je fais de travailler avec un zèle persévérant à me rendre de plus en plus digne de Sa suprême satisfaction.

J'ai l'honneur d'être avec le plus profond respect,

De Votre Eminence,

le très humble et très obéisant serviteur.

F. Liszt

Document No. 2. ASV, SS, 1859: Rubric No. 220, fasc. 3, leaf No. 142. October 29, 1859. Draft of Antonelli's letter to Liszt, forwarding to him the commission of Commander of the Order of St. Gregory the Great. Italian (1 page).

<Rubric No.> 220/3

To: Commander Franz Liszt,

Weimar.

October 29, 1859

As I wrote to you in my previous letter, I am sending you today the enclosed papal brief certifying your rank as Commander of the Order of St. Gregory the Great, which the Holy Father was pleased to confer upon you. His Holiness, to whom I transmitted the expression of deep grati-

220/3

Al Sig[nor] Commend[ator] Francesco Liszt,

Weymar.

29 ott[obre] 1859

In conformità di quanto significai a V[ostra] S[ignoria] I[llustrissima] con l'anteced[ente] mio foglio, Le invio oggi qui accluso il breve comprovante l'onorevole distinzione di Commenda[tor] dell'Ord[ine] di S[an] Gregorio M[agn]o che piacque al S[anto] Padre di

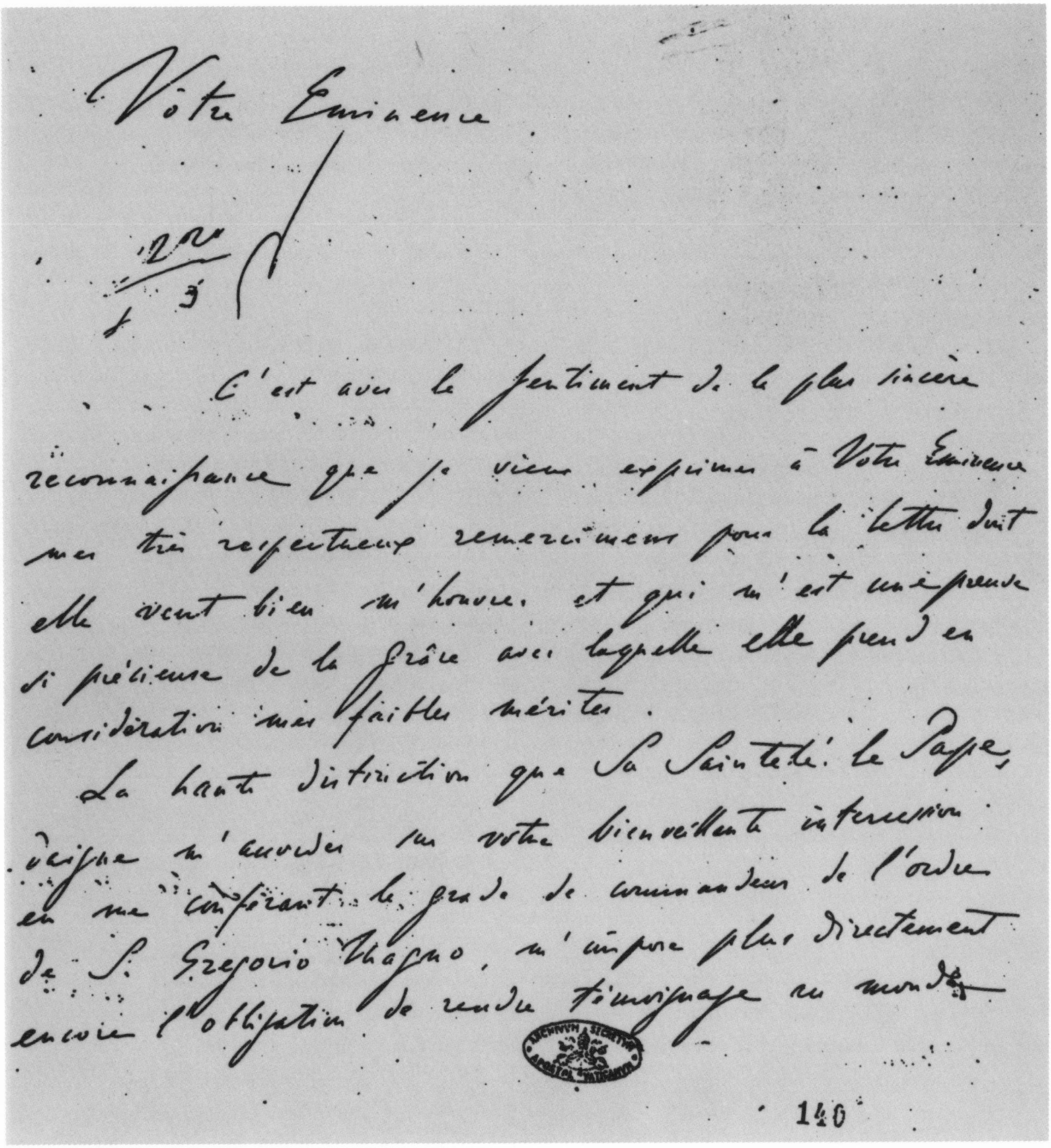

Plate 14. Facsimile of a letter from Liszt to Cardinal Antonelli, dated "Weimar, August 25, 1859," upon being elevated to the rank of Commander of the Order of Saint Gregory the Great..."A valuable proof of the favor with which you look upon my modest merits."

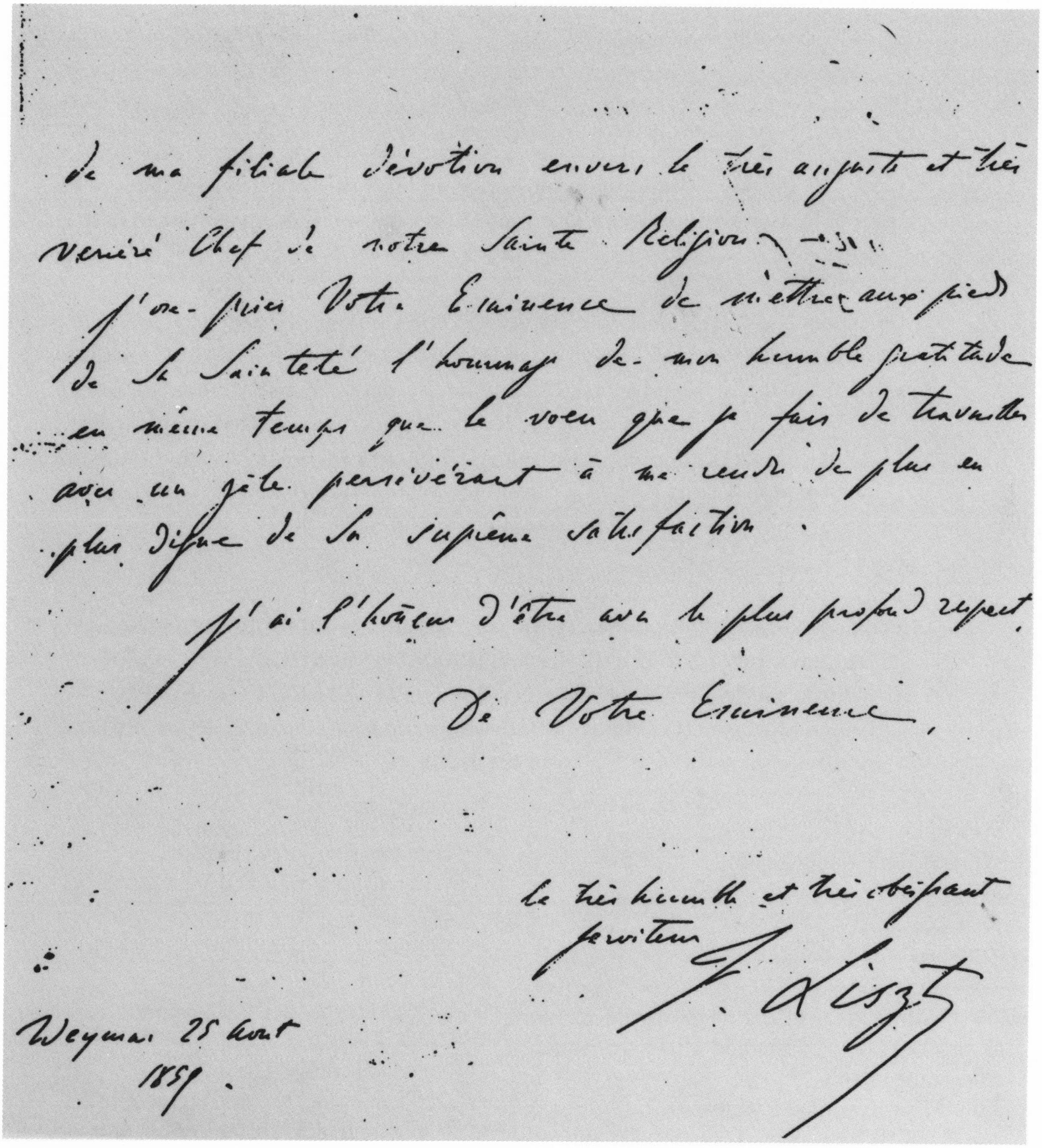

de ma filiale dévotion envers le très auguste et très vénéré Chef de notre Sainte Religion. —

Je prie Votre Eminence de mettre aux pieds de Sa Sainteté l'hommage de mon humble gratitude en même temps que le voeu que je fais de travailler avec un zèle persévérant à me rendre de plus en plus digne de Sa suprême satisfaction.

J'ai l'honneur d'être avec le plus profond respect,

De Votre Eminence,

le très humble et très obéissant
serviteur
F. Liszt

Weymar 25 août
1859.

Plate 14. (cont.)

tude communicated to me in your letter of August 25 last, was much gratified by it. In the act of giving you this news, it is my privilege ...

<Giacomo Cardinal Antonelli, Secretary of
     State>
Brief enclosed.

concederle. La S[antità] S[ua], cui rassegnai e' sensi di profonda riconoscenza da Lei manifestatimi con la Sua lettera del 25 ag[os]to p[rossimo] p[assa]to, ne ha provato piena soddisfazione. E nel darle di ciò contezza mi pregio etc.

<Giacomo Cardinal Antonelli, Segretario di
     Stato>
Con Breve.

Document No. 3. September 1859. The ASV, SS catalogue lists under Prot. No. 6076, Rubric 220, the papal commission conferring on Liszt the title of Commander of the Order of St. Gregory the Great. This commission, however, is not contained in that volume.

Document No. 4. December 1859. In the ASV, SS catalogue there is a reference to a document with Prot. No. 7549/3, dated December 1859 and described as a petition pertaining to the Iwanowska case. Unfortunately, that document cannot, at present, be found, since the indication of the the Rubric Number was omitted by the Archivist at the time. It might very well be the same petition to reopen her case that Carolyne presented in August 1859 or a copy of the September petition presented by Marie about her legitimacy.

Document No. 5. ASV, SS, 1860: Rubric No. 247, fasc. 2, leaf No. 204. The original of De Luca's July 14, 1860 letter to Antonelli (See ASV, NV Doc. 24) enclosing Żyliński's letter of May 24, 1860 (NV Doc. No. 21 and ASV, CC Doc. No.31). Italian (2 pages). It contains the following salutations customarily omitted in the draft:

Protocol No. 1057
Wittgenstein-Iwanowska Marriage Case
247

Vienna, July 14, 1860
.....

     With feelings of the deepest respect I bow to kiss Your holy purple and I have the honor of confirming myself
Your Most Reverend Eminence's
most humble, devoted and obliging servant,
Antonino <De Luca>
Archbishop of Tarsus
Apostolic Nuncio
Enclosure

N. 1057
Oggetto: Causa matrimoniale
Wittgenstein-Iwanowska
247
Vienna, il 14 luglio 1860
.....

     Co' sensi del più profondo ossequio m'inchino al bacio della S[anta] Porpora mentre ho l'onore di confermarmi
Dell'Eminenza Vostra Reverendissima
Umilissimo, devotissimo, obblig[atissi]mo Servo
     v[er]o
Ant[onino] Arciv[escov]o di Tarso,
N[unzio] Ap[ostolic]o
(Con inserto)

Document No. 6. ASV, SS, 1860: Rubric No. 247, fasc. 2, leaf No. 205. Draft of Antonelli's July 24, 1860, letter to Quaglia forwarding the copy of Żyliński's letter to De Luca (ASV, NV Doc. 21 and ASV, CC Doc. No. 31). See ASV, CC Doc. No. 30. Italian (1 page).

Document No. 7. ASV, SS, 1860: Rubric No. 267. The ASV, SS catalogue lists, under the date of December 7, 1860, a document pertaining to Władislaw Okraszewski's delivery of a package to the Nunciature in Vienna. The document was not found in that volume.

EPILOGUE

The Rome of Pius IX and Gustav von Hohenlohe

by ALAN WALKER

I

When Liszt arrived in Rome, on October 20, 1861, the Catholic Church was in the middle of the gravest crisis of its long existence. There was a dark side to life in the Eternal City which today is all but forgotten, especially in biographies of Liszt. The higher clergy within the Vatican itself was hopelessly divided into factions whose manner of doing business with one another included conspiracy, violence, assassination, and suicide. Papal Rome had become a battlefield in which Franciscans strove against Dominicans, Jesuits against Liberals, "Blacks" against "Whites." Liszt was to live in Rome for eight years (1861–69) during which time he became a cleric. He could hardly remain immune to the life-and-death struggles that faced the church. What were they, and how did they come about?

Pius IX had been elected Pope on June 16, 1846, and his elevation to the Holy See had been greeted in Italy with an outpouring of joy. The restrictive policies of his predecessor Gregory XVI, and the latter's secretary of state Cardinal Luigi Lambruschini, had brought the Papal States to the verge of revolution.[1] "Young Italy," in particular, saw in Pius its last best hope, a national leader who would succeed in untying the bonds that had fettered the Italian states to the House of Habsburg for generations. The cry "Viva Pio Nono!" was soon on everyone's lips, and the drive towards a unified Italy appeared to carry the pope's sanction. It was the first time in history that a "liberal" pope had occupied St. Peter's, and the heads of state in France, Austria, Prussia, and England trembled to think of the consequences. They did not have to wait long to find out. One of Pius IX's first political acts was the granting of a general amnesty to political prisoners and exiles, on July 16, 1846, less than three weeks after his coronation in the Basilica of St. Peter's. He naively supposed that this would have a healing effect and utterly failed to realise that these same revolutionaries, some of whom pursued assassination as political policy, would simply continue their fight to have the Vatican itself swept aside and establish a democratic government in its place. Within a short time Pius found himself besieged by problems and had to act against the very people he had so recently pardoned. In his encyclical *Qui pluribus*, of November 9, 1846, he laments the intrigues against the Holy See, the machinations of the secret societies, the emergence of communism, and the calumnies of the

[1] Giovanni Maria Mastai-Ferretti (1792-1876) had never wanted to be pope. Nor was he considered to be the strongest candidate for the pontificate. He had only received the red hat in 1840, and through his charitable work as cardinal priest of Santi Pietro e Marcellino he had become known as a friend of the common people. This made him suspect at a time when the "common people" were toppling thrones all over Europe. Everyone remembered that it was Mastai-Ferretti who, as Archbishop of Spoleto, had persuaded 4000 Italian revolutionaries who were fleeing before the Austrian army to lay down their arms, and had then induced the Austrian commander to pardon them for their treason. In consequence of this act, Mastai-Ferretti had made many friends among the revolutionaries, whose cause he appeared to support. After Gregory XIV's death the mounting frustration of the Italian nationalists, and the fear that Gregory's repressive Secretary of State, Cardinal Lambruschini, might be elected as his successor, prompted a group of liberal cardinals, headed by Bernetti, to

block his election. On June 14 fifty cardinals assembled in the Quirinal Palace for the conclave. They were divided roughly between the Absolutists who favored a continuance of the temporal powers of the pope, and the Liberals who wanted greater flexibility in the Church's dealings with Italian national aspirations. At the first scrutiny Lambruschini acquired more votes than Mastai-Ferretti, but not enough for the necessary majority. It was not until the fourth scrutiny that Mastai-Ferretti emerged as the clear candidate. Even then, he would never have been elected pope if Cardinal Gaysruch of Milan had not arrived too late to make use of the right of exclusion vested in him by the Austrian government. Had that happened, the subsequent history of the papacy might have been entirely different. But with the elevation of Mastai-Ferretti to St. Peter's, the dramatic confrontation between Church and State, which was to characterise so much of his reign, began to unfold. It was also the longest papacy in the history of the Roman Catholic Church, lasting for thirty-two years.

press. One of the most powerful of the secret societies was the fanatical "Circolo Romano" which, under their leader Ciceruacchio, instituted mob rule and brought Rome to the brink of riot. They demanded a constitutionally elected govern-

ment, a lay ministry, and a declaration of war against Austria. To this last demand Pius was unable to accede, whereupon he was denounced as a traitor to Italy and marked for death.

II

Nothing better sums up these turbulent times than the assassination of Pellegrino Rossi, the Prime Minister to Pius IX. On November 15, 1848, Rossi was on his way to the legislative assembly in the Palazzo della Cancelleria to explain the pope's new program of administrative reform. He had just seated himself in his carriage when an assassin's dagger was plunged through his neck, and he expired almost at once. The killing was carried out at the behest of one of the secret societies. Rossi's murder triggered an attack on the Quirinal Palace the next day. Palma, a papal prelate who was standing at a window, was shot, and Pius was forced to escape the palace in disguise. He and many of his Cardinals fled the city and assembled in Gaeta, in the Kingdom of Naples, from where he issued appeals for help to France, Austria, and Spain. During the pope's exile a Roman Republic was proclaimed, but it was short-lived. On June 29, 1849, French troops entered Rome and restored order. When Pius himself returned to the Vatican, on April 12, 1850, he was no longer a liberal.

Studying theology in Rome at this time was the twenty-eight-year-old Frédéric de Mérode, who later became a close personal friend of Gustav von Hohenlohe, and was also acquainted with Liszt. As a young man, Mérode had military training in Algiers. When he heard of Rossi's death he took off his cassock, donned a pair of pistols, and rushed over to the Quirinal Palace in order to defend the pope. Mérode was one of the clerics who accompanied Pius to Gaeta, during the dark days of the Roman Republic. In acknowledgement of his loyalty, the pope made Mérode his chamberlain and war minister. In this latter role Mérode found himself perpetually at odds with Antonelli (whom Pius had named his Secretary of State in 1848), who preferred diplomacy to arms. Mérode became the papal Almoner to Pius IX, in succession to Hohenlohe when the latter was made a cardinal in 1866.

After his return to Rome, in 1850, Pius clung tenaciously to his waning authority. Since he was unwilling to give up any of his temporal possessions they were taken from him one by one, by force. The Piedmontese ruler Victor Emmanuel, and his anti-papal prime minister Camillo Cavour, wanted a united Italy with Rome as its capital, and they worked unceasingly towards the dissolution of the pope's domains. This objective was difficult to achieve so long as the House of Habsburg supported Pius and kept its military garrisons within the Papal States.[2] But in 1859 Austria and France went to war with one another. They clashed at Magenta on June 4, and then at Solferino on June 24. During this last battle, in which the two armies were led by their respective monarchs, the Emperor Franz Josef and Napoleon III, approximately 150,000 soldiers on each side confronted one another. While the engagement was in progress, a torrential downpour of rain turned the battlefield into a swamp and mired both man and beast in mud. At the end of the day the Austrians had sustained 23,000 casualties, while the French and the Piedmontese had suffered 12,000 and 5,500 respectively. The carnage on the Austrian side obliged that army to withdraw not only from the field of battle but from all its garrisons as well, and Victor Emmanuel demanded that the defenceless Papal States be ceded to Piedmont. Pius IX refused to give up his territories (he called them "the robe of Jesus Christ"), so Victor Emmanuel prepared a military campaign against him. He finally defeated the newly-raised papal army at Castelfidardo on September 12, 1860, and again at Ancona on September 30. Meanwhile, Victor Emmanuel had met Garibaldi on September 26, who had proclaimed him King of Italy. For the next ten years it was the French garrison in Rome that protected the patrimony of St. Peter's—all that was now left of Pius IX's temporal possessions. It was not until 1870, when France was preoccupied with its disastrous war

---

[2]The Papal States included the following domains: Romagna, Umbria, the Marches, Sabina, and Emilia, over which the popes had ruled as sovereign monarchs for centuries.

against Germany, that Victor Emmanuel marched into Rome and made it the capital of a united Italy. Church and State were now officially separated. Although the so-called Law of Guarantees recognised Pius as a sovereign, and made him a financial provision of more than three million lire annually, Pius refused the conditions and remained a self-imposed prisoner in the Vatican for the rest of his life—as, for that matter, did his successor Leo XIII. There-after, it was the official policy of the Vatican to have no formal diplomatic ties of any kind with the government of Italy, many of whose members were excommunicated; indeed, the church sometimes excommunicated its own clergy if they breached this rule. It was not until 1929, with the arrival of Mussolini, that the Concordat between the Vatican and Italy was signed, and the Roman question was settled.

III

The enormous political pressures that were exerted on Pius IX during his long and tragic pontificate help to explain some of his doctrinal reforms, which were designed to help the church during its crisis. His celebrated encyclical *Quanta cura* (December 1864) was an attack against liberalism, and was issued with a *Syllabus errorum* which listed 80 of the "principal errors of our times." And at the First Vatican Council (1869-70), which took Pius and his advisors several years to plan, the doctrine of Papal Infallibility was adopted, although not without acrimonious debate, during which more than eighty of the cardinals voted against it and then left the city. Henceforth, the pope was empowered to make *ex cathedra* statements on all matters involving the interests of the church and claim that his authority came from God.

Some of the liberal cardinals who had been swept into office with the election of Pius IX now found themselves isolated, and (for such was the temper of the times), physically endangered. They included cardinals Franchi, Schiaffino, and Hohenlohe, all of whom died under mysterious circumstances and were generally believed to have been poisoned. Their enemies, the Jesuits, were known to be expert in the preparation of the *acquetta*.[3] Their most famous victim was Father Antonio Rosmini, one of the greatest religious leaders the Catholic Church ever produced, who incurred the implacable hatred of the Jesuits for his support of a unified Italy and the clear separation of Church and State. His central thesis was that the true business of the church was the saving of souls, not the pursuit of political power. The Jesuits eventually denounced him and condemned his ideas through the Inquisition. The last entry in Rosmini's *Diario della Carita* is dated February 25, 1852:

> Ash Wednesday. A man, dressed in black, with a blue overcoat, came into the garden at Stresa, and inquired of Antonio Carli [Rosmini's lay-brother] if he looked after the Abate Rosmini. He answered that he did and the man said that he had a small request to make, which if agreed to would be rewarded with a great sum of money. He took out of his pocket a small phial, and asked him to pour its contents into the coffee or chocolate that the Abate Rosmini took in the morning. Astounded, Carli refused, and the stranger at one replied that it was no matter, and coolly walked out of the garden and went straight to the shore opposite the house, where there was a boat waiting with three or four boatmen. He boarded it and was gone.[4]

During the months that followed Rosmini suffered from intestinal pains, vomiting, and haemorrhaging. After developing jaundice and dropsy, he died a lingering, painful death in 1855. He was fifty-eight years old. Even the Wittgenstein-Iwanowska file bears witness to these troubled times, and to the unusual measures that had to be taken when it was necessary to communicate in secret. On May 10, 1860, we find Gustav Hohenlohe writing to Monsignor De Luca: "I enclose herewith ... some other letters that I am asking you to forward to their destination. I am sorry to inconvenience you so often, but what can one do in these times so unsafe for gentlemen and their letters?!"[5]

---

[3]The *acquetta di Perugia* was a cup of slow-acting poisoned chocolate, possibly with an arsenic base.
[4]LR, p. 466.

[5]See p. 48 of the present volume. There is evidence that Liszt, too, was caught up in the cloak-and-dagger atmosphere of Rome, and that he communicated "sensitive" material to the outside world through his many diplomatic channels there.

IV

In fact, Gustav von Hohenlohe is an interesting case, and not merely because of his special connection with Liszt. The best information about his private life comes from his longtime friend and colleague Primo Levi, the editor of Rome's *Tribuna*.[6] Hohenlohe was a liberal who was given a cardinal's hat in 1866—thanks in part to his powerful family connections in a largely Protestant Germany, connections which Pius hoped to manipulate to his advantage.[7] But Hohenlohe's profound disillusionment with Pius caused him to leave Rome for an extended period (between 1871-76). Indeed, his liberal views had created a solid wall of opposition within the Vatican's secretariat, and it became impossible for him to function there. It was not until Leo XIII was elected pope, in 1876, that Hohenlohe returned to the Eternal City. In 1878 he was appointed Archbishop of Santa Maria Maggiore, one of the most important dioceses in Rome, and a year later he became Bishop of Albano. These distinctions were possible for him only because it was Leo XIII's official policy to indulge in window-dressing: that is to say, Leo adopted the outer trappings of liberalism while cleaving to the conservative traditions he had inherited from Pius IX. But he reckoned without Hohenlohe's outspokenness and his readiness to resist him. Hohenlohe had many connections within the new Italian government, and he used them constantly, in defiance of the papal injunction forbidding any diplomatic contacts with these arch enemies of the Vatican. He found it hypocritical that Leo censured him for this while doing exactly the same thing himself, albeit surreptitiously. Several times Hohenlohe was reprimanded by Leo through the latter's intermediary, Cardinal Mariano Rampolla. The conflict between the pair is symbolized in the famous letter that Hohenlohe wrote to Leo on July 24, 1889.

> Today we can no longer isolate ourselves in Chinese fashion from the personages of the Italian Government. God has so ordained that the Church can never again get back her temporal power. The salvation of souls requires that we resign ourselves to this fact, that we keep quietly within the ecclesiastical sphere and perform charity by giving of our substance and by teaching the faithful.
>
> There is talk of quitting [Rome]. Now his Excellency Crispi [Minister for External Affairs] told me the other day to inform your Holiness that, if you wish to go, he will not oppose it and will have you escorted with all honors, but that your Holiness will never return to Rome; that if your departure should stir up a war—for example on the part of France—religion would lose immensely thereby; that Italy would not make war unless France attacks her; that in the case of war the Italian Government guarantees the safety of the pope at Rome, but that the pope must cherish no illusions: let him depart, and he shall never return to Rome, and the Holy See will suffer a terrible shock.
>
> ... We cardinals have the strictest right to speak the truth to the Pope; therefore listen. In the time of Pius VI the five million crowns stored by Sixtus V [reigned 1585-90] in the Castle of St. Angelo were lost, and nevertheless, up to 1839, every new cardinal had to swear to preserve those five millions which no longer existed. It was only Cardinal Acton who in 1839 protested against that oath, and Pope Gregory found Acton's reasons just. Likewise, today also, cardinals are made to swear things which they cannot perform. Therefore it is time to find a remedy.[8]

This last point must have been deeply resented by Leo. What Hohenlohe was complaining about was the fact that every new cardinal was still made to swear an oath to preserve intact the inheritance of the Holy See, which theoretically included those temporal powers which had been lost forty years earlier and would never be restored. It took courage to write such a letter, and Hohenlohe himself believed that he might well fall victim to the assassin's dagger or the equally deadly *acquetta*. On December 5, 1891, the newspaper *Il Messagero* carried a notice that he was ill, although this was not true. Hohenlohe told Primo Levi that the news had been inspired by the Secretariat of the Vatican in order to prepare the public for his death.[9] Not long afterwards, Hohenlohe was summoned to his family home at

---

[6]LC. See also LK.

[7]It was Hohenlohe who helped to negotiate the treaty between Bismarck and the pope, which ended the *Kulturkampf*.

[8]LC, pp. 11-12.

[9]LK, p. 12.

Rauden, where his youngest brother Victor, Duke of Ratibor, lay on his deathbed. He refused to travel with the priests that the Vatican wished to appoint as his travelling aides (whose job was ostensibly to protect him), because he could not trust them, and asked Signor Levi, a Jew, to recommend someone else—a situation that one of his biographers has rightly characterised as "dramatic."[10] Levi selected for this purpose Monsignor Bignani, priest at the royal villa in Monza, whom he knew to be above suspicion.[11]

Hohenlohe believed that his particular enemies were the Jesuits, and with good reason. At the time of their unremitting assault on the teachings of Rosmini, it had been Hohenlohe who had emerged as one of that priest's strongest champions. As long as Pius IX lived, this had caused him no real harm; Pius had been sympathetic to Rosmini, to the extent of promising him a cardinal's hat, although the Jesuits had blocked the nomination. But with the accession of Leo XIII, the Jesuits suddenly found in the occupant of St. Peter's one of their staunchest allies. In 1892, the Vatican press issued a posthumous attack against Rosmini[12] which the *Osservatore Romano*, the official organ of the Jesuits, praised without stint. When he read it, Cardinal Hohenlohe wrote a satirical reply to the *Osservatore*, in which he told Rosmini's anonymous accusers that they were doing harm to the Church, and, in the unlikely event that the criticisms came from Leo XIII himself, the episcopate "would find itself in the hard necessity of deposing him," since the utterances of Pius IX on these matters would make Leo guilty of propagating a false doctrine. By uttering such a statement, Hohenlohe was deliberately standing in harm's way.

IV

But what made Hohenlohe such a perceived threat to Pope Leo and his cohorts was his deep friendship with Francesco Crispi, Minister for Foreign Affairs in the new Italian government. It was well known that Hohenlohe entertained Crispi in his private apartments in the Santa Maria Maggiore, and that the two talked politics. Hohenlohe did nothing to quell the gossip. Once, at a wedding reception for one of Crispi's lieutenants at the Foreign office, Hohenlohe playfully removed his crimson beretta and placed it on the head of Crispi. "When I am pope," joked Hohenlohe, "I will make you my secretary of state." Not long afterwards, Hohenlohe was present at a reception given by Crispi in the magnificent Sciarra Palace. In the course of the dinner Hohenlohe caught Crispi's eye, lifted his glass, and silently toasted him with champagne. The whole of Rome talked about that incident the following day.[13] Such behavior, however good humored it was meant to be, created consternation at the Vatican,[14] and Leo was obliged to administer a severe rebuke to his renegade cardinal. In his defence, Hohenlohe pointed out that he was the brother of the Chancellor of Germany,[15] and this made it impossible to evade certain social responsibilities. The interview, according to Levi, "was not absolutely pacific," and Hohenlohe left Rome for several months. The displeasure of the pope was not diminished when he learned that Hohenlohe had sent a personal representative to Milan in order to attend the unveiling of Luca Beltrami's monument to Rosmini. Had Hohenlohe been well enough to make the trip in person he would have done so. But he had meanwhile succumbed to a mysterious sickness. Levi saw him at Tivoli in August 1896, and he had already entered that strange cycle of illness and health that marked his final weeks. First he was unwell, then he would recover, and his doctors could not say with certainty what was wrong with him. But nothing prepared his friends for the shock of the announcement from Santa Maria Maggiore that he had suddenly expired "of a heart attack" on

---

[10]TCH, p. 295.

[11]LK, p. 13. It was Monsignor Bignami who, eight years later, had the sad honor of giving the last rites to the assassinated King Umberto of Italy.

[12]*Rosminianarum propositionum, quas S.R.U. Onquisitio, approbante S.P. Leone XIII, reprobavit, proscripsit, damnavit, Trutina theologica*, 1892.

[13]What added fuel to the fires of speculation was that Hohenlohe was considered to be a possible candidate for Pope by some of the cardinals. The playful exchange of words with Crispi masked a deadly game.

[14]TCH, pp. 299-300.

[15]Prince Chlodwig von Hohenlohe was appointed Chancellor of Germany in 1894, and had been the right hand man of Prince Otto Bismarck.

October 30, 1896. Levi hinted at poisoning, but he refused to elaborate because the Hohenlohe family declined to order an autopsy.[16] They had good reason to make this decision, according to Levi, because two earlier attempts to poison Hohenlohe had convinced them that on this occasion he might well have been a victim. And had foul play been proved, they would have been obliged to launch an inquiry into the identity of his enemies. The impact that such an inquiry would have had on the Catholic church in Germany and Austria would have been incalculable.

Hohenlohe was laid to rest in the little German cemetery at Santa Maria. Over his tomb they placed a marble slab bearing an inscription from his eldest brother, Chlodwig.

HERE RESTS IN PEACE
MONSIGNOR GUSTAV HOHENLOHE,
CARDINAL OF THE HOLY ROMAN CHURCH
AND TITULAR PRIEST OF ST. CALLIXTUS,
PRINCE OF THE GERMAN EMPIRE
AND A PRIEST OF THE BASILICA LIBERIANA.
BORN OF A NOBLE FAMILY WITH AN EVEN
    NOBLER MIND,
LOYAL TO CHURCH, COUNTRY, AND
    FRIENDS,
HE WAS A LOVER OF THE ARTS AND A
    FATHER TO THE POOR.
HE DIED IN THE LORD, AGED SEVENTY-TWO,
ON OCTOBER 30, 1896, IN ROME.

CHLODWIG, PRINCE VON HOHENLOHE AND
CHANCELLOR OF THE GERMAN EMPIRE,
ERECTED TO THE WORTHY MEMORY OF HIS
    BROTHER.

V

Even during the 'seventies and 'eighties, when Liszt was no longer in permanent residence in Rome, he tried to spend three months out of every year there. And since he could count among his intimate friends some of the leading players on the chess-board of the Vatican, it would be unthinkable to suppose that he would remain unaffected by their views—to say nothing of the political upheavals that went on around him. We know, in fact, that Liszt was a fervent supporter of Pius IX, and he accepted without question the findings of the First Vatican Council, in particular the doctrines of Papal Infallibility and the Immaculate Conception. He expressed it thus: "Our church is not strong, and she must exact total obedience. We must obey, even if we hang for it ... That is why all the princes of the church will adhere to it: not one of them can remain outside."[17] (This prediction turned out to be absolutely correct. Those cardinals who had left Rome because of the dispute over Papal Infallibility did eventually submit to the authority of the Church.) And on another occasion he wrote: "I submit and give my support [to the *Syllabus errorum*], as Catholics are duty-bound to do."[18] When Pius died, Liszt described him as "a saint." All this makes Liszt sound like a conservative. Yet he sided with the liberals on a number of fundamental issues, including the separation of Church and State. And his admiration for revolutionary figures such as Lamennais and Rosmini was unbounded, although he was far less sympathetic to their followers.

In fact, it was Liszt's liberal ideas that linked him to Hohenlohe, and that help to explain the friendship that developed between the pair in the 'sixties and 'seventies—their earlier differences about Carolyne's annulment notwithstanding. Liszt genuinely admired Hohenlohe's liberal stance and his willingness to stand up and be counted. Still, it remains true that he wrote very little about the great issues which held Rome in thrall. When the Republican Army attacked the Vatican troops defending Rome, on September 20, 1870, Liszt was in Hungary and all he could say was: "The huge events that startle the world also bear on my little existence. I had planned to return to Rome during the first days of October; but considering the actual state of things ... it wasn't much of a task for them to persuade me to prolong my stay in Hungary."[19] Liszt, in short, was like the proverbial diplomat who thinks twice and then says nothing. On other moral issues, however, he was easier to fathom. Liszt was against the death-penalty. He did not believe that the state should terminate life. This comes out most strongly in a letter he wrote from Italy in January 1882, in which he re-

---

[16]LK, p. 142; and LCH, pp. 49-50. Although Levi was close to Hohenlohe, his writings reveal him to be anti-clerical in general, and anti-Jesuit in particular. The poisoning theory has never been corroborated.

[17]SZM, p. 258.
[18]LLB, Vol. 7, p. 171.
[19]HLSW, p. 144.

ferred to the death penalty as "an abominable social crime ... It is obvious that we are all more or less guilty, deranged, or crazy, but it does not follow that we ought to be guillotined, hanged or, as an act of mercy, shot."[20]

For Liszt, life was sacrosanct, which is why he was against suicide as well. Nor was this merely a theoretical stance, imposed upon him because of his obligations to the church. It is well known that in the late 1870s Liszt entered a severe depression and contemplated suicide—an act of despair from which only his devout Catholicism saved him:

> "... I am extremely tired of living; but as I believe that God's Fifth Commandment 'Thou shalt not kill' also applies to suicide, I go on existing."[21]

> "Last Friday I entered my seventieth year. It might be time to end things well—all the more since I have never wished to live long. In my early youth I often went to sleep hoping not to awake again here below."[22]

The darker side of Liszt's personality has long been suspected, but it has never been more clearly revealed than in these letters.

Liszt was certainly the most famous musician to have resided in Rome up to his time, so it was natural that there was much talk about him angling for the position of director of the Sistine Choir. He certainly discussed the reform of church music with Pius IX, but there is no evidence that the Pontiff was about to dismiss Salvatore Meluzzi from his post at St. Peter's. Nor did Liszt covet such a position. He once said that he "neither expected nor wished for an appointment or title of any kind at Rome." And he added that he was "under no illusion as to the difficulty and vexations of such a task."[23] In fact, Liszt's music was considered by many of Rome's leading clerics to be far too advanced for the taste of the Church.

For the rest, Liszt's long sojourn in Rome was not harmful to his work. He completed some of the greatest masterpieces of his old age in the city and its environs, including his oratorios *Christus* and *St. Elisabeth*. Instrumental music also flowed from his pen in great abundance, including the Two Franciscan Legends (based on episodes from the lives of St. Francis of Assisi and St. Francis of Paulo, the latter being Liszt's patron saint) and some of the pieces in the last volume of the *Années de pèlerinage*. These last compositions were written mainly at the Villa d'Este in Tivoli, the magnificent residence that had been placed at Liszt's disposal by Cardinal Hohenlohe in 1868 so that Liszt could escape the hustle and bustle of Rome whenever he wanted to compose.[24] Its gardens were one of the wonders of the world. Here, amidst their hundreds of splashing fountains and majestic cypress trees, Liszt himself confessed that he felt at one both with God and nature.

Not long after Liszt arrived in the city, he apotheosized it in his "Memento Journalier" with an immortal phrase: "Oh Rome! My country; city of the soul; the Niobe of Nations." The words, of course, are Lord Byron's,[25] but they expressed Liszt's deep feelings about a place he came to love. Rome offered Liszt the prospect of personal happiness, a new life, and a harmonious existence such as he had not known for many years.

---

[20]WLLM, p. 418.
[21]WLLM, p. 299.
[22]WLLM, p. 384.
[23]LLB, Vol. 7, p. 73.

[24]Contrary to popular belief, the Villa d'Este never belonged to Cardinal Hohenlohe. He leased it from the Dukes of Modena, a branch of the Habsburgs. What is a fact, however, is that when Hohenlohe took over the property it was badly neglected, and he spent large sums of money restoring the fountains and the gardens to their former beauty.

[25]They come from *Childe Harold*, Canto 4, Stanzas 78-79.

INDEX TO THE ANNULMENT DOCUMENTS

**A. From the Secret Vatican Archive, Nunciature of Vienna, 1860–61, Vol. 427.
The file pertaining to the Diocese of Fulda as kept by Cardinal De Luca
and consisting mainly of the "Special Annex: The Matrimonial Case of
Wittgenstein versus Iwanowska."**

Document No. 1: Inscription on the spine of the volume containing De Luca's file from Vienna.

Document No. 2: File Title. Italian. Leaf No. 76.

Document No. 3: De Luca to Kött, April 11, 1860. Latin. Leaf No. 77.

Document No. 4: Kött to De Luca, October 31, 1860 (answer to Document No. 3 with note on the verso penned by De Luca). Latin. Leaves No. 78-79.

Document No. 5: File Title. Leaf No. 81.

Document No. 6: Copy of Żyliński's annulment decree, February 24 (O.S.) = March 7, 1860 (enclosed by Kött with Document No. 11, Kött to De Luca, April 10, 1860). Latin. Leaves No. 82- 83-84. For the text see ASV, CC Doc. No. 28.

Document No. 7: Copy of Father Guidi's letter to Kött, March 29, 1860 (enclosed with Document 8: Kött to De Luca, April 3, 1860). Latin. Leaf No. 86. For the question of bribery, see ASV, CC Docs. No. 16 and 17.

Document No. 8: Kött to De Luca, April 3, 1860, with note on the verso penned by De Luca. Doc. No. 7 is enclosed. Latin. Leaves No. 87-88.

Document No. 9: Quaglia to De Luca, April 4, 1860 (with note on the verso penned by De Luca). Enclosed with Doc. No. 10. Italian. Leaves No. 90-91. The draft of this document is in ASV, CC, Doc. No. 18. For the context, see ASV, CC Docs. No. 16, a petition by Mons. Hohenlohe; and 17, a memorandum to the Pope on the question of bribery. De Luca's answer, not preserved in this file, is in ASV, CC Doc. No. 21.

Document No. 10: Hohenlohe to De Luca, April 6, 1860, with note on the verso penned by De Luca. Enclosing Doc. No. 9. Italian. Leaves No. 92-93.

Document No. 11: Kött to De Luca, April 10, 1860 (enclosing a copy of Document No. 6, a Copy of Żyliński's decree. See Doc. No. 6 and ASV, CC Doc. No. 22. The text of the latter is in ASV, CC Doc. No. 20). Latin. Leaf No. 94.

Document No. 12: De Luca to Kött, April 14, 1860 (answer to Document No. 8: Kött to De Luca, April 3,1860). Latin. Leaf No. 96.

Document No. 13: De Luca to Kött, April 19, 1860 (answer to Document No. 11: Kött to De Luca, April 10, 1860). Latin. Leaf No. 97.

Document No. 14: Hohenlohe to De Luca, April 19, 1860, with note on the verso penned by De Luca. Italian. Leaf No. 98-99. De Luca's answer is not in the files.

Document No. 15: De Luca to Żyliński, April 29, 1860. Latin. Leaf No. 101.

Document No. 16: Kött to De Luca, April 25, 1860 (answer to Documents No. 12 and 13: De Luca to Kött, April 11 and 14, 1860). Document No. 17, a copy of Stichling's letter to Kött, April 23, 1860, is enclosed. Latin. Leaf No. 102.

Document No. 17: Copy of Stichling's letter to Kött, April 23, 1860 (enclosed with Document No. 16: Kött to De Luca, April 25, 1860). German. Leaf No. 103.

Document No. 18: Quaglia to De Luca, May 3, 1860. The original draft is in ASV, CC Doc. No. 27, which contains an additional paragraph that was not included in this document.

For the context see also ASV, CC Docs. No. 23, 24, and 25. Enclosed with Doc. No. 19. Italian. Leaf No. 107.

Document No. 19: Hohenlohe to De Luca, May 10, 1860, with note on the verso penned by De Luca. Leaves No. 108-109. De Luca's answer is not in the files.

Document No. 20: De Luca to Kött, May 21, 1860. Latin. Leaf No. 110.

Document No. 21: Żyliński to De Luca, May 24 (O.S.)=June 5, 1860 (answer to Document No. 15: De Luca to Żyliński, April 24, 1860). Enclosed with Doc. No. 23: Balabine to De Luca, June 24 (O.S.)=July 6, 1860. Latin. Leaves No. 111-112.

Document No. 22: Kozlowska to De Luca, November 23, 1860, with note on the verso penned by De Luca. German. Leaves No. 113-114.

Document No. 23: Balabine to De Luca, June 24 (O.S.)=July 6, 1860, with a note on the verso penned by De Luca. (Doc. No. 21, Żyliński to De Luca, May 24 (O.S.)=June 5, 1860 is enclosed). French. Leaves No. 117-118.

Document No. 24: De Luca to Cardinal Antonelli, July 14, 1860, in response to Document No. 18: Quaglia to De Luca, May 3, 1860, and with reference to Document No. 23: Balabine to De Luca, June 24 (O.S)=June 5, 1860. (A copy of Doc. No. 21 is enclosed. See ASV, CC Doc. No. 27, and also No. 26 whereby Antonelli sends it to Quaglia.) Italian. Leaf No. 119.

Document No. 25: Quaglia to De Luca, September 25, 1860. See ASV, CC Doc. No. 43. For the context, see also ASV, CC Docs. No. 41 and 42. Italian. Leaf No. 120.

Document No. 26: De Luca to Kött, October 10, 1860. Latin. Leaf No. 121.

Document No. 27: Hohenlohe to De Luca, October 11, 1860. Italian. Leaves No. 125-126. De Luca's answer, not included in this file, is in ASV, CC Doc. No. 41.

Document No. 28: Kött to De Luca, October 15, 1860 (answer to Doc. No. 26, De Luca to Kött, October 10, 1860). Latin. Leaves No. 127-128. A copy of this letter will be sent by De Luca to Quaglia. See in this file Doc. No. 34, and ASV, CC Docs. No. 46 and 47.

Document No. 29: Hohenlohe to De Luca, October 16, 1860 (anticipates Liszt's request in Doc. No. 30, Liszt to De Luca, October 16, 1860). Italian. Leaves No. 129-130.

Document No. 30: Liszt to De Luca, October 16, 1860, with note on the verso penned by De Luca. French. Leaves No. 131-132.

Document No. 31: De Luca to Quaglia, October 18, 1860 (answer to Doc. No. 25, Quaglia to De Luca, September 25, 1860). See ASV, CC Doc. No. 45. Italian. Leaf No. 133.

Document No. 32: De Luca to Borowski, October 19, 1860. Latin. Leaf No. 134.

Document No. 33: De Luca to Żyliński, October 20, 1860. Latin. Leaf No. 135.

Document No. 34: De Luca to Quaglia, October 24, 1860. See ASV, CC Doc. No. 46 (Doc. No. 28 from this file is enclosed. See also ASV, CC Doc. No. 47). Italian. Leaf No. 136.

Document No. 35: Borowski to De Luca, October 31 (O.S.) = November 12, 1860 (answer to Doc. No. 32: De Luca to Borowski, October 19, 1860). Doc. No. 36, an abstract of the proceedings of Luck-Zhitomir, is enclosed. Latin. Leaf No. 141. De Luca forwarded a copy of this letter to Rome (ASV, CC Doc. No. 62).

Document No. 36: Borowski's abstract of the Luck-Zhitomir proceedings concluded on October 19 (O.S.) = October 31, 1852. Enclosed with Doc. No. 35: Borowski to De Luca, October 31 (O.S.) = November 12, 1860. On the verso of the last leaf a note penned by De Luca. Latin. Leaves No. 142-143. See also ASV, CC Doc. No. 63, a copy sent by the Luca to the Pope together with a copy of Doc. No. 35 (ASV, CC Doc. No. 62).

Document No. 37: Żyliński to De Luca, October 31 (O.S.) = November 12, 1860, with note on the verso penned by De Luca (answer to Doc. No. 33, De Luca to Żyliński, October 20, 1860). Latin. Leaves No. 145-146.

Document No. 38: Hohenlohe to De Luca, December 1, 1860, with note penned by De Luca. Italian. Leaves No. 147-148. De Luca will follow Hohenlohe's advice and send copies of Docs. No. 35 and 36 directly to Mons. Stella, the Pope's Secretary. See ASV, CC Docs. No. 60, 61, 62, 63.

Document No. 39: Quaglia to De Luca, January 16, 1861, with note on the verso penned by De Luca (answer to Doc. No 31, De Luca to Quaglia, October 18, 1860, and Doc. No. 34, De Luca to Quaglia, October 24, 1860, which enclosed a copy of Doc. No. 28, Kött to De Luca, October 15, 1860. See ASV, CC Doc. No. 47). For the draft of this letter which contains passages not to be found in the present document, see ASV, CC Doc. No. 68. Italian. Leaves No. 149-150.

Document No. 40: De Luca to Kött, February 6, 1861. Latin. Leaf No. 151.

Document No. 41: De Luca to Kött, June 5, 1861 (follow-up to Doc. No. 40, De Luca to Kött, February 6, 1861). Latin. Leaf No. 152.

Document No. 42: De Luca to Cardinal Antonelli, June 9, 1861. A copy of Doc. No. 40 is enclosed. See also ASV, CC Doc. No. 69. Italian. Leaf No. 153.

Document No. 43: Kött to De Luca, June 11, 1861 (answers Doc. No. 40, De Luca to Kött, February 6, 1861, and Doc. No. 41, De Luca to Kött, June 5, 1861). Latin. Leaf No. 154.

Document No. 44: De Luca to Cardinal Antonelli, June 20, 1861 (follow-up to Doc. No. 42, De Luca to Cardinal Antonelli, June 9, 1861). A copy of Doc. No. 43, Kött to De Luca, June 11, 1861, was enclosed. (ASV, CC Doc. No. 71), together with a note for Quaglia (ASV, CC Doc. No. 70) not included in this file. Italian. Leaf No. 159.

B. From the Secret Vatican Archive, shelf mark Z60, Diocese of Zhitomir in Ukraine. The case file of the Holy Congregation of the Tridentine Council, 1859–61.

Document No. 1. August 2, 1859. Letter from Mons. Hohenlohe to Mons. Quaglia: Okraszewski's appeal to reopen Carolyne's case. Carolyne's Latin Petition (Doc. No. 2) and Okraszewski's power of attorney (Doc. No. 3) are enclosed. Italian (2 Pages).

Document No. 2. Undated, but August 1859. Carolyne's petition to Pope Pius IX (Prot. No. 2390) Latin (2 pages).

Document No. 3. Undated. Memorandum. Okraszewski's power of attorney in Carolyne's case. French (1 page), August 1859.

Document No. 4: Okraszewski's visiting card, probably attached to the above.

Document No. 5. June 13, 1859. Letter. Archbishop Żyliński to Władislaw Okraszewski (Prot. No. 1146, also 766). Russian (3 pages). Enclosed with Doc. No. 3.

Document No. 6. June 13, 1859. Legal translation of the above approved by the Russian Government (Prot. No. 1146, erased 766) French (3 pages).

Document No. 7. July 4, 1859. Authentic copy of the 1852 Mohilow sentence, notorised by the Russian Government, consisting of the majority resolution of the Consistory, the minority opinion of Vicar General Laski, and the formal approval of the latter by Archbishop Holowinski (Prot. No. 11020). Russian (38 pages).

Document No. 8. July 14, 1859. Legal translation of the above done by Okraszewski, with Russian Government approval. French (34 pages).

Document No. 9. Undated, but first week of August 1859. Draft. Memorandum to the Pope from Monsignor Quaglia, Secretary of the Holy Congregation, outlining the merits of the case. Italian (4 pages).

Document No. 10. August 8, 1859. Draft of the Papal Rescript authorising Archbishop Żyliński to review Carolyne's case. In Quaglia's own hand. Latin (1 page).

Document No. 11. September 1859. Petition by Marie von Sayn-Wittgenstein to Pius IX, requesting a declaration of legitimacy (Prot. No. 6733I), with draft in Quaglia's hand of papal answer dated September 13, 1859. Latin (2 pages).

Document No. 12. September 10, 1859. Letter by Monsignor Cardoni to Quaglia enclosing his legal opinion on Marie's petition. Italian (1 page).

Document No. 13. September 10, 1859. Monsignor Cardoni's expert opinion on the issue of Marie's legitimacy. Latin (5 pages).

Document No. 14. September 1859. Draft. Quaglia's memorandum to the Pope on the merit of Maria's petition with a report on Cardoni's opinion. Italian (3 pages). For the response to the petition, see end of Doc. No. 11.

Document No. 15. November 26, 1859. Petition to Quaglia from Hohenlohe (Prot. No. 6733/I) to duplicate documents sent to Żyliński that have been lost in the mail. Granted on that date. Italian (2 pages).

Document No. 16. March 1860. Petition. Monsignor Hohenlohe petitions the Pope to move the review of the case to Rome on account of possible bribery in Mohilow. With note on action, in Quaglia's hand, dated March 26, 1860. Latin (4 pages).

Document No. 17. March 26, 1860. Draft. Memorandum to the Pope on the question of bribery (the date is elicited from Doc. No. 23). Italian (4 pages).

Document No. 18. April 4, 1860. Draft letter from Quaglia to De Luca with corrections in Quaglia's own hand (See ASV, NV Doc. No. 9). Italian (8 pages).

Document No. 19. April 12, 1860. Letter from Archbishop Żyliński to the Pope enclosing a copy of his February 1860 sentence of annulment. Latin (2 pages).

Document No. 20: Enclosed with Doc. No. 19. A copy of Żyliński's decree verified by Monsignor Proniewski (his name is mis-spelled Prosciewski in copies originating from the one made by Kött). See ASV, NV Doc. No. 6 and ASV, CC Doc. No. 22. The text of the decree is given in ASV, CC Doc. No. 28.

Document No. 21. April 14, 1860. Letter, in De Luca's own hand to Quaglia, enclosing a copy of Żyliński's decree received from Kött. This letter is not in the ASV, NV file. Italian (1 page).

Document No. 22. Enclosed with Doc. No. 21. De Luca's copy of Żyliński's decree made from the one sent to him by Kött. See ASV, NV Doc. No. 6; both these copies provide the wrong spelling Prosciewski for Proniewski. See ASV, CC Docs. No. 20 and, for the text, No. 28. Latin (4 pages).

Document No. 23. April 30, 1860. Draft. Memorandum from Quaglia to the Pope suggesting the suspension of the February 1860 sentence and the necessity of an appeal against it on the part of the Defender. The date is elicited from Doc. No. 25. Italian (4 pages). Contains references to ASV, NV Docs. No. 9, 13, 15 and ASV, CC Doc. No. 21.

Document No. 24. April 1860. Memorandum addressed probably to Cardinal Cagiano de Azevedo, prefect of the Holy Congregation of the Council, on whether to send orders directly to Kött. Refers to ASV, NV Docs. No. 16 and 17. Italian (2 pages).

Document No. 25. April 30, 1860. Papal order to Quaglia to write to De Luca. See ASV, NV Doc. No. 18.

Document No. 26. May 3, 1860. Draft of letter by Quaglia to De Luca. For the text See ASV, NV Doc. No. 18.

Document No. 27. June 3, 1860. Petition by Carolyne to the Pope on removing the impediments against her new marriage. The case is to be reviewed again. French (3 pages).

Document No. 28: Copy of Żyliński's decree made from the official original dated February 24 (O.S.) = March 7 (N.S.), 1860, given by the Archbishop to Carolyne. Enclosed with Doc. No. 27. Latin (4 pages).

Document No. 29. July 1860. Princess Carolyne's formal presentation of her case for the Congregation's review as drafted by Okraszewski. Italian (11 pages).

Document No. 30. Undated. Memorandum with comments on Carolyne's presentation of the case. Italian (5 pages).

Document No. 31. July 24, 1860. Letter from the Secretary of State, Cardinal Antonelli, to Monsignor Quaglia forwarding to him a copy of Żyliński's letter of May 24 sent him by De Luca on July 14 (See ASV, NV Doc. No. 24). Italian (2 pages).

Document No. 32. Enclosure. Copy of Żyliński's letter to De Luca, dated May 24 (See ASV, NV Doc. No. 21). Latin (5 pages)

Document No. 33. Undated. Memorandum to the Pope on Żyliński's defense, the Concordate, the status of the case. Responds to Docs. No. 31 and 32. Italian (8 pages).

Document No. 34: Undated. An expert opinion on the legal status of the February 1860 sentence of annulment issued by Archbishop Żyliński. Latin (10 pages).

Document No. 35. August 1860. Draft Memorandum to the Prefect of the Congregation, Antonio Cagiano de Azevedo, or to the Pope reviewing the nature of the 1860 Mohilow sentence and the terms of the Russian Concordate. Italian (8 pages).

Document No. 36. August 22, 1860. Monsignor De Ferrari's letter enclosing the Princess's answer to a request for additional documentation. See Doc. No. 30. Italian (1 page).

Document No. 37. August 1860. Enclosed with Doc. No. 36. Carolyne's answer to a request for additional documentation.

Document No. 38. August 1860. Memorandum probably addressed to Cagiano De Azevedo. Comments on Doc. No. 37 and the enclosure of a copy of the Princess's presentation of her case (Copy of Doc. No. 29) and a copy of Doc. No. 37 without the introductory paragraph. Italian (4 pages).

Document No. 39. Enclosure. Copy of Doc. No. 29. Italian (9 pages).

Document No. 40. Enclosure. Copy of Doc. No. 37. Italian (3 pages).

Document No. 41. September 2, 1860. Letter in De Luca's hand to Hohenlohe suggesting that Quaglia should request the records of the 1860 Mohilow proceedings and order the Bishop of Fulda to suspend the wedding. With a note in Latin, in Quaglia's hand, dated September 24, about writing to De Luca in terms of the resolution passed by the Congregation on September 22 and approved by the Pope. Italian (2 pages)

Document No. 42. September 22, 1860. Printed documentation for the meeting of the Congregation on that date, consisting of the following documents enumerated in alphabetical order:

A) Statement of the case and the eventual decision of the Congregation, recorded in Quaglia's hand, to uphold the Mohilow sentence. Italian (6 pages).

B) Enclosure No. 1. Printed transcription of Doc. No. 29, Carolyne's presentation of her case for upholding the 1860 Mohilow sentence issued by Żyliński. Italian (6 pages).

C) Enclosure No. 2. Printed transcription of Doc. No. 8, the French translation done by Okraszewski, of the 1852 sentence issued at Mohilow with Monsignor Laski's minority position which was upheld by Archbishop Holowinski. French (24 pages). Okraszewski's statement about the accuracy of the translation is not reproduced.

D) Enclosure No. 3. Printed transcription of Doc. No. 6, the French translation of Żyliński's letter to Okraszewski, dated June 13, 1859. French (2 pages).

E) Enclosure No. 4. Printed transcription of Doc. No. 2, Carolyne's 1859 petition to the Vatican to authorise the Archbishop of Mohilow to reopen her case. Latin (2 pages).

F) Enclosure No. 5. Printed transcription of Żyliński's Mohilow sentence dated February 1860. See Docs. No. 20, 21, 28. See the latter for the complete text. See also ASV, NV Doc. No. 6. This copy derives

from De Luca's copy (Doc. No. 21) in turn made from ASV, NV Doc. No. 6, where Proniewski's name is spelled Prosciewski. Latin (3 pages).

G) Enclosure No. 6. Printed transcription of Doc. No. 32; see ASV, NV Doc. No. 21, Żyliński's letter of May 24, 1860, to De Luca protesting the accusation of bribery. Latin (3 Pages).

H) Enclosure No. 7. Printed transcription of Doc. No. 40, a slight variation of Doc. No. 37, Carolyne's response to the Congregation's request for authentic copies of the sentences of Mohilow (1851) and Zhitomir (1851). Italian (2 pages).

Document No. 43. September 25, 1860. Draft of Letter from Quaglia to De Luca, informing him of the decision of the Congregation. See ASV, NV Doc. No. 25. Italian (2 pages).

Document No. 44. September 28, 1860. Carlo Modesti, a Roman attorney, petitions on Carolyne's behalf for the return of the original of the 1860 Mohilow sentence. Granted by Quaglia on the same day. Italian (2 pages).

Document No. 45. October 18, 1860. Letter from De Luca to Quaglia raising questions about the September 22 decision of the Congregation. For the text, see De Luca's draft in ASV, NV Doc. No. 31. Italian (2 pages). It bears the prot. No. 1819/1.

Document No. 46. October 24, 1860. Letter from De Luca to Quaglia enclosing a copy of Kött's letter of October 15, 1860. See De Luca's draft in ASV, NV Doc. No. 34. Italian (2 pages).

Document No. 47. Enclosure. Copy of Kött's letter to De Luca, dated October 15, 1860. See ASV, NV Doc. No. 28. Latin (2 pages).

Document No. 48. December 2, 1860. Memorandum. Caterini, the new prefect of the Congregation, writes to Monsignor Berardi requesting documents from the Office of the Secretary of State. Italian (1 page).

Document No. 49. December 3, 1860. Berardi responds to Caterini. Italian (1 page). The documents originally enclosed are not in the file, but they are reproduced in Docs. No. 59C, D, and E.

Document No. 50. December 3, 1860. Draft. Memorandum from Caterini to Quaglia about the documentation necessary for the December 22 meeting of the Congregation. Italian (1 page). The enclosed documentation, not kept in the file, was reproduced in Docs. No. 59B, C, and D.

Document No. 51. December 10, 1860. Draft of Memorandum from Quaglia to Cardinals D'Andrea, Silvestri, Marini, and Mertel on whether they intend to be present at the December 22 meeting of the Congregation and whether they still have the printed documentation for the September 22 meeting. Italian (2 pages).

Document No. 52. December 10, 1860. Draft of memorandum from Quaglia to Cardinal Milesi for the same reasons presented in Doc. No. 51. Italian (2 pages).

Document No. 53. December 10, 1860. Draft memorandum from Quaglia to Cardinal Villecourt along the same lines as Docs. No. 51 and 52. Italian (2 pages).

Document No. 54. December 10, 1860. Memorandum from Quaglia to Cardinal Bofondi with the latter's answer on the same sheet. Italian (1 page).

Document No. 55. December 11, 1860. Cardinal Mertel's answer to Doc. No. 51. Italian (1 page).

Document No. 56. December 11, 1860. Note providing Cardinal Milesi's answer to Doc. No. 52. Italian (1 page).

Document No. 57. Cardinal De Silvestri's answer to Doc. No. 51. Italian (1 page).

Document No. 58. December 21, 1860. Note by Cardinal Cagiano De Azevedo to Quaglia about the meeting of December 22. Italian (1 page).

Document No. 59. December 22, 1860. Printed documentation for the meeting of the Holy Congregation of the Council, consisting of:

A) Position paper about the case together with the decision in Carolyne's favor and the voting record written in Quaglia's hand. Italian (4 pages).

B) Enclosure No. 1. Printed observations on the merit of the case. Italian (8 pages).

C) Enclosure No. 2. Additional summary: No. 1. The Russian proposal on the levels of jurisdiction. French (2 pages).

D) Enclosure No. 3. The Vatican's acceptance of the Russian proposal on jurisdiction in ecclesiastical cases. Italian (3 pages).

E) Enclosure No. 4. French (1 page). A communication from the Russian Government to the Bishops of the Empire.

Document No. 60. December 26, 1860. The Pope's secretary, Monsignor Stella, sends De Luca's letter of December 6 (not in ASV, NV) to Quaglia. It encloses Borowski's letter of October 30, as well as his resume of the Zhitomir trial of 1851. Italian (1 page).

Document No. 61. December 6, 1860. De Luca's letter, in his own hand, to Monsignor Stella. Italian (1 page).

Document No. 62. Enclosure. Copy of Borowski's letter, dated October 30, 1860. De Luca's mistake: the original; see ASV, NV Doc. No. 35, is dated unequivocally (October 31, 1860). Latin (2 pages).

Document No. 63. Enclosure. Copy of Borowski's resume of the Zhitomir proceedings of 1851. See ASV, NV Doc. No. 36. Latin (6 pages).

Document No. 64. Undated. Memorandum from Quaglia to the Pope about De Luca's and Kött's concern about repercussions in Germany, should Liszt and Carolyne get married there. Suggestions about performing their marriage in Vienna or in Rome. Italian (5 pages).

Document No. 65. Undated, but probably from the Spring of 1861 (See note to Doc. 66). Memorandum in Quaglia's own hand to Caterini with comments in margin by the latter presenting the draft of the Congregation's final decision, originally dated January 8, 1861.

Document No. 66. January 8, 1861. See AVR Doc. No. 1. This draft, enclosed with Doc. No.

65, contains at the end a deleted passage that was not included in the final document kept in the Vicariato file and containing the decree of the Holy Congregation of the Council, dated January 8, 1861, after the Pope's approval on January 7. Latin (4 pages).

Document No. 67. January 7, 1861. Papal authorisation to write to De Luca. Latin (1 page).

Document No. 68. Draft of the January 16, 1861 letter to De Luca. See ASV, NV Doc. No. 39. The draft was originally written on the 13, and the date was subsequently penned over to read January 16, after the text was presented for approval to the Pope on January 14. The draft, in the hand of one of Quaglia's scribes (not the same who wrote the actual letter in the ASV, NV file), contains corrections and insertions in Quaglia's own hand and notes to the extent that these were suggested by the Pope himself. Italian (4 pages).

Document No. 69. Unsigned copy of De Luca's letter to Kött, dated February 6, 1861 (see ASV, NV Doc. No. 40), sent by De Luca to Antonelli in his dispatch No. 1291 (see ASV, NV Doc. No. 42). Latin (3 pages).

Document No. 70. De Luca's letter to Quaglia, dated June 22, 1861, not included in the ASV, NV file and originally enclosed with ASV, NV Doc. 44, a letter to Antonelli (Dispatch No. 1304) whose draft date was June 20, 1861. Italian (1 page).

Document No. 71. Enclosure in the Dispatch from Vienna No. 1304. De Luca's copy of Kött's letter to him, dated June 11, 1861. See ASV, NV Doc. No. 43. Latin (1 page).

Document No. 72. Monsignor Hohenlohe's letter to Caterini indicating new evidence in favor of the validity of Carolyne's marriage, with a note about its inclusion in the Secret Archive's file. Italian (3 pages).

Document No. 73. An article from a newspaper referring to the strange outcome of Carolyne's efforts to obtain an annulment in order to marry Liszt.

C. From the Archive of the Vicariato di Roma, in St. John Lateran. The file containing the marriage application pertaining to the marriage of Liszt and Princess Carolyne von Sayn-Wittgenstein, 1861. Shelf mark N. 4477, L/41.

Document No. 1: Certified copy of the final judgement of the Holy Congregation of the Council (December 22, 1860), dated January 8, 1861, which upholds their earlier decision of September 22, 1860 and the Russian annulment issued by Archishop Wenceslas Żyliné ski on February 24 (O.S.) = March 7, 1860 (See ASV, NV Doc. No. 6, and ASV, CC Docs. No. 20 and 22; see No. 28 for the text). For a paragraph not included here, see the draft of this Doc. in ASV, CC Doc. No. 65. Enclosed with Doc. No. 2. Latin (2 pages).

Document No. 2: Princess Carolyne's and Liszt's marriage application, addressed to Pope Pius IX, dated September 18, 1861, referred by the Holy Congregation of the Council to the Office of the Vicar General of Rome. Italian with Latin notes (3 pages).

Document No. 3: Liszt's Baptism certificate, dated May 22, 1848 (enclosed with Doc. No. 2). Latin (1 page).

Document No. 4: A deposition from Father Anton Hohmann, the Roman Catholic priest from Liszt's parish in Weimar, certifying his unmarried status since 1848, dated July 18, 1861. Latin with notes in German (2 pages).

Document No. 5: A deposition from Carolyne testifying to Liszt's unmarried status up to the year 1848, dated September 18, 1861 (enclosed with Doc. No. 2). Italian (1 page).

Document No. 6: A request in Notary Erasmo Ciccolini's hand to waive the reading of the marriage banns, probably included with Docs. Nos. 7 and 8. Italian (2 pages).

Document No. 7: An instrument of interrogation bearing the names of Liszt and Carolyne, dated October 20, 1861, in which the penalties for bearing false witness are set forth. Pertaining to Doc. No. 8. Latin (2 pages).

Document No. 8: A sworn deposition from Liszt and Carolyne, written in the hand of Notary Erasmo Ciccolini, testifying to the fact that they were both single, dated October 20, 1861. Enclosed with Doc. No. 6. Italian (1 page).

Document No. 9: A bill signed by Notary Erasmo Ciccolini for services and the writing of instruments required for getting married. Italian (1 page).

D. From the papers of Cardinal Antonelli, Secretary of State.

Document No. 1. ASV, SS, 1859: Rubric 220, Fasc. 3, leaves No. 140-141. Liszt's letter of thanks to Antonelli upon being informed the Holy See has made him a Commander of the Order of St. Gregory the Great. French (2 pages).

Document No. 2. ASV, SS, 1859: Rubric No. 220, Fasc. 3, leaf No. 142. October 29, 1959. Draft of Antonelli's letter to Liszt forwarding to him the commission of Commander of the Order of Saint Gregory the Great. Italian (1 page).

Document No. 3. September 1859. The ASV, SS catalogue lists under Prot. No. 6066, Rubric 220, the papal brief conferring on Liszt the title of Commander of the Order of St. Gregory the Great. This brief, however, is not contained in that volume.

Document No. 4. December 1859. In the ASV, SS catalogue there is a reference to a Doc. with prot. No. 7549/3 dated December 1859 and described as a petition pertaining to the Iwanowska case. Unfortunately, that document cannot, at present, be found since the indication of the Rubric Number was omitted by the Archivist at the time. It might very well be the same petition to reopen her case that Carolyne presented in August 1859 (See ASV, CC Doc. No. 2), or a copy of the September Petition presented by Marie about her legitimacy (See ASV, CC Doc. No. 11).

Document No. 5. ASV, SS 1860: Rubric No. 247, Fasc. 2, leaf No. 204. The original of De Luca's July 14, 1860 letter to Antonelli (see ASV, NV Doc. No. 24) enclosing Żyliński's letter of May 24, 1860 (ASV, NV Doc. No. 21 and ASV, CC Doc. No. 31). Italian (2 pages).

Document No. 6. ASV, SS, 1860: Rubric No. 247, Fasc. 2, leaf No. 205. Draft of Antonelli's July 24, 1860, letter to Quaglia forwarding him a copy of Żyliński's letter to De Luca (ASV, NV Doc No. 1 and ASV, CC Doc No. 31). For the text see ASV, CC Doc. No. 30.

Document No. 7. ASV, SS, 1860: Rubric No. 267. The ASV, SS catalogue lists, under the date of December 7, 1860, a document pertaining to Władislaw Okraszewski's delivery of a package to the Nunciature in Vienna. The document was not found in that volume.

SOURCES
CONSULTED IN THE PREPARATION OF THIS VOLUME

ASV, NV   Archivio Segreto Vaticano. Nunciatura di Vienna, 1860–61, No. 427. Documents from the archives of Cardinal Antonino De Luca, papal nuncio to Vienna.

ASV, CC   Archivio Segreto Vaticano, Rome. Documents from the Holy Congregation of the Council (1859–61). Shelf mark Z60. Diocese of Zhitomir.

ASV, SS   Documents from the archives of Cardianl Antonelli, Secretary of State.

AVR   Archivio Storico del Vicariato di Roma, St. John Lateran, Rome. Documents pertaining to the marriage of Liszt and Princess Carolyne von Sayn-Wittgenstein (1861). Shelf mark N. 4477, L/41.

BLTB   Bernhardi, Theodor von. *Aus dem Leben Theodor von Bernhardis*. 9 vols. Leipzig, 1893-96.

DA   Darmstadt Archive. Originale der Briefe Liszts an eine Freundin. Hessische Landes- und Hochschulbibliothek, Darmstadt.

EKFL   Eckhardt, Mária P., and Knotik, Cornelia, eds. *Franz Liszt und sein Kreis in Briefen und Dokumenten aus den Beständen des Burgenländischen Landesmuseums*. Eisenstadt, 1983.

EHC   Eubel, Konrad. *Hierarchia Catholica medii et Recentioris aevi*, Vols. VII-, Patavii, MCMLXXIX.

GRT   Gregorovius, Ferdinand. *Römischer Tagebücher, 1854-1874*. Stuttgart, 1892.

HL   Haraszti, Emile. *Franz Liszt*. Paris, 1967.

HLC   Hamburger, Klara. "Franz Liszt and Michelangelo Caetani, duc de Sermoneta." *Studia Musicologica Academiae Scientiarum Hungarica* 21 [Budapest] (1979), pp. 239-65.

HLSW   *The Letters of Franz Liszt to Marie zu Sayn-Wittgenstein*, translated and edited by Howard E. Hugo. Cambridge, 1953.

HSD   Herwegh, Marcel. *Au Soir des dieux*. Paris, 1933.

LAG   La Mara (ed.). *Aus der Glanzzeit der Weimarer Altenburg*. Leipzig, 1906.

LC   Levi, Primo. *Il Cardinale d'Hohenlohe nella Vita Italiana*. Turin-Rome, 1907.

LDML   La Mara. *Durch Musik und Leben im Dienste des Ideals*. 2 vols. Leipzig, 1917.

LK   Levi, Primo. *Kardinal Prinz Hohenlohe. Persönliche Erinnerungen eines Italianers*. Deutsche Revue, January–March, 1907, issue no. XXXII

LLB   La Mara, ed. *Franz Liszt's Briefe*. 8 vols. Leipzig, 1893-1905.

LR   Leetham, Claude. *Rosmini. Priest, Philosopher and Patriot*, with an introduction by Guiseppe Bozzetti. London, 1957.

LSJ   La Mara, ed. *An der Schwelle des Jenseits: Letzte Erinnerungen an die Fürstin Carolyne Sayn-Wittgenstein, die Freundin Liszts*. Leipzig, 1925.

MAL   Melegari, Dora. "Une Amie de Liszt, la Princesse de Sayn-Wittgenstein." *La Revue de Paris*, September 1, 1897.

RGS   Ramann, Lina ed. *Franz Liszts gesam-
           melte Schriften.* 6 vols. Leipzig, 1880-83.

RL   Ramann, Lina. *Lisztiana: Erinnerungen
           an Franz Liszt in Tagebuchblättern,
           Briefen und Dokumenten aus den Jahren
           1873-1886/87,* herausgegeben von Ar-
           thur Seidl; textrevision von Friedrich
           Schnapp. Mainz, 1983.

RLKM   Ramann, Lina. *Franz Liszt als Künstler
           und Mensch.* 3 vols. Leipzig, 1880-94.

SZM   Schorn, Adelheid von. *Zwei Men-
           schenalter: Erinnerungen und Briefe.* Ber-
           lin, 1901.

TCH   Thayer, William Roscoe. *Cardinal Ho-
           henlohe—Liberal.* Italica. Cambridge,
           MA, 1908.

TOS-W   Troisier de Diaz, Anne. *Emile Ollivier et
           Carolyne de Sayn-Wittgenstein. Cor-
           respondance, 1858-1887.* Paris, 1984.

VLKN

           Végh, Gyula. "Liszt Ferenc kiadatlan
           naplója: Memento Journalier, 1861-
           1862." *Muzsika* (Budapest) nos. 1/2
           and 3 (1930).

WA   Weimar Archives. Liszt Collection
           now held by the Nationale Forschungs-
           und Gedenkstätten der Klassischen
           Deutschen Literatur in Weimar. Das
           Goethe- und Schiller-Archiv, Weimar.

WFL   Walker, Alan. *Franz Liszt (vol. 2): The
           Weimar Years, 1848-1861.* London and
           New York, 1989.

WFLR   Wohl, Janka. *François Liszt: Recollec-
           tions of a Compatriot,* translated from
           the French by B. Peyton Ward. Lon-
           don, 1887.

WLLM   Waters, Edward N., (ed.) *The Letters of
           Franz Liszt to Olga von Meyendorff,
           1871-1886.* In the Mildred Bliss collec-
           tion at Dumbarton Oaks. Translated
           by William R. Tyler. Dumbarton Oaks,
           1979.

GENERAL INDEX